KV-193-252

TROUT. FISHING
A Guide to New Zealand's South Island

TROUT FISHING

A Guide to New Zealand's South Island

Tony Busch

David Bateman

Basic Services for International Anglers

The South Island, as with any trout fishing region, is serviced by fishing guides, accommodation and self-drive vehicles of varying standards. I have been professionally involved in the hunting and fishing sphere since the 1970s and as a matter of course have associated with fellow Kiwis and sportsmen from the 'four corners'. Years, and plain experience, have moulded a group of proficient New Zealand guides – individualist outdoorsmen motivated by nature to share her domain, their intimate knowledge and a special fishing experience with international anglers.

I solicit inquiries regarding these three services from anglers desirous of professionalism and, if requested, will supply a suggested fishing itinerary encompassing the South Island and will make all the necessary reservations which require only the usual nominal booking fee deposit. Visit the website: www.flyfishnewzealand.com for guiding, literature and personal assistance with your accommodation, transport and associated services.

Tony Busch

Busch Fishing Safaris
25 Tresillian Avenue
Nelson
NEW ZEALAND
Telephone/Fax (03) 545 0660
tony.busch@xtra.co.nz

Opposite title page: The author using a dry fly to a rising trout, Nelson District.

First published in 1994 by David Bateman Ltd, 30 Tarndale Grove, Albany, Auckland, New Zealand

Distributed in the United States by Stackpole Books, 5067 Ritter Road, Mechanicsburg, PA 17055

Reprinted 1997, 1999, 2001

Copyright © Tony Busch, 1994, 1997, 1999
Copyright © David Bateman Ltd, 1994, 1997, 1999

ISBN 1 86953 184 1

This book is copyright. Except for the purpose of fair review, no part may be stored or transmitted in any form or by any means, electronic or mechanical, including recording or storage in any information retrieval system without permission in writing from the publisher. No reproduction may be made, whether by photocopying or by any other means, unless a licence has been obtained from the publisher or its agent.

Cover design by Errol McLeary
Photography by Tony Busch
Printed in Hong Kong through Colorcraft Ltd

Contents

The Paringa River, West Coast.

Introduction

Although the two islands of New Zealand are administered as a single entity from Wellington, they contrast in many respects. They may have similar vegetation, insects and birds, but their geography, waterways, climate and fish species are different.

Both islands have extensive mountainous regions. Those of the North Island are more or less confined to the central section, where there are several areas of volcanic activity. The South Island, on the other hand, has a continuous chain of mountains in the Southern Alps extending from one extremity to the other. This bisects the wind currents of the Southern Hemisphere, resulting in generous rainfall in the western and southern regions.

The rivers of the South Island flow from the mountain peaks across the plains, to converge with the Tasman Sea in the west, or the Pacific Ocean in the east. Unlike the North Island, the lowlands are formed from rocks and gravel in open country, across which wide rivers and streams gently flow. Naturally, some sections pass through native forests which, although dense, are not as impregnable as those in the North Island and access to the water's edge is usually possible.

The South Island is more or less circumnavigated by the main highway system, which provides countless public accesses to good fishing rivers. There are also many lakes, where good results may be obtained with rainbow trout, brown trout and, in many instances, land-locked quinnat salmon. The South Island should, however, be considered a wild brown trout fishery and is quite unsuitable for the fish husbandry practiced in the 'rainbow country' of the North Island by government agencies.

The river habitat throughout the Island is subject to constant and careful management from the controlling Fish & Game Councils, to ensure the continuity of an excellent brown trout fishery.

One difference between the fishing of the two islands is that in the North anglers usually travel to a specific destination for the sole purpose of trout fishing, whereas the South offers 'story book' conditions allowing tourists to drive through the countryside and enjoy all the scenic attractions while taking advantage of good fishing at positions only a few hours apart.

Although the waterways of the South Island are well stocked with brown trout, visiting anglers should realize that they are hard to catch and that four fish per day is a typical result. They should not expect to catch large trout (over 2.2 kg) with any degree of regularity either — the average would be 1.3 kg. There are certainly many locations where large trout may be caught, but these are generally off the beaten track, and the services of professional guides are essential to ensure success.

Geography

The South Island has five distinct geographical and climatic zones, and an appreciation of this will assist with the preparation of a fishing vacation which the weather may make or mar. The Island is only one day's drive long, so anglers should plan a schedule which will permit them to move quickly from one district to another at short notice. There is little point in sitting the weather out when a short drive of two or three hours would provide a location where the water and weather conditions are good enough to provide reasonable fishing.

The Nelson Province

Situated at the northern extremity of the island, this boasts the best weather in the whole of New Zealand. It offers good brown trout fishing in numerous clear-watered streams and rivers, many of which are parallel to or crossed by the highway system.

The weather during summer (November to February) is generally hot, dry and settled, but there are intermittent days of scattered rain. These make conditions unsuitable for fly fishing but generally improve water levels and colour for anglers practising the spinning method. Lightweight summer clothing is essential when fishing during the summer months,

Mikonui River, West Coast.

when the unaccustomed may receive severe sunburn unless precautions are taken.

Although all techniques of trout fishing are practised throughout the district, it is ideal for fly fishing, especially during January and February. The weather at this time is generally very hot, with calm mornings and afternoon sea breezes, followed by breathless twilights providing good fly-fishing conditions until about 10.30 p.m.

The West Coast

This is a narrow section of land, with an average width of 20 km, situated between the Southern Alps and the Tasman Sea. It extends from Karamea in the north to Jackson Bay in the south — a distance of some 400 km. The province receives excessive rainfall, with moderate temperatures, and is extremely verdant. There are huge areas of native forest and swamps, as well as numerous streams and rivers.

Anglers visiting the region should be prepared with good waterproof garments, insect repellent and — if visiting a remote section of the province — an emergency supply of food and water. The weather can change quickly anywhere on the coast, and it is possible to become weather-bound miles from anywhere.

The area is sparsely populated and, with the possible exception of Greymouth and Hokitika, has limited motel/hotel accommodation. Pre-booking is therefore advisable.

Earth banks and encroaching vegetation restrict access to many otherwise excellent fly-fishing positions on a number of lakes and rivers, but provide perfect conditions for the spinning method. Keen anglers should carry equipment for both fly-fishing and spinning techniques, as weather and water conditions will frequently dictate which method may be applied.

Central Lakes

This district extends from Queenstown northwards to Tekapo and includes Lakes Wakatipu, Hayes, Wanaka, Hawea, Dunstan, Benmore, Ohau, Pukaki, Ruataniwha, Tekapo and many rivers.

It is close to the tussock-covered foothills of the Southern Alps, where the altitude creates frequent strong winds. It is essential to use protective lotion to prevent sunburn. It seldom rains during the summer, but visitors should be prepared with warm clothing for the surprisingly cold temperatures that may be experienced at any time of the year.

The majority of these rivers and lakes have open and accessible shores, providing good trout fishing conditions for all techniques. Although fishing locations are considerable distances apart, the good road system permits fast travelling between them.

Southland

Extending from the West to the East Coast, this is a verdant province of bush-covered hills, grassed lowlands, and numerous lakes, rivers, and streams, most of which are extremely well stocked with both species of trout.

Although it undoubtedly provides the best brown trout fishing in the South Island, the province unfortunately has the most inclement weather in New Zealand. There are seasons where even the most dedicated fly angler is able to count the number of fishable days on his fingers. You should try to fish there, but be prepared to move on quickly if the weather closes in.

Canterbury

This is on the East Coast and contains some of the most delightful small fly-fishing streams imaginable. Skilled dry-fly anglers are provided with superb conditions for quietly walking upstream and fishing to visible trout feeding in clear water beneath overhanging willow trees.

The province has a very dry climate, which causes many of the smaller streams to dry up completely at the height of summer — a problem that is aggravated by the extraction of enormous quantities of water from the larger rivers for irrigation purposes. There is, however, alternative fishing available in many of the lakes that are accessible from the highways servicing the inland reaches of the province.

The settled nature of the climate eliminates the need for special clothing or medical provisions, apart from light summer shirts and moisturizing lotion for protection against sun or windburn.

The Queen's Chain

Anglers fishing South Island waters will experience a phenomenon unique to New Zealand — the Queen's Chain.

At the inception of the colony in 1840 Queen Victoria instructed Governor Hobson to 'set aside a chain (22 yards) along the rivers, lakes and sea coasts for the recreation and amusement of the inhabitants of any town or village'. This surveyed marginal strip of land

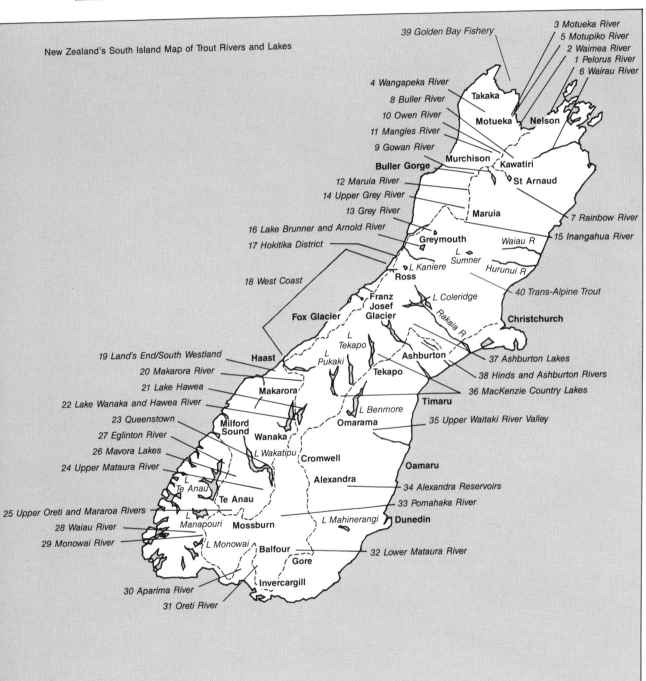

New Zealand's South Island Map of Trout Rivers and Lakes

39 Golden Bay Fishery
3 Motueka River
5 Motupiko River
2 Waimea River
1 Pelorus River
6 Wairau River
4 Wangapeka River
8 Buller River
10 Owen River
11 Mangles River
9 Gowan River
12 Maruia River
14 Upper Grey River
13 Grey River
16 Lake Brunner and Arnold River
17 Hokitika District
18 West Coast
7 Rainbow River
15 Inangahua River
40 Trans-Alpine Trout
19 Land's End/South Westland
20 Makarora River
21 Lake Hawea
22 Lake Wanaka and Hawea River
23 Queenstown
27 Eglinton River
26 Mavora Lakes
24 Upper Mataura River
25 Upper Oreti and Mararoa Rivers
28 Waiau River
29 Monowai River
30 Aparima River
31 Oreti River
37 Ashburton Lakes
38 Hinds and Ashburton Rivers
36 MacKenzie Country Lakes
35 Upper Waitaki River Valley
34 Alexandra Reservoirs
33 Pomahaka River
32 Lower Mataura River

Takaka
Motueka
Nelson
Murchison
Kawatiri
St Arnaud
Buller Gorge
Maruia
Greymouth
Waiau R
L Sumner
L Kaniere
Ross
Hurunui R
Franz Josef Glacier
L Coleridge
Fox Glacier
Rakaia R
Christchurch
Haast
L Tekapo
L Pukaki
Ashburton
Tekapo
Timaru
Makarora
L Benmore
Omarama
Milford Sound
Wanaka
L Wakatipu
Cromwell
Oamaru
L Te Anau
Te Anau
Alexandra
Mossburn
L Manapouri
L Mahinerangi
Dunedin
L Monowai
Balfour
Gore
Invercargill

is not visibly indentifiable but nevertheless exists on about 70 per cent of all river, lake and sea shorelines. Currently (1994), Government action has been instigated to include the 'missing' strips into official recognition. This will, hopefully, be completed in 1995.

However, this right of access along shorelines does not allow freedom of approach across private land to reach the 'Queen's Chain' and anglers must seek permission from property owners before passing through gates or fences.

As a rule of thumb, it may be assumed that where there are no fences between the road and a river, or there are signs depicting camping, picnicking, or fishing, there is public access.

If it is necessary to cross a fence to gain access to the water's edge, it must be assumed that someone owns the land up to the river bank and occasionally to the centre of the stream itself. Anglers should obtain permission to cross such land from the nearest dwelling. It is seldom that such an approach will be rebuffed.

Meticulous attention has been given to the classification of the fishing positions described in this book. They may be considered 'public', but the author accepts no responsibility as to their legal status.

Licences and Regulations

The regulations pertaining to fishing are adequately explained on the licences issued by the separate Fish and Game Councils throughout New Zealand. The licences are reciprocal between districts but local requirements are quite complex and varied. Visiting anglers should obtain detailed information regarding the regulations of each district by examining a licence held at any local sports/fishing shop.

Fishing Etiquette

There should be no need to mention this subject, but some anglers do not demonstrate courtesy.

The 'rules' are few and simple:

(1) If practicing the spinning method, do not cast a minnow near water which is obviously going to be fished by a fly angler.

(2) When an angler is already in position and fishing, leave him or her as much undisturbed water as you would normally desire yourself.

(3) Do not disturb trout by visible or audible movement in front of people who are fishing, whether they are fly anglers working upstream or spin/streamer fly anglers working downstream.

(4) Acknowledging a fellow angler's presence by a word or wave makes for fellowship.

Water Safety

Most New Zealanders are used to their environment, and many have fished for eels, whitebait and trout in the rivers and lakes since childhood. They tend to take for granted the skills necessary for survival in the back country.

The most important safety factor for visiting overseas anglers is probably an appreciation of the clarity and depth of the water in the rivers and lakes. Misunderstanding these can kill the angler unaccustomed to New Zealand conditions.

Do not step into water until you have determined its depth, especially on river beds where there is no gravel beach. The large stones and solid rock formations of many mountain streams disguise the depth of the water. This is often a light turquoise colour, and the sparkling segments of mica on the bottom of the pool are likely to a 3 m below the surface, not a few centimetres as they may appear.

The effervescent appearance of the water in rapids may also coax the unwary into trouble. Not only will the water be deeper than it appears, it will also be surprisingly swift. Once entered, rapids of this nature tend to be almost impossible to back out of, forcing the angler to go with the current and complete the river crossing

Many anglers, especially those from overseas, make use of a wading stick. This practice is to be commended. People wearing thigh boots (or especially chest waders) in deep or swift water should always carry a pocket knife within reach. This is a most important and essential tool for slashing your waders and releasing trapped air if you are swept off your feet and upended.

Many visiting anglers use lightweight packaway waders with wading shoes or boots. This is an excellent system, though boots rather that shoes are recommended, These provide better support and protection for the ankles in the waterways, which are predominantly of loose gravel, stones, and rock. Ideally these boots should be fitted with felt soles, as they provide a good grip on the stones that are slippery with weed and slime in midsummer. Lightweight waders should be the type that can be repaired with a patch from a portable kit.

Although most of the terrain through which the rivers flow is quite open, there will be occasions when it will be necessary to force your way through patches of scrub and briar — vegetation which will play havoc with clothing.

Clothing

The clothes worn by spin anglers do not affect results, because the trout are beyond visual range, but those worn by fly anglers are very important. Since they fish within casting range of their quarry (apart from the streamer-fly technique), they are also within their visual range. Experienced fly anglers therefore wear drab clothing, especially hats.

There is little use in wearing dull grey, green or brown clothing which blends into the vegetation if the whole effect is spoilt by gaudily-coloured headgear. A cap with a brim is essential to prevent sunglasses reflecting sunlight, but the remainder of it should be quite nondescript.

Sabine River.

South Island Techniques and Practices

Spinning

Spinning (or threadlining) is a simple and effective method of catching trout which is widely practiced throughout the South Island. It is merely a matter of casting a small metal or plastic lure into the water and retrieving it slowly so as to imitate a small fish or insect.

The technique permits ample opportunity to study the terrain and water conditions as well as the habits of the fish and the insects on which they feed. This information will prove invaluable should you decide to fish with a dry or wet fly on future occasions. Spinning is therefore an ideal introduction to trout fishing.

Rods

Spinning rods are available in two basic materials: fibreglass (solid or hollow) and carbon fibre (or graphite). The solid-glass models are extremely strong and robust with a relatively stiff action in comparison to rods made of hollow glass or graphite. For this reason, they need to be slightly longer, 2-2.2 m, in order to provide the whip necessary for casting light lures.

Hollow fibreglass rods are much lighter that solid models but, although equally strong when in use, require more careful handling when being transported or stowed. Most anglers prefer hollow rods because of their lightness and 'whippy tip' action, which allows small lures to be cast with a flick of the wrist instead of the more tiring full-arm motion required with solid glass. The ideal length for this type of rod is 2 m.

Graphite has a higher tensile strength than fibreglass and is considerably more expensive. Rods manufactured from this material combine the three properties most desired by anglers: strength, lightness and a certain degree of stiffness. Their action often feels stiffer than rods constructed of solid glass, yet they are more sensitive and enable lures to be cast further with less effort. This is an important consideration when casting into a headwind. The recommended length for a graphite spinning rod is 1.8 m.

Spinning rods are usually available in two basic styles: with a pistol grip or a straight butt. Pistol-grip rods are only used when fishing the overhead multiplier (level wind) or closed-face reels. The reel seat and grip are designed so that the rod can be held like a handgun, as only one hand is employed when casting. Pistol-grip models are extremely light and rarely more than 2 m in length, with a medium-action tip capable of casting lures between 7-21 g.

Reel and Line

Over the years the open-faced, fixed-spool reel has become established as the most popular and versatile reel used by spin anglers. It is simple to use, reliable and capable of casting light lures further than any other type of reel. The open-face spinning reel is designed to couple with standard straight-butt rods, and is used beneath the handle.

It should be used with enough nylon line to fill the spool almost to the edge. The ideal breaking strain is 2.7 kg.

Two other types of reels are also used for spinning, and both have their advantages. The closed-faced fixed-spool reel minimizes tangles and permits one-handed operation when casting. It is ideal for junior or disabled anglers. The overhead multiplier reel, (level wind) with its superb drag system, is generally used for long-distance fresh water salmon fishing.

However, a top quality open-faced spinning reel is recommended for all-round freshwater fishing, and will last indefinitely with routine maintenance.

Jim Glenn fishing in the Nelson District.

Spinning Operation

Spinning and fly fishing require entirely different equipment and techniques. The spin angler relies primarily on the intricate design of the reel for casting efficiency as the line is carried out by the weight of the lure. The ability to retrieve the line at varying speeds with a spinning outfit is also an advantage when fishing the different sectors of a river.

The fly angler, on the other hand, uses the weight of the line as the propelling force when delivering a minute feather-like imitation to the water; the reel is not used during this operation.

The spinning reel requires only two vital adjustments: the anti-reversal lever, which stops the handle rotating backwards, must be left in the activated position at all times; and the clutch or drag adjustment must be set in accordance with the rod's capacity and the breaking strain of the line.

Before assembling the outfit, always ensure that the bail arm is in the closed position by rotating the reel handle one complete turn. Attach the reel to the rod and thread the nylon line under the bail arm, through the rod rings and tie it to a lure. The clutch must now be set to allow a smooth even drag when the line is withdrawn from the spool. At this stage I suggest that the novice attach the lure to an immovable object and, after lifting the rod tip to a vertical position, pull against it. The rod tip must bend quite noticeably as the clutch slips, asserting a smooth even pressure to the line. This adjustment must not be altered during fishing, even though it will slip madly while playing a fish in the initial stages. While it is slipping, continue winding the handle to eliminate the momentary slack line which usually occurs as the fish suddenly stops its headlong rush and turns towards you. This is a critical moment, when the fish can throw the hook if it is allowed slack line.

Too tight a clutch setting, or attempting to tighten it while playing a fish, will probably lose the fish, either through line breakage or by the hook tearing out of the fish's mouth.

Casting Procedure

The rod butt is gripped with the stem of the reel between the second and third fingers to permit positive control and to allow the tip of the forefinger to hold the line prior to the casting stroke.

Rotate the handle of the reel until the bail arm faces to the right, pull off line with the free hand (note the even clutch pressure) until the lure hangs about 25 cm below the rod tip. Lift the line with the tip of the forefinger of the hand holding the rod, then open the bail arm to the left. The line will now lead from the spool, over the fingertip and through the rod rings where it will be held taut by the weight of the minnow. Bend the wrist backwards to bring the rod tip slightly behind you and cast quickly forward, stopping the rod in the direction of the target — this action should be accomplished by wrist rather than arm action.

Start winding the reel handle the instant the minnow hits the water; delay at this moment may cause the lure to sink and lodge on the river bed. Practice will determine the best speed of wind, so watch the minnow as it is retrieved to gauge its action. Too fast a wind will bring it to the surface, while a wind that is too slow will cause it to sink and lodge or bounce over the stones on the river bed.

When a fish strikes, set the hook with a slight but firm flick of the wrist holding the rod; too hard an effort may tear the lure from the fish's mouth and send it hurtling like a bullet straight at you. Always play the fish out completely before attempting to bring it to the net and while doing so, ensure that the rod is held vertically so that it bends quite noticeably to provide a shock absorber for the line — this is essential.

Fishing Positions

Spinning is effective in all types of trout water, with the possible exception of the clear, tranquil pools which are normally regarded as the domain of the fly angler. Check the local regulations: spinning is not permitted in all waters.

All flowing trout water, from shallow ripples only a few inches deep to turbulent white water, will yield results if the lure and the manner in which it are worked are appropriate. Start by casting across the current towards the opposite bank of the river, in a slightly upstream direction, so that the lure is retrieved against the current in a sweeping arc and passes over the most likely holding stations of the trout. If you are uncertain about where the fish may be holding, alter the angle of each cast by a few degrees until all the water within casting range has been thoroughly covered.

Some of the most productive areas are those which occur at each end of a rapid, especially where large eddies and swirling backwaters flow up against the faster-moving current. Trout favour a feeding position just inside the slacker water, at the very edge of the main stream. When working the upper reaches of these areas, cast into the main stream and retrieve slowly so that the lure moves along the fringe of the swirling backwater.

At the lower reaches of the rapid the current will slow down, offering smooth flowing water that has spread out across the river bed. Ideally, these glides should be fished at their lower extremity just where the current accelerates over the bar to commence another fast run. This is a favourite holding station for trout. They are extremely alert when feeding in such positions and the angler must use long casts from an upstream position to avoid detection. Cast across the river, a little ahead of the bar so that the lure is carried naturally by the current in a sweeping arc into, and through, the feeding area. This should be done several times, as you walk slowly downstream, until the final cast retrieves the minnow through the actual broken water at the head of the rapid. Once again, practice will determine the best speed of wind.

The use of a high-speed retrieve reel is advantageous in these circumstances as it allows the angler to stand on the edge of the broken water below the fall and cast upstream. The rapid retrieve enables him to keep the lure off the bottom as he works it down stream towards the feeding fish.

Although spinning will often yield spasmodic catches throughout the day when conditions are favourable, the best times are dawn and dusk. Trout are always most active at these times and generally feed more intensely on a wider range of food.

Fly Fishing

Fly fishing is a general term to describe a complex art containing four distinct categories — dry fly, nymph, wet fly and feather lure (streamer) fishing — all of which employ similar equipment but slightly different techniques. Regardless of which method is used, tackle requirements will vary according to the type of water being fished. For instance, a long, heavy rod is not suitable on small streams less than 6 m wide, and a fly rod designed to cast heavy lines a long distance is unsuitable when fishing a 'rise' with a dry fly, where delicate presentation is essential.

Rods

Today, the accepted fly rod is constructed of graphite. They have surpassed the fibreglass models in weight, action and are only slightly more expensive.

The split-cane fly rod still remains the symbol of fly fishing excellence and there are many enthusiasts who would fish with nothing else. While I acknowledge the meticulous craftsmanship in the manufacture of these rods, and the superb action which is only attainable from the use of nature's natural materials, I cannot recommend them for general use.

Hollow glass fly rods are much lighter than cane models and, generally speaking, have a more pronounced tip action that requires wrist movement when casting, rather than the traditional 'elbow-in, stiff-wrist' method used with the former. The quick action and resilient nature of fibreglass usually permits the one rod to be used for the four methods of fly fishing. The ideal average fibreglass rod for South Island conditions is 2.6 m long, and designed for a weight 5 line. This combination is light enough for a ten-year-old child to handle.

Available at a slightly higher price than fibreglass, fly rods manufactured from hollow carbon fibre (graphite) can only be described as superb. On the first encounter, these rods appear so fragile that one is hesitant to handle them, but the ultra-light weight and incredibly fast tip action makes them a delight to use. Although these rods are capable of handling floating lines two weights either side of that recommended by the manufacturer, I would strongly advise using a sinking line one weight lighter than the one specified. The rod blank lacks the overall resilience and power to lift a heavy sinker from beneath the water.

Whereas a fibreglass rod gains its powerful action from overall flexibility, a graphite rod relies on the energy storage capacity of the last two feet of the tip enabling it to shoot line like a slingshot. In order to master this action one must forget past habits and start afresh by concentrating on wrist action. One should lay the index finger along the tip of the rod (a technique I have always advised in any case when using light rods), and roll the wrist. This action ensures a smooth transmission of power by bending the rod quickly from the butt upwards to the base of the whippy section. At the very instant the forward movement reaches this point, stop the wrist. The length of line that can be shot using this method is quite astounding. There is one very important rule when using a graphite rod: never strike with the rod at the moment of take. The tip action is so quick that the result would be either a broken leader or the hook pulled out of the fish's mouth, often with a section of jawbone attached to the barb. Always tighten the line firmly with the free hand before activating the rod.

The most outstanding feature of these rods is not so much their ultra-lightness or strength, but rather their amazing line-handling ability. After a few hours' practice the fly can be delivered with unerring accuracy and lightness under the most difficult conditions and with lightning speed to 'holding pockets' in turbulent white water. This technique allows a dry fly to float naturally for a few seconds before being 'whisked-away' by line drag and will often 'lift' an opportunist feeder — especially the brown species.

Reels

These are quite different from those used for spinning and all other forms of fishing which employ monofilament nylon. Fly reels have a simple centre pin drum featuring an adjustable brake on the spool to slow down the run of the fish. All good quality models have interchangeable spools, and their construction is such that they are easily adjustable for either left- or right-handed winding action.

Modern fly reels are designed with perforated spools to reduce weight and to allow air to circulate and dry the line. The size of the reel is assessed by its external diameter and the width of the spool. The width of the spools are narrow, medium or wide depending on the type of line being used. Wide to medium spools are generally employed with the heavier sinking lines used in deep lake or large river fishing when employing the feather lure technique, whereas the narrow spool is the most common when fishing streams. The reel does not play a major part in casting, and in fact the experienced fly fisherman usually plays small fish by retrieving or releasing the line through the fingers of his free hand. When playing large fish in rough water however, the efficient drag system fitted to quality fly reels is essential to permit a smooth and continual resistance on the line when in the withdrawal mode. In such circumstances a momentary hesitation of breaking action, and the ensuing jerk as it 'takes-up' again, will often break a leader or bend a hook, losing the fish.

When casting and retrieving, the line is either held in the hand or dropped onto the water or ground. This procedure is necessary because there is no weight on the line to pull it off the reel during the cast. For the initial cast this has to be done by stripping line from the reel by hand.

Lines

All fly lines have a braided synthetic core covered with a plastic material, and are designed to either float or sink. They are manufactured in four separate styles and are available in various qualities.

Although a high quality line is softer and more manageable both in the air and in the water, I advise the novice to start with a cheaper line because for the first season, until the art of casting is mastered, the line will frequently crack in the air similar to a whip. Whenever this occurs a minute fracture is caused in the plastic covering which permits water to enter the core. This will not affect the strength of the line to any degree but causes it to become heavy, unmanageable and to sink.

Level line: When the diameter of a line is uniform throughout its length it is said to be parallel or level. Level lines are normally sold in lengths of 23 m (75 ft) and are cheaper than other types of fly lines. They are available in a full range of weights from 3 to 10 in both sinking and floating models.

Double-tapered line: Fly presentation is greatly improved when a tapered line is used. Because of the taper, the line gradually slows down during the final stages of the cast and the fly lands more softly on the water than is possible with level line.

Double-tapered line is the most widely used, and as implied by the name, tapers from the centre evenly to both ends, allowing it to be reversed on the reel and doubling its life. These lines are available in a full range of weights in both sinking and floating models. The sinking models are also available in several densities, which determine the depth desired for fly presentation.

Weight-forward line: This type of line is also double-tapered, but the taper is more pronounced at one end so that the weight of the line is unevenly distributed. In other words, at one end the line tapers from its thickest section to the tip in about 4.51 m, whereas at the opposite end the taper extends over about 18 m. The line is designed for use with the sharply tapered end attached to the leader and the gradually tapered section attached to the backing, hence the name.

I have favoured this style of line for several years, finding that it rolls beautifully and presents a fly delicately. Less effort is required in the casting action, which makes the weight-forward line ideally suited in situations where extremely short distance casts are necessary, when casting into a head wind, or when working in confined positions and unable to false cast. This model is also available in both sinking and floating styles.

Sinking tips: By varying the quantity of air bubbles in the core or plastic covering of any section of fly line it can be made to float or sink. Lines designed to sink do so at different rates and are described as fast, medium or slow sinkers. A combination of these properties produces lines which are part floater and part sinker, the forward end being constructed to sink and the remainder to float. A line of this kind is referred to as a sinking tip line, and the sinking section is usually about 6 m long. These lines are extremely effective when used as directed.

Shooting heads: Heavy sinking models, tapered at one end only (which is designed for attaching to the monofilament nylon backing), are referred to as 'torpedo heads' or 'shooting heads'. These lines are much shorter than other types and are designed to facilitate long-distance casting. They have limited application, such as on deep lakes and North Island rivers where streamer flies are widely used, and are not otherwise generally used by anglers.

Coloured line: All lines are available in vivid colours and for years I agreed with the consensus that light green was the best. This notion was undoubtedly based on the assumption that what was difficult for the human eye to see was also less likely to be noticed by the fish. After conducting many extensive tests on different types of trout water, using a variety of the most gaudy and brilliantly coloured lines available, I am now thoroughly convinced that, unless it is fluorescent, the colour of the floating line makes no difference whatsoever to the fish. Fluorescent lines impart a reflection similar to a mirror in the sun.

Classification of Line

From the foregoing, it will be clear that fly lines vary enormously in weight and diameter and must be matched or balanced with a rod of suitable strength in order to be fully effective. Because of the variety of lines available, an international system of coding is used by all manufacturers for the specification of their products. Thus, irrespective of its diameter, each line with the same numbering is suitable for use with the same rod. Initially a series of numbers was used to indicate the weight of line: 2-10 being the standard range. These numbers only indicated the weight and conveyed no information about the type of line. To overcome this problem a series of letters (corresponding to the initials of the words used to describe the types of lines) were added to the number to give this data.

Letters placed before the number refer to the type of taper, whereas those placed after the number refer to the floating or sinking properties. For example, a DT7F can be recognized immediately as a double taper (DT) floating line (F), for use with a rod suitable to a size 7 line. Similarly, a WF5F/S is a weight-forward (WF) or sinking tip (F/S) size 5.

The standard length of double-tapered lines is 27.5 m, and they are intended for use with about 50 m of backing to allow for those all too infrequent occasions when large fish make extensive runs.

Modern synthetic fly lines require very little maintenance. Their plastic coating tends to accumulate various types of foreign matter such as minute particles of grit and algae, especially towards the tip section where the air-impregnated coating is finest. Tiny cracks in the plastic coating allow moisture to penetrate into the core, increase the density of the line and eventually cause it to sink. Periodic cleaning of the line with fly-float grease (mucilin/silicon type) will remove these damaging particles and prolong the effective life of floating lines. The better quality lines are sold with a small container of cleaning agent specially formulated by the manufacturer.

Leader and Tippet

The tip of the fly line is attached to a tapered monofilament nylon leader which should be tied to the eye of the fly hook. A leader is essential and has a twofold purpose: it serves as an inconspicuous link between the fly line and the fly rod, and because of its small size, it enables the fly to be presented gently and naturally to the surface of the water.

The following chart gives the American Fishing Tackle Manufacturers Association (AFTMA) standards which are based on the weight of the first 30 feet of fly line, exclusive of the tip (approx. 6″ (150mm) section.)

LINE NUMBER	WEIGHT	
	grams	ounces
1	60	.14
2	80	.18
3	100	.23
4	120	.28
5	140	.32
6	160	.37
7	185	.43
8	210	.48
9	240	.55
10	280	.64
11	330	.76
12	380	.87

LETTER CODE;

L	level line (no taper)
DT	double taper
WF	weight forward, forward taper
ST	shooting taper, torpedo head

The following letters are always placed after the line number.

F	floating line
S	sinking line
F/S	sinking tip line

The upper reaches of the Wairau River, also known as the Rainbow River.

The length of the leader is most important and should never be shorter than 2 m, to avoid alerting the fish when presenting a fly. An ideal length is 2.7 m. The finest end of the leader (which is tied to the fly) is known as the tippet, and its diameter and breaking strain should vary to suit different waters and conditions.

The opposite end is known as the butt and its diameter should be slightly less than the end of the fly line. A limp leader is awkward to lay out straight on the surface of the water and makes effective fly presentations almost impossible. For this reason the leader must always be fairly stiff at the thick (or butt) end.

The strength of the tippet is influenced by the type of water being fished, the feeding pattern of the fish and the size of the fly to be used. You must remember that the entire outfit depends on the strength of its finest section. The breaking strain at the point where the tippet is attached to the fly is a crucial factor, as it is less than at any other part of the line. Tippet sizes are shown on the following table.

Leader specifications alter slightly between manufacturers but the 'Cortland 333' listed here exemplifies the average rating.

SIZE	BUTT DIAMETER	TIP DIAMETER inches	mm	TIP TEST lb	kg
7X	.021	.004	.10	2.4	1.1
6X	.022	.005	.13	4.0	1.8
5X	.023	.006	.15	4.6	2.1
4X	.024	.007	.18	6.0	2.7
3X	.025	.008	.20	7.9	3.6
2X	.026	.009	.23	10	4.5
1X	.026	.010	.25	13	5.9
0X	.027	.011	.28	15	6.4

The majority of experienced fly anglers now insert a short section of tippet material between the leader and the fly. The advent of extremely fine monofilament has provided a deception unknown to fly anglers only a few years ago.

Backing

Backing is a special braided line that is attached between the fly line and spool arbor. Its primary function is to provide extra length as insurance against losing those trophy sized fish that strip the entire main line from the reel. Linen lines are normally employed as backing because of their soft qualities, which provide a compressible arbor when loaded onto the reel. The compressible quality of the braided line allows the main line to be wound on under heavy strain with less risk of spool-spread or damage to the reel which may happen if monofilament is used. Another useful function of the backing is that it fills up any surplus space on the drum, thereby increasing the reel's capacity to retrieve line quickly.

The backing and leader may be attached to the fly line by various means. For many years I have used the small plastic leader link, which is a simple and efficient method enabling leaders to be changed in seconds and ensures a smooth joint which eliminates the possibility of leader tangle when casting. This unit is also ideal to cover the knot attaching the backing to the fly line and will slide (often extremely quickly) through the rod rings when a large fish makes a dash for it — a most important factor. Many anglers splice an eye on the end of the line which allows easy attachment of the leader by tying or interlacing the two loops. Others use a nail knot or glue a butt into the line's core. However, the accepted method of joining the backing to the fly line is to remove the outer synthetic coating from about 2.5 cm at the end of the line and whip both lines together with binding silk. The binding is then sealed with glue which is rolled smooth as it dries. This joint will also pass through the rod rings without any difficulty.

Principles of Fly Casting

Of the various skills that are required for the enjoyment of fly fishing, none is more important than fly presentation. A degree of mystique surrounds it, and many exponents regard it as an art rather than a skill. But the majority of fly fishermen are mainly interested in the thrill of playing a fish and are satisfied with their casting ability so long as it allows them to enjoy this experience regularly.

Holding the Rod: There are two main methods of holding the butt of a fly rod. The most common is the thumb grip, so called because the thumb is placed along the top of the grip. The alternative method is known as the foregrip, with the index finger along the top of the butt. The chief advantage of the thumb grip is that it permits more power to be transferred to the rod, as is necessary with heavy equipment and long-distance casting. It was the only grip suitable for handling the rods of bygone years. With the advent of lightweight rods, however, the necessity and desirability of this style of grip is questionable.

Although used less frequently than the thumb grip, the forefinger technique is the method that I personally recommend. The foregrip assists accurate casting, and while permitting free wrist action, also checks the common error of taking the rod too far back during the back cast. The forefinger should be kept slightly bent rather than forced flat on the butt. This enables the fingertip to exert both power and directional pressure during the final stages of the delivery (shooting) stroke, a technique that I consider imperative to gain the maximum efficiency from a light graphite rod. I also find the foregrip more comfortable.

The degree of firmness used to grip the rod is also an important factor. Too tight a grip will impede the smoothness of action and soon result in forearm fatigue, whereas a grip that is too loose will prevent adequate control. Regardless of which grip is used, always ensure that the thumb or index finger is as far forward on the butt as comfortably possible.

Casting Procedure: Start by assembling the rod, reel, line and leader. The reel is positioned beneath the rod — ensure that the line feeds out from the bottom of the spool. Thread the line through the rod rings and, after attaching a small dry fly, pull out about 6 m of line and lay it out reasonably straight on the water (or ground) in front of you.

Adopt a balanced stance, with the left foot (if you're right-handed) positioned directly ahead of the right and pointing in the general direction of the cast. Lower the tip of the rod until it is almost touching the surface of the water and, using your free hand, pull off about 2 m of line from the reel and let it fall to the ground. Reach forward and grasp the line near the bottom ring, lowering it until it is by your hip. While doing so let the line slip through the fingers with just enough pressure to keep the line taut through the rod rings to its extremity on the water. During the casting manoeuvre the free hand will follow the hand holding the rod butt in unison, insuring that there is no slack line between it and the fly at any time — this is most important if the rod is to be loaded correctly.

From a horizontal position, lift the rod swiftly and smoothly until the tip reaches the one o'clock position. When done correctly the weight of the line will make the rod bend and store spring-type energy, especially in the upper section. This will swiftly accelerate the line backwards from the moment the rod stops its arc, and cause it to travel under its own weight until the loop finally straightens out. The rod tip will bend backwards and be loaded for the forward thrust.

Importance of Timing: At the moment the rod is fully loaded with the weight of the line at the completion of the back cast, the caster applies forward pressure by bending the rod swiftly and smoothly forward until its tip reaches the ten o'clock position. This action causes the line to roll over itself, forming a loop in mid-air as it changes direction and shoots forward. The efficient looping of the line in the air is enhanced by the use of a tapered line and leader which, owing to their narrower gauge and lighter weight, travel more slowly than the main section of the line. The transition from the back cast to the forward cast occurs at exactly the moment the rod is fully loaded, with the line extended as far backwards as possible. This necessitates a momentary but distinct cessation of rod movement by the hand.

Good timing is essential, both to cock the rod correctly and ensure a powerful forward cast, and when the line is returned to the back cast. The arc followed by the rod is of extreme importance and should only exceed the ten o'clock and one o'clock positions at the delivery stage. The hand holding the butt of the rod must travel parallel to the ground, and once this motion is perfected it will be noticed that the line in the air also follows a parallel course.

The rod must be moved in a positive but smooth manner — jerky actions must be avoided. The hand action in driving the rod on each stroke should be one of continuous acceleration, which will cause the upper section of the rod to bend noticeably and function like a slingshot in shooting the line.

Before progressing to the next stage you should practice the foregoing techniques until you can lift the line from the water and work it in the air. Concentrate on executing the back and forward casts until you develop a sense of timing, feel and control. Only then attempt the next manoeuvre — shooting the cast.

Shooting the Cast: Practice at keeping the line in the air is never wasted as it is an important aspect of fly fishing known as false casting. False casting allows you to shorten or lengthen your line until you have the length to place the fly exactly where required. It is also an important and effective means of drying a fly and also facilitates changing the direction of a cast.

Shooting the cast is simply a matter of timing. Perform the movements of the back cast and the beginning of the final forward cast, but continue past the ten o'clock position and finish the stroke with the rod tip just below the nine o'clock position. The line will then shoot forward, parallel to the water, until a loop is formed. Just as the loop straightens out, open your free hand and the loose line will be pulled through the rings by the weight of the straightening line.

Do not aim the rod tip at the desired position on the surface of the water, but well above it, to permit the line to straighten out completely in the air and fall gently to the surface.

Considerable practice is necessary before the rod and line can be handled efficiently and effectively as a synchronized unit, and it may take years before casting becomes a totally coordinated and natural motion. It is therefore advisable to become reasonably adept at false casting and shooting the cast before attempting to fish for trout with a fly. The expense of reaching good trout water and the limited time available for fishing are too valuable to be wasted on casting lessons which could have been learned at home. It can be very depressing to have the fly repeatedly snagged in briars and trees, not to mention frightening every fish on station. During the many years that I have given practical instruction, I have found that even one hour's tuition saves the novice many hours of frustrating trial-and-error practice in casting procedures. Seek help from an experienced fly fishing angler if possible.

One word of advice before practising; break the point and barb off the fly hook to eliminate the chance of accidental injury — to yourself, or to amused onlookers.

The Dry Fly Method

The strategy of catching trout with a dry fly demands stealth, deceit and countless hours of practice. Although it is generally considered a form of fishing that is visual in every respect, the experienced angler will frequently 'lift' a trout from the depths by the skilful use of the artifice and rod/line handling technique. The expertise required, however, will take many years to perfect, during which time an instinct regarding atmospheric pressures and conditions, insect habits and ability to read the water will develop — knowledge that only experience can provide. Therefore, the average fisherman should regard the dry fly method in the short term as practice — expertise will follow naturally.

On one hand, the angler must conceal himself from the fish's sight by quietly stalking through cover and using camouflage, and on the other hand his approach depends very much on what he can see on the water's surface.

The circles produced by feeding fish as they lift to the surface to take insects is known as the rise. This type of feeding behaviour suggests the dry fly method, and will normally occur between dawn and noon, ceasing during the heat of the day and resuming in the early evening. This is naturally only a guide: the rise may occur at any time during the day and continue for several hours, or not happen at all, depending on the hatch.

Sometimes a fish is taken on a dry fly without any rise being apparent, and it should be assumed that the fish was engaged in intermittent surface feeding and may have risen shortly before the angler came along, the ripples caused by the rise having vanished.

In any case, the novice should follow the general principle that when surface indications are absent it is advisable to fish with a nymph.

Should the fish be surface feeding on nymphs or wet flies, their behaviour will be quite different.

Rise Forms

Most of the various rise forms displayed by trout will fall into one of two categories: that of a fish rising 'on station', or that of a 'cruiser'. Only occasionally fish will rise in no discernible pattern.

The fish 'on station' takes up a holding position which can be maintained in the current with minimum effort. This may be anywhere in the river. Brown trout especially have a habit of using vortex forces to hold in seemingly impossible places as they rise to take food swept downstream into its cone of vision. The cruiser on the other hand continually moves around on a regular beat, which may comprise a rather complex pattern. Cruisers are more common in larger pools and the deeper, slower-flowing sections of a stream.

The techniques employed in any situation will generally be determined by watching the feeding patterns of the fish. For this reason, an understanding of the significance of different rise forms, and an ability to recognize them, are an immense help to the angler.

The rise is most apparent in calm water as a fish lifts quietly to the surface and sucks in a tiny insect, causing gentle rings on the surface. In rough water an unusual swirl will be noticed in the turbulence as the fish fights the current. Under certain light conditions its wonderful colouration rather than the shape of the fish will be quite visible.

The wet rise is generally characterized by noisy action. This is particularly so during the evening, just preceding dark, when the fish frequently jump clear of the water. During the daylight hours the wet rise is less spectacular and is often mistaken as a dry one by the inexperienced. In these instances the fish will cause a minute splash on the surface but seldom break water, and it is advisable to use a thin-bodied wet fly of the Greenwell's Glory (size 12/14) style. This fly may be fished to the rise or used in the manner of a feather lure, that is, across and down, with a slow retrieval against the current.

In quiet water on calm days it is quite common to see fish breaking the surface of the water with their backs. This feeding pattern is referred to as humping, head and tailing, or the porpoise rise, and occurs when the fish are feeding just below the surface, usually on nymphs as they float upwards to hatch in the surface film. As this pattern indicates that food is not being taken on the surface, it is unsuitable for fishing with a dry fly and a very small nymph should be presented.

Fly Selection

Trout generally feed very selectively. During a rise they may actively feed on only one particular species of insect and then at a specific stage of its life cycle. Casting to a rise in such circumstances requires an imitation that closely resembles the insect, although even a skilfully tied artificial may be ignored on still clear pools. An alternative is to move to a location where there are sections of broken water, as the fish have less time to recognise the artificial fly where the current is turbulent and strong.

The opposite of this behaviour is when the fish are not feeding selectively and various fly patterns prove equally effective. It frequently happens that two or more anglers catch fish on the same expanse of water, each using two or more completely different flies. Here the fly is taken because it looks as though it may be food rather than because it closely resembles any particular insect.

Such indiscriminate feeding may account for the success of many 'impressionistic' flies which bear no resemblance to natural trout foods. Such patterns are sometimes tied with scant regard for the general shape, colour and size of common aquatic or terrestrial insects. There are occasions when these flies can be very productive and, for all anybody will ever know, every fly fished might fall into that category at some time or another.

Manner of Presentation

Dry flies are tied to represent surface food, and ideally should ride cocked or balanced on the surface film and never become water-logged. Apart from the question of which fly to use, the appropriate manner of presentation must also be assessed. The way in which a fly is delivered to the surface can contribute to your success in attracting fish. For example, where grasshoppers are observed near the water's edge, the grasshopper pattern is a logical fly to select, and the best method of delivery is to splash it down as heavily as possible beside an undercut bank.

Another example is the typical approach to fishing with a hatching caddisfly. In this case, the newly hatched insect flutters and skitters across the surface before taking off. It has survived the journey from the bottom of the pool encased in its pupal membrane and, on reaching the surface, it struggles to free itself from the encumbering covering, wriggling and skittering in the process. By presenting an imitation that closely resembles the size of the hatching insect, and then skilfully simulating its frenzied movements on the surface, the angler enhances his chances of taking fish.

These two examples clearly illustrate the principle that the action of the fly can be just as important as the fly itself. In both cases keen observation and the skilful use of streamside knowledge plays a significant role.

Investigation of Stream Ecology

While knowledge is accumulated in a piecemeal fashion with the progress of time, simple studies can hasten the understanding of the stream ecology. Making a post-mortem examination on the first fish taken from a stretch of water is an important practice. Through this procedure the relationship between insect activity above the surface and the feeding behaviour of the fish soon becomes apparent. The procedure may be taken one step further by actually studying the insect in its aquatic environment. One will soon learn to recognize the nymphs of the mayflies, stoneflies and the larger dragonflies and damselflies. The caddisfly larvae, in their small cases made of sand, sticks and vegetable material, are also readily recognized. With experience, it is possible to identify the various stages of the life cycles and finally, to reach conclusions as to the time of hatching and other valuable details.

Equipped with a knowledge of life cycles, the post-mortem becomes more meaningful. With a small jar of methylated spirits in the fishing vest, each catch becomes a step towards more successful fishing in the future. Careful observation will enable an accurate assessment of the feeding activity of the fish at the moment of capture.

As a further study, one might take successive comparisons from within the same stretch of water. Over a period of time, a knowledge and understanding of the behaviour and the life cycle of the various insects will result. As a general rule, each species has a particular time of the year for each new stage in the life cycle. Furthermore, there is a special time of day when the changes occur.

Time spent on the stream, whether fishing or simply observing, contributes towards a better understanding of the whole stream environment and ultimately the chance of taking fish. This undoubtedly has much to do with the way locals always seem to be able to take fish. They learn where the best pools are, where the fish lie, what fly to present and what action to give it.

However, despite all possible study and understanding, there are times when even the most experienced angler cannot raise a fish. Good fly fishing is therefore largely a matter of being in the right place at the right time, for even the most accomplished dry fly angler may as well fish in his bathtub or languish in the nearest pub if the fish aren't feeding.

Creating an Artificial Rise

In certain circumstances it is sometimes possible to trigger a rise by casting continually to one spot so that the fly repeatedly falls inside the circular window of a trout on station. If this is done skilfully, the trout may be induced to rise as if a natural hatch were occurring. This unlikely technique has been known to succeed and is definitely worth a try if all else has failed — it eases the frustration that we all experience at times.

Trout feed when food is most available. They are opportunistic predators and unlike more evolved life forms that seek food when hungry, trout feed by instinct. If food is present they will feed, and the more plentiful it is, the more voraciously they will feed.

Dry Fly Technique

Assuming that a promising stretch of water has been chosen and the weather and time of day are suitable, the angler's strategy will make the difference between success and failure. Much will depend on the angler's ability to deliver his fly lightly to the water in the correct spot. The technique employed will be largely determined by the nature and strength of the current, and the necessity to fish upstream. The dry fly angler is obliged to fish upstream because trout spend most of their time facing that direction. Laying downstream would cause respiratory difficulties for the fish because of their need for a continuous flow of oxygenated water into the gills. Facing into the current also means that food is swept into the holding station, necessitating a minimum amount of effort on the fish's part when feeding. If the angler were to position himself ahead of the fish and cast towards them, his obvious presence would alert them.

Types of Water: Trout streams flow in runs and pools. The runs may be either fast or slow, deep or shallow, and are termed rapids, white water, riffles or glides, according to the nature of their flow. Sometimes a stretch of water contains two or more of these features and allows versatile anglers an opportunity to practice all aspects of their art.

Smooth, shallow glides are regarded as the ultimate trout water by dry fly anglers. This is so because the gentle flow brings a constant supply of surface food to the waiting fish, which are able to maintain stations with minimum effort, and still watch a wide expanse of stream. The smooth, unbroken surface of such glides enables the fish to see the insects riding in the surface film and to time their rise accurately.

Pools, even the smallest ones, are conveniently divided into three sections — the head, the body and the tail — each with its own set of characteristics which require a different approach. The head is where the water enters the pool, slowing down toward the body, which is the deepest and slowest section, then accelerating in the tail and eventually becoming a run to the next pool.

The fact that good trout water is generally crystal clear allows the angler to see the quarry, observe its feeding pattern, present a fly and watch as the fish rises and actually takes the fly into its mouth — a thrilling moment for even the most experienced dry fly fisherman.

The Problem of Drag: A constant problem when presenting a dry fly is line drag. In fly fishing terminology, the word drag is used to describe what occurs when a faster or slower current flows between the angler and the fly, making it behave in an unnatural manner. Drag can also be caused by wind when fishing dry flies on still water.

The natural insect always travels with the current, unless attempting to leave the water, or affected by strong wind. This is not the case with the angler's fly, however, which is tethered to the leader and line. If any part of the line between angler and fly floats faster than the tip of the leader, the fly's natural drift is affected causing it to be dragged unnaturally across the surface.

Trout are cautious, selective feeders, alert to any variations in their food supply. Since their feeding pattern at any particular time depends on the uniformity of appearance and behaviour of their food, it is crucial for you to ensure that your fly floats in exactly the same manner. If the fly is travelling faster than the line, drag is more easily controlled — all that happens is that the line between the angler and the fly becomes slacker, and can be adjusted by rapidly retrieving surplus line.

Drag presents more difficulty on some types of water than on others. For instance, when fishing the head of a pool on a large stream, drag is rarely a problem because the line is nearly always moving faster that the fly, which allows the angler to control the cast by taking in line more rapidly. The body of a pool and smooth glides are likewise easily fished on large steams, and it is only when attempting to fish the tail that drag becomes a serious problem. However, on small streams the problems of drag are more acute, because you cannot restrict your line to a uniform current. The smaller the stream, the more distances are compressed, and the more the problem of drag is compounded. Drag can never be totally eliminated, but its effects can be minimized. One method of overcoming drag on small streams is to stalk as close as possible to a feeding fish. It is usually possible to approach fish more closely on small streams than large ones. This is because the narrow or confined water makes it difficult for fish to see anything beyond the streamside vegetation, thus providing you with excellent cover. With less line on the water, there is much less likelihood of variations in the current.

The key to solving the problem of drag lies in ensuring that there is sufficient slack in the line to enable the fly to drift over the stations of feeding fish before the line tautens. The moment the current causes the slightest tension on the line, drag will occur. There are various ways of creating the required amount of slack line and the most common is mending the line, so-called because it occurs after the cast has been made. Mending the line is a technique that is easily learned and involves flicking loops of line either upstream or down, as the situation demands. A quick roll-over of the wrist is all that is required, as a good floating line lifts readily from the surface and follows the rod tip. On long casts it is sometimes necessary to raise the whole arm before flipping the wrist.

A more difficult method is to stand well back from the bank and cast almost directly across the stream so that the fly lands slightly upstream from the fish's window. Those who cast well can produce an upstream curve in the line so that the fly has a longer drag-free drift.

The 'Feeling of Touch': Master anglers develop in their fingers over the years the sensitivity of a surgeon. Until the angler develops at least the fundamentals of this sensitivity many of the other fishing skills may be of little use.

It seldom comes naturally or quickly. It requires a lot of concentration, no mean feat when one considers the many distractions of the sport: the beauty of the surroundings, the constantly changing light, the need to keep an eye on the hatch, not to mention the sight of feeding fish.

Night fishing is practiced extensively in the South Island, and is the ideal way to acquire what I call 'the feeling of touch' so vital in fly fishing.

Night Fishing: Before fishing a new area at night it is sound policy to reconnoitre the stream in daylight, carefully noting the position of relevant features such as backwaters, tributaries, obstructions and variations in current, and then spend the intervening daylight period fishing elsewhere in order to avoid disturbing the fish population. On returning to the spot in the late twilight it is much easier to take up a predetermined position and cast into the darkness with reasonable certainty of placing the fly correctly.

The rod tip should be held low, pointing at the fly as the line swings in a slow arc across the pool. The index finger should rest along the top of the rod butt to detect the slight touch, while slack line is smoothly retrieved by stripping it over the crook of the second finger — a technique that keeps the line taut, yet allows it to be seized instantly when necessary.

In the dark, bite registration is a delicate affair that requires patience and skill to detect. Often it is scarcely discernible and feels like excess current drag on the line. Then the free hand must tighten the line in a smooth, firm, continuous motion. Never strike with the rod: this basic rule is of paramount importance, and applies to all fly fishing techniques.

All senses must be constantly on the alert for the slightest sensation of current drag, at which the free hand smoothly and firmly retrieves the line. It is frequently necessary to strip three or four sections (arm strokes) of line before it becomes apparent whether or not a fish has been hooked. If a fish has taken the fly it will pull back hard, generally with a double jerk.

Only at this moment should the rod be lifted from the horizontal position to point straight up at the stars, where it will remain until the fish is played out.

The fighting characteristics of a night-feeding brown trout are often spectacular. By day they are surely the most vigorous underwater opponents, but by night their manner of resistance is even more active and frequently acrobatic, with the fish seeming to spend much of the fight above the water. Sometimes a fish will circumnavigate the pool, and occasionally the legs of the angler, in a desperate attempt to throw the hook or snag the line. This can have dire consequences if one happens to be perched precariously on a submerged rock in midstream.

Rings of the Rise: The dry-fly technique is generally practiced during the daylight hours in calm or slow-flowing water wherever fish are found to be feeding from the surface. This manner of feeding is indicated by the appearance of rings on the surface, created as the fish rise cautiously and suck insects from it.

Rising fish will either be feeding at random (cruising), or on station. When taking food from the surface it is more common for them to move at random, rather than stay on station as is the case when feeding on nymphs. However, there are two situations where this general rule does not apply: the first is in the smooth water of a bar, just before the start of a rapid; the second is at the tail of a rapid where the faster current meets the quieter swirl of a backwater.

As the fish on station remains in a fixed position, rising occasionally to take an insect then returning to the same spot, you are able to observe its lie very carefully before presenting your fly. Having decided on the best vantage point, allowing for drag and obstructing streamside vegetation, you approach stealthily and cast. The fly should be delivered to the water slightly upstream of the fish's position, remembering that the current tends to make the rise seem a little further downstream than it really is. The perfect delivery ensures that the waiting fish sees the fly as it falls lightly on the edge of its window and then drifts naturally in the surface film, with none of the fly line and only a small part of the tapered leader visible.

A Trout's Cone of Vision: Because of the effects of refraction, a fish will always appear larger and closer to the surface than it actually is. It also appears to be further away than is the case. These facts should always be taken into account when casting to a fish that can be seen. A fly, cast to a trout from a downstream position, will float over the fish's window provided it is delivered accurately to the spot where the fish appears to be.

The 'window' is the term used to describe the circular area of the surface which falls within the range of the fish's vision. No matter how much a trout whirls around, it cannot alter the attitude of its window, which is always poised above its head like an inverted cone.

The size of the window varies according to the depth of the fish, and is estimated to be about 1.8 m in diameter when viewed by a trout 1 m below the surface. When seen from the depth of only 15 cm, the window is barely 15 cm in diameter. From this it can be understood that the closer trout are feeding to the surface, the greater the degree of accuracy required when casting a fly.

Sometimes it is very difficult to estimate the depth and true rise position of a trout on station. To overcast the line would almost certainly alert the fish to your presence so in such circumstances, it is better to err on the first cast by delivering the fly short, or behind the fish. You can always follow up with a slightly longer cast, until the fly is placed within the rising circle of the fish; but if the fish is frightened by the fly entering its range of vision, all hopes of capture must be abandoned for several hours.

When employing this practice it is imperative to let a misplaced fly drift well back from the fish before lifting it from the water. The sucking sound of a fly being pulled quickly off the surface will spook a brown trout several metres away in either direction.

Fishing for Cruisers: The difficulty of determining the position of a fish and predicting its movements makes casting to cruisers more exacting. A cruiser moves over a set beat according to a schedule so, when one is found, it is important to observe its behaviour from a distance until its route is discerned. Once this pattern is understood, you can predict the approximate path and speed of the fish and present your fly accordingly. It may take anything from a couple of minutes to half an hour of careful observation in order to be reasonably certain of the pattern of the cruising. Once a predictable circuit is established you can work out a strategy for casting from behind the fish. As with casting to a trout on station, it is safer to drop the fly short of the predicted path rather than cast beyond it.

Repeated attempts may be made, providing the fish is never frightened by the line falling across its field of vision.

Patient Observation: Time spent just watching the water is rarely wasted and, to a trained eye, will yield an abundance of useful information. Patient observation not only reveals the fish's beat but also the type of hatch and thus the food source on which the trout is most likely to be feeding. Particular note should be taken of the surface disturbance created by the rise. If gentle rings are evident there is little doubt that the fish is feeding dry, but should the rise be even slightly splashy or disturbed, it is probable that very small wet flies are being taken from the surface film. It is quite difficult at times to differentiate between a dry and a wet rise, and it may be necessary to experiment with different flies until a pattern is found that deceives the fish. A fish surface-feeding on nymphs rarely breaks the surface with its head. Rather, its back fin and tail will create a visible disturbance.

Timing of the Strike: Having chosen an attractive pattern and placed it correctly on the water in the right spot, the chances of deceiving the fish are good. If the fly is skilfully delivered so that it lands on the edge of the fish's window, or is given a slight twitch as the fish moves in for a closer inspection, the chances of success are excellent.

Presenting a carefully chosen fly and watching as the fish rises and takes the imitation into its mouth is a thrilling moment indeed, but the pause of the strike must surely rank as the most thrilling aspect of all. The timing of the strike is very important and must be slow, with a pause of two or three seconds before attempting to set the hook. This is always done by smoothly applying pressure with the free hand. Never strike with the rod, as there is too great a risk of snapping the leader or tearing the hook from the fish's mouth. An average interval for the strike is a slow count of three from the moment the fish is seen to take the fly.

In some circumstances, as with large cruising fish, the delay is extended to a slow count of five. In others, when the trout are small and feeding actively in the current, it is made almost instantly.

There are no hard and fast rules concerning timing, but as a general guide the slower the water and the larger the fish, the slower the strike. Of course, there are many instances when the size of the fish is unknown, and experience alone will enable an angler to determine the correct pause.

Avoid Alerting the Fish: The behaviour patterns of brown and rainbow trout show certain variations. Whereas rainbows have a preference for rough water, the browns will inhabit the whole river and seem more inclined to cruise than rainbows. The larger the fish, the greater will be its tendency to cruise.

The favourite position of each species should certainly receive priority attention but care must be taken to avoid disturbing the fish that are off station. The cruisers are generally more alert than fish on station and, when frightened, they have a tendency to swim away in panic. This behaviour generally puts every other fish in the vicinity on guard.

I have yet to understand thoroughly the puzzling antics of brown trout when they are on the alert. At times they will dart around the pool as though possessed, take off for parts unknown and unattainable, or just freeze in position. On several occasions over the years I have actually resorted to prodding them in the ribs with the tip of the fly rod to check that they were indeed still alive — they lost no time in proving the point. Once a fish has been disturbed it will obviously be on the alert, so no further time should be spent on it and new prey should be sought.

Hearing and Vision: Trout are normally extremely vigilant and easily disturbed by unfamiliar sights and sounds. They cannot hear human voices, which is perhaps fortunate when I recall some of the colourful expletives bellowed at trophy sized specimens that break the leader or throw the hook. Nevertheless, trout do have acute hearing, and water transmits sound waves five times faster than air. Although sound waves in the air are not transmitted to the water, a tiny pebble accidentally kicked into a quiet pool, the sound of feet dislodging riverbed stones or trudging along the bank, will alert every fish in a radius of about 10 m or so.

Their sight is also remarkably sharp, and enables them to see objects above the surface for considerable distances. The range of their vision depends on various factors, such as smoothness of the surface, light, brightness of objects and streamside foliage. But under normal daylight conditions they seem capable of detecting anything that moves within a

Al Holmes, from Seattle, preparing to release a big brown trout.

distance of 9 m, except when approached from a narrow strip directly behind the fish, which permits a skilful stalker to approach within about 3 m. In bright conditions their vision can detect shiny objects for much greater distances than 10 m, especially if the objects glint in the sun.

I have one fishing companion who is meticulous about eradicating sun reflections, even to the point of camouflaging the shiny rings on his cane rod with unsightly black paint. His rationale is based upon a thought-provoking observation — the number of occasions when, believing himself to be alone along a stretch of river, the first indication of the presence of another angler has been the glint of chrome or polished steel in the distance. If the human eye can detect such reflections so easily, so can the wily trout's.

Stealth and Camouflage: The importance of exercising stealth and caution when approaching a body of trout water cannot be over-emphasized, particularly in the height of summer (January through March) when the South Island streams are running low with warm clear water. Under these conditions, the trout leave their customary feeding stations in the shallow areas adjacent to the main current, to seek shelter and shade beneath overhanging foliage, undercut banks, fallen logs and the leeward side of large boulders. From such obscured positions the fish have the advantage over the angler, who is invariably in the sunlight.

Clothing is of the utmost importance. Besides being loose and comfortable it should be appropriately coloured, either green or brown so that it blends in with the natural surroundings and offers good camouflage. Many of the available fishing garments, while excellently designed for carrying all kinds of fishing accessories, are often rendered useless by incorporating bright colours and chromed buttons or belt buckles.

Wading: There are many situations when it is either necessary or advantageous for you to position yourself in the stream. Some streams are so heavily timbered on both banks that wading offers the only method of approach. In other situations, wading can enable the angler to avoid troublesome drag.

There is more to wading than simply walking up the centre of a stream. As previously mentioned, sound vibrations travel faster through water than air, greatly amplifying any disturbance created by clumsy feet. Wherever possible, always move up the side of a stream and always through water previously fished. If it is necessary to wade into mid-stream, do so slowly and with great care. The ripples and vibrations created by the legs will alert fish at an astounding distance, so it is always necessary to cast to the chosen spot well before any surface disturbance reaches it.

Some basic safety precautions must also be considered when wading. The foremost is the need to maintain a secure footing at all times — never lift one foot off the bottom until the other is firmly planted. Always move slowly, and when placing a foot on the bottom after taking a step, make sure your foot is settled before transferring your weight on it.

White-Water Fishing: The South Island offers abundantly stocked trout water of every description, including the roughest, wildest rapids imaginable. Fishing white water is a most exhilarating experience, calling for perfect rod and line control, extreme casting accuracy when placing the fly in the smallest of broiling backwaters, and very fast line retrieval. The common idea that this type of water is shunned by the brown trout and favoured by the rainbow is incorrect.

I take delight in watching the expression of sheer disbelief on the faces of overseas anglers each time I guide them to one of these spots. Not only is the roar of the torrent unnerving, but the surging, tumbling white water gives the impression that nothing could survive in such conditions.

When choosing a position in these areas, I locate water of between 6 cm and 3 m deep, that is well broken with protruding rocks and stones. While it is possible to fish this water by feel, I have always found that better results are obtained by watching the fly as well. It is essential to keep the line taut at all times and to strike quickly.

The recommended equipment for this style of fishing is a 2.7 m rod that ensures positive control of a weight-forward weight 5 floating line, both in the air and in the water. A 2.7 m leader of 2 kg breaking strain used with a well-hackled, thin-bodied dry fly is a very effective combination. The actual fly pattern is unimportant but for what it is worth, I favour the Blue Dun. Full bodied patterns tend to become water-logged and sink.

Brown trout inhabiting these waters are, of necessity, extremely fit and active. They fight as viciously as the turmoil in which they live.

I would recommend this white-water fishing only to those who have mastered the art of rod and line control, and are experienced in rivercraft — it certainly calls for quick reflexes, and a stable footing.

Wet Fly Fishing

This extremely versatile method of fishing is probably the easiest way to catch trout with a fly. It certainly has a much wider application than is generally believed or implied by the so-called 'across-and-down' method, which is only one of various applications.

Before continuing, I would like to clarify a couple of further points concerning wet fly terminology. Many fishermen from the North Island of New Zealand share the opinion of their overseas counterparts that the wet fly used in the South Island is actually the feather lure (streamer fly). This classification is incorrect. The description of a wet fly in the South Island is basically a flat, backward-facing winged variety in hook sizes 8 to 18. There are of course countless variations: winged or wingless, thin or thick bodies, gaudy or plain coloured, each style representing a particular submerged food source.

Conventional wet flies are usually tied and fished to imitate dead terrestrial flies, large underwater insects, tiny smelt and in several patterns of emergers (insects in the process of emerging from their chrysalis stage).

Nymphs, which are tied to imitate living aquatic insects between the egg stage and hatching, are also fished below the surface, but in a different manner from that used when fishing wet flies. Nymph fishing is regarded as the most skilful method of fly fishing and is the subject of a separate section.

The Evening (Wet) Rise: There is no doubt that if one desires to just catch a fish during normal atmospheric conditions, the evening rise should be fished. This rise starts in the late twilight about ten minutes before complete darkness, and lasts for barely fifteen minutes. The onset of the rise occurs simultaneously over the whole stretch of water and ends in the same manner, as if one had thrown a switch. The precision of this synchronized feeding phenomenon is truly amazing, and baffles the rational mind. The rise is generally preceded by the cessation of all fish movement for a period of about half an hour and followed by a similar interval, prior to the start of the after-dark dry fly rise. During the wet rise the fish frequently leap clear of the water, splash continuously and act as though they had not eaten for a week.

Tackle and Flies: Fine tackle is not as important when fishing the evening rise with a wet fly. A standard-length rod and floating line with a tapered leader of immaterial length will suffice. The fly pattern is also unimportant, although I have found that prior to complete darkness a size 12/14 fly of the thin-bodied, dark-coloured variety (Twilight Beauty, Kakahi Queen, Greenwell's Glory and so on) gives excellent results. If one possesses the self-control to stop fishing for a few minutes just as complete darkness falls, and to switch the fly to a size 8 thick-bodied pattern, the fishing session will extend a few minutes past the cessation of fish activity which generally signals the end of the rise.

It is of paramount importance to hold the rod firmly. Under these circumstances the fish have a tendency to strike with considerable force, so much so that on many occasions I have almost had the rod wrenched from my hand by the impact of the initial take. Naturally, the 'feeling of touch' technique previously described in the section on dry-fly fishing, does not apply in this style of fishing — rather it is rough, tough and active.

Wet Fly Technique: As with all forms of fly fishing, much depends on the choice of suitable water for fishing the night rise. The ideal position for wet-fly fishing is on the bar of a lake, or the tail of a large pool where the fish swim up against the current and enter calmer water. The actual flow of calm water into a confined run tends to concentrate the food supply.

The technique required is quite simple, and is merely a matter of casting slightly upstream, then quickly retrieving the line over the index finger of the hand holding the rod until it is taut. The line is held with the free hand as the fly is swept downstream to cover the width of the stream in a wide arc, until it reaches the end of its drift. At this point the fly is very slowly retrieved until a comfortable casting length is attained, during which period it is often taken by a fish.

John Garnett from the
United Kingdom holds one
of the West Coast's wily
brown trout.

Do not keep the rod tip pointed directly at the fly during this style of fishing, but at a slight angle from the line drift to allow it to act as a shock absorber. If the rod is pointed at the fly, as when dry fly or nymph fishing, the sudden jerk caused by the strike will invariably break the leader and, at times, even the hook itself. The tip of the rod, however, should be pointed down at the water until the moment of strike, at which stage it is raised into a vertical position after tightening the line with the free hand. The rod should remain vertical until the fish is played out.

At the conclusion of the night rise, it is often worth changing the fly to a streamer pattern of the Craig's Night-time or Black Phantom variety, and to continue with the same technique for another half an hour — there's generally one more fish left in the run.

The Dawn Rise: Early risers are well rewarded when using appropriate wet-fly patterns in sizes 12-14 at dawn. The most successful ties seem to be thin-bodied with light-coloured wings, similar to Dad's Favourite, Greenwell's Glory, Molefly and Kakahi Queen. It is necessary to be in position just as the light strengthens enough to silhouette the trees against the dawn sky.

The fish will feed quietly, but are quite visible. In fact, they will frequently lift their heads right out of the water, unlike the noisy splashing and jumping behaviour of the night before.

The wet rise in the morning usually lasts about an hour, after which time the fish start feeding on nymphs, and continue with this activity throughout the day. There is usually a two hour suspension of nymph feeding during the late morning, when the fish switch over to a dry fly. However, a wet rise may occur at any time of the day, especially in settled weather, so it is expedient to always carry a few wet patterns in the flybox.

Impromptu Rises: If a wet rise occurs during the day and is of a splashy or aerobatic nature, the night rise technique should be practiced. On the other hand, if the rise form is very quiet, the fish should be approached from behind if possible and long-distance casts employed to avoid detection with the presentation of a small nymph or dry fly. Casting proficiency is a real asset in this situation, as the best results are obtained when the fly is placed about 50 mm to one side and slightly in front of the fish's head. Such a presentation invariably causes the fish to move and snap instinctively without inspecting the imitation.

This technique necessitates that the rod be kept pointed at the fly, which is attached to a 2.7 m leader at the end of the line. The 'feeling of touch' is of the utmost importance if a successful hook-up is to be achieved. At the slightest indication of vibration, or current drag, transmitted through the rod to the ball of the index finger resting softly on the top of the grip, the free hand must smoothly harden the line. The instant a fish is hooked, the rod is lifted into a vertical position.

The Art of Fishing Blind: Productive fishing is possible throughout the day by casting a fly close to an undercut bank concealed by branches from overhanging willows. Shallow, shaded areas on the edge of a rapid are also likely spots where fish can be caught at odd times during the day. These sections of water are best worked by slowly walking upstream and casting a short line ahead, then stripping continually to keep it taut. With experience this manoeuvre will be executed by moving the rod tip backwards (instead of stripping) to keep a taut line — false casting should be avoided when fishing this method.

Practice and careful observation will gradually improve one's ability to read the water and detect fish in the most likely places. In many instances it is possible to see fish on station and present a fly accordingly, but lack of sighting should by no means deter you from blind-fishing. This manner of fishing calls for accurate timing of the strike, positive reflexes, and the 'feeling of touch' that I have frequently emphasized. The line must be continually retrieved and kept taut, yet in such a manner that the natural drift of the fly is not affected.

Nymph Fishing

The nymph is a comparatively recent addition to the methods of fly fishing. This highly effective technique has created a new breed of angler: the amateur entomologist who beguiles the dyed-in-the-wool dry/wet fly enthusiasts with science — and results.

The word 'nymph' refers to the larvae of common aquatic-bred insects such as mayflies, dragonflies, damselflies, stoneflies and so on, which live underwater between the egg stage and hatching. During this period of their life cycle, which may last from a few months up to several years, the nymphs are heavily preyed upon by trout, and in some regions constitute up to 80 per cent of a fish's diet. In fact, nymphs are the major food source of trout in all parts of the world where the species has been acclimatized, so it is obviously why anglers imitate them with such care.

Perhaps the greatest advantage of this method is that it means productive fishing can be practised throughout the day regardless of weather conditions, instead of waiting for the customary rise forms. This is possible because trout will accept food almost continually if it is carried to them by the current. Nymphs are therefore ideal as they can be presented throughout the hottest parts of the day to trout that are sheltering below the surface or beneath obstructions.

Life-like Replicas: Because artificial nymphs are imitations, they must appear very life-like if they are to deceive the fish, especially if they are used in still or slow-moving water where trout have plenty of time to inspect them. Fishing with a nymph is undoubtedly one of the most exacting and rewarding methods of fly fishing, and the nymph would certainly be the fly par excellence for catching all species of trout anywhere in New Zealand, were it not for the skill required to master some aspects of the technique.

I have spoken at length on the 'feeling of touch'. This so-called sixth sense is more crucial to success when using nymphs than in any other method of fishing, with the exception of dry-fly fishing after dark. Anyone who has observed a nymph specialist at work will testify to the miraculous ease whereby he catches trout. A fish is sighted on station and a single cast made — it looks as easy at that. But, by the same token, the majority of these anglers would seldom bother to use a dry or wet fly and could almost be described as fanatics.

Many types of material are used to dress the bodies of artificial nymphs, but the most common are seal's fur, wool, or a mixture of both. Some are tied almost entirely with fine copper wire and feather fibres. There are literally hundreds of different patterns to choose from in the nymph range, which is enough to bewilder most conventional wet/dry anglers who feel themselves already overburdened with the choice of regular imitations. I personally use only about six varieties, in a range of sizes. With constant experimentation I hope to narrow this down even further — but then I am not a fanatical exponent of the nymph, although rather in danger of becoming one.

Nymph Techniques: There are several ways of fishing with a nymph. In many respects, they can be used in a similar manner to the conventional wet fly — that is, either by casting upstream in moving water, or across and down (the latter method works, despite what the experts say). Nymphs may also be fished like miniature lures, with a lifelike action imparted to their movement by flicking the rod tip to create an erratic retrieve. This technique is particularly effective in still or slow water. The speed and manner of retrieval should be varied until a successful combination is found.

The dead drift application is popular on small streams where trout are visibly cruising, or feeding in positions where it is not possible to present a fly by conventional casting.

A variation of this technique has also proved successful on larger rivers and lakes, but requires lightning reflexes and, above all, an uncanny knack of knowing the precise moment when a fish has taken the fly. It is rare for the fish or fly to be visible when applying this method in larger waterways, so the strike must be timed by the 'feeling of touch' or what mystified observers sometimes describe as extra-sensory perception. Occasionally, for no apparent reason, the masters of this technique will suddenly apply pressure to the line and a fish is inexplicably hooked.

Many anglers now use a floating strike indicator sized to the leader or line at a distance from the nymph approximately equal to the depth of water to be fished. This is an ideal technique, which once mastered will result in a greater catch-rate. Various materials are used as an indicator, from fluorescent self-adhesive pads to knitting wool and natural wool fibre found on paddock fences. When fishing it is merely a matter of watching the floating indicator and striking quickly at any time the indicator is pulled beneath the surface.

Nymphs are suitable for use in all types of water, especially when there is no obvious hatch, and may be fished just beneath the surface or at great depth. The selected fishing depth will be determined by various factors such as observable or assessed feeding level, strength and nature of the current, depth of water and so on. Fish porpoising occurs when trout are taking nymphs just prior to the stage when they grow wings. At such times a floating line is employed with the leader greased to within a short distance of the fly. When fish can be seen feeding well below the surface, a floating line with a sinking tip is best. Weighted nymphs or sinking lines are necessary when fish are observed to be feeding very deep, or when no feeding activity of any kind is apparent.

Shallow Broken Water: Rough water lends itself perfectly to the nymph, particularly in shallow runs where it is possible to walk upstream slowly to locate trout holding and feeding in a food channel or fish blind, by casting a short distance ahead. This manoeuvre requires competent line stripping and horizontal rod control to maintain tautness of line and avoid drag. False casting directly upstream must be avoided in clear conditions as it can alert the fish. It is better to gain distance by casting across the river and then make one delivery stroke to the visible fish or the desired position. Particular attention should be given to the edges of the current, especially in broken water caused by large rocks, fallen logs or trailing willow branches. Feeding fish prefer these areas where they may lie on the edge of the current with minimum effort and feed discriminately on what is brought down. The common idea that trout will always be on station behind protruding rocks in broken water is incorrect — they will frequently hold a position in the current just ahead of the rocks in a vortex — pay special attention to these areas.

The habit of spotting a trout before presenting a fly pays dividends. Once seen, the battle is half over and with a little self-control it is possible to stand undetected for quite some time and 'throw the flybox' at them.

Deep and Turbulent Water: When fishing turbulent deeper water, the practice is to wade into the current as far as possible and cast upstream into the broken water behind an obstacle. My policy is to place the nymph on the very edge of the current and allow it to drift naturally into the eddy. If this method is unsuccessful, it is possible to fish across and down, as with a wet fly.

During these manoeuvres it is essential to keep a taut line at all times, which is no mean feat in places where the current is strong. When fishing from a downstream position the fish will be comparatively easy to hook by swiftly tightening the line with the free hand. When fishing from an upstream position, timing the strike is much more difficult and the 'feeling of touch' is of paramount importance.

Another extremely important and productive position on any river is at the base of a rapid along the very edge of the main current, just where it flows against the quieter swirls of a backwater, or just below the last upthrust of water as it levels off into a deeper pool.

Continuing to Cast into the Same Area: These deep agitated water positions should be fished consistently for at least ten minutes, even when no sign of fish movement is evident — not, as many fishermen do, 'three casts and we're off'. The large-bodied weighted nymphs that are commonly used in this type of water should be changed at intervals, until a successful pattern and size is found. When the first fish is caught, it usually pays to remain on station and continue casting into the same area — in many instances there will be several trout feeding in the run.

This latter point was graphically demonstrated to me by my son. He stood in the same position for about an hour, changed his nymph twice and hooked five big fish, but lost four of these owing to leader failure in the wild water. It was a hot afternoon under a blazing sun, and we had been chiding each other regarding the merits of his nymph versus my large Blue Dun dry fly, on which I caught the first (and only) large fish. While Ray could have fished downstream from this position, the nymph would not have been presented correctly, as the water was about 2.4 m deep and the drag on the line would have caused the nymph to float too high in the current and not drop into the hole behind the rock. The downstream method is better suited to slightly shallow water.

The nymph specialist generally chooses water of a different hue than I have just described. It will be crystal clear, knee-deep and flowing smoothly over stones rather than rocks. This type of water is well suited to fish-spotting with the use of polarized glasses that filter out the surface glare and reveal the sub-surface terrain clearly. When trout are feeding in this environment, they move slightly from side to side to take nymphs carried down by the current, then return to their holding station. The angler stealthily approaches from the rear to within about 6 m of his quarry, and casts the nymph so that it lands to one side and slightly behind the nose of the feeding fish — just within its vision. To allow the trout time to study the presentation minutely as it drifts back will invariably result in it being spurned — it is seldom that a nymph is a perfect replica of the real thing.

Setting the Hook: This action separates the master from the apprentice. The fish will blur for a fraction of a second as it turns, snatches the nymph, then returns to its station. During this short interval the hook must be set. Preceding the take, the line must be taut so that the strike can be made with the free hand at the very instant that the touch is registered. The strike should be instantaneous for the fish will immediately eject the fly on realizing that it is a fraud. For this reason, it is quick reflex action and the sixth sense that distinguishes the expert nymph angler.

Discerning the Rise Form: It is not unusual for experienced anglers to occasionally mistake a wet rise for a dry one. This generally happens when fish are found quietly surface-feeding in broad daylight. If careful attention is paid to the disturbance pattern created by the feeding fish at the surface, the true rise form should become apparent. If the surface disturbance is anything other than gentle smooth circular ripples, then the chances are that the rise is wet, and that very small nymphs (size 16-18) are being taken from the actual surface film

The author on a tributary of the Aparima River after the successful presentation of a dry fly.

of the water. Close observation will generally reveal a slight splash at the moment of take if the fish is feeding on small wet flies.

Fish feeding off the surface in this manner are extremely alert, and extra care must be exercised when judging the distance of the cast. If the line is allowed to pass over the rise it is almost certain that the fish will be instantly alerted and cease feeding. In such circumstances I use a small-bodied Pheasant Tail nymph with a few straggly hackles running backwards from the head, attached to an extra long 3.0 — 3.6 m leader with a tippet strength of about 1 kg.

Occasionally I use a nymph after dark when applying the across and down method, with satisfactory results. However, I do not consider that this is as effective as either the dry fly or feather lure (fished wet). The fish will take the nymph so presented in a positive manner, and invariably hook themselves.

Feather Lure Fishing

This effective method of catching trout utilizes a very large 'exciter'-type streamer fly, known as a feather lure (streamer fly). As a rule this type of lure is designed to represent a small fish, and is tied with brilliantly coloured materials aimed at exciting the killer instinct of large trout.

This technique is widely used in the North Island of New Zealand, where most of the larger rivers and lakes are stocked with mainly rainbow trout. The diet of these trout consists largely of the prolific quantities of smelt that inhabit the waters, whereas in the South Island the abundant insect life is the principal food source. So it will be readily understood why this technique enjoys such wide-spread popularity in the North Island, where it is generally called wet-fly fishing, although this is a misnomer according to traditional terminology.

Angling with a feather lure is certainly the easiest of all the fly fishing techniques. As this type of fly represents small feeder fish, many of which grow fairly large, it is usually tied on large, long shank hooks. When cast and retrieved with the correct action and speed, it performs the same function as the metal minnow used during spinning. In practice, this technique is similar to the conventional across and down wet-fly method, with the addition of a very slow retrieval against the current.

Heavier Tackle Necessary: Many traditionalist fly anglers look upon this technique disdainfully, regarding it as unsporting because of the heavy tackle (by South Island standards) that is employed. Nevertheless, in certain weather and water conditions the feather lure is the only effective means of catching fish. For instance it is ideally suited for fishing very deep water, or when streams are in flood and discoloured, on exposed windswept lakes and during the hours of darkness.

The technique is usually practised on large rivers and deep lakes where long-distance casting is desirable, not only to permit the line to sink to the bottom when necessary, but to provide the best and longest retrieval route for the lure. Maximum casting distance is achieved with the aid of a long heavy rod, and either a weight-forward or shooting head line, attached to monofilament backing line. The sheer weight of this equipment and the physical effort required for casting calls for a different method of holding the rod.

Whereas previously I have advised using a grip with the index finger on the top of the butt to facilitate rod and line control, I now recommend that the thumb be placed in this position and the index finger used to control stripping, retrieving and seizing. This grip will ensure that the main muscle of the hand is used to provide maximum power for long-distance casting. Accuracy of the cast is now a secondary consideration.

Most Suitable Conditions: The deep, quietly flowing stretches of a river, especially the areas against an underwater overhanging shelf, are perfectly suited for this technique. These positions frequently harbour the largest trout, but are generally quite difficult to fish when using the other three fly fishing methods. The streamer fly retrieved deep and close to the bank will usually entice the fish into action. Earlier I described the merits of fishing deep and turbulent water as well as the base of a rapid with the nymph. Both of these positions are also ideally suited for the streamer fly, but it must always be used across and down. In such circumstances the sinking line employed ensures that the lure runs deep.

Few anglers realize that the rough water side of a wind-swept lake often provides excellent results with the feather lure. During inclement conditions, most anglers invariably choose to fish the quiet water of the sheltered shore (which also produces good results). It is generally unpleasant to stand in the pounding surf and cast a long line into the teeth of a strong wind, but the results are frequently very rewarding. Under these conditions the line should be retrieved with reasonable speed to permit the lure to travel well above the bottom and through the agitated water. Trout that congregate in this position will feed with gay abandon.

Deadly Action: Anglers working the sheltered side of the lake will make long distance casts, wait until the lure has sunk to the required fishing depth, and then begin the retrieval in the usual manner. When using a feather lure, this is done by quickly stripping about 10 cm of line over the index finger, pausing momentarily, then repeating the 10 cm strip. This method of retrieval imparts a life-like pulsing movement to the soft feathery dressing of the lure, causing the feathers to alternately flatten against the body during the forward movement, and fluff out during the brief pause. This type of action proves particularly deadly, as it simulates perfectly the shape and swimming characteristics of small fish. It should always be applied when using a feather lure, regardless of the type of water being fished.

Slow Rate of Retrieval: The feather lure will frequently capture above-average sized trout, but because most large fish lie in, or close to, deep water and are slower swimmers than the younger specimens, it is important that the lure is not retrieved too fast. The speed of the current must always be taken into account when assessing the optimum retrieval rate. Often big fish are lost simply because they are unable (or unwilling) to chase a lure against the current. Large trout are more inclined to conserve their energy by adopting the easiest feeding strategy. They will rarely give chase to a lure that is travelling much above their feeding level, particularly if it is climbing steeply towards the surface. To keep a lure down at the required depth during the retrieval, especially where the current is fairly strong, it is necessary to use a heavy sinking line and sometimes (when local regulations permit) wind strips of lead or copper wire around the finished body of the fly. Many anglers achieve the same effect by attaching extra weight to the leader a short distance ahead of the fly. This must be done in such a manner that it does not interfere with the natural movement of the feather lure. Where the flow is fairly brisk, it is advisable to slow the retrieval right down, and allow the current to do the work.

Peculiar Soft Take: Contrary to what one might expect, the manner in which large trout pounce on a feather lure is seldom felt as a strong solid take. Instead, it is generally experienced as what has been termed a kind of pluck at the end of the line. Prior to the strike, the rod should be kept lowered and pointed to one side of the line retrieval. At the moment of strike two vital actions must occur simultaneously. The line must be hardened instantly with the free hand as the rod is lifted smoothly into a vertical position, where it can act most efficiently as a shock absorber. The index finger will seize the line until the manoeuvre is completed, at which stage the fingers of the free hand will grip the line and let it slip whenever excess pressure is applied by the fish, until the excess line is expended and the fish is on the reel.

The reel drag should be very carefully balanced with the action of the rod when using this technique. Every season I use and test many fly rods of both questionable and superb quality, with the conclusion that there is no hard and fast rule for drag setting; it has to be set to suit the individual rod.

I stand to be corrected by the feather lure experts, but my limited experience with this particular technique has narrowed the necessary range of lures to the following selection: Mrs Simpson (cockabully); Hamill's Killer (dragonfly larva); Parson's Glory (smelt); Jack's Spratt and Grey Ghost (whitebait); and Craig's Night-time and Pukeko (used after dark).

The feather lure is used extensively for trolling behind a boat while employing the same rod, line and leader as used in rivers. This method performs the same task as a spinning outfit with metal minnows and is referred to as 'harling'.

Artificial Flies

The word 'fly' is applied to many different forms and may be defined as a hook covered (dressed) with assorted materials in such a manner as to deceive the fish into mistaking it for food. Thus, a fly can represent aquatic as well as terrestrial insects. They can also represent a host of other creatures such as tadpoles, frogs, nymphs, minnows, mice, or any other small animal whose habitat is close to the water and which is small enough to be taken by a fish. Some 'exciter' patterns do not represent any living thing and are designed purely to arouse the aggressive instincts of a fish and induce it to strike.

I am not convinced that a large range of patterns is necessary and that every flying thing should have its imitation. A small selection in various sizes generally suffices. The presentation of the fly is of far greater importance than the emulation of the food source, and most fishermen have at some time wondered why the contents of a fish's stomach reveal a completely different diet to the fly taken at the time of capture.

Artificial fly patterns are divided into two basic groups: wet and dry. As their names suggest, the dry fly is designed to float above the surface of the water and the wet fly is designed to float in the surface film itself — similar to a half submerged leaf. The floating or sinking characteristic of a fly is determined by the different materials used in its construction. The dry fly is made from lightweight materials and treated with a water repellent such as silicone spray or cream mucilin. Heavy materials that quickly absorb water are employed when fashioning wet flies.

The Art of Deception

Since the art of fly-tying became a gentlemen's pastime during the early eighteenth century, an estimated total of 16,000 patterns have been published, the majority being originally developed for conditions in the United Kingdom, Europe and America. Strangely enough, a number of patterns were found to work extremely well regardless of where they were used and subsequently have became immortalised around the world as outstanding fish catchers.

Although the most popular styles are readily available through tackle shops, many anglers prefer to tie their own flies. In order to do this some basic knowledge of insect anatomy is necessary. Fly tying is not overly-concerned with producing life-like replicas, but relies on a realistic silhouette to deceive the fish.

Fly tying is a skill of its own and one which I have yet to master. I would advise anglers wishing to pursue this interesting pastime to search for specialised information in one of the many excellent books written on the subject.

Gowan River.

Both brown and rainbow trout appreciate the clear, invigorating water of the Pelorus River.

| Pelorus River

Although actually situated in the province of Marlborough, the Pelorus River is popularly regarded as part of the Nelson province because of its proximity to Nelson city. It is an interesting 45-minute drive away through the native and exotic forests of the Whangamoa and Rai Reserves.

The river begins in the beech forests of the Mount Richmond Forest Park and emerges from a gorge to flow into the Pelorus Sound at Havelock, some 25 km away. Despite the length of this river, access is limited to a 10-km section running parallel to Highway 6. The public accesses described here will provide several days of fishing, and anglers wishing to try other sections must obtain permission from nearby farm houses before crossing private land to reach the river.

The gentle terrain of the valley creates a large stream of clear water drifting quietly through big, wide pools and occasional rapids. The banks are covered with grass and shaded by avenues of deciduous trees. It is a photogenic area in autumn and an audible haven for native birds in spring.

Long sections of the river drift quietly between high banks, and wading is necessary to reach trout that are more alert than most anglers — they'll take evasive action the instant you make a faux paus or even tie a fly to a leader. The extensive lower reaches of the Pelorus are extremely deep, slow flowing and quite inaccessable, thus providing a natural hatchery and flood haven, ensuring the continuity of the fish population.

I suggest that you fish this river before the sea breeze ruffles the water at noon as this makes fly casting difficult in exposed places and the accurate delivery of a fly to trout feeding beneath overhanging vegetation impossible.

At dawn, large trout will take a weighted nymph drifted through deep water beneath overhanging willows, and their smaller counterparts will snatch at any small wet fly bounced over ripples in a shallow rapid. Try a size 12/14 Greenwell's Glory, Peveril o'Peak or March Brown. The heat of mid-morning sun will induce trout to cruise the shallows and feed on hatching aquatic insects, and you should watch for the slightest surface disturbance among the protruding stones or against a grassy bank. Fish feeding in this way may be taken on a softly presented 16/18 Adams/Kakahi Queen dry fly or the smallest Pheasant Tail (Sawyer's pattern) nymphs floated in the surface film.

Boisterous rapids and runs should be fished at midday and in the early afternoon with 10/12 dry fly patterns Molefly, Kakahi Queen, Humpy and Wulff. Revert to a size 10 Hare & Copper or Stonefly nymph during poor light conditions or if the river is running high.

Throughout summer, the twilight hour offers the most pleasant interlude imaginable. Preceding twilight the wind generally drops, and the lengthening shadows will herald an

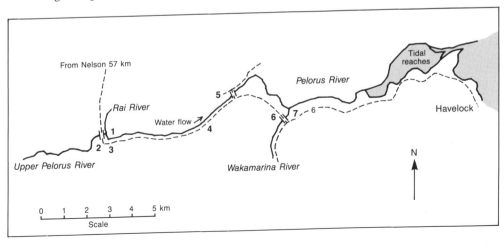

evening rise that has few equals anywhere in the South Island. The atmosphere is charged with anticipation for the first splash and the fly fisherman is 'in his element'.

The Pelorus River system and Lake Rotoroa, with its Gowan and Sabine Rivers, are the only waterways in the district to hold both rainbow and brown trout.

(1) Pelorus Bridge: 56 km from Nelson

Leave Nelson on Highway 6 to Blenheim, pass through the settlement of Rai Valley, drive over the Pelorus Bridge and stop in the large parking area on the left. A signposted walking track leads downstream to a gravel beach where there are rock formations forcing the river to turn right and converge with the Rai River tributary. This offers several fishing options. You may walk to the left over huge rock buttresses extending into the river and cast to rising fish (early morning and evening) or blind fish into the rapids flowing swiftly over clean, fresh alluvium.

It is possible to walk directly ahead onto a contoured gravel beach and fish the glide and turbulence of the confluence. This is an appealing position in the late twilight as the hush of darkness magnifies the call of the morepork and the screech of the possums goads the fish into a frenzied wet rise.

(2) Totara Reserve: 1 km from (1)

Turn left off the highway as it veers left into this elevated and sheltered camping site overlooking an immense surge pool. This pool is well stocked with trout which rise prolifically night and morning and provide the spin fishing angler with superb conditions during the day.

It is possible for fly anglers to fish the ripple at the head of the pool by following tracks through bush on the left to reach the obvious outcrop of rock — a small but good venue.

The large gravel beach opposite is reached via a signposted walking track leaving Highway 6 and passing over a swingbridge one kilometre south of the Pelorus Bridge. This offers access to the only acceptable fly fishing stance on the pool, while the bar downstream is accessable from position (3). The excellence of this venue, nestled in a reserve of virgin totara forest, is frequently marred by frustration 'if only I could reach those rising fish!'

(3) Riverbed Access: 200 m from (2)

Further on along Highway 6, there is a wide gravel verge on the right-hand side, opposite a gravel track leading beneath some trees towards the river. Park on this verge and walk the track before driving down, as it is occasionally washed-out. It is necessary to complete the descent of this access track to turn a vehicle, as the gradient and loose gravel surface makes reversing uphill impossible.

This is a good venue with varied water conditions and an open riverbed of stony terrain suited to all fishing techniques. The large pool described in (2) is visible upstream and its glide, forming the rapid extending across the river ahead, is loaded with trout.

Success on the Pelorus River, position (4).

Generally there are fish rising quietly on the apex of this fall, and fly anglers should stand downstream in the rapid itself and cast ahead to drift a very small nymph or dry fly over the disturbances. Try a size 16/18 Adams, Dad's Favourite or Black Spider dry fly and a similar sized Peacock Herle or Sawyer's Pheasant Tail nymph.

These resident trout have been fooled by experts, are easily spooked and delight in throwing down the gauntlet to fly anglers.

A large weighted nymph, say a Hare & Copper or Stonefly, should be cast 'across and down' in the descending turbulence, as it is too rough to fish large nymphs upstream, and drifted into the shallows of the pool in view. It is quite probable that you will pickup a small, stupid rainbow trout in this impossible-looking section.

The large pool beneath the high cliff is well stocked, but you must fish it upstream with a long line to avoid detection. The trout are quite difficult to locate visually here because of poor natural light conditions, especially in the afternoon.

The pool exits into a long rapid flowing vigorously over stones and rocky shelves offering excellent blind fishing with a large, high-floating dry fly. The rough and steepish banks are quite negotiable and provide good casting positions, but the current makes sighting fish difficult.

The occasional small, shallow inlets and glides should be examined minutely for a barely detectable stationary grey shadow, which should be tempted with a very small lightly tied nymph or dry fly of say the Grey Darter or Adams variety.

The rough water in this rapid calls for a positive fly fishing approach and the whole expanse should be covered with the fly being drifted through the same ripple two or three times. This is a good position from which to use a size 8/10 weighted nymph tied to a dropper beneath the dry. One or the other will goad a feeding trout into at least exposing its position.

Spin anglers will have easier going as they walk slowly downstream and cover the whole river with a slim, heavy minnow placing special emphasis on the turbulence to leeward of the rocky shelves extending into midstream.

(4) Anglers' Access Strip: 5 km from (3)

The river is visible through the roadside trees en route to this position and the wide, calm expanse, deeper this side beneath the willows, will be clearly discernible. It is quite normal to see rises from the moving vehicle.

A fringe of rough, impregnable scrub precedes and almost obscures the small Anglers' Access sign. When sighted, park on the roadside and pass through the fence. I suggest you walk downstream along the top of the bank and examine the rippling and calm water for rises before clambering onto the riverbed. Overhead power lines above the river locate the start of a wide shallow rapid that is always well stocked with (generally small) trout. They will provide hours of pleasure for any fly angler.

The wide expanse of sparkling ripples and the reflection of avenues of weeping willows and tall golden poplars sighing constantly to the clouds drifting above make this a picturesque spot. Fishing is but a bonus in such a setting.

The only 'jinx' here is the slippery round stones beneath the knee-deep water. Felt-soled boots help and aluminium strap-on cleats are perfect. Also a wading stick will eliminate the possibility of you using your rod as a walking stick, with dire results. Start fishing the rapid in the upstream manner from the bar of gravel at its lower extremity, and work your way across the current with a size 12 high-floating dry fly or Hare & Copper nymph into the deep channel beneath the trees on the other side of the river.

Fish this location well, and float your fly down the fast water entering the deep section against a high bank. Fish the whole rapid thoroughly, as even 15-cm deep ripples between protruding stones can hold a 500 g to 1.5 kg rainbow or brown trout which will be quite invisible until the fly flashes by.

The gentle glide at the head of the rapid extends at an angle across the river just upstream of the power lines. Fish it gently with 16/18 dries and nymphs. A stealthy approach and fly presentation are essential once you reach the upper extremity of the rapid. The sombre water beneath the willows on your left side is an excellent 'lie' for feeding trout, and you should fish it upstream until the depth restricts further progress. Cross the river and likewise fish the shallows into deep water.

(5) Daltons Bridge Anglers' Access: 1.8 km from (4)

Drive over the bridge and use the stile on the other side to reach the river. You'll have already examined the water in both directions from the bridge, seen the large trout swimming below, and decided that they're out of reach until the evening rise brings them into the shallows to feed.

A Twilight Beauty wet fly will suffice nicely then, but in the meantime walk upstream and fish from the shallow gravel beach on the right side with size 16/18 dries and nymphs tied to a very fine leader.

Spin anglers have perfect conditions for long distance casting and a deep water retrieve beneath the overhanging vegetation on the right side of the river downstream from the bridge. This is a venue for big trout.

The trees on the opposite bank overhang the slow-moving current, which is a particularly good fish-holding location. It is almost out of casting reach for fly anglers, who are assured of results from the presentation of a size 8 weighted Stonefly nymph during twilight. It is, however, an easy target for spin fishermen at any time of the day, and those large rainbows fight like crazy.

(6) School Road Access: 2.1 km from (5)

Drive through the gate this side of the school and follow a rough track through stands of scrub to the river where there's a small turning position. Park where possible.

The river is confined into several runs by alluvium, which alters the course of the river with every flood, but the large pools at either end of the broken section are well stocked with trout and they replenish the rapids when the high waters recede.

The general area should be 'fished over' and emphasis placed on the deeper flow against the stopbank on the opposite side of the river. This good trout-holding location must be fished stealthily from a downstream stance as the water and atmosphere are extremely bright and clear.

Miles of fishing water are available upstream for anglers willing to walk through gorse and blackberry bushes and ocasionally wade the rapids. The upper section of the large pool visible downstream is accessible from here, while its lower extremity is reached from the access (7).

(7) Wakamarina River Access

Drive over the highway bridge a few hundred metres past the school, turn left (away from the pub) and follow a narrow gravel road to its end beneath some trees a short distance ahead. Turning and parking (in order to avoid restricting gate access) is difficult here and anglers wishing to spend several hours fishing should perhaps consider parking near the hotel and returning on foot.

The road follows the Wakamarina River to its convergence with the Pelorus where there is (generally) a shallow but inaccessible bar extending the full width of the main stream. The plentiful stock of trout in the gut beneath this bar feed deep during the day and enticements, both fly and metal, must be presented at the correct depth to make contact.

The dull light of dawn and twilight will provide an active rise, and fly anglers will revel in the action that follows a take on a size 10/12 Greenwell's Glory, Dad's Favourite or Twilight Beauty wet fly. There are some large rainbow trout in this position.

At normal or low water levels it is possible to walk downstream for a mile or so and enjoy particularly good fishing in fast rapids, gentle ripples and quiet pools. It is necessary to wade the river beneath tall willow trees on the left bank to reach the long shallow gravel beaches downstream, as there is no public access from here down to the tidal reaches of Pelorus Sound.

The trout in this watershed suffer frequent disruption from flash floods. The river channel can be likened to a giant sluice box, especially in the solid rock gorges of the upper reaches, and there are times when trout numbers are depleted in any one location.

Their recovery from this temporary, but regular, occurrence will be aided by your practise of catch, photograph and release.

2 Waimea River

This gentle river bisects the Waimea Plains of Nelson, after gaining its source from three tributaries in the surrounding hills. The upper reaches are stocked with large trout, limited in numbers by a pristine environment. The water is filtered to incredible clarity by mountains of mineral rock. This creates a habitat of visual appeal, but means that the water is incapable of sustaining mosses, weeds or aquatic insects. The lower reaches, on the other hand, provide good conditions for anglers practising either the spinning or fly fishing method. They are well stocked with brown trout (not withstanding floods or droughts) and are accessible from a gravel road paralleling the river between stopbanks.

The Waimea is subject to occasional and often severe flooding, which alters the water channels. This should be taken into account when reading my description of the region. All the accesses shown are public.

The river is bridged in two positions by major highways leaving Nelson; Highway 6 at Brightwater, 24 km inland, and Highway 60 at Appleby, some 19 km west of Nelson city. These divide the river into three distinct sections.

The area below the Appleby Bridge is influenced by the tide and flows over a wide gravel bed in open terrain. The course of the river over the plains is lined (one side or the other) with willow trees which do not provide the shade or shelter one would expect. The environment is actually too open to be described as a perfect trout habitat. Shoals of smelt and minnows infest the river from the sea up to the Appleby Bridge, and trout have to compete with kahawai and mullet for this source of food. It is quite possible for anglers to catch these sea-run predators right under the bridge, some 3 km inland. This causes confusion when fishing the immediate area during twilight, when some fish charge frantically in all directions chasing smelt while others remain 'on station', feeding sedately. Fly anglers who are fishing positions where trout are chasing sub-surface food should use a sink-tip or full sinking line with the streamer fly technique, even if a large weighted nymph is necessary to emulate a tiny minnow.

The perfect time to fish the area downstream from the bridge is during twilight when a high tide coincides with darkness, but you must ensure that your 'escape route' remains open. The tide can quickly entrap the unwary in thigh-deep water.

Good fishing is available from dawn until mid-morning, at which stage the inevitable sea breeze will ruffle the leaves, create surface ripples and make fly casting impossible within an hour.

The deep pools and shaded areas beneath the willows in the mid section between the highway bridges may be fished throughout the day. These positions provide spasmodic results during low-water conditions in midsummer, but the opposite is the case when the river is rising or running full as result of back-country rain.

The deeper sections of rapids frequently hold feeding trout that have moved-up from the head of the pool. Always examine these positions before walking upstream to fish.

The upper section of the river, from Highway 6 bridge to the weir at Max's Bush, offers 2 km of delightful fly fishing, where experienced anglers may expect to locate holding trout visually or lift cruisers with a strategically placed dry fly.

The water here is considerably colder than that of the mid and lower regions which have warm pools. The terrain is rougher, and vehicle access is limited. Consequently the trout are less disturbed by the swimming fraternity but more alert to untoward incidents. A stealthy approach is paramount here.

Spin anglers should use 7-g (or lighter) Spoons, Tangoes, Mepps or Veltic-type minnows in subdued or yellow colours, but fly anglers have a difficult choice. The stable food source for trout in this river is smelt and cockabullies (scolpins) supplemented by insects, the majority of which are terrestrial. Use normal streamer fly patterns Grey Ghost, Jack's Spratt in or near the tidal reaches and Yellow Dorothy, Mrs Simpson and Parson's Glory elsewhere. Standard nymph patterns, Pheasant Tail, Hare & Copper or Stonefly, in sizes suited to the prevailing conditions will suffice anywhere in the river system.

Dry flies should be of the sparsely tied varieties Adams, Greenwell's Glory, Partridge & Yellow or Hardies Favourite. The twilight hours should be fished wet with Greenwell's Glory, Dad's Favourite, Peveril o'Peak or Twilight Beauty in sizes 12 to 16.

The Lower Section: Appleby Bridge to the Sea

(I) Queen Street Access

Turn right at the traffic lights on the Nelson side of Richmond, follow Queen Street through its intersection with Landsdowne Road, a distance of 4.5 km, and pass over the visible stopbank 1.2 km away. Drive slowly along the gravel vehicle track (which may be muddy in odd places) to the shingle bed of the river (about 500 m).

En route there are several distinct but half overgrown bulldozed tracks leading towards the river and terminating on the stopbank constructed of hewn rock. The deep water flowing against this embankment is well stocked with brown trout holding between the slabs of rock and feeding on minnows and whitebait swimming upstream.

Restrictive vegetation permits spinning only. Such anglers should cast as far downstream (or upstream when the tide is receding) as possible and retrieve their minnow close to the rock wall. Spoons, Tangoes, Daffies or Tobies coloured black, gold or yellow will suffice and an imitation whitebait minnow should be used when the bait is running in September/November.

Your first sight of the river reveals a wide shallow bar guiding the water towards the stopbank and offering an easy knee-deep river crossing. Fly anglers should casually fish the current upstream and ahead while wading across. The slightly agitated water, compressed into a narrowish channel at the base of the bar, provides an excellent evening/full-tide fishing venue, when trout (and predator sea fish) act as though they've been starved for a month.

As darkness settles and the tidal flow begins to wane, the immediate vicinity explodes with jumping and splashing fish rushing helter skelter all over the place, oblivious to everything except food. I've even had them hit my legs when in pursuit of smelt, such is their feeding frenzy.

The streamer fly method surpasses all techniques in these circumstances. But the fly must be retrieved at exactly the correct depth to succeed — 10 cm (4 in) beneath the surface. I've found that the best line to produce consistent results is a sink-tip floater. Although the fly is of lesser importance than the line (and depth of presentation) the following four patterns tied on a size 2 hook may be considered the basic selection; Yellow Dorothy, Parson's Glory, Jack's Spratt and Grey Ghost.

Anglers should be ready to fish at the first sign of a rise. The action is fast and furious, but lasts barely half an hour, and it will cease as abruptly as it started.

These trout are sea-run browns which take the fly violently and, once hooked, will head towards the open sea with the speed and strength to test the very best equipment — ever had a screaming spool fly off its arbor?

Reasonably good daylight fishing is available during full/high water conditions as far as the bridge visible upstream. The river runs deep against the overhanging willows on the far bank and fly anglers fishing from the shallow side should wade into the stream and make long casts to permit a fly or nymph to brush the foliage as it drifts naturally downstream.

Examine the water near trailing branches carefully; large trout are masters at concealment when dominating a food channel, and feed with incredible dexterity. Generally only a fin or nose will reveal the holding station of a mature brown trout.

The breathless hours of dawn and twilight coax resident trout to wander at large through the large expanses of mirror-surfaced water and they take with scarcely a ripple. Locate your quarry by its bow wave, and place a 16/18 Hare's Ear nymph or Adams dry fly 15 cm (6 in) ahead of the apex — as softly as falling thistledown.

The two shallow rapids separating the pools below the bridge will seldom hold trout during daylight hours in summer months unless the river is running high. The fish will be in the shade and sanctuary of the banks overgrown with scrub and willow trees. They will, however, move into the broken water to feed as darkness settles and remain on station most of the night.

The groynes of rock beneath the willows on the other side of the river are accessible from an access road leading downstream from the visible bridge. These provide good spin fishing venues.

Instead of returning to Queen Street, it is possible to drive up the riverbed (or rough gravel track beneath willow trees) to the bridge where there is parking and easy foot access to conditions suited to spin or nymph fishing, in a deep channel of water flowing along a bank beneath tall trees.

(2) Tidal Reaches: The West Bank

Drive west over the highway bridge and turn right into an access road leading past a grassy reserve and terminating on the tidal riverbed 2 km downstream (don't leave your vehicle unattended on the final 400 m of smooth gravel if the tide is coming in). Along this road there are several indistinct footpaths going through rough vegetation towards the river, in addition to one well-used vehicle track leading onto an open gravel beach. Finally, there is a parking area between trees where the road turns onto the riverbed itself. This parking position is opposite, and provides quick, dry-foot access to the evening fishing channel described earlier in this chapter.

The river from here downstream is visibly tidal and provides a different fishing aspect to the one generally associated with trout fishing. Anglers of either technique are assured of an interesting interlude if they walk well downstream early on a sunny morning and fish upstream just ahead of the tide.

All water movement ceases momentarily preceding the tide-flood and concentrated inspection will usually reveal almost-transparent fish cruising quite purposefully in search of food. These fish will swim in and out of casting range and may be taken with a small Mepps/Veltic spinner, or a number 6 light drab-coloured streamer (similar to a rabbit tie) or size 8 wet fly (Blue Dun/March Brown). This is absorbing fishing: harassed by screaming terns while watching your footing and the encroaching tide, you spy ghostly shapes of something that may be a big sea-run brown trout if the shadow beneath it is any indication of size.

The spaciousness of these lower reaches offers good overnight parking positions for those with self-contained vehicles, and the gentle terrain will surely entice adventurous anglers to walk quietly upstream in the dead of night and cast a size 12 Twilight Beauty dry fly towards stars reflected in 'the ring of the rise'.

The Mid Section: Between Highways 6 and 60

When returning from the lower section, turn left onto Highway 60, cross the Appleby Bridge, drive on a further 1.2 km and turn right into Blackbyre Road. If travelling direct from Nelson, continue straight through the Richmond traffic lights on Highway 6, drive 1.6 km and turn right at an intersection to follow the Motueka highway. The Blackbyre Road junction is on the left, 4 km away.

Blackbyre Road passes over the stopbank 900 m ahead and follows the river for 6 km before merging with Clover Road which crosses Highway 6 near Brightwater and leads to the upper section of this river (see below).

(3) Riverbed Access: 1.5 km from Blackbyre Junction

Drive over the stopbank, turn right, and follow the road downstream down an obvious track onto the riverbed. If the road is blocked by a pile of gravel (occasionally left by the crushing plant operator) it will be necessary to turn and park near three tall blue-gum trees on the roadside and walk through the fringe of trees to reach the river.

The road embankment forms the stopbank along which fly anglers should walk furtively, while examining the deep water flowing quietly over huge slabs of hewn rock.

Stealth and patience are the keynote here — there are a few large brown trout domiciled in this pool. They are shrewd, alert and swim with gracious disdain of the anglers' presence, but they are sitters for a perfectly presented size 18 Grey Darter or Ostrich Herle nymph. They bask in the sun, suspended motionless mid-depth and midstream, to all intents and purposes asleep, but skilled anglers will notice the white of their lips opening and closing as they take sub-surface nymphs.

During the day only small fish will be found in the rapids and fast water at the head of the pool, but evening hours bring forth the larger trout. Anglers wishing to fish here in the evening should continue up the road and follow an obvious vehicle track onto the riverbed itself — parking in terrain that provides easy walking to the water's edge. It will be necessary to cross a shallow ripple to reach the gravel bank of the pool.

(4) Riverbed Park Access: 2.4 km from (3)

En route to this extensive section of open riverbed, the road once again skirts the perimeter of a constructed embankment where similar conditions to those prevailing at access (3) will be found. This pool, however, is considerably longer than the previous one, contains swifter water and holds a larger number of average-sized trout which succumb to skilled fly anglers.

Anglers intending to fish this pool should park on the roadside near three overhead power lines, step through stunted scrub and examine the whole expanse of water as they walk upstream. Unless trout are feeding actively, they will be difficult to locate beneath surface swirls and will appear as transparent apparitions — you may have to locate them by their shadows during sunlit conditions.

This is a fly anglers' venue unless the river is high or slightly discoloured. A spinning minnow deployed during normal conditions would mobilize every trout in the vicinity away from the angler. Spin anglers may, however, expect results at dawn and again in late twilight after the evening rise has finished, especially if fishing from the gravel bank opposite. Follow the vehicle track (800 m ahead of the power lines) through a fringe of trees onto the riverbed where there are good overnighting and picnicking positions a short distance from the pool.

Upstream, a rock groyne confines the river into a crescent-shaped flow of runs and boisterous rapids which provide lively fishing conditions for anglers using either method.

(5) Picnic Flat Access: 1.7 km from (4)

Drive past the crushing plant, ignoring the tracks leading towards the river, and take an access through trees at the distance given above.

This section of regenerating riverbed has a smooth surface with established shade trees offering sheltered positions for picnicking close to good trout water. Nearby there is a willow-shaded pool, and 800 m downstream there are gentle rapids at the convergence of the Wai-

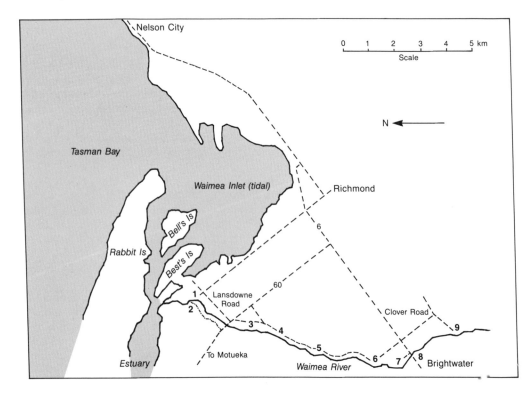

iti River. The ripple upstream is the outlet from the Holmes Pool, an excellent section of fly fishing water.

The river around the perimeter of this flat provides conventional trout stream conditions and may be fished similarly, but the Holmes Pool rates special attention. It is probably the best stocked section of water holding the largest brown trout in the entire river. It may be fly fished from the right-side gravel bank in the usual manner by casting to rises or just fishing blind with a weighted nymph or dry fly (the former technique is pertinent with a wet fly during the evening rise). But the upstream stalking approach, described on the two pools earlier in this chapter, is really warranted here. The difficulty experienced when scrambling through trees and prickly scrub on the road embankment to gain casting positions in this venue is surely a small price to pay for the opportunity to fish for such trophy-sized and quite visible brown trout.

(6) Blackbyre/Clover Roads Junction: approx. 3 km from (5)

Blackbyre Road ends at a vehicle access (an extension of Clover Road) leading through rough vegetation to the riverbed. The river from here to the Brightwater Bridge some 2 km upstream descends a distinct gradient through a bed of stones and it is necessary to walk the river and examine holding-pockets in turbulent water.

A grey smudge or flash of colour will identify feeding trout which should be tempted — and caught — with a size 12/14 Humpy/Wulff/Molefly dry fly or size 10/12 Hare & Copper, Stonefly or Pheasant Tail nymph.

This active and intensely absorbing search for something in the current is relieved occasionally by calm pools, where a leisurely interlude readies an angler for the next rapid.

(7) Highway 6 Access: 2.2 km from (6)

Follow Clover Road from the farm gate (leave it open or shut, as you found it) for 1.6 km, turn right at the intersection and drive towards the elevated highway bridge.

Travel 400 m only and turn right into a narrow farm-type access road which leads downstream, veers towards the river, then parallels it for 1.4 km and terminates among unkempt patches of broom and stunted trees and grass. This extensive parking area has walking tracks through vegetation to a rough flood-prone riverbed, offering good fishing

The typical terrain and waterflow of the Waimea River.

in boisterous water conditions, where visual inspection of holding-pockets will often reveal the shape of a trout.

It is possible for two or more anglers to 'leap-frog' fish the river between accesses (6)-(7) and (7)-(8). It takes only a short time to reconnoitre the region by car and familiarize yourself with the local geography.

The Upper Section: Highway 6 to Max's Bush Weir

(8) Brightwater Bridge (Highway 6) Access: 200 m from (7)

Return to Highway 6, turn right, cross the bridge, turn left into a gravel storage enclosure and park unobtrusively on the far side where there is a track leading onto the riverbed.

There is 2 km of excellent fly fishing water from here to the final access position upstream, and anglers should contemplate spending 3 or 4 hours fishing quietly upstream to meet their transport there.

This section is typical of a South Island trout fishing river; clear water effervesces over rapids, meanders through mirror pools and caresses an occasional buttress of clay or rock. It is a venue which is generally sunlit, but cooled by afternoon sea-breezes, providing idyllic upstream dry fly (or small semi-floating nymph) blind fishing while ever searching for the tell-tale twitch of a fin, swish of a tail or surface swirl of a feeding brown.

Small Kakahi Queen, Blue Dun, Yellow Humpies and Adams dry flies, and Grey Darter, Peacock Herle-style nymphs, are the order of the day here.

(9) Max's Bush Access: 4 km from (8)

Travel back over the Brightwater Bridge, turn right at the first intersection, follow Clover Road for 1.7 km and turn right into Haycocks Road. Follow the road through a couple of signposted gates to a carpark beside a powerhouse 2 km away.

Before this building the road descends steeply to cross a grassed flat surrounded by trees and overarched by heavy overhead power lines. Follow the vehicle track leading from the road (unless it's muddy) and park directly ahead beside a fence. (Ideally, you should continue driving along the road first and reconnoitre the area from the elevated carpark.)

Step through the fence (be careful, it may be electrified) and follow the vegetation-shrouded track to the riverbed of large stones directly beneath the power lines.

The concrete and rock weir visible upstream terminates the Waimea River and is preceded downstream by 300 m of the most delightful water imaginable. Golden-coloured knee- to thigh-deep water rushes quite swiftly over and between large stones and shelves of solid rock creating the perfect fly fishing venue — a location to excite the most staid of anglers, and surely a fitting finale to the 'river of the plains'.

3 Motueka River

Nelson is on the edge of the Waimea Plains, which are surrounded by mountains on three sides and ocean on the other. The area is serviced by two river systems: the Waimea River flows through the centre of the plains and the Motueka River skirts the base of the Tasman Mountains. Both possess a maze of tributaries, most of which rise from clear-watered springs in remote valleys.

This chapter deals with the Motueka River from the sea coast to the convergence with the Wangapeka River, its major tributary, near Tapawera, some 50 km inland. The Wangapeka is conceived in virgin forests in the North-West Nelson Forest Park and the headwaters of the Motueka weep from wind-savaged mineral deposits of stark and grotesque beauty on high alpine slopes in the Mount Richmond Forest Park. These dissimilar waters merge to create one of the best brown trout fisheries in New Zealand: a gentle river likened to a large stream as it follows a shallow gradient through a gravel course over prime agricultural land.

Most of the valley floor is surveyed into small free-hold properties, many of which possess riparian rights, which means that the occupier owns the land up to the centre of the river and is entitled to refuse access. Anglers wishing to fish sections of river not described here should request permission from the nearest house.

The river is over-stocked (despite some displacement due to floods) with brown trout which, despite an abundance of food and a perfect habitat, average only 1 kg (2.2 lb) in weight. While both spinning and fly fishing methods are successful, the river must be considered a fly anglers' utopia, where large expanses of clear water drift quietly through pools shadowed by avenues of deciduous trees. The smooth glides, sparkling ripples and boisterous rapids are all well stocked, and even the swift runs through clefts in solid rock generally have an extremely fit and active brown trout holding in seemingly impossible conditions.

The unique beauty and serene atmosphere of this river belie the characteristics of its fish. Brown trout are recognised internationally as an adversary equal to the skills of the most accomplished fly anglers, and the trout of the Motueka are masters of the art and unquestionably New Zealand's most difficult fish to catch. I know of only one other river (the Jackson River, Haast) in which brown trout demonstrate the same acute vigilance, cunning and fastidious choice of insects, and it's also a river sourced by mineral terrain. However, these trout may be caught off-guard during rising and slightly dirty water conditions resulting from heavy rain in the hills. But if barometric pressures are falling at the same time, then just go home.

Fly anglers must use the smallest and lightest hackled flies available, and a 2 m (9 ft) small diameter leader with a fine tippet added. Dry fly patterns Pheasant Tail, Adams, Greenwell's Glory and Twilight Beauty during the day, with the two latter patterns in wet for the twilight rise, would be a good basic fly selection.

Nymphs will be used frequently — at any time of day, and, once again, the smallest sizes that will cajole a trout into a take without spooking should be presented. The Sawyer's pattern Pheasant Tail may be considered the basis of your selection which could also include Grey Darter, Hare & Copper, Gold-ribbed Hare's Ear, Greenwell's Glory and Twilight Beauty in sizes 10-18.

Spin anglers should fish the roughest, fastest water in sight with a 7- or 10-g Toby/Tinker coloured gold, black or yellow, and use the same coloured 7-g Spoon, Tango or Daffy in the ripples. The debris-littered backwaters and the apex of glides will produce results with a small Mepps, Veltic or similar blade-type minnow. **But please** use single hooks or cut two prongs off those mouth-mutilating trebles.

Long-distance casting is frequently necessary to reach fish rising midstream, and meticulous presentation is essential when trout are quietly feeding on willow grubs hatching on a single leaf trailing in the water.

The precise line and fly control necessary to catch fish regularly in this waterway may only be achieved with the use of quality equipment. Personally I use Sage exclusively and find the LL series in either weight 3 or 4 (depending on wind strength) ideal. The two rods are unsurpassed for soft and accurate (and surprisingly long distance) delivery.

The proximity of the open sea and encircling mountains create a generally predictable daily weather pattern in midsummer. An awareness of this will help anglers to plan successful forays, avoiding unnecessary travelling and wasted fishing time. Dawn breaks about 4 a.m., the air is calm until 11 a.m. Then the sea breeze wafts upstream, increasing in strength and blowing surprisingly strongly between 1 p.m. and 6 p.m. It then decreases gradually and ceases altogether, around 9 p.m. The calm period lasts until the ocean recalls its wayward breeze from the mountains about midnight.

Spin anglers are assured of results at this time when fishing anywhere with almost any small minnow, but should move into swift water as the light strengthens and concentrate their efforts in similar positions all day.

Fly anglers should use small wets, (say sizes 14/16 Greenwell's Glory) for a couple of hours from dawn, changing to small nymphs as the sun incubates the hatch in shallow water and attracts trout to feed surreptitiously. This nymph rise will change to a surface one about an hour before the sea breeze.

Fly anglers should endeavour to fish the following two particularly interesting and pleasant periods each day. Sunrise will bring forth a positive but subdued rise in gently flowing sections all over the river, especially where overhanging willow branches brush the water. Examine the surface closely for the merest ripple indicating a fin or lips of a trout sucking a tiny insect emerging from the nymph stage.

When the inevitable afternoon sea breeze ceases as daylight fades, the swallows will suddenly materialize and summon the fish to a tumultuous rise. It lasts barely an hour but offers frenzied and exhilarating action for all participants.

(I) Whakarewa Street Access: 3.7 km from Motueka town centre

Drive along Highway 60 into Motueka and turn left to follow Whakarewa Street inland from an intersection on the east end of the town itself. Watch carefully for the street sign, it is erected on the wall of a building, and not a post as is usual.

The street terminates beside an access gate, just over the raised grass covered stopbank. The river flows deep against the embankment, which curves left (downstream) from its down-valley course and disappears behind some trees. This spot provides many hours of fishing suited to all techniques, but access necessitates scrambling through rough vegetation. The visible run upstream of your stance is extremely well stocked with trout in the deep water close to the bank rather than in the shallows on the opposite side of the river. Fly anglers should walk slowly upstream, step down the bank here and there and drift a fly/nymph

Position (3), Motueka River.

through water disturbances midstream as well as hard against the overhanging grass of the stopbank. Their spin fishing counterparts should walk along the stopbank to the source of the glide — a rough fast rapid — then apply the downstream technique using heavy, deep-running minnows.

Do not be fooled by the apparent absence of fish, or their visible movement, they're here alright. The last 10 minutes of twilight will prove it with an incomprehensible number of actively rising and jumping trout.

Excellent water, beaches and unrestricted casting conditions await downstream. Follow the stopbank, cross it where possible and 'follow your nose' through restrictive scrub, walking onto the gravel riverbed at the end of the stopbank. A long, wide gravel/stone beach slopes gradually into the most perfect pool, glide, rapid and turbulent deep-watered swirl-pool you'll ever see — and it's full of fish too! This extensive area also extends around the corner downstream where several upstands of solid rock create all types of water conditions. Actually, the entire location provides far too much water to be fished properly in a single day.

The water is easily enough read by the experienced angler, but may I suggest that the long rippling shallows on the edge of the rapid be fished thoroughly with a small dry or nymph applied in the upstream manner. The water here is only a few inches deep, but it is an exceptional food bed (as is the thigh-deep flow midstream) and holds a lot of fish.

(2) Highway 60 Bridge Access: 58 km from Nelson

Return to the intersection in Motueka, turn left and follow Highway 60 through the town. Cross over the river bridge, turn left onto a roadside gravel storage area and follow the vehicle track over the stopbank. While you may park anywhere here, and fish nicely rippled water with either method, the sheer size of the river renders this venue better suited to spinning.

The rough track passes beneath the bridge, follows the river downstream and terminates in unkempt vegetation near the tidal reaches. En route several openings offer walking access to the river, which may be crossed at odd positions where braided channels and gravel bars separate the volume of water. It is an interesting location providing several good fly fishing and spinning spots and it should be visited by those with a few hours to idle away.

(3) Gum-tree Corner Access: 4 km from (2)

Continue along Highway 60, driving straight ahead, until reaching an intersection signposted 'West Bank Motueka River'. Turn left and follow this road for about 1 km, where, on a sharp right-hand turn, there is a lone, large gum tree on the left side. The gate beside the tree bears the inscription 'Private Property, please shut the gate'. Park on the roadside and step over a fence stile which offers walking access down a grass-covered bank to the river.

Here you will find a well-stocked run of perfect fishing water flowing between flood-control stopbanks, over occasional outcrops of solid rock, gravel bars and through deep pools against the road embankment. The gentle gradient and varied terrain create perfect breeding conditions for aquatic insects and minute fish, so the area is a natural feeding ground for trout. They cruise as the sun gathers strength in the morning and again at twilight. During the hot, bright afternoons, however, they cease feeding to seek shelter.

The spin angler visiting this position should fish the faster sections of water and leave the pools and shallow rippling runs for fly fishing. There is room enough here for everyone. There is a particularly good spin fishing position upstream, providing a stance on rocks below the road embankment, from which to retrieve a minnow close to the bank through deep, productive water. Walk (or drive) along the road for 100 metres or so and locate a track leading from the road verge to the river below. This is positioned where the road veers slightly right and immediately downstream from the bend in the river.

(4) Rocky Creek Access: 7.7 km from (3)

Cross the bridge and park on the verge. You may walk down the creek itself or follow an indistinct track (Motueka side) through rough vegetation and driftwood onto a high sand bank sloping into the water near several large rocks where there will be cruising trout with eyes like hawks.

The immediate locale is well stocked and offers good fishing for both spin and fly anglers. The pool, the deep water behind the half immersed rocks and the shallow run (accessible with waders) over the line of boulders midstream is a perfect fly fishing venue. The fast-running water towards and below the creek convergence is ideal for spin fishing as is the entire width of the main stream, and from here it is possible to lay a line into the shallows on the opposite side of the river.

Fly anglers only: Step through the creek, walk stealthily upstream on the clay bank and carefully inspect the surface ahead for cruising trout. They will take a small, lightly hackled nymph if you're experienced enough to drift the fly like a phantom and present it as softly as thistledown — these trout are spooky... and big.

(5) Alexander Bluff Bridge Access: 300 m from (4)

Park on the bridge approach and use the elevated structure as an observation platform. There is a long, shallow, gravel/stone beach on the right side downstream, where fish will probably be rising in the ripple near the trees. Access to this venue is via a short rough vehicle track just downstream from the bridge. (Examine it before driving down, as it may be washed-out.) The beach continues around the corner and provides many hours of fishing when either fly fishing or spin fishing.

The sandy beach upstream extending into a long, underwater bar is reached from a track leading under the bridge on the opposite side of the river. It is necessary to park on the road as the vehicle access has been closed.

The bar, its glide, shallow ripple and deep, swirling pool are all good fish-holding positions but, with the exception of the shallows upstream, necessitate a blind fly fishing or 'chuck-and-chance' spin fishing approach. Examine the run downstream from the pool where it flows smoothly beneath overhanging willows. There are usually a few trout holding motionless on the bottom and feeding sedately on nymphs as they drift along the visible riverbed channels. You can reach a casting position, albeit long distance, from beneath the bridge itself. Drift a size 14/16 weighted Hare & Copper nymph down the channel and watch the action.

It is possible to walk upstream along this bank for a considerable distance and enjoy good fishing all the way, but a quiet, stealthy approach over stones and beneath trees is essential. The trout will be feeding in a few inches of water, and they will be alert.

Our fishing route parallels the river's upstream bank, but if you wish to stay overnight drive over the Alexander Bluff bridge and turn right. There is large, sheltered public reserve on the banks of the river a short distance upstream, which provides an excellent fishing base for anglers.

(6) Herring Stream Access: 2.9 km from the Alexander Bluff Bridge

This access to the riverbed is difficult and leads from an obvious parking space between a power post and a small, white bridge, where the road turns left. Scramble through thick undergrowth towards a tall willow tree on the left side of the creek. Here you will find a distinct foot track leading down the 3 m bank into the creek bed. You may either follow the creek to its convergence with the river or clamber up the other side and walk through low scrub on the bank overlooking a section of intriguing water. Should the undergrowth be impregnable, you may follow the creek itself to the Motueka River after stepping down a bank into its bed just downstream from the road bridge.

This area of fissured rock shelves, calm pools, gravel bars and sparkling ripples exemplifies the diversity of South Island brown trout rivers and accentuates the clear atmosphere, crystalline water and emerald colours of New Zealand. Large fish will be seen cruising and feeding in clear shallow water here where the smooth, clean, solid-rock bottom magnifies their colouration and every movement. The deep sections with small, swirling cataracts of floating debris will induce trout to surface feed and reveal their whereabouts.

Long-distance casting and perfect presentation of minute nymphs or sparsely hackled dries is essential for success. It is not a novice's arena, and even the expertise of the most experienced anglers will be put to the test here.

A gravel bar paralleling the current separates the rapids from the calm section and provides a perfect stance for spin fishing the former and fly fishing the latter. The lower and upper portions of this venue are similarly divided, and spin anglers should concentrate on the egress and leave the top section with protruding rocks for fly anglers.

(7) Enclosed Access: 2.2 km from (6)

As the road descends slightly and veers right to parallel the river, it is flanked by an avenue of trees on its left side. Watch carefully for a vehicle access in the trees. Drive in, park and walk a short track to a glide at the lower end of an immense pool covering the entire width of the river. The glide and its fast but gentle rapid is guided downstream by a stone beach, providing good conditions for spin fishing with a slim, gold-coloured minnow that must travel through the current without breaking the surface in 30 cm (12 in) of water. The trout will be holding in the shallows beside the fast current.

Fly anglers should sneak downstream from the access track and fish the shallows upstream close to this side with the delicate application of a size 16/18 Sawyer's, or Gold-Ribbed Hare's Ear pattern nymph until the depth of water near some overhanging willows restricts further progress — some 100 metres or so. You must move like a shadow and examine the shallows ahead for feeding trout, while perhaps nonchalantly casting abreast into midstream and letting the fly drift over rises just in case. There will be trout here unless you, or someone else, has just spooked them. It is, and has been for many years, an outstanding position.

Now, walk upstream through the trees and carefully examine the deepish water near the bank. You will see large trout cruising and feeding against the overhanging grass or just beneath willow branches trailing in the water. This very difficult fly casting position will test the expertise of a master.

The section terminates in a pool between two large, upstanding rocks. Cast a weighted size 10 Hare & Copper nymph into the turbulent current on the outside of the backwater and see what happens. After fishing, you may climb the embankment here and walk back down the road to your car instead of scrambling between the trees again.

(8) Peninsula Bridge Access (junction): 1.7 km from (7)

Follow the road to Ngatimoti at this junction, and park in the paddock beside the bowling green. The river descends a steady gradient between the trees, flows over a shallow bar and enters a large, deep pool, which extends several hundred metres downstream from the bridge. A track leads through the trees to the visible sandbank, where spin anglers may

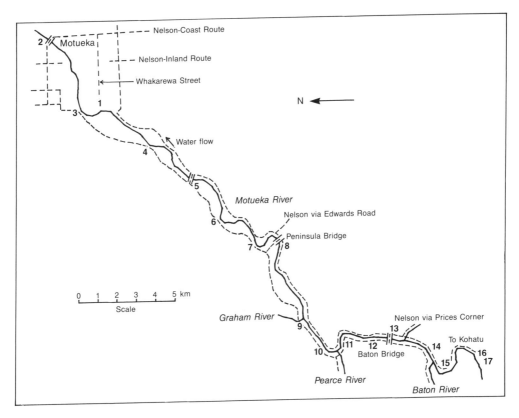

stand and dredge the turbulent depths paralleling the bar. Fly anglers should fish this bar thoroughly before working their way upstream on their side of the river.

The deep water under the bridge on the other side of the river will have large fish visibly cruising in search of food, and challenging all anglers to have a go. While it is possible to scramble down the steep bank beside the bridge and endeavour to catch these trout, you should be warned that they've been frustrating experts for years.

Energetic anglers would do better if they walk downstream along the highway and scramble through thick vegetation to reach one or other of the large rock formations visible from the bridge. These offer good fishing to exponents of either spinning or fly fishing. The difficult access restricts fishing pressure here.

While you're on that side of the river, continue along the road and walk behind an old building at the junction. Locate an indistinct foot track leading over the bank and through grass to the river's edge. Step into knee-deep water and cast a fly (or minnow) upstream into the convergence of a small creek, where there will be trout feeding on station beside overhanging scrub. This excellent venue is spoiled only by the depth of the water, which occasionally restricts fishing methods to spinning. In normal circumstances, however, the glide and bar may be successfully fished with a fly or nymph and the area is extremely well stocked with residential trout.

There is also good fishing upstream from the bowling green back on the western side of the river. Just follow the trees, step over a fence, walk through unkempt grass on the bank and clamber into shallow, but reasonably swift, water to positions of your choice. The section near the visible rock outcrop upstream is worthy of close attention by the exponents of either spinning or fly fishing.

Return to the west bank road.

(9) Graham River Access: 4.7 km from (8)

Turn left this side of the small bridge and follow a vehicle track paralleling the creek to a large picnic area, shaded by tall willow trees, beside the convergence of the Graham and Motueka Rivers. This sheltered enclosure allows easy access to spots providing many hours of fishing for anglers using any technique.

The tributary enters a fast rapid, providing ideal spinning conditions close to the bank this side, in the main stream. Fly anglers should however, from a downstream position, cast a size 10 weighted Pheasant Tail nymph into the crystal-clear Graham River and let it drift into the honey-coloured Motueka water at their convergence. This position and its environs will hold feeding trout — unless they've been recently disturbed.

Spin anglers should fish their way downstream with a 7 to 14-g Tinker/Toby minnow coloured gold or black (it is too fast here for Mepps or Veltics). Fly anglers will fish upstream through the wide ankle- to knee-deep rippling fall with a size 12/14 high-floating dry and change it to a size 16 or 18 small-bodied nymph when casting to fish visible in the glide, a location well stocked with smallish browns.

The 2-km long pool covering the full width of the river at the head of the glide is a great example of the perfect brown trout river. Avenues of willow trees frame the stream, virgin native forests engulf those on the western side, and the hint of white water rapids at the head of the pool emphasises the backdrop of mountains and cloud-washed blue sky. This is not only the most photogenic scene imaginable, it is also the best stocked section of brown trout water in the Motueka River system, boasting fish numbers equalled by only two other rivers in the South Island (the Mataura and the Deans Bank section of the Clutha), according to official annual survey results.

The river is waist-deep midstream, and there are thigh-deep wadeable sections along each bank. Fly anglers must 'wade wet' or wear chest waders to fish this location properly.

The western bank receives the early morning sun and produces a hatch of both aquatic and terrestrial insects that attracts feeding trout from all over the river. Ideally, this side of the river should be fished from sunrise to noon by walking upstream in thigh-deep water, casting to obvious rises or visible trout and paying special attention to the willow branches trailing in or drooping just above the water.

It will be necessary to clamber up a bank occasionally and dodge a few trees while working your way upstream. Take care wading across the river, there is a distinct channel of deeper

The noon rise should be fished with lightly dressed Adams, Dad's Favourite or Pheasant Tail dry flies. The fish will generally feed in this manner until the sea breeze ruffles the water's surface in the early afternoon, when the heat from the sun is usually so intense that they seek shelter beneath rocks and overhanging trees and cease feeding altogether until the cool of the evening.

This is a particularly good spot for the evening rise, when it is possible to walk slowly against a gentle current and cast to fish feeding in the shallows ahead, while at the same time being in range of surface trout feeding in the midstream current or against the grass bank on the other side of the river. A few trout will feed stealthily before the evening rise, and anglers should use either a very small unweighted nymph, such as a Gold-Ribbed Hare's Ear or a size 16 Twilight Beauty dry fly. These patterns must be replaced with size 12/16 Twilight Beauty or Greenwell's Glory wet flies immediately the multitude of fish start their noisy, splashy evening rise a few minutes before complete darkness, and it's too dark to see the eye of the hook.

Anglers fortunate enough to stay overnight in this reserve should drive 500 m upstream from the entrance and park on the road shoulder at the apex of a sharp right-hand curve. This is opposite a gap in the trees offering a panoramic view of an immense, deep, swirling pool in which large trout will be seen drifting and feeding in the sub-surface eddies. These monstrous residential browns (even by New Zealand standards) have studied many admiring anglers standing on the cliff above, spurned every careless presentation, inspected every type of fly ever tied and disregarded spinning minnows which frequently pass within eyesight. Skilled fly anglers, however, have an even chance of a hook-up if they study the fish's beat and apply the appropriate technique. A rock slide (now covered with foliage) has recently provided precarious access to the upstream section of the pool and it is possible to stand on the water's edge and cast up-current to trout actively sub-surface feeding in an agitated manner. You should inspect this location carefully from below the skyline, look beneath the visible trout and you'll be surprised at just how many more are poised above the bottom rocks ready to dart out and take an opportune size 16 weighted Hare & Copper nymph presented in the correct current channel at the right depth. In other words, do not become hypnotized by those extrovert trout, look further afield for those displaying maturity.

The section of river upstream from this pool is a 2-km long crescent-shaped run of water, flowing deep beneath arched willow trees growing at the base of the road embankment. The opposite side of the river is shallow, with a bed of gravel presenting perfect fishing conditions for exponents of both techniques. Spin anglers should work downstream while casting directly across the current to land their minnow beneath the overhanging willow trees, permitting a long and slow retrieval from the depths to the shallows of the beach. Fly anglers, on the other hand, should walk slowly upstream in knee-deep water and search for trout feeding on nymphs being hatched by the morning sun, at the same time keeping an eye on the surface right across to the other side of the river for a swirl indicating a fish feeding on station. Access to the shallow side of this long run is possible only during summer, when the water is low. At this time it may be reached by wading the main river just above the entrance to McLeans Reserve.

The upper end of the run is a wide and shallow rapid extending the full width of the river opposite the convergence of the Stanley Brook Stream. It is reached by driving along Highway 61 for 2.1 km from the entrance to MacLeans Reserve and watching carefully for an old vehicle track leading off the highway into the scrub on the right just before the road curves to the left. There is restricted parking room where the track ends near the river and it is only necessary to walk a short distance through a fringe of tangled vegetation to reach the small gravel beach at the convergence of the Stanley Brook Stream. The wide rapid is knee deep, surprisingly swift and necessitates care when being waded.

The ideal manner in which to fish this long and well-stocked run of water would be to leave one vehicle near the Stanley Brook Stream access and drive back to MacLeans Reserve with the intention of spending a leisurely day fishing the whole section properly.

There are several very good spin fishing positions under the willow trees along the road embankment. The agile angler should drive along the highway, park on the wide shoulder, search for indistinct tracks leading down the steep bank, and scramble to a position on the edge of the deep river. Minnows to use here are a 14-g (½-oz) Tinker/Toby, in a gold, black or yellow colour, supplemented with a 21-g (¾-oz) Dinky-di during high and/or swift water conditions. The minnow should be cast as far as possible across and downstream and retrieved very slowly against the current directly beneath the overhanging willow trees.

Some very interesting fly fishing to visible trout is available upstream from the Stanley Brook convergence, but it should be visited only by physically agile anglers. It is necessary to cross rapids to reach pools, runs and deep water broiling between upstands of solid rock where large, fat browns nonchalantly enjoy sunlit seclusion. Walk up the riverbed, but do not walk along the vehicle track which traverses private property above the left side of the river.

(16) Hinetai Road Access: 9.1 km from (15)

Follow Highway 61 over the Stanley Brook Hill. The descent will reveal the willow-lined course of the Motueka River and Hinetai Road leading downstream from the acute corner visible ahead. Follow this road for 2.2 km and just before the hill drive through an arch in the willow trees onto the riverbed (slowly, the river may have changed course). Here is miles of lovely water in both directions: runs, rapids and pools with a small flow of gin-clear water descending a bed of stones with scattered clumps of nuisance scrub.

The bright atmosphere and clear water favours the fly fishing technique, and while those anglers must approach the river and fish with the stealth of a ghost, their spin fishing counterparts may stand well back from the bank and lay a long line to present a very small Mepps, Veltic or Spoon minnow in the shallow rapids and runs.

Fly anglers are advised to walk down the riverbed and start fishing at the convergence of the Wangapeka River. The first rapid below the junction is well stocked with active fish which offer good sport when blind fishing with a weighted size 10/12 Pheasant Tail or (rough) Hare & Copper nymph — trout are difficult to locate visually in this tumultuous water. It is also a very good spin fishing venue.

Stealth is paramount in this area, careless walking on stones or approach to the water will frighten trout into instant flight and put all nearby fish on guard. It is indeed a pleasant area and worthy of the delicate touch from a SAGE weight 3 rod, 5X leaders and size 14/18 flies.

(17) Tapawera Access: 4.9 km from (16)

Continue along Highway 61 to Tapawera and turn right at the junction preceding the township. You will pass a motor camp on the left en route to the bridge which offers an observation platform to examine the river and its environs.

The rough road on the right side preceding the bridge may be followed well downstream and provides easy walking access to the open riverbed of stones and gravel with water conditions comparable with those encountered at the last described access position. Once again, the bright and open nature of this environment creates fishing conditions best suited to fly fishing techniques.

The Motueka River must be considered one of New Zealand's South Island brown trout gems. It has provided thousands of anglers with incalculable hours of fishing pleasure since the 1800s. The quality of fishing we still enjoy today is by no small means due to the endeavours of genuine sportsmen, long forgotten, to retain a unique heritage for posterity.

Please acknowledge the dedication of our forebears by practising and demonstrating conservation.

Instead of retracing the journey down the Motueka Valley to return to Nelson City it is possible to continue along Highway 61 to Kohatu Junction, turn left and follow Highway 6, the main Nelson/West Coast route.

4 The Wangapeka River System

The Wangapeka is a wilderness river sourced by rain water filtered through the mosses of virgin mountain forests in the North-West Nelson Forest Park. The headwaters of this beautiful river are stocked with large brown trout, and they live in a pristine environment typical of the remote regions of New Zealand's Southern Alps. An internationally acclaimed walking track follows along the upper section of the river. Unfortunately there are positions where the fish are frequently harassed, and eaten, by the back-packing fraternity. This has intensified the inherent wariness of the fish, but has also provided more food for the survivors and so created trophy brown trout of superb physique, unique colour and inconceivable strength.

The lower 10-km section of the river bisects an open, farmed valley through a stable course of rock and clay which forms repetitive sections of runs, rapids and pools in a bed of gravel and small stones. It is a vigorous water flow, calling for a similar fishing approach by anglers using either the spinning or fly fishing methods. The large population of smaller sized fish in this lower section inhabit the whole spectrum of water, and fly anglers must resort to a considerable amount of blind fishing in conjunction with sight fishing technique, rather than rely solely on the latter.

This lower section, and its convergence with the Motueka River, is within an 8-km drive of the Tapawera township, some 60 km from Nelson city. The upper reaches of the Wangapeka necessitate a long journey from Tapawera on secondary roads which traverse a saddle and cross two small tributaries. The road then follows the river's course en route to the entrance of the North-West Nelson Forest Park.

Public accesses to the river are more or less restricted to those described here, and anglers wishing to visit other venues must seek permission to cross private land from nearby farmhouses.

Leave Nelson towards the West Coast on Highway 6 and turn right at Kohatu Junction, this side of the curved bridge crossing the Motueka River — a distance of 52 km. You will now follow Highway 61 to Tapawera, 7.3 km away.

The Lower Wangapeka River

(I) Confluence Motueka/Wangapeka Rivers: 8.6 km from Tapawera

Pass through Tapawera, turning left at the junction and crossing the Motueka River bridge. Then turn right and follow the Wangapeka road, which clearly parallels the course of the Motueka River downstream. This road ends at the head of the Wangapeka Plains 18 km away after more or less following the river for 10 km upstream from its convergence with the Motueka.

There are four walking accesses through the roadside trees to the Motueka River en route to the confluence and all offer good fishing in this small, clear-watered stream. The first access is a grassed vehicle track leading directly ahead as the road turns sharply left 6 km from the Tapawera Bridge, and over the next kilometre another three appear as indistinct openings in tangled vegetation beneath willow trees.

After travelling 8 km from Tapawera, drive straight ahead at the junction and follow the Pikamai road for 400 m, parking on the apex of an acute left turn before the Wangapeka River Bridge barely visible through trees. There is a concreted fire/barbecue stand in this small rest area which offers a sheltered and strategic position to remain overnight for those with self-equipped vehicles.

This delightful position is only a few steps from the bank of the Wangapeka River, which flows through a deep pool between stable banks of rock and clay covered with vegetation.

The rapid visible downstream converges with the Motueka River. The high-arched bridge upstream may be closed to vehicular traffic by a locked gate, but this does not prohibit foot access, or a steep scramble down the bridge approach on the opposite side of the river to reach the water. Remember that a stealthy approach to the water's edge is necessary to avoid disturbing the trout visibly swimming within casting range. The riverbed is light-coloured sand which lifts the fish and their shadows into sharp relief as they cruise on a feeding 'beat' between large shelves of solid rock.

This spot is ideal for the fly fishing method, but such anglers must exercise extreme stealth and competent presentation of small (16/18) nymphs or lightly hackled dry flies to succeed. It is a difficult position, with challenging fishing, for novice anglers to master.

Walk downstream beneath the trees and across the gravel riverbed of the Motueka to reach the actual confluence, where the combined water flows surge against a cliff face and swirl into an immense pool. This location offers good fishing to the exponents of either method who must apply their technique according to prevailing conditions. Generally speaking, both rivers converge over wide rapids, with a wadeable shingle bar paralleling the Wangapeka flow. The whole expanse of water is well stocked with small, very active brown trout which take with a ferocity equal to their habitat, so ensure that your equipment is in perfect condition.

Fly anglers should fish the rapid sections with a size 8/10 weighted Hare & Copper, Stonefly or Pheasant Tail nymph in the early morning and late afternoon or during overcast/dull periods of the day. Well hackled, high-floating dry flies, say Molefly, Kakahi Queen, Blue Dun or Humpy in size 10/12, would be a wise choice in the same rapids during the warm and bright late morning/early afternoon hours. The calm sections of the area should be fished with size 16/18 Adams, Greenwell's Glory or Dad's Favourite dry flies when trout are visibly cruising and feeding sedately.

Spin anglers are advised to fish their way down the Wangapeka rapid, through the convergence, while retrieving their 14-g (½-oz) black, gold or yellow Tinker/Toby minnow deep beneath the turbulence swirling against the base of the cliff. The time necessary to fish this whole area of disturbed water properly will result in just rewards for the dedicated.

Agile anglers will encounter challenging fly fishing upstream from the bridge, where there is difficult, steep access. It is necessary to cling limpet-like to sheer rock or wade through thigh-deep water to reach the left bank upstream, but once there you can fish excellent runs where trout may be located visually by fishermen experienced in this technique.

Occasional outcrops of solid rock divide the gravel bed into sections where feed currents are formed by broken water flows. Here, skilled fly anglers can read the water and place a size 14/16 Hare & Copper, Gold-ribbed Hare's Ear or Pheasant Tail nymph strategically in front of a trout noticeably holding in the stream. Naturally, the trout feeding voraciously in a fast current will be 'fed' with a size 10/12 Twilight Beauty or Grizzly Wulff dry fly.

Several hours of fishing can be had at this venue, where it is necessary to remain in the riverbed unless permission to cross adjoining private land is obtained.

(2) Roadside Access: 2.4 km from (I)

Return to the Pikamai Road junction and turn right to travel up the valley. The road embankment forms the riverbank for 700 m after passing farmed paddocks. The rough roadside vegetation restricts access in all but two places, and these can be difficult to locate. The more obvious one is beneath tall black birch trees on the road verge itself. This is unexcelled trout fishing water: a stable riverbed with stones, gravel and fissured rock shelves create a multitude of delightful runs, eddies and ripples of clear, boisterous mountain water.

This instantly appealing section of river will provide anglers using either technique with hours of pleasurable fishing, and may be fished all the way upstream to the next access.

(3) Bluff Access: I km from (2)

Park where the road curves left to pass through a cutting and inspect the immediate area from an elevated position. Clamber down the rocky bank and fish the turbulent water with either a slim, deep-running, gold-coloured spinning minnow or a heavy-weighted size 8 Green Stonefly, Swannundaze or rough textured Hare & Copper nymph, preferably tied to a sink-tip floating fly line.

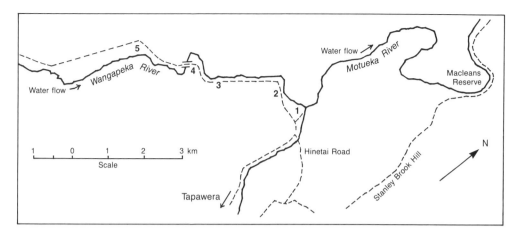

Wangapeka River.

The deep pool below the high bank contains a good number of fish, constantly harrassed by ambitious anglers and their swimming kids who cause them to lay low during the day then feed at dawn and again during the twilight hours. The only chance of catching one of these shrewd inhabitants in daylight is by presenting a very heavy, black-coloured spinning minnow, or similar performing large roughly woven nymph, and dragging it along the bottom of the pool.

The rough rapid entering this pool follows the road embankment for some 400 m, providing a rough, precarious bank on which to walk upriver, cast ahead and drift a fly back downstream close to the edge of the grass and stones.

This venue, although difficult to fish with the fly technique, is well worth the effort for agile anglers. Spin anglers, on the other hand, may walk along the road, fish back while employing their downstream method and expect to catch a real fighting fish in this tumultuous run of sparkling water.

(4) Wangapeka Bridge Access: 1.1 km from (3), 12.1 km from Tapawera

A slow drive over this bridge reveals a pool upstream against a hill with a nicely rippled run extending from its glide to pass beneath the bridge. The ripple then forms a rapid and descends a positive gradient over fissured rock shelves in a wide riverbed where it veers to the right and disappears from view. A captivating scene, not only for fishing but picnicking as well, the sandy beach extending from an elevated shaded bank is a good position to keep the others quiet (and out of the way) while you indulge in a little stealthy fly fishing.

The area is well stocked with smallish browns; the large ones are nonchalantly cruising out of range in the deep water of a miniature gorge just around the corner upstream.

The pool and glide should only be fly fished (with small flies or nymphs) if trout are visibly cruising or rising in the clear water, but the ripple and rapids from here downstream should be fished thoroughly, whatever technique is used, as both methods are successful in this location.

Spin anglers should work downstream and cover the whole expanse of reasonably shallow water with 7-g Tango, Daffy or Spoon minnows coloured yellow, gold or brown. It will be necessary to cross the river downstream of the bridge. Be careful though, as the bottom is often slippery.

Fly anglers would be wise to walk downstream and start fishing from the shallow shelf below the bridge all the way back to the exit glide of the pool. Use a size 14/16 Greenwell's Glory, Twilight Beauty, Peveril o'Peak dry fly during the hot and sunny period of midmorning and a similar sized Pheasant Tail, Hare's Ear or Speckled nymph at other times of the day. It is possible, although difficult, to visually locate trout in this slightly agitated water flow.

(5) Willow Tree Access: 1.1 km from (4)

This access is clearly identifiable as a large opening beneath tall willow trees on the left just past a road bridge crossing a small creek, and it offers easy walking access to a wide riverbed of stones and beaches of fine gravel.

Many hours of fishing can be enjoyed at this venue as this accessible waterway, bisecting open terrain, may be fished for several kilometres up to and past the sheer rock bluffs visible on the left side upstream. The river flows quite boisterously through successive rapids and pools, which alter character occasionally when the river floods, and it's quite possible to find that your favourite run has disappeared on subsequent visits. Nevertheless, the whole area is well stocked and provides good conditions for both fly and spin fishing, when similar enticements, and techniques, to those used downstream should be applied.

This position is the last public access to the lower Wangapeka River and anglers wishing to go further upstream should remain in the riverbed unless they approach local residents for permission to cross private land.

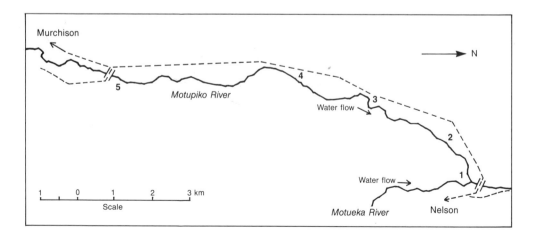

5 Motupiko River

This invaluable spawning tributary of the Motueka River is within an hour's drive of Nelson city and provides 10 km of delicate dry fly fishing equal to the best available anywhere in New Zealand. Knee-deep water ripples through a gravel bed, occasionally arched with deciduous willows. The river skirts the base of alluvium hillsides that shelter the environs of a gentle valley from the savagery of Nelson's daily sea breeze. The river seems to be misplaced, and deserves to flow through the soft contours of the Canterbury Plains, rather than the undulating, austere Nelson countryside. But be that as it may, it is a quality fly fishing venue.

The geography of the riverbed provides shallow, sparkling ripples, calm pools and smooth glides, many of which extend into standing willows and provide trout havens. The channels of loose gravel often change course during floods and it is occasionally necessary to walk long distances and reconnoitre the river to locate displaced trout before commencing to fish. The necessity in this instance, however, is a pleasurable experience in itself; the riverbed is generally covered with brilliantly coloured native wildflowers and, although the gravel is sometimes a little rough underfoot, the walking is quite easy up an almost imperceptible gradient. Long avenues of tall trees reflect the sunlight, block out the horizon and provide a perfect windbreak, factors which combine to create good fish-sighting conditions.

The trout are well conditioned, quite large, and their average weight of 1.3 kg (3 lb) typifies the spawning stock that move into the headwaters of the South Island's lowland rivers each winter. Strangely, many perfectly proportioned fish then choose to remain in the isolation of these small streams and endure the warm low-water levels of autumn instead of returning to the sanctuary of the main rivers. They form the nucleus of this river's sportfish.

Stealth of approach and lightly delivered, perfectly placed small flies and nymphs are essential for success in this river and the rudiments of fly fishing techniques should be mastered before attempting to fish here.

Experienced fly fishermen will sight their trout in the calmish sections and place a size 16/18 Gold-ribbed Hare's Ear, Grey Darter, or Ostrich Herle nymph in the correct position to take a stationary sub-surface feeder. The quiet riser may be tempted with a similar sized Pheasant Tail, Adams, Molefly, Coch-y-Bondhu or Greenwell's Glory dry fly during the day and a Twilight Beauty, Peveril o'Peak or Dad's Favourite in the twilight. Cruising and feeding trout will react to a strategically placed size 16/18 Hare & Copper nymph one way or t'other. Generally speaking, boisterous rapids rushing through newly formed gravel channels between 60-cm high banks devoid of vegetation, are unlikely to hold fish or provide suitable conditions for sighting sub-surface trout. But do not discount such water in this river (unless it is low due to dry weather) as the trout adopt nomadic habits following floods or preceding heavy rain. A size 10/12 Grizzly Wulff, Humpy (red or yellow), Kakahi Queen or Blue Dun dry fly bounced quickly over the surface turbulence will certainly reveal the presence of any fish in transit.

The river and Highway 6, separated by 300-400 m of farmed land, run parallel in a north/south direction for 11 km and of the five public joining strips just one is identifiable. Use only the four accesses described here, or seek permission from adjacent houses to cross private land.

(1) Convergence Access: 50 km from Nelson

Leave Nelson, and head south on Highway 6, and pass over the curved Motueka River Bridge beside the Kohatu Hotel 52 km away. Travel a further 100 m, turn left off the highway into a nondescript foliage-enclosed vehicle track leading beneath the bridge, and follow it slowly to its end on the riverbed. This is the confluence of the Motueka and Motupiko Rivers. The Motueka River, in both directions, is small and appealing, as it flows through ripples, runs and pools along the base of rock groynes. Unfortunately the open, bright environment restricts reliable fishing results to the evening/twilight period.

The Motupiko River emerging from the right is also small and generally flows through a deep run against and under a foliage-covered bank opposite. Trout will be in residence here, unless they've just been disturbed, or caught. The Motupiko River may be walked and fished for 2.5 km to the next access upstream through terrain that characterises the waterway for the next 10 km or so.

(2) Quinney's Bush Access: 2.1 km from (1)
Turn left at the small roadside sign, and follow the road through the camp. Park near the walking track ascending the low stopbank towards the river. It'll be necessary to walk upstream on the riverbed for a short distance to escape the children who are swimming there and scaring every trout in the immediate vicinity.

(3) Public Access Alley: 2 km from (2)
Watch carefully on the left side for this alley-style gravel vehicle track leading between farm fences to the riverbed, lined with avenues of trees, 220 m away. Drive slowly, this track occasionally floods, and leave the gate either open or shut, as found.

This position generally provides a positive flow of water running towards and against a bluff directly ahead of the entrance gate. This pool should be approached from a downstream direction to avoid alerting any surface-feeding trout. The other pools and wide expanses of water visible downstream should also be approached and fished likewise. There are several good runs upstream that merge into stands of willow trees and provide interesting opportunities to fly fish for visible trout.

(4) Porthouse Culvert Access: 2.3 km from (3)
A clearly signed and identifiable highway bridge offers ample roadside parking and easy access to a usually dry creek-bed, which should be followed on foot to its convergence with the river. The fishing conditions here are nothing short of perfect, and any fly fishing angler should deem himself or herself fortunate indeed to have the opportunity to visit such a venue.

A small stream of clear water descends a gentle gradient through successive ripples, quiet glides and willow-backed pools. These conditions, together with the tranquil environs of a natural watershed, must surely exemplify the essence of fly fishing. The brown trout are but a bonus here.

(5) Korere Bridge Access: 6.2 km from (4)
Turn left at a major junction, follow the St Arnaud/Lake Rotoiti road and pass over the bridge. Turn left (upstream) through a gate situated half-way down the approach. This provides access to a wide grassed space on the left just inside the gate and an access road that parallels the river, obscured by scrub, downstream for about 600 m. Anglers should walk this road, step through a barbed wire fence preceding a watercourse near the base of a hill ascended by the road, and fish the river back to the bridge.

This is delightful dry fly water: a small stream descending a gentle incline over wide rapids, long, shallow, willow-backed runs and an occasional small pool. Despite the small proportions of this river it holds large-sized brown trout of good physique. Their unobtrusive rise to a size 16/18 Adams or Dad's Favourite dry fly will often take an angler by surprise, as will the tenacity of the ensuing duel.

It is quite possible, and indeed desirable, to walk further downstream along the riverbed from the gate to gain more good fishing water. This must be accomplished without disturbing the fish as you pass.

Anglers, this is a most pleasant stream-sized river which replenishes its stock of trout each spawning season. Unfortunately, such stock has been regularly depleted by expert fly anglers — who should know better — for many years. Your contribution to conservation education through a demonstration of catch and release will help reverse this old-fashioned approach to trout fishing. I solicit your participation and welcome you to the Motupiko River.

Above: Late spring in Nelson's back-country, when the initial heat of summer incites the trout to nymph voraciously.
Below: This beautifully conditioned brown trout was visually located and taken on the first cast with a size 10 Hare & Copper nymph.

NYMPHS   *Top Line:* Black Gnat, Blue Dun, Coloburiscus, Greenwell's Glory.
                Middle Line: Hare & Copper, March Brown, Mayfly, Peacock & Purple.
                Bottom Line: Pheasant Tail, Sawyer's Pheasant, Twilight Beauty, Wasp.

STREAMERS   *Top Line:* Parson's Glory, Mrs Simpson, Hamill's Killer.
                Middle Line: Grey Ghost, Black Pete, Jack's Spratt.
                Bottom Line: Black Phantom, Red Setter, Craig's Night-time.

WET FLIES

DRY FLIES

WET FLIES *Top Line:* Blue Dun, Black Spider, Black Gnat, Coch-y-Bondhu.
Middle Line: Dad's Favourite, Greenwell's Glory, Grouse & Purple, Kakahi Queen.
Bottom Line: Love's Lure, March Brown, Peveril o'Peak, Twilight Beauty.

DRY FLIES *Top Line:* Blue Dun, Black Gnat, Yellow-tipped Governor, Dad's Favourite.
Middle Line: Greenwell's Glory, Grouse & Purple, Kakahi Queen, Love's Lure.
Bottom Line: March Brown, Molefly, Peveril o'Peak, Twilight Beauty.

Above left and right: The Grey River's protruding boulders provide a perfect habitat for hatching nymphs, brown trout and fly fishing anglers using small nymphs.
Below: Jim Glenn of the United States, the author's fishing companion of many years, displays the results of a successful stalk and presentation.

6 Wairau River

The St Arnaud Ranges separating the Nelson, Marlborough and Kaikoura Provinces source three large rivers, providing literally unlimited kilometres of brown trout fishing. The Buller, Wairau and Clarence Rivers however present contrasting water, terrain and climatic conditions. The Wairau River offers good fishing for over 100 kilometres. The lower portion is reached via a subsidiary road, the mid section parallels Highway 63 (Blenheim/Murchison), and the upper reaches flow through the Rainbow Valley. Here the river is mistakenly called the Rainbow River, and I describe it in the following chapter.

Although roads run along the lower and mid sections of the river they provide only restricted public access due to the extensively farmed valley floor. However, once access to the open riverbed is gained there is unlimited fishing in both directions.

Eighty-odd kilometres of water flows through frequently braided channels of gravel, sand and small boulders, providing unrestricted foot access to repeated sections of sparkling rapids, deep runs and smooth glides with venues suited to fly, streamer and spin fishing techniques.

The clear water is faintly tinged snow-blue, the weather is generally fine and the heat of the sun, often accentuated by wind, necessitates the use of protective clothing, brimmed hats and moisturising lotion. Whereas the actual fishing terrain is geographically ideal for the use of light fly rods of, say, 8'6" (2.5 m) in weight 4, the inevitable wind demands the use of powerful and positive rods of, ideally, a SAGE 9 ft (2.7 m), using a weight forward number 5 line.

Standard fly patterns work well. My choices are Pheasant Tail, Stonefly, Hare & Copper and Gray Darter nymph with Grizzly Wulff, Coachman, Molefly or Twilight Beauty dries in sizes to suit the prevailing conditions. However, fly patterns used must be influenced by the knowledge that 'naturals' in venues subjected to constant wind seldom float on the surface but rather are whisked-off the moment they hatch. Use well-hackled high-floating dry flies that do this upon presentation.

The calm early twilight should be fished with dry size 14/16 Twilight Beauty, Greenwell's Glory or Adams flies, to be replaced with similar wets as darkness settles and the fish start splashing.

Spin anglers have an easier choice with golden or light brown coloured minnows. Use the slender shapes for fast water and blade-type (Veltic/Mepps) in quiet sections irrespective of the wind.

A typical scene on the Motupiko River.

Lower Section

Anglers spending a night or two in the Blenheim area should consider fishing accesses (1) to (5) below. Those driving direct to the West Coast via Lake Rotoiti are advised to try positions (6) to (12), and the Pelorus River described in Chapter 1 is perfect if you are travelling to Nelson on Highway 6.

(1) Gravel Pit Access

Leave Blenheim (or Spring Creek) on Highway 1 heading towards Picton, turn left into an indistinct road immediately preceding the Tuamarina Bridge (which spans the Wairau River) and follow it onto the riverbed where there is heaped gravel. There is easy walking to the water's edge, where conditions are suited to spin fishing during the day and fly fishing in the twilight, when fish move into the shallows to feed. Spin anglers should cast right across the current into the deep section of water flowing against the road embankment opposite.

(2) Anglers' Access Sign: 4 km from (1)

Drive over the bridge and turn left into Tuamarina Track which more or less follows the river upstream for the next 12 km. The road climbs and curves right around the base of a hill, providing a panorama of the river en route to an old sign reading 'Fishing OK but no wood'. This sign is beside a rough, grassed vehicle track leading beneath tall trees. Don't drive along it before visual inspection as it has several occasionally muddy branches. The various accesses lead to an open riverbed offering venues suitable for both methods of trout fishing. Restricted roadside parking is possible here if the track is impassable.

(3) Roadside parking: 2.7 km from (2)

The road curves right again revealing a flow of excellent fishing water directly below the embankment. Once again the parking is restricted, but the effort of clambering down a short, steep bank will be rewarded with easy foot access to an interesting location with challenging ripples, runs and glides. Calm atmospheric conditions will enhance the presentation of small nymphs (16/18) or dry flies here during the mid-morning and evening rise, and the spin angler may concentrate on fast or rippled water at any time of the day.

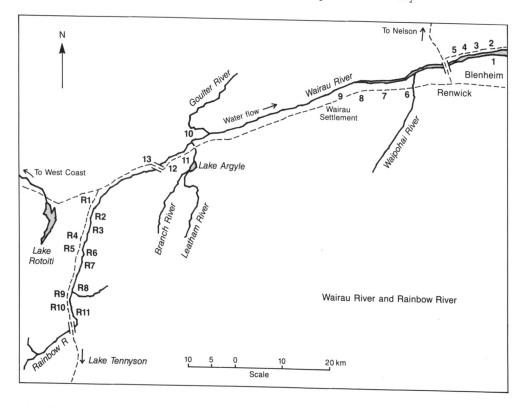

Wairau River and Rainbow River

(4) Fishing Access Sign: 1.2 km from (3)

A short distance before this sign (adult/kid/rods, blue against a white background) the open terrain reveals the river flowing quite deep in an arc beneath a rock groyne near the road. Note the wide expanse of flat bank on the other side of the channel providing a perfect upstream stalking/casting platform that is quite accessible from a track leading though the gate near the access sign. An interesting and demanding fishing venue.

(5) Highway 6 Bridge: 7 km from (4)

Continue along Tuamarina Road to the intersection, turn left and follow Highway 6 over the Wairau Bridge. Turn left on the other side of the bridge and follow the vehicle track over the stopbank to an open riverbed with several accessible channels of water providing fishing conditions suited to all techniques. It is possible to park in the shade beneath the bridge to escape the searing sun.

Camping is prohibited in the immediate vicinity, but it is only a few hundred metres to Renwick and about 8 km to Blenheim; a short journey surely to reach good trout water as the sun lifts a hatch to trigger a rise in the morning and again at twilight.

Mid Section Wairau River

Highway 63, the direct route from Blenheim to the West Coast via Lake Rotoiti, eventually merges with Highway 6 at Kawatiri Junction on the Buller River, a distance of 163 km. This highway runs the length of the Wairau River on its southern side, but provides very few public accesses. The following six positions offer transient anglers unlimited fishing adjacent to several good overnight camper van parking venues. This is a popular route with the American R.V. enthusiasts who frequently travel in convoy and enjoy the back-country of the South Island to its full extent.

The following portion of the Wairau River is described from Renwick, the junction of Highways 63 and 6, 11 km south of Blenheim.

(6) Waihopai River Access: 6.5 km from Junction

The bridge reveals a clear-watered stream flowing over a rough bed of stones. Turn right to follow the stream down towards its convergence with the Wairau River approximately 1 km away. It is possible to park beneath the bridge, walk downstream along the stopbank to fish the Wairau River for the day, then 'stalk' the Waihopai River upstream when returning. The stopbank road is occasionally washed-out, making vehicle access impossible to the main river.

The Waihopai, while not a recognised trout stream, does in fact hold fish in rapids and the runs entering and exiting pools, and provides good sport to fly anglers using very small dries and nymphs.

Although the unstable nature of the riverbed makes for an unreliable trout habitat, it does provide a pleasant venue to camp overnight, especially for those with children as there is usually a good swimming hole near the bridge.

(7) The Narrows Access: 2.4 km from (6)

Turn into this access that follows a row of pine trees leading from the highway on the right just south of a farmhouse signposted 'The Narrows'. Be careful — it's easy to miss if you are driving too fast. Follow the gravel road, driving through the gate 300 m ahead bearing an Anglers' Access sign, and park at its termination. It is only a few minutes walk along a gravel track leading between tall, rough vegetation to reach the riverbed.

The channel of water is generally quite close to this position, and usually flows hard against the groyne constructed of hewn solid rock in view downstream. This venue offers ideal spin fishing conditions, especially in the flow of agitated water near the groyne and the several deep rapids nearby, where slim, deep-running minnows coloured gold or brown should be used.

Fly anglers should present weighted nymphs (sizes 8/10 Hare & Copper, Stonefly or Pheasant Tail) in these deeper sections, and similar patterns in sizes 16/18 in the shallows at the tail of pools, where trout will be quite visible holding station while feeding quietly side-to-side in the accelerating current.

As the heat of the mid-morning sun lifts the hatch, fish will feed with barely a surface ripple and dry fly patterns Adams, Twilight Beauty, Molefly or Greenwell's Glory in sizes 16/18 would be a wise choice.

Anglers wishing to stay overnight in the immediate area should consider parking near the gate mentioned above, as there is more room here than at the road's end, and it is only a short stroll to the river to fish an evening rise.

(8) Anglers' Access (Road) Sign: 7.4 km from (7)

A row of old pine trees at right angles to the road marks this gravel access road originating from posts on the roadside displaying an Anglers' Access sign. This track traverses an old riverbed, and it is rough, passing through a couple of gates (leave as found), crossing a small, open creek (it has a good solid gravel bottom) and climbing the stopbank which has a rough vehicle track along its summit. Do not drive along the stopbank road without prior inspection as it is occasionally washed-out or made impassable by encroaching vegetation.

Parking is restricted near the stopbank, and although it's possible to leave your car between the willow trees on the southern side or among broom bushes opposite, I'd suggest parking on open, dry and solid old riverbed gravel terrain on the upstream side of the unfenced access road a few hundred metres back towards the highway.

(9) Wairau Township Access: 6.2 km from (8)

Turn right into the gravel road immediately before the township, and follow it around a right-hand curve, parking beneath the tall trees. Locate the foot track on the left side of a disused vehicle access and follow it over a precarious plank bridging a small stream, through a short section of swampy ground, then beneath willows onto the open riverbed. Conditions similar to the last access will be found here.

Instead of parking beneath the trees, you may continue along the gravel road for a further kilometre when it ends against a stopbank. This provides easier foot access across an old, dry water channel onto the open riverbed. Trees overhang the water channels in several places in this locality, providing not only shelter but a food source for trout as well. It is indeed a position worthy of your attention, and cold liquid refreshments are available in the township exactly 2.5 km down the road in case the weather's too hot.

(10) Lake Argyle Recreation Area: 29.3 km from (9)

There is no public access to the Wairau River over this distance. Although it parallels the highway, it is separated by wide tracts of farmed land. One kilometre before the Recreation Area the highway descends a low plateau and reveals a canal of water flowing towards you and turning right towards a building visible across the plain above the river. This canal carries a good head of fish and originates from the powerhouse at the foot of the Lake Argyle Dam some 2.5 km away.

The section of canal opposite a wide gravel road verge has an overflow weir midstream and it is a good fishing venue. It is merely a matter of stepping over the fence, walking across flat grassed terrain and presenting a well-hackled dry fly. Terrestrial rather than aquatic flies are trout food here and sizes 8/10 Humpy (red body), Red-tipped Governor, or Kakahi Queen patterns will do nicely. Spin anglers could expect results with almost any type of minnow — try something bright, a silver/red Veltic or Mepps perhaps.

Follow this section of canal downstream along its servicing road. The canal offers good fishing wherever foot access is available and the large terminating pool at the powerhouse is well stocked with frequently rising fish. This position calls for very long-distance fly casting and is actually better suited to the spinning method.

The environs of the power station provide a panoramic view of the Wairau Riverbed where access tracks leading to the edge of the water channels are quite discernable. The spillway channel converging with the river below the power station is well stocked with fish and frequently produces good results. It is essential, however, to keep out of sight and not disturb the trout before fishing with the upstream technique using a size 12 high-floating dry fly.

Many hours may be spent here fishing the canal from Highway 63 to the powerhouse, its spillway on the lower plateau, the main Wairau itself and even a tributary on the opposite side of the river when the main stream is low enough to wade across.

(11) Lake Argyle Recreation Area: 1 km from Highway 63

Return to Highway 63, and turn left at the signposted road junction ahead to follow the canal to the powerhouse. This canal is only about 300 m long, and it holds a good number of fish that are generally visible from the vehicle. But it is difficult to fish owing to the steep and slippery banks. Continue up the hill to Lake Argyle, where signs explain the area, the fish stocking program and current regulations. This constructed dam provides good fishing, due to the considerable effort that has been made creating a recreational asset for the general public by the Marlborough Electric Power Authority.

The road on the opposite side of the lake ends at a boat launching ramp near the visible ablution shed overlooking the inlet canal from the Branch River. There is good spin fishing on the delta of a generally dry creek half way up the lake shore opposite here and the flats at the head of the lake provide a reasonably good fly fishing venue.

An old road follows the inlet canal a short distance upstream from the ablution building, offering an elevated path from which to locate trout and salmon feeding in the swiftish current. Examine the edges of the water flow carefully, especially just underneath patches of overhanging grass, as the fish will be difficult to identify beneath the surface ripples.

Follow the road on this side of the inlet canal to the Branch River 1.5 km ahead where concrete dams control water levels and gravel movement. For an interesting change, inspect the turbulent water cascading from a weir into the head of the canal. Careful observation will reveal fish swirling and fighting the holocaust of broiling, clear water, sparkling white foam and surging whirlpools — now try and catch'em!

(12) Kowhai Reserve: 5 km from the sign 'Recreation Area'

This reserve is an ideal base from which to fish the Lake Argyle Recreation area for a day or so. It's approximately halfway between the road junction to the Lake Argyle Recreation Area and the final fishing access in this section of the Wairau watershed, the Wash Bridge.

The river flows against the Kowhai Reserve's rocky peninsula and good fishing positions may be located during a stroll along the road instead of walking the riverbed. The gradient of the valley floor is slightly steeper here than it is downstream and calls for a more positive and active approach to fishing by both fly and spin fishing anglers. Good trout water extends all the way upstream to the Wash Bridge, and anglers should consider spending a whole day walking and fishing this section to be met there by their companion and driven back to base at the Kowhai Reserve.

(13) Wash Bridge: approx. 5 km from (12)

This final access provides literally miles of fishing in both directions. There is good sheltered parking on grassed flats between stands of manuka trees on the upstream left-hand side of the bridge approach as well as on an old gravel road on the opposite downstream side. Foot access is identifiable and quite easy to an open riverbed where the river is confined to narrower, deeper and more stable channels than those prevailing downstream.

Fly anglers should fish their way upstream slowly, visually searching the shallows on the edge of the river for a slate-grey shadow barely discernible against similar coloured stones.

Spin anglers may 'work' in the opposite direction with their minnows and enjoy the scenery in this long river valley unique to the top of the South.

Nelson's Buller River is 20 km away.

7 Rainbow River

The upper reaches of the Wairau River are often mistakenly called the Rainbow River, derived from the name of its first tributary which dwarfs the main stream. This remote river bisects a wide valley floor in a northerly direction for 30 km, then veers east, and becomes the Wairau River. Its snow-tinged water flows forcefully over a bed of boulders and coarse gravel, occasionally rushing madly between outcrops of solid rock that create deep, inaccessible pools with impossible fishing conditions hosting visible, large, cruising fish. This primeval terrain of jagged peaks, forest-covered mountain slopes, huge shingle slides and hidden waterfalls is an environment habitable by only the most tenacious of fish — large, wild brown trout.

While the river can not be described as well stocked, it does hold a reasonable number of large brown trout and an increasing number of salmon, the latter due to an ambitious stocking program and state-of-the-art spawning beds constructed during the early 1990s in a tributary of the true Rainbow River. Personally, I consider that this region has more appeal to outdoorsmen who use trout as a reason to visit virgin terrain rather than to those who just want to go fishing.

The gravel road is negotiable and traverses isolated mountainous terrain between the Nelson and Canterbury districts. Caution is essential when using this route as there are several open watercourses that flood and wash out during heavy rain. It is now a private road and a key must be purchased (semi-refundable deposit) from farmhouses situated at each end. Inquiries may be made here regarding its condition.

(I) Access Key: II.7 km from St Arnaud (Lake Rotoiti)

Follow Highway 63 towards Blenheim, turn right at the sign Rainbow Station (ignore the Rainbow Skifield entrance), drive a further 2.6 km and follow the sign regarding an access key.

(2) Merry Stream Access: 7.6 km from (I)

The road is higher than and separated from the river and passes through several stands of native forest, crossing two watercourses en route to this first fishing access.

Ford the Merry Stream then park on the wide gravel road verge. The Wairau River is within view and quite accessible following a short walk down the stream bank. The river tumbles over a bed of boulders creating a disturbed but steady flow of water descending a distinct gradient and offers spin fishing rather than fly fishing conditions. There is literally miles of fishable water here and anglers may wander at will in either direction over the wide and open gravel riverbed.

(3) Road/River Convergence Access: I.5 km from (2)

The road descends to the same level as the river after crossing Rough Creek (a concreted ford) and you may park on the roadside, walk 20 m and examine the current close to the bank for fish holding station or actively feeding in a disturbed flow.

If the light is poor or the water too cloudy to permit fish sighting then by all means fish blind using the upstream technique: initially with a large, well-hackled dry fly (sizes 8/10 Humpy, Wulff, Irresistible, Black Gnat) and change to, or use on a dropper, a heavy, large-bodied size 8 nymph in the absence of action.

Here again, the open riverbed permits both fly and spin anglers to wander at leisure and choose terrain with water conditions suited to their personal expertise.

(4) Dip Flat Access: I.6 km from (3)

The road crosses a concreted ford through Woolshed Stream en route to a road junction. Turn left towards the Military Personnel Training Establishment (only used periodically), and follow a vehicle track leading from the road and clearly ending on the quite solid gravel riverbed. The gradient in this location is quite gradual and creates shallow ripples, wide pools and smooth, deep runs. The open nature of the valley floor and the smooth water conditions combine to present a good fish-sighting venue, at least, to those versed in this art. But at times atmospheric conditions will make this task difficult even for the proficient and blind casting should be applied in the absence of sighted trout, which will be a darkish brown shade here.

(5) Second Dip Flat Access: 2.5 km from (4)

The road now climbs and skirts the edge of a plateau directly above the river to provide vantage points to scan for fish. It is necessary to push through the few feet of soft native brush between the road and cliff edge — be careful or you'll end up sky-diving as the plateau is high and ends abruptly.

If the fish sighted are large enough to warrant the effort, you should mark their position with a landmark, drive along the road to the next access, walk back and catch them. It is quite possible to see 3.5-4.5 kg (8-10 lb) fish anywhere in this river.

The road descends, and a narrow grassy flat separates it from the river, where a wide, shallow run glides over and through large protruding stones. This is an absolutely perfect trout habitat, specifically created for fly anglers experienced in the technique of wading ever so slowly upstream in knee-deep water, locating a motionless trout by the twitch of its fins or tail, then placing a size 16 or 18 Sawyer's, Miracle, or Grey Darter unweighted nymph 'bang on its nose'. That is if the fish aren't rising, in which case they will be easier to locate and catch with a similar sized Adams, Coachman or Twilight Beauty dry fly.

(6) Six-Mile Creek Access: 2.1 km from (5)

This elevated ring-road leads through forest and provides an opportunity to study the geography of the river before descending to rejoin the main valley road 1 km ahead. You will pass the Rainbow Ski Field junction en route to the concreted Six-Mile ford just before which there is an access road leading to the main river. This venue provides deep and boisterous water confined to stable channels where spin anglers should fish across and down with a 14-g (½-oz) deep-running minnow coloured black or dark green/brown. Fly anglers will find the next access more to their liking — it's a beaut.

(7) St Ronan's Well Access: 5.3 km from (6)

Drive carefully down the steep incline to pass over a narrow bridge, carry on a few yards and stop on the road verge to reconnoitre the river valley below; this will assist with your next fishing approach.

The road levels off parallel to the river which is now only 50 m away across a grassy flat. Turn into the next vehicle track and follow the indistinct wheel marks through long grass downstream to the shingle slide conveying St Ronans Stream into the Wairau River.

After admiring and perhaps showering under the waterfall, fly anglers should saunter to the river and fish upstream through the wide and quietly flowing pool with a size 14/16 nymph (dry fly, if a rise is apparent) up and into the base of the rapid ahead. Now, fish in the upstream manner with a well-hackled size 8 dry fly. This good trout water should be fished thoroughly by applying the blind technique over the whole expanse of turbulence — it's impossible to spot fish in these boisterous conditions.

Trout will be holding in the current beside a feed channel, and anything that even resembles food will be taken impulsively — and vigorously. Ensure that your leader is free of wind knots.

(8) Hamilton River Access: 1 km from (7)

The Wairau River becomes evident as you drive over this bridge. Continue a few metres, turn left, drive over the grassed clearing between trees, and park on the far side where there is a most delightful, sheltered camping position.

Several foot tracks lead through open bush onto the river. The one leading upstream to the right terminates on a small sandy beach near the base of a rapid, while the one to the left follows the river downstream and in odd places permits an elevated view of a swift deep pool and the backwater created by confluence of the Hamilton River.

Close observation will probably reveal a couple of large trout holding in the current or slowly cruising in the depths and it will be necessary to place your enticement at the same level held by the fish to induce a take.

Spin anglers are at an advantage here; they may stand well back, cast ahead of the fish with a heavy, deep-running minnow, and determine the depth of retrieval by the speed of the wind.

Fly anglers may have to resort not only to weighted nymphs, but also to lead shot seized to the leader and/or the sink-tipped floating lines.

Although this may be a lot of trouble to go to to catch one fish, the sight of such a quarry nonchalantly exposing itself in the crystal waters of a sunny pool will be challenge enough for any fisherman. The best fish holding station here is on the opposite side of the river, immediately upstream from the converging current of the Hamilton River, where trout will lay close to the solid rock buttress, motionless and almost invisible.

(9) Sliprails Access: 2.4 km from (8)

There are several accesses to the river over this distance. One beside a gatepost across the road, from where a steep but short scramble down a bank beneath trees provides an excellent section of water flowing over protruding boulders. A second is reached by walking over grassed terrain on Irishman's Flat to easy water, descending a gentle incline in open surrounds.

A road-sign, 'Sliprails', identifies this position where the river once again flows over protruding boulders as it arcs to the right within a short walking distance of the road. This very good venue is suited to both spin and fly fishing, and is one worthy of close attention.

(10) Homestead Flat Access: 600 m from (9)

Drive through the gravel-bottomed Shroders Creek ford and park near the gate before the old Rainbow Homestead. Walk along the grassed track a few hundred metres to the river near the bush visible over open paddocks.

Leave the vehicle here — it will be easier to walk back along the road after fishing, than stumble back along the riverbed and over fences.

There are more than 2 km of good fly fishing water here which offers two anglers the opportunity to walk abreast on either side of the river and enhance each other's fishing by sighting trout and offering casting instructions. The odd scramble around a few trees and up and down banks will be of little consequence compared to the enjoyment that awaits.

The river follows a shallow 'S' bend ,the gradual incline produces gentle ripples, sparkling runs and smooth glides, while the open nature of the valley provides better natural light conditions than those prevailing downstream. This venue receives unhindered sunlight from sunrise to sunset. This is truly an outstanding fishing spot. Fish the quiet and shallow sections with sizes 14/16 lightly dressed nymphs or dry flies and replace them with larger bodied, full-hackled varieties in swift, broken or wind-agitated water.

Pay special attention to the calm water downstream to the right of where the river veers away from its course along the base of the high roadside bank. It widens and becomes shallow, submerging a flat area of round boulders to form a perfect feeding venue for brown trout.

Good fish sighting conditions exist here for fly anglers, where only long and accurate casting with sizes 16/18 nymphs will ensure results. Stealth is the order of the day in this well-stocked location.

Trout will be holding station and feeding quite noticeably in rough pockets and glides over the following 300-400 m of river, necessitating a different approach from the one used in the gentle reaches downstream. Anglers fishing upstream on the right should climb up the high bank and visually examine every inch of water ahead of their stance as they progress upstream.

The trout will be quite large and reasonably easy to locate by the proficient, but anglers lacking this expertise should perhaps occasionally have a quick look and concentrate on blind fishing, as is also necessary for anglers fishing on the other side of the river.

Concentrate on fishing along the base of this bank right up to the convergence with O'Connors Creek — it is good fish holding water in its entirety. Follow the creek to the road and return along it to your vehicle.

(11) Rocky Bluff Access: 3.4 km from O'Connors Creek gate

The elevated road converges with the river's course a few metres before this very visible overhanging bluff, and anglers should park on the roadside and then walk ahead to examine the clear water in the pool beneath their feet. Examine the wide, shallow tail of the pool carefully for a tell-tale shadow before rushing madly ahead to look in the swirling deep backwater for a larger one.

This is a good finale to an excellent river as this pool ends the fishable section of river. The Rainbow tributary convergence is only about 2 km upstream, and the fine alluvium of that river also drifts this far down the Wairau and renders both waterways unsuitable as a trout habitat.

The precincts of the last two described accesses will, however, provide many pleasurable hours of fishing activity. The terrain is open, of a gentle gradient and provides easy foot-access to good trout water.

The road continues over Island Pass, providing access to Lakes Tennyson and Tarndale, along the upper reaches of the Clarence River and terminates at Hamner after traversing Jacks Pass. It is rough and very scenic in fine weather.

Rainbow River, position (5).

8 Lake Rotoiti — Buller and Travers Rivers

This is the freshwater playground of the Nelson/Marlborough provinces, with excellent camping facilities and a modern motel-style lodge, boasting a good climate, a small township and clear water well stocked with brown trout.

A popular lake for all water sports, it is extensively fished by the trolling method. As with most lakes, however, the fish come close inshore to feed during early morning, and again in the evening, offering fly anglers an entirely different challenge to that of the Buller River.

The shoreline of the peninsula separating Kerr Bay (St Arnaud) and West Bay is rough, rocky and unsuitable for shore fishing. However, both bays have shingle beaches providing easy walking access to relaxed fishing in the calm of the dawn and again in the twilight, when small flies and nymphs should be used to attract the cruising trout.

If you have a boat, good fishing may be had anywhere along the shoreline, especially in the evening, when the rise is generally quite prolific. During calm early morning hours, you should quietly paddle the boat along the shoreline until a cruising fish is seen, then place a small nymph or wet Coch-y-Bondhu fly in its path. Use a floating line and leader of at least 2.7 m (9 ft) in length.

Head of the Lake

There is boat access only to this location, which has two Park Board huts complete with beds and cooking facilities. You will, however, need to bring your own sleeping bag and cooking utensils. Approach the Park Board Headquarters at St Arnaud for permission to use the huts. The shore of the lake between the river and stream that enter it here is shallow, muddy, and covered with an underwater weed.

Excellent results await the stealthy angler who can cast a size 14 or 16 Pheasant Tail nymph accurately. During the dawn hours there are numerous intently feeding but extremely alert fish, while twilight brings forth the dry feeders preceding and following the 20 minute wet rise at nightfall. During this rise the trout will frantically take wet flies of the Greenwell's Glory, Twilight Beauty, or almost any other pattern — they're not fussy at that hour.

The twilight also brings forth millions of annoying buzzing insects as the sandflies retreat with the daylight, so ensure that your insect repellent is handy.

Travers River

Access is no problem in this beautiful 8 km valley, with its grassy flats and wide gravel bed. For those of a more adventuous nature, it is possible to follow the bush track for a further 3 km, while fishing the river all the way to the John Tait Hut. Here you will find a stove, fuel, bottle-gas cookers, and 16 beds. Apply to Park Headquarters at St Arnaud for further details.

This river provides fishing equal to its beauty, and the gentle water conditions are worthy of matching equipment. The SAGE 9 ft (2.7 m), two-piece, weight 4 rod will deliver the necessary size 14 to 18 flies and nymphs with the delicacy and accuracy that these 2-kg (4½-lb) brown trout demand — and have come to expect!

The same rod will soothe the frenzied panic of the hooked fish with the smooth and positive control necessary to permit its early, unharmed and passive release.

Outlet of the Lake

The bar of Lake Rotoiti, as the source of the Buller River, offers good fishing all day and excells at dawn and twilight. The former period should be fished with minute nymphs or Greenwell's Glory wet flies, the daylight hours with Hare & Copper/Pheasant Tail style nymphs, and the evening with Twilight Beauty or Peveril o'Peak wet flies.

It is a small flow of water when compared with the expanse of the lake and is often shallow enough to cross when wearing waist-high waders. The glide forms a rapid in a stable bed of stones which passes under the road bridge providing access to the Mount Robert Ski Basin, and is within walking distance of the West Bay Motor Camp.

Although subject to considerable fishing pressure during holiday periods, this venue seldom fails to produce trout for competent anglers using either technique.

Buller River

Few rivers in New Zealand offer the delightful conditions of the Buller. Emerging as a small stream from Lake Rotoiti in Nelson, it joins the sea some 150 km away at Westport. Despite its length, however, it becomes too big for fly fishing after about 60 km, though sections of the lower reaches offer excellent spinning.

The entire river is well stocked with wild brown trout, and the large lower section provides an enormous natural hatchery, which supplements the fish population upstream of the lake itself. The 50-odd km of water described here is crystal-clear and traverses a long valley in a westerly direction to converge with its two longest tributaries near Murchison.

Four other tributaries, rivers in their own right, merge with the Buller over this distance and they will be identified and described under their own names. The whole spectrum of trout fishing water is provided by this vibrant waterway with the best climate in New Zealand. It is paralleled by the highway in its entirety and entices the angler, with glimpses of easy access, to azure blue pools, sparkling rapids and sweeping runs.

But the trout demand skilled adversaries; one careless footfall on the gravel, a reflection in the wrong place or a fly delivered carelessly and it's all over for the angler.

The initial 7 km of headwaters provide unbelievably fast and violent conditions to which it is difficult to gain access, let alone reach casting positions. This is, nevertheless, the most exhilarating and best stocked section of water in the Nelson province, with few equals in the South Island. Averaging only 1.5 kg in weight, these fish fight like the very devil and will test the skill of the most experienced fly angler.

This section calls for perfect rod and line control, agility, and sure-footedness in the swift current rushing over slippery rocks. Although spinning is permitted and practised here, it is better suited to fly fishing techniques with the presentation of a large-bodied, size 8, weighted Stonefly, Hare & Copper nymph, or (preferably when the sun enhances the sparkle of a rapid) a similar sized Grizzly Wulff, Humpy, Molefly or Kakahi Queen Palmer-hackled dry fly.

It is almost impossible to wade these upper reaches, and the occasional shallow crossing must be treated cautiously — the stones are coated with slippery green moss. Felt soles are of little help, the only safe footing provided by aluminium cleats and the use of a robust wading stick.

The mid-section of the river extends for approximately 20 km and provides contrasting water and terrain. The birch trees and impregnable stands of manuka lining the rocky channel are slowly replaced with tussock grass growing on low banks with round stones reaching into the water.

There are still occasional clumps of manuka and matagouri, native briar versed in the technique of plucking fly lines from midair and tangling them irretrievably in their inch-long thorns. They also play havoc with careless anglers, clothed or otherwise: give them a wide berth.

Swift water traverses open terrain through a succession of rapids, glides and fast pools with swirling backwaters. There are few calm pools as such anywhere in this section, which holds fewer but larger trout than the headwaters.

The stony bed frequently conveys the water into the tussock grass beneath the anglers feet and this, combined with a turbulent surface, creates very difficult fish-sighting conditions. These 40-90 cm deep runs hold many fish and should be fished blind with a large dry fly while straining the eyes to locate a long grey shadow holding stationary near the bank or suspended just beneath the surface in the midstream current.

This harsh terrain is gradually replaced by contoured gravel beds and wide river-flats descending a gentle gradient in an open valley. This location offers some of the most pleasant brown trout fishing venues in the South Island.

The elevated highway provides a panorama of clear water sweeping through long gentle arcs which are framed in ash-grey gravel and fringed with golden tussock grass highlighted by stands of weeping willows.

Surely the ultimate dream of a perfect fly fishing river, and within easy reach of several overnight riverside camping positions.

Highway 6 runs beside the lower reaches from Kawatiri Junction to Murchison, offering 30 km of vigorous water flowing over gravel beds, restricted between solid rock embankments and passing beneath overhanging native trees.

(1) The Source of the Buller River: 86 km from Nelson

Leave Nelson in a southerly direction on Highway 6, travel 35 km and turn left at a road junction signposted 'Wai-iti Valley/Lake Rotoiti/St Arnaud 51 km'. The road bisects the Golden Downs Forest and converges with Highway 63 from Blenheim, 5 km before the St Arnaud settlement. Continue through St Arnaud for a kilometre or two, turn left and follow the Mount Robert/West Bay Road for 1.4 km and then park in the gravel-pit just past the second motor camp entrance and within sight of the Buller Bridge.

The smooth, swiftly flowing water directly ahead provides good fishing. Use a nymph in the early morning, a dry fly mid morning to late afternoon and again after dark, when the trout stop their 'splashy' wet rise. Twilight should be fished with a size 12/16 wet fly.

This section of river is well stocked with small brown trout with an average weight of 1 kg, and are so easily caught that the position is described as the learners' pool. Suitable fly patterns here, and in other calm, shallow sections are: nymphs Hare & Copper, Gold-ribbed Hare's Ear, Grey Darter and Pheasant Tail; dry flies Adams, Blue Dun, Greenwell's Glory, Molefly; wet flies Greenwell's Glory, Twilight Beauty, March Brown in small sizes of say 14-18. Use larger sizes when the river is high or when fishing fast broken sections of water.

The track entering the bush downstream leads to position (2) and provides access to the river. Water and terrain conditions over this section are extremely rough but it is well stocked with trout that rise savagely for a dry fly and take a nymph with enthusiasm. It should be fished by experienced, physically fit and agile anglers only.

Walk towards the lake through the trees to reach the shallow bar which is generally negotiable with the use of hip boots. You should stand on the bar itself, cast slightly upstream and let the fly tumble over the ripple to swing downstream with the current. Keep a taut line and be ready for a take when retrieving the fly — it will be a very vicious strike. I have found that the best time to fish this position is during the evening rise, 10 minutes before and after complete darkness, when the fish rise wet. There's often a good dawn rise.

Small as they may be, it is a delightful way to spend a warm summer evening — catching and releasing 'young-uns' within a few minutes walk of the West Bay Motor Camp, an ideal overnight base for anglers using tents or campervans.

(2) Upper Buller Bridge: 2.9 km from (1)

Return to Highway 63, turn left, drive 1.5 km and park on the apex of the curve within sight of the bridge. Good fishing prevails in both directions but the restrictive bush-covered terrain and violent water can only be described as a 'holocaust' — it is a venue for fit, agile and experienced fly anglers (and trout) only.

Walk over the steel barrier and follow the track to a grassed clearing 50 metres upstream, where the elevation provides a view of rough water tumbling and roaring madly over a shallowish section of boulder-strewn riverbed.

This is one of the calmest sections in the 2 km of river up to the outlet that I described under position (1) — let the unprepared retreat and the proficient ready themselves for an experience!

Rig your 9-ft (2.7-m) SAGE graphite weight 5 rod with a WF floating line, a 3-lb test tippet leader, and a size 8 or 10 dry fly, well-dressed with silicon flotant. Pattern is of less importance than high-floating, vibrant action and my choice would be Grizzly Wulff (elk hair), Yellow Humpy, Molefly, Kakahi Queen or Black Gnat — the last three patterns should be Palmer-hackled (double-hackled).

Follow a faint track through knee-high vegetation and wade a short distance into the water to allow for back-casting room. Cast upstream and cover the whole surface — trout in these headwaters frequent even the most unlikely feeding positions and will snap at the fly as it flashes by. A nymph may be used here effectively, but personally I favour the dry in these shallow turbulent conditions and use a weighted nymph in the deep pockets of water between large boulders and slabs of solid rock.

Return to the clearing and follow the track upstream. The only large pool in this section of river is about 400 m upstream, just after the track crosses a miniature ravine. There is also a very good, but small, fishing venue at its convergence with the river which may be fished in passing.

Step down the low bank, through a narrow cleft, and walk a few feet into the river. Cast a large, well-hackled dry fly a few times slightly up and across the tumbling mass of frothing water. Fish caught here certainly take some landing.

Return and cross the ravine, follow the track a short way, then sidle your way over the crest and down the bank beneath manuka trees onto the horizontal plain and follow your nose to the river. There is a faint track leading through a small patch of grass on the edge of the water about three quarters of the way up the pool. The shallows at the tail should be fished blind with a small dry fly and rising fish in the current tempted with the same pattern (use larger size if spurned).

The width of water at the head of the pool is restricted by solid rock buttresses: it is deep and calm this side and the current enters opposite. Work your way upstream (it is difficult but possible along a narrow ledge of stones beneath trees) with a large weighted nymph and cover all the 'dead' water between the bank and current. This hole holds a good head of trout but it is important to present your nymph at the correct feeding depth to make contact.

The rough, rocky section immediately above the the pool will not produce a fish but the next calmer section of water emerging from a right-hand curve will. Scramble through the prickly undergrowth, slip and slide through the shallows to reach casting position, and work your way upstream with a high-floating dry fly until the terrain bars further progress. The track now provides elevated views of the river in its tortuous bed. If you can, clamber down and fish with a large dry as the whole expanse holds fish.

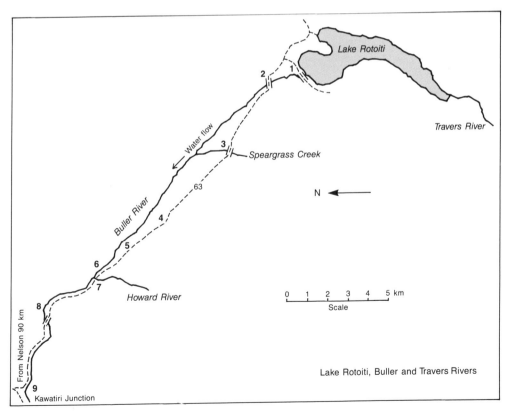

Lake Rotoiti, Buller and Travers Rivers

The track descends to the level of the river after about a kilometre, and immediately following a sharp left-hand turn the river can be seen through a narrow opening in the small manuka trees. This is an excellent venue and will provide an hour or two of concentrated fly fishing with a dry or nymph.

Walk a few metres downstream and start fishing back from the acute right-hand bend. The swift run on the opposite bank is generally good for a trout, and in fact the whole stretch of water upstream to where it curves to your right is a perfect brown trout habitat — work it over thoroughly.

There are more intresting nooks and crannies holding feeding fish in this unique waterway than I have space to describe. It is indeed a challenging venue — answer the call and explore.

Both sides of the river downstream from the bridge are paralleled by walking tracks through restrictive vegetation, and it is a matter of finding your own way into water. The flow here, while still swift, is slightly smoother than the upper section. Use the same fishing technique as upstream in this location, where it is also possible to float the fly down the current and swing it into the swirl of a backwater — something that doesn't exist in the 'holocaust' upstream.

(3) Speargrass Creek Access: 3.1 km from (2)

The river veers right and separates from the highway over this section. Although it is possible to follow boundary fences across the wide plateau, down two levels and reach good trout water, I would suggest driving to this easier access. Stop and park in the Speargrass Creek depression.

Follow the creek bed to the river and make your way along an animal track to reach water of your choice. The flow is swift and broken. Access along the grassed riverbank is restricted by vegetation, but this difficult venue is certainly worth fishing. It is well stocked with very agile, wary trout that are difficult to sight, and it will be necessary to fish blind with a high-floating dry fly.

It must be considered a position for experienced, fit fly anglers — the going, and the fishing is 'rough 'n' tough'.

(4) Homestead Creek (Anglers') Access: 4.5 km from (3)

Step over the Anglers' Access stile beside the sign positioned where the road veers left, to pass through the creek depression and walk across the wide plain to the river. The river still flows swiftly over stones but the riverbank is less restricted by vegetation here than it is upstream.

Lake Rotoiti, position (1), the source of the Buller River.

Anglers should consider fishing this section all the way to Speargrass Creek, which may be followed up to the highway, which can be walked back to their vehicle instead of retracing the journey back down the rough riverbed.

Actually, this mode of approach may applied to all accesses between the lake and Kawatiri Junction: positions (1) to (9).

(5) Power Pylons (Anglers') Access: 2.4 km from (4)

Park near the Anglers' Access sign beneath the power pylons. Another long walk over the plateau is necessary but its elevation offers a panoramic view of some excellent fishing water, where the river meanders over a wide bed of gravel in a valley floor devoid of restrictive vegetation. The tussock-covered terrain, though a little rough underfoot, offers easy access to the water's edge.

The open environment makes the trout extremely vigilant, and although fewer in number they are larger than their counterparts in the tumultuous water upstream and as a matter of course are also shrewd, alert and shy.

This is good water to fish by slowly walking upstream, casting blind with a size 10 or 12 dry fly while visually examining the current for holding or feeding trout. A nymph, size 8 Pheasant Tail, Stonefly or Hare & Copper, works well here when fishing blind, but sighted fish should be tempted with similar patterns in sizes 14/16 first and the size increased if spurned.

Caution in approaching the water and careful presentation of the line now replaces the physical aspect of casting, retrieving and controlling the fly so necessary upstream. Watch the shadow of your line while casting, it will spook the trout as quick as a flash.

(6) Anglers' Access Sign: 2.1 km from (5)

As the highway descends to cross the Howard River Bridge it presents a captivating view of the valley, especially during the bright sunny period of the day. Turquoise river water bisects the valley floor over a wide bed of light-coloured gravel, curving graciously as it descends gentle inclines covered with golden tussock. Note the ease of approach to the long, shallow ripples, the quiet water in the pools and the lack of casting restrictions -indeed, the perfect fly fishing venue.

Continue to the lower level where there is an Anglers' Access sign beside a stile on the right. It is only a short distance from the river and offers a starting position for a morning's fishing terminating at the pylon (5) access — a very good section.

(7) Howard River Convergence Access: 500 m from (6)

Drive over the Howard River Bridge, turn through the roadside gate, and follow one of the vehicle tracks towards the river. The one upstream terminates in an old gravel-pit, the two downstream lead to the willow trees in view. Drive through the grass slowly; it is quite often wet and boggy.

This good overnight position is strategically placed to provide interesting fishing in unexcelled brown trout water. Cross the river and walk downstream for a kilometre or so to where the river curves to the right, away from its course along the base of the highway embankment.

From here downstream the river descends quite steeply through a rapid. Fish your way back to your parking/camping position by starting at the long glide in which trout will be quite visible around the underwater outcrops of solid rock. This is good water, well stocked with 'spooky' fish which require a very small-bodied, size 16 nymph, an invisible 4X tippet leader and a presentation as soft as thistledown. Then again these fish may be rising, in which case use a similar sized Adams, Pheasant Tail or Coch-y-Bondhu dry fly.

The several ripples, rapids and deepish runs from here on up are good fish habitat, and will provide many hours of pleasurable and successful fly fishing.

If staying overnight, use a size 12 Twilight Beauty wet fly in the first pool upstream from the Howard River convergence just as the twilight surrenders to darkness — it's a beaut spot.

(8) Harley's Rock Bridge Access: 3.4 km from (7)

The road is quite narrow as it skirts the base of a hill to this position and offers a panorama of river and environs to equal the one described under position (6). En route two Anglers' Access signs, with limited parking room beside them, are positioned to allow a leisurely examination of access, terrain and water conditions before proceeding to the river, and it is time well spent.

The valley turns left here and the road gently descends to Harley's Rock Bridge over the Buller River and presenting a view across the wide grassed valley floor to the river which skirts the base of bush-covered slopes. This water will be fished from the next access. Note the runs, ripples and occasional smooth glides; there are no pools as such here.

The backwater between the river and hill is always worth stalking carefully; its stock of cruising trout is generally replenished with every flood.

An elevated small gravel flat on the upstream (St Arnaud) side of the bridge, offers a good parking and observation position. It is an easy walk from the highway to the river, which may be fished upstream for as far as desired, from accessible and open terrain. This is a good venue for spinning in the rapids and fly fishing along the edges of calmer sections.

Good fishing is also available from the gravel road on the other bank. Drive over the bridge, turn hard right and follow the road as it runs along the river to opposite the two anglers' accesses described above. The road is adjacent to, but separated from, the river by a narrow strip of native bush, but careful observation will reveal foot access to the water's edge.

Parking is limited — look for an old gravel pit on the left and an obscure vehicle track to the right leading onto a most delightful grassed clearing right on the edge of the river. The track to this good overnight camper van position should be walked first — it may be muddy.

Interesting fly fishing is to be had from this latter position by walking upstream on a narrow ledge below the small cliff just above the high-water mark. Use either a large, heavy nymph or high-floating size 8 dry fly by casting upstream and floating it back right against the overhanging grass or solid rock formation. A difficult but challenging venue.

There is also good fishing available downstream from Harley's Rock Bridge after walking to the riverbed from its upstream approach. It is a good idea to reconnoitre the whole area from the bridge itself before commencing to fish. There will be large trout to be seen visibly holding in the current below.

(9) Kawatiri Junction Access: 3.3 km from (8)

It is possible to park on the roadside en route to the next venue, search the river for feeding trout and then clamber down the steep embankment and catch them. Watch carefully for a vehicle access leading from the highway to a stand of manuka scrub on the riverbed, opposite a high bank where the river curves right. Inspect the area before driving down the steep access road (it is rough), locate your picnic or camping position then note the fishing water suited to your preferred technique. The excellence of this venue will be quite apparent, and a good head of trout frequent all types of water here.

(10) Keystone Reserve Access: 2.6 km from (9)

Highways 63 and 6 converge 1 km further on. Follow the latter and turn left at the sign (as the highway veers right) into this overnight base equipped with only the most basic of amenities but strategically positioned to offer good fishing for both spinning and fly fishing enthusiasts.

The disturbed run of water flowing along the perimeter of the long grassy flat is too deep to wade. It does, however, provide perfect spin fishing conditions when walking along the water's edge at the base of a 2-m high bank.

Fly anglers should follow an indistinct track through tall vegetation at the lower end of the reserve and emerge onto a small gravel beach offering access to an area of contrasting fishing conditions. Water rippling over shingle bars, bouncing against rocky outcrops and rushing through deep runs with fast rapids to create conditions demanding thoughtful and competent application of several fly fishing techniques.

Hours may be spent fishing this extensive area, downstream and around the corner, where the hassle of gaining access is rewarded by a venue where a nymph or dry fly will prove equally effective if applied correctly in relevant current flows.

Above left: This fish, located visually feeding on emerging nymphs in shallow water, was taken on a size 16 Peacock Herle nymph.
Above right: Although of modest size, this is a trophy befitting the unique environment of the West Coast.
Below: The discoloured spring flow of Southland's upper Mataura River: just 48 hours later it was a sparkling run hosting visible trout 'rising dry'.

Above: Fairytale fishing conditions prevail at the Motueka River's convergence with the Baton River.
Below: The upper Buller River provides a testing environment for both angler and trout.
Opposite: The Borland of Southland: a silent 'arena' demanding stealth and perfect presentation of minute dries and nymphs.

Above: The beauty of this scene belies the savagery of the Gowan River. This tumultuous waterway is unique in New Zealand and emits a challenge to fly anglers that the foolhardy will accept.
Below: The 'Browns of the Gowan': the author's son holds his 'nymphed' trophy.

(11) Washout Creek Access: 2.4 km from (10)

This small bridge is crossed while following a right-hand bend leading through native birch forest. Watch carefully for a bush-framed vehicle track leading left about 50 m past the bridge and follow it to a large parking/camping area on the old railway track. Follow an indistinct foot track over the low embankment towards the river, veer slightly left through open bush, then between a short section of thick scrub beside the creek. You'll exit over white marble alluvium onto a wide riverbed.

This venue provides good water for both fishing methods. The river descends a gentle gradient through a series of rapids, glides and pools in open terrain which provides unrestricted foot access and casting positions. This is a most pleasant area to park, picnic or camp. The whole clearing is completely enclosed beneath an umbrella of forest, enhanced by the sight and sound of native birds.

(12) Grassy Parking Area: 1.2 km from (11)

Pull onto this grassed area within sight of the sign 'Gowan Junction' a few hundred metres past the confluence of the Gowan Tributary and Buller Rivers. A short walk through native bush will present swift, broken water ideally suited to spin fishing only, from fairly restricted accesses.

(13) Buller Bridge: 1.6 km from (12)

Turn left at the junction, follow the road to Lake Rotoroa, and park near the bridge offering an elevated view of the river in both directions. The large pool extending from the bridge offers good spinning, as does the next long rapid downstream. The water upstream from the bridge is quite broken and turbulent but fly anglers agile and experienced enough to handle rough terrain should expect results fishing the edges with a well-hackled size 10 dry fly. This latter section is unsuitable for novice fly anglers or spin fishing enthusiasts.

(14) Roadside Rest Area: 4.7 km from Gowan Junction

The highway descends a slight depression where a rest area complete with picnic table is positioned on the left beside a stand of trees. Several rough vehicle tracks lead towards the river and it is merely a matter of driving along one or the other to park within walking distance of the river.

The water flow is quite forceful here necessitating a similar approach by anglers, be they fly or spin exponents. It will be necessary for the former to make long casts with a large dry fly or heavy nymph, and the latter to use a slim, deep-running minnow with a very slow retrieve along the edge of the current.

There is a section of very well stocked water at the first right-angled bend in the river downstream.

(15) Raites Road Access: 3.3 km from (14)

Turn left at the sign, pass through the gate before the bridge, and park beside willow trees. The water flowing along the perimeter of this alluvium flat alters character with every other flood making it necessary to 'roll with the punches' and either spin or fly fish as prevailing conditions dictate. It has always been a well-stocked venue and a pleasant area to rest awhile.

(16) Owen River Park: 2.2 km from (15)

As the highway descends to pass the Owen River Tavern, veer left, drive past the building, follow the access onto the reserve and park on the far side near the confluence of the Owen Tributary and Buller Rivers. This is a good overnight camper van base.

(17) Grassy Parking Area: 7 km from the Owen Tavern

The highway descends and veers right before traversing a small flat. Just before it veers left to ascend a rise, pull onto the large flat grassed area on the left and park under the tree. This is just preceding the Nuggety Bridge turn off to your left, in case you don't stop in time.

Step through the bush, down a short bank and onto the riverbed, where there is the most perfect natural groyne imaginable. Two long rocky outcrops protrude into the swift, deep stream. The slack water between them will hold fish either on the cruise or holding station just where the current enters a backwater.

Fish the area from a concealed stance with a sizes 14/16 Adams, Humpy, Molefly dry flies or an unweighted Hare & Copper or Hare's Ear nymph. Spin anglers should use a black 14-g Tinker/Toby minnow or, if there are autumn leaves floating on the surface, a yellow-hued 7-g Tango or Spoon.

(18) Buller Bridge-Matiri Valley turnoff: 7 km from (17)
Follow the Matiri River Valley road for 400 m and park between trees on the left just where the road turns left. Tracks from here follow a small cascading creek to the level of the Buller River and terminate on a large horizontal rock shelf. This is an ideal venue for spin fishing or in which to use weighted nymphs with a sink-tip fly line.

(19) Mangles River Bridge: 2.7 km from (18)
There is a large reserve on the right side as you approach this bridge, which offers a sheltered rest area beneath tall conifers. There are several steep foot tracks leading over the bank through vegetation to some fast, clear, productive water for spin fishing only.

There is a well-defined foot track leading from the far corner to the convergence of the Mangles and Buller Rivers. This is a small but good spin fishing position.

(20) Murchison Motor Camp: 2.8 km from (19)
This motor camp provides all amenities for the travelling/camper van fraternity, is within sight of the township and is strategically positioned to use as a base from which to fish the Buller and its tributaries.

The township is only 2 km further along the highway.

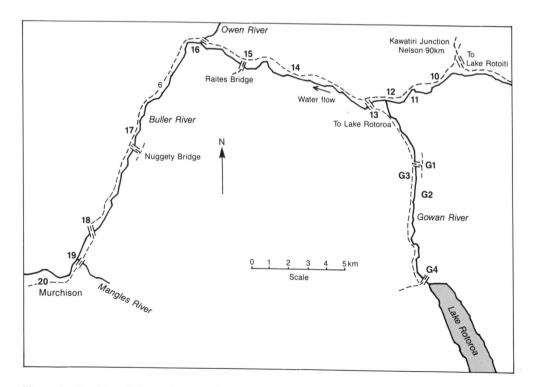

9 Lake Rotoroa and Gowan River

Situated in a high rainfall area and guarded by millions of vicious sandflies, this isolated, bush-fringed lake lies cradled in mist-shrouded hills dwarfed by a backdrop of towering mountain peaks. Its placid waters are reserved for trout fishing and give source to one of the wildest and most exciting rivers in the South Island.

The lower end of the lake is only a 15-minute drive from Highway 6. You will find a large grass parking/camping area right on the lake shore, providing an ablutions block and 'open shelter' hut complete with large fireplace.

The small settlement at this end of the lake also includes a National Park ranger station, to which inquiries should be made regarding permission to use either of the two huts (capacity 22 people) near the two rivers at the head of the lake. When using these huts it is necessary to provide your own sleeping bag and cooking and eating utensils.

Road access stops at the lower end of the lake. The head can only be reached by boat. There are no shelves to fish from on the sides of the lake, although very good fishing will be had from a drifting boat: stop once the fish are seen and cast towards them with a size 14 Hare & Copper nymph or wet Coch-y-Bondhu fly.

The waters of the lake are well stocked with brown trout and a small population of rainbows. With ultra-keen eyesight, these fish are fastidious in their choice of flies and minnows.

Outlet of the Lake — Gowan River

Walk from the bridge or jetty along the Flower Brothers Memorial Walk to the edge of the river. It is usually possible to walk in the water some distance onto the actual bar, which provides good fishing, especially in the early morning and evening at which stage the fish become very active on the surface (as do the sandflies).

Fly patterns in dark colours work best in this location: Black Gnat, Black Spider, Pomahaka Black and Twilight Beauty for example. The style, wet or dry, will be determined by the type of rise.

The streamer fly, in dark or yellow hues, is a good fish-attracter in the smooth, 2-m deep water flowing over the weed bed of the bar, and anglers fortunate enough to have a boat should anchor it just upstream from the stand of flax on the other side of the river. This is an excellent fish-holding position.

Smooth Glide

Walk to the left from the jetty through a small stand of native bush and onto the long shallow shelf which extends well out into the lake. Careful perusal will locate fish cruising slowly over the low bottom weed, unless there is an obvious hatch on. Use a small Pheasant Tail-style nymph, 3X leader, and floating line for these bottom-feeders. Rising trout should be tempted with Sawyer's Pheasant Tail nymph, Black Gnat, Twilight Beauty or Adams dry flies — in the smallest size available.

Convergence of the Sabine River

Access to the head of the lake is possible by boat only, and excellent fishing conditions await anglers fortunate enough to visit the area, especially if they stay overnight in one of the huts on the D'Urville and Sabine Rivers.

The lower reaches of this river flow through rough scrubby terrain which creates difficulty in reaching some productive positions; they are frequently cluttered with logs and flood debris, making the predominantly rainbow trout complacent and susceptible to artifical flies. It is, however, an intriguing area to explore in a small boat while drifting around the shoreline through bays sheltered by forests and water broken by fish rising with incredible delicacy. A different experience to that of bouncing in the wind-chop while trying to fish the Sabine River's current as it enters the lake over a shingle delta.

The waters of the lake intrude slightly into standing trees and patches of small rushes on the shoreline. Although walking progress is slow and difficult, some very good fishing is available to fly anglers wishing to stalk, and catch big trout cruising sedately through their chosen territory. This is enthusiasts' country.

Convergence of the D'Urville River

Although also situated at the head of the lake, this river offers a different atmosphere to that of the sombre surrounds of the Sabine. The river flows over a much wider gravel bed, the whole area receives more sun so the foliage and shoreline are naturally lighter and brighter. The fish, still plentiful and quite visible, are generally of the brown species and even more difficult to catch than those in the precincts of the Sabine tributary. The D'Urville River offers good fishing in a truly back-country environment.

Gowan River

Unique in the South Island, at first sight this is an impossible and forbidding venue for trout fishing. A roaring, raging torrent surging over slippery stones between rocky banks from Lake Rotoroa to the Buller River. Ten kilometres of hostile terrain with difficult access to fishing positions where scrub and precarious footing create impossible casting, fish playing and landing conditions.

Once over the past few years this river officially recorded more brown trout per mile than any other river in the South Island, and although seasonal fluctuations in the environment have seen this claim placed elsewhere, it retains a similar rating to the Motueka, Mataura, Clutha and Pomahaka Rivers. However, it is not a venue for the novice or faint-hearted, rather it is a realm for active, adventurous and experienced fly fishing anglers wishing to test skills unattainable, and indeed unnecessary, in accepted trout fishing streams.

The Gowan converges with the Buller River beside Highway 6 at Gowan Junction, 99 km south of Nelson (27 km north of Murchison). Although the river is accessible upstream on the right (western) bank as far as its source at the outlet of Lake Rotoroa, it is necessary to cross its only bridge to reach most of the fishing positions.

(1) East Bank Bridge: 5 km from Gowan Junction

The road is in proximity and parallel to the river for 3.4 km preceding this bridge and reveals a close-up view of the turbulence in the Gowan. The first fishing position is reached after travelling 1.6 km up the valley from Gowan Junction. The river comes towards you from the left to flow against the road embankment where an 'anglers' access' sign is clearly visible (on a gate), which also offers vehicle parking recommendations.

There is easy access to the horizontal gravel riverbed (extending upstream from the road) which offers good conditions for walking upstream while applying the 'upstream fly fishing' technique. Use a large size 8/10, palmer-hackled Molefly, Blue Dun or Kakahi Queen (well dressed) dry fly or similar sized weighted Hare & Copper, Stonefly or Swanundaze nymph. These enticements will of necessity be presented blind because the water flow is too rough to allow the sight fishing technique.

You should examine the shallows ahead while walking upstream — there are a few 'windows' in the current that may well reveal a 'holding' trout. There is a distinct vortex (visible from the entrance gate) between two current flows running parallel to the road just downstream from where the river veers right (downstream direction). While the 'window' clearly reveals a bed of fine gravel, the distance is too great to see the trout that will undoubtedly frequent this position to 'hold' and feed in the slack water. Both fly and spinning anglers should 'work' this section thoroughly with either a large size 8 weighted nymph or heavy blade (gold/black) minnow. Unfortunately the river is generally too deep and swift to permit foot crossing.

A few hundred metres further along the highway the river once again flows hard against the road embankment where there is another 'anglers' access' sign. The water is deeper here as it strikes five rock groynes extending into the stream from the road embankment. Spinning anglers should 'fish their way down' from groyne to groyne and dredge the convergence of the current with the vortex. Fly anglers should do the same with a dry fly (Black Gnat/Blue Dun/Humpy Yellow or weighted Stonefly/Swanundaze nymph) heading upstream. Do not walk along the road to examine the slack water between the groynes; the trout will 'spook' quick as a flash at the first sign of movement. This location offers an angler a pleasant position to park the car in a space at the upstream extremity of the venue. Encroaching bush renders the in-flowing section of river unsuitable for fishing.

Study the environs from the bridge. The downstream flow descends a continuous gradient in a long straight rapid between encroaching trees — it is good dry-fly water and access is possible through the scrub from the road leading downstream from the gate (with the anglers' access sign) on the eastern bank. It is necessary to take a step or two into the river itself to cast ahead and across with a high-floating dry fly. You must fish 'blind' because the water turbulence here, as over much of the river, renders the sighting of fish impossible. While a weighted size 8 Stonefly or Hare & Copper nymph works well anywhere in this river, there are positions, such as this one, where these applications can be enhanced if used on a dropper below a strike indicator or preferably a large dry fly. It is possible to drive downstream along the east bank road to a small, rough creek that may be followed to its convergence with the river. This spot offers particularly good fishing by either the spinning or fly technique.

If spinning, work downstream using a 14-g Black Tinker (or similar slim, deep running minnow), by casting across the current to the opposite bank and slowly retrieving: the minnow will follow the vortex of a fast current. The fly fishing technique may be employed in either the upstream (very fast retrieval) or wet fly (across and down with a slow retrieval) mode using a heavy, large-bodied nymph or well-hackled and dressed size 8 dry fly. Patterns are less important than action. The nymph should be heavy enough to tumble in the eddies behind protruding upthrusts of water or stones and the dry fly should bounce over small turbulences and submerge through foaming cataracts of white water. The sight of a brown trout flashing from several feet away to 'savage' a dry is a revelation of streamlined beauty and strength. This violent take, peculiar to the foaming cataracts of the Gowan and upper Buller Rivers, is rarely seen in average waterways. The rod should be held at an angle to the line retrieval in order to cushion the sudden take by the fish — they will hit hard and play as 'rough and tough' as the water they live in. Strong, robust leaders are essential to handle the turbulence, and fish, of this river. This is SAGE country.

(2) East Bank Mid Section Access

The upstream view from the bridge reveals a small channel of water merging with the main stream on the right-hand side — there is often a fish holding in this small, calmer position. The main channel of boisterous water flows noticeably against a low grassy flat in a small depression a few metres upstream at the origin of the high scrub-covered bank. This position is accessible from the other side of the farm gate (anglers' access sign). Stop and examine the river upstream (ideally from the elevation of your vehicle's bumper or floorboard) and you will notice the river flowing over a comparatively wide and level rocky shelf on the left. This particular position cannot be seen from anywhere else and provides excellent fly fishing in fast, shallow water, but it has very restrictive scrubby access. It can, however, be reached by obstinate anglers — it is rough and tough going but worth it.

I suggest you start fishing with a large dry from a stance on the grass bank, just inside the gate where the small creek enters the river. There is generally a fish or two working the current near the willow tree on the opposite side. And no, you cannot cross the river, you will have to land your fish this side ... somehow.

The road traverses farmed river flats for 1.8 km and terminates at a locked (anglers' walking access) gate after passing through two other gates also signed 'anglers' access'. The river, while flowing close to the road, is out of sight below the plateau and you may park anywhere (be careful of hidden boulders off the road) and walk the few metres to examine its flow. This unlikely looking water certainly holds fish, unseen but quite susceptible to a deftly manipulated dry fly. Try a size 8 yellow-bodied Humpy, Grizzly Wulff, Kakahi Queen or well-dressed and greased Coachman, and hang on.

I'm unable to locate the best position with a landmark, but I suggest you walk, examine the river between the gate accesses and fish from any position attainable. This is challenging fishing at its best: rough, difficult footage on loose boulders along the base of a 2-m high rocky bank, a fast flow of tumultuous water overpowering the sigh of the wind with its roar, and the sandflies are really something!

Continue up the road and park where indicated by the sign on the locked gate, step over the stile and walk past the stand of open bush which reveals a glimpse of the river close by. The water now follows several small channels, but these are too small to hold fish (except during floods or high water conditions).

The track veers right, then gradually turns left and appears to terminate against the foot of a plateau. The river becomes visible through a few scattered trees on the right as you walk upstream revealing an excellent fishing venue. Two separate, fast flowing pools are divided by a short rapid and provide good fishing. Personally, I prefer the upper one, which is accessible by crossing a small, deep creek. It is possible to stand in knee- to thigh-deep rushing water and cast a fly right across the current and drift it along the perimeter of a low moss-covered bank beneath overhanging manuka trees. This is a natural position for trout to hold and feed on passing insects.

Fish the pool thoroughly with either a size 10 or 12 high-floating dry fly or a size 8/10 weighted Hare & Copper or Green Stonefly nymph. Start at the exit glide and gradually work upstream through its wide body, the depths of the in-flowing rapid-chute and the gravelled shallows of backwater on your left side. This pool demands and indeed deserves a dedicated, vigorous and positive fishing approach. It has consistently produced the best conditioned brown trout I have ever caught in the South Island and I request sportsmen to treat this particular area as a trophy venue. Please catch and release these magnificent specimens.

My philosophy in revealing the location of such outstanding positions is influenced by a simple quote uttered to me while fishing in Yellowstone National Park, Wyoming, USA, 'The more to share — the more to care'. (Kiwis take note: those Americans know how to manage their resource and have certainly taught me a thing or two about conservation.)

Now, try the upper rapid. It is fast, slippery, rough-going and difficult enough to negotiate let alone fish, but it is a well-stocked run of water descending a slightly steeper gradient than downstream. The water is shallowish, very tumultuous and offers ideal large well-hackled dry fly conditions. Don't bother with a tight line here as the current will do it for you once the fish snatches the fly.

(3) Gate Access: 1.6 km from East Bank Bridge

Drive 1.3 km from the bridge, stop on the elevated road and examine the river traversing an 'S' bend between native bush in the valley below. The dominating feature is a wide, deep, fast-flowing pool offering restrictive access, casting and playing conditions. It is a must in an angler's book — an unnerving, invigorating and exciting venue to fish.

Continue down the hill and park beside a gate on the apex of a right-hand bend, a distance of only 300 m. The river is a few metres away enclosed by trees. Step into the water carefully, it is slippery. The river is quite open and completely arched over by virgin forest as it descends a gentle gradient towards your stance. This is a superb but shaded fly fishing water where you can't locate trout by sight or sound and you will need to apply the upstream blind fishing technique. It is necessary to walk upstream in knee-deep water, cast well upstream with a dry fly or nymph and 'strip like hell'. The trout in this enclosure are not overly large but they fight like demons.

The downstream section divides into braided channels that flow into the head of the pool viewed from the road. Restrictive vegetation creates difficulty in gaining access and it is a matter of fighting your way through formidable scrub the best way possible.

The terrain actually creates a good spinning venue with runs, turbulence and a natural fish haven beneath driftwood and overhanging vegetation. The pool is very well stocked, but when standing in thigh-deep water keep an eye out for eels (big 'uns), they are very territorial in this location and will challenge strangers with a long, lingering, twisting 'kiss'.

(4) Rotoroa Lodge Access — Upper East Bank: 4.6 km from (3)

En route to this position anglers may stop on the elevated road and reconnoitre the valley below. The river emerges from an enclosing bush 'tunnel' to follow a crescent-shaped course and exit down a very rough rapid downstream. The undulating countryside opposite offers easy access to the open riverbank, almost devoid of access and casting restrictions.

The water descends gently through a continuous glide for several hundred metres, deepening from an accessible and shallow beach to pass over submerged weed and flow beneath native ferns and miscellaneous trees against the cliff opposite (just out of fly casting range). This is the Gowan; sombre, quiet, forceful and full of trout that rise actively. It represents a normal river, unlike the 'holocaust' downstream, and radiates an instant fishing invitation to all anglers.

The access vehicle track visible near the pylons on the hill opposite is private and out of bounds, but there is a walking track (originating from the bridge upstream) that follows the open riverbank downstream, offering excellent fishing access to this outstanding piece of water.

Continue up the road and cross the bridge spanning the outlet (Gowan River) of Lake Rotoroa. Rotoroa Lodge, a licensed establishment visible on the other side of the bridge, provides full accommodation to tourists and anglers and is certainly strategically positioned to provide a 'stop-over' base from which to fish the venues described in this chapter, in conjunction with the Owen River (pages 88-89) and the Buller, pages 74-82. There are 'anglers' access' signs on the other side of the bridge indicating the start of the track following the river downstream as described above.

The banks within reach of the track offer good access to deep water in several places and a careful approach through the grass that obscures the river bank's edge is essential if an unscheduled swim is to be avoided.

Spinning and fly fishing will provide good results anywhere over this long section of river and accepted spinning techniques may be applied with 7- or 14-g spoon (1/4-1/2oz), blade or Mepps/Veltic minnows in subdued colours and fitted with a single barbless hook.

Fly anglers may revert to established fly patterns — Humpy, Wulff, Greenwell's Glory and Twilight Beauty in sizes 12 to 18 — but still use large nymph patterns unless trout are feeding on the surface beneath overhanging foliage, cruising a calm backwater or sipping emergers midstream. In the latter cases, use a size 16 or 18 slim-bodied Pleasant Tail or Peacock Herle nymph from here up to and including the bar of the lake.

Lake Rotoroa and the source of the Gowan River is a short distance from the Lodge and a walking track follows the outlet stream and provides several small fishing positions.

The Flower Brothers Memorial Walk originates from the carpark near the jetty and terminates on the large grassy lawn in front of the lodge. It offers the non-fishing members of the party an opportunity to stroll through and enjoy the small stand of virgin forest along the animated waters of the lake.

10 Owen River

This, the most delightful fly fishing stream of the Buller River system, has only two equals in the Nelson district. It is a short stream of clear water flowing exuberantly over a gravel bed. It rises from the slopes of Mount Owen to converge with the Buller River bordering Highway 6 some 100 km south of Nelson. The fish are large, quite easy to locate in the bright environs, and are as alert as their mountain counterparts. Their fastidious choice of flies, together with a wary and tenacious nature, is all that delays their extinction. This is an extremely fragile fishery.

The river receives considerable pressure during holiday periods by vacationers who fish for the table and have no interest in sport fishing or the preservation of a unique heritage. Education and example alone will save this fishery. Please help demonstrate your concern by using a catch and release policy in this river.

I have described the several public accesses from the road which follows the river upstream, but anglers must obtain permission to pass through fences and cross private land elsewhere.

(1) Owen River Reserve: 109 km from Nelson

Located by access (16) in the Buller River text (Chapter 8), it is a good camping base from which to fish both the Buller and Owen Rivers. The Owen flows along one perimeter of the reserve and provides good fishing from the confluence up to and past the highway bridge. Access along the bank is difficult and restricted by long grass and overhanging trees, and the water flow is generally slow and often waist-deep. The physical effort required to reach casting positions is warranted, however; this is a good run of water, especially in the twilight when the 'lunkers' cruise and take size 14 Twilight Beauty wet flies.

(2) Vehicle Access Track: 500 m from highway junction

Turn right off Highway 6, past the hotel but before the bridge, follow the gravel road around the first bend, and watch carefully for an overgrown walking track leading through the willow trees. The river here runs swiftly over a bed of slippery stones that create difficult wading conditions (even with felt-soled boots). Fly anglers should walk upstream in the knee-deep water and cast a small dry fly ahead so that it drifts back under the grass and vegetation on the right-hand bank.

This venue is well stocked with smaller than average sized trout that, like their larger counterparts upstream, prefer small flies and nymphs. Adams, Greenwell's Glory and Dad's Favourite dries for shallow or calmish water and Coch-y-Bondhu, Molefly, Grizzly Wulff or Humpy in the rippled sections. Size 16 Hare & Copper, Gold-ribbed Hare's Ear or Pheasant Tail (weighted) would be a wise choice of nymphs.

This section of river extends for 1 km or so then veers left away from the road embankment to pass through private property. You should clamber up the bank about here and return to your vehicle.

(3) Branch River Access: 3.5 km from (2)

The road ascends and traverses an elevated plateau for 3 km and provides a panorama of two large, grassy river flats around the perimeter of which the course of the river can be traced by sighting its water or overhanging trees. This is private land. Do not enter without approaching the occupants of the first house up the valley on the left side for permission.

The road turns sharp right to follow the toe of a hill and parallels the trees that obviously line the riverbed around the perimeter of the large paddock. Park near the corner and follow the short length of fence to the cliff edge overlooking the gorge. A pool below locates the convergence of the branch stream approaching from the valley directly opposite your stance. This pool heralds the start of a 1.5-km section of gorge with steep, wooded but negotiable sides; fast, tumultuous water, slippery stones, rock buttresses, scrub-restricted access and good fishing for the physically fit angler. Do not contemplate fishing here unless you fit this category as it is rough and tough and an exhilarating but very exhausting experience.

(4) Roadside Access: 1.4 km from (3)

The road passes over a cattle stop, descends to the level of the river and reveals a horizontal run of excellent boulder-strewn trout water. Parking space is restricted here, so drive a further 800 m, pull off the road just past an old shearing shed and walk back to fish the river upstream.

The 2.5 km of accessible river available from this location is perfect brown trout habitat and should be fished thoroughly with the smallest of flies (be the fish visible or otherwise). The run immediately below the convergence of the tributary emerging from the other side of the river is a particularly good trout holding and feeding venue.

(5) Tributary Access: 1.7 km from (4)

The road provides a panoramic view of the river emerging from a wide valley and veering right to flow towards the last described position. Continue through the cutting, turn left into a rough track immediately before a bridge, park and walk to the river that spreads wider and flows quieter than has been the case downstream.

Extreme stealth and competent presentation of the fly fishing technique is now paramount if trout are to be caught. They will be quite visible: large, beautifully proportioned, golden-hued, almost close enough to touch, and docile.

This venue is the last accessible section of the Owen River, although the public road continues up the valley for several more kilometres. Anyone desirous of fishing further upstream must seek permission to cross private property from the occupants of nearby farmhouses.

Great scenery and great fish attract thousands of overseas anglers every year.

11 Mangles River

This is a small spawning tributary of the Buller, flowing from the east to converge with the main river 125 km south of Nelson and 4.5 km before Murchison. Three rivers, the east and west branch of the Tutaki, and the Tiraumea, merge to source the Mangles River some 14 km inland from Highway 6. Whereas the rivers individually have a summer water flow too small for fishing, their combination as the Mangles River holds a good head of trout and offers anglers hours of precision fly fishing.

This river calls for the use of light rods, fine-tipped leaders, small flies/nymphs and an accomplished skill in fly fishing techniques. The 5-km long upper reaches typify a South Island trout stream as they flow over beds of stones and gravel, ripple down gentle rapids and drift through long pools between grassy farmland banks. Easy walking access to perfect casting positions is possible in this section but stealth is paramount. Sight or sound of the angler, his line false casting through the air, or striking the water, will put the trout to instant flight. This alertness is even more apparent in the deep, tranquil pools of the gorge section downstream.

The lower 10 km surges between rocks and stones, swirls violently against solid buttresses and caresses sheer rock walls in terrain devastated by earthquakes early this century. There is a tangible silence within the bush enclosures of this gorge, a dank and brooding environment, where even the river muffles its song with slippery moss and lichen to prevent anglers reaching fishing venues dry and unscathed. The large browns residing in the pools are quite visible as they cruise and take quietly from the surface film, challenging the most experienced and competent fly angler to a frequently one-sided duel. This location offers an interesting interlude in a river with varied temperaments and holds an established but fragile stock of large trout. Please treat this waterway as a catch and release only venue.

Turn inland off Highway 6 4.5 km north of Murchison and follow the Tutaki Valley/ Matakitaki Lodge road.

(1) First Gorge Access: 1.3 km from Highway 6

Drive over a small bridge 800 m from the junction, and park in a large area near a white marker post after travelling 1.1 km. Follow an indistinct foot track through the trees and down the steep bank to a large, slippery rock just above the water.

The river flows through a gorge of solid rock which creates miscellaneous pools, runs and occasional gravel bars. It is possible to wade the small rapid ahead of your stance to reach the long pool visible upstream. Examine the glide in passing for trout.

Approach the pool stealthily, and fish the immediate area thoroughly while concealed before standing on the skyline to examine the depths for 'cruisers' (pay particular attention to the in-flowing ripple and its vortex). Determine the trout's feeding 'beat', then place a size 16 or 18 lightly-dressed nymph in its path.

There are also several good fishing positions upstream, but to reach them involves a struggle over rock formations and steep banks — it is a venue suited to physically agile anglers only.

(2) Birch Tree Access: 1.7 km from (1)

Just before this access point you will pass Walker Road leading left to a bridge. Inspect the river from here, and although it does not provide access, it will assist in planning your next move. It is possible to walk down the riverbed from the next venue 300 m upstream and fish to trout which are probably visible in the current either side of the bridge.

The next access, 300 m along the road, is identifiable by two tall birch trees growing close together just inside the boundary fence. Step over the fence, walk a few feet to the trees and follow an old track descending the bank in a downstream direction. The river now runs over stones, gravel, low outcrops of rock and through a few small pools. It may be followed in either direction, and should be fly fished with larger dries or nymphs than those used in the gorge section downstream. The good fishing water visible upstream may be fished around the corner and up to its termination at a large, very good spin fishing pool next to to the road 900 m away.

(3) Old Swingbridge Access: 2.3 km from (2)

Park near this old bridge, where there is walking access from the roadside approach to the riverbed of stones and slippery rock. This venue provides a section of good fly fishing water, incorporating the pool at the Blackwater River convergence which actually produces better results when spinning.

(4) Roadside Access: 2.7 km from (3)

The road descends from its elevated position to follow the river on the same level for a short section, allowing you to park on the verge and step through a fringe of trees to a riverbed of boulders, gravel bars and banks covered with long grass. This good, but physically demanding, spot calls for the positive application of an upstream fly fishing technique and the use of sizes 8/10 well-hackled dry flies or weighted nymphs. Naturally these large flies should be replaced with much smaller ones when a trout is sighted feeding quietly in the shallows or on the smooth shoulder of a glide.

This section of river originates from open valley terrain 1.1 km upstream and offers good fishing all the way. The occasional difficult obstacle to clamber over and around is of little consequence when the quality of the fishing is considered, and it is possible to return along the road to your vehicle.

(5) Locked Gate Access: 1.1 km from (4)

The elevated road parallels the river and provides views of the excellent trout water between accesses (4) and (5). It is quite possible to park on the roadside and walk to any particular position which may appeal in passing. The locked gate on the left, close to a right-hand bend in the road, is inscribed 'private property' as a deterrent to shooters. Trout anglers are permitted to fish the locality by the property owner Ray Borcovsky residing in the next house up the valley. But you must leave your vehicle on the road and walk through the gate after visiting the residence and requesting permission to wander over the property. The effort required to extend this courtesy is a small price to pay for the privilege of fishing the next few kilometres of superb fly fishing water.

Fly anglers will be enthused with the river here. A knee-deep flow of clear water ripples over a gravel bed retained between grass-covered earth banks with occasional trees overhanging deep runs. The trout are difficult to sight in the boisterous water conditions and blind fishing should be practised while walking upstream.

This is initially dry fly country, where a size 10 or 12 Grizzly Wulff, Humpy (yellow), Blue Dun or Molefly will lift a fish from beneath the ripples. If it fails, replace it with a size 10 weighted Hare & Copper nymph.

This excellent venue extends for some 3 or 4 km to the next access, the Tutaki Bridge, which ends the fishing in the Mangles River.

(6) Tutaki Bridge Access: 3.1 km from (5)

Park on the other side of the bridge. From here you can clamber down the approach and walk downstream to the convergence of the west branch of the Tutaki River and then fish back using the upstream technique. This is a good venue, with a nice flow of water, open terrain with varied and interesting water conditions in the most pleasant surrounds imaginable; a verdant valley that has actually been enhanced by the touch of mankind. A refreshing difference indeed.

12 **Maruia River**

Without any doubt this is one of the best rivers in the northern section of the South Island. The Maruia can be reached 12 km south of Murchison and it offers good fishing for some 72 km through to Springs Junction. Highway 65 more or less follows the river most of the way, and although there are a multitude of access points, some of them necessitate scrambling through impregnable vegetation laced with blackberries and briar. Many banks are high and steep and frequently rise out of deep water — something of an anticlimax following a 10-minute struggle through heavy bush. I would advise those unfamiliar with the river to fish from the ten accesses I describe below.

The section of river below the falls, some 10 km upstream from the Buller convergence, holds brown trout only, while the upper section holds both rainbow and brown species. The water is generally clear, running over a gravel bed lined with native bush and willow trees, most of the way to Shenandoah Saddle. The gravel bed of the upper section is frequently braided and traverses a wider valley floor of grass and tussock with occasional stands of willow trees.

(1) Corner Access: 3.4 km from O'Sullivans Bridge

Drive off the wrong side of the highway at the apex of a sharp left-hand bend (the second one from O'Sullivans Bridge; note mileage given) and park on a grass-covered, gravel-based clearing. This is large enough to hold several vehicles. The river is audible but obscured by native bush. Step over the low fence, walk about 5 m to the edge of the bank and locate a steep track descending to a small gravel beach 10 m below. The river flows quite swiftly here and provides very good spin fishing conditions with deep-running, slim-bodied, dark-hued minnows.

Fly anglers should walk upstream from the car, following the old vehicle track carefully between blackberry vines and sidle over the bank at the first opportunity onto the gravel riverbed. This small position is productive for sizes 8/10 full-hackled dry fly patterns — Humpy, Kakahi Queen, Blue Dun, Grizzly Wulff — or sizes 8/10 weighted Hare & Copper/Stonefly nymphs drifted correctly down the shallow edges of the rapids.

(2) Awapiri Bridge Access: 1.7 km from (1)

The bridge offers an observation position from which to view the river in both directions. The trout seen cruising or rising in the depths nearby are only accessible to spinners casting from the rocks beneath the bridge. Those rising at the head of the pool upstream are sitters for an experienced fly angler using small nymphs or dry flies.

The tail of the pool, visible downstream, provides excellent fishing for anglers using either method. An hour or two is required to fish this particular location properly. It is necessary to walk along the highway and clamber down a steep bank beneath native bush to reach the riverbed.

(3) 'S' Bend Access: 2.5 km from (2)

The highway veers sharply left, follows a short straight, then veers sharply to the right opposite a two-storey farmhouse on the left of the second curve. Stop before this curve opposite a grassed flat on the right side of the road, where a deep stormwater ditch and track lead through the trees to the river bank. The flat offers off-road parking in dry ground conditions only, and is only a few steps from a riverbed of gravel, sand and tussock grass offering easy access to excellent fishing water. If the small creek is flooded return and walk up the road, from where there is also ample access to the riverbed just around the corner.

The river flows fast near the access bank and ends a 2-km section of rapids, ripples and pools extending from the base of the Maruia Falls. This long venue contains the full spectrum of trout fishing conditions, and anglers with plenty of time should perhaps consider residing overnight at the following access.

(4) Maruia Falls Access: 2 km from (3)

Follow the access road to its termination beneath the falls. This extensive and undeveloped camping area has basic amenities, excellent camping and camper van parking positions between sheltering trees and an honesty box payment facility. It is an ideal stopover for a night or two beside fishing water unexcelled anywhere in New Zealand.

Spin anglers may spend hours fishing in the turbulent pool at the base of the falls, where skill is necessary to cast between floating driftwood. It is well stocked with brown trout. Fly anglers should walk downstream and fish the edges of the rapid flowing from the pool with either a size 10 or 12 Humpy, Wulff, Blue Dun dry fly or size 10 Hare & Copper, Stonefly or Speckled nymph.

It is necessary to cross the river a couple of times when fishing the 2-km section between positions (3) and (4), and this is quite possible during normal conditions. The ripple entering the long, large pool beneath the high roadside bank downstream is a particularly good position for large brown trout which will challenge even the most accomplished fly angler. It is a duel with almost no chance of success for the angler during daylight hours, but the evening rise reverses the conditions — trout beware!

(4a) West Bank Bridge: 2.3 km from (3)

Turn to the right and after crossing the bridge turn left and follow the bush-enclosed road. After about 1 km it emerges onto open farmland and follows the river for a further 10 km. The varied types of water from here upstream offer good fishing by either method. Gin-clear water, unrestricted casting room, good stocks of both rainbow and brown trout and pleasant surroundings — what more could an angler ask for?

The initial view of open farmland reveals the river flowing from your left. It is followed downstream to the corner ahead by a vehicle track from a farmhouse where access permission may be sought. Follow the track downstream to the corner and fish the most delightful flow of water imaginable to a good head of very alert trout. The river flows against the road embankment in several places from here upstream and offers easy public access to good water. You must ask the residents of nearby houses for permission to cross their land to fish other venues. It will be readily granted. This valley is a particularly good fishing location and anglers have enjoyed an excellent relationship with the farmers for many years. I implore strangers to acknowledge and respect this privilege of unrestricted access.

(5) Culvert Access: 6 km from (4)

There are two worthy fishing venues en route to this access, namely Pea Soup Creek and Bluff Creek positioned at 3.6 km and 1.8 km respectively. Both necessitate scrambling down a steep tree-covered bank and standing in water while fishing. The gravel bars so characteristic of these two positions for many years have disappeared, but although this

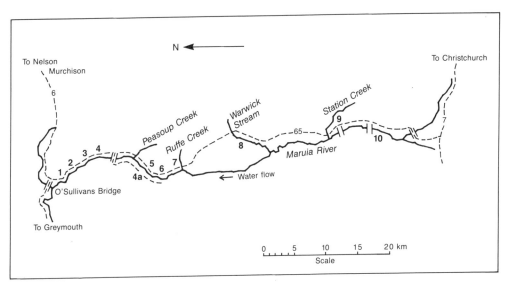

detracts from access, the quality of fishing and trout habitat is unaffected. They should now, however, be considered as spinning rather than fly fishing venues.

Accesses (5) and (6) are difficult to locate as they are both situated on nondescript sections of highway, so watch your odometer carefully. Position (5) is preceded by an dilapidated building on a high bank with two boundary gates 100 m or so further along the road. Stop between the gates, walk along the right shoulder of the road and locate the culvert flowing from a concrete wall. A large grassy flat on the opposite side of the culvert offers off-road parking. Walk beneath the trees down the short, steep bank onto a gravel beach where you will find excellent fishing water. Any further words of elaboration would only detract from this captivating fishing venue; it warrants the effort to locate it and is certainly worthy of an hour's fishing time.

(6) Culvert Access: 700 m from (5)

Drive a further 700 m along the road and look for a high bank on the left side of the highway opposite a grassy site immediately upstream of a small stream fringed with scrub between the road and the Maruia riverbank. Clamber down the bank of the creek, which is cascading over rocks to enter the Maruia River beside a huge boulder. A deep channel of swift water flows along the outside of the boulder. A small gravel beach extends downstream from its 'toe' to merge into a wide, shallow expanse of stable, moss-covered stones. This is perfect brown trout habitat.

Anglers should walk downstream without disturbing the trout in the channel and fish with the upstream technique. Stealth of approach is important here. The resident browns will be extremely alert and holding in a food channel beside the boulder. Fly anglers may perhaps try a small dry a couple of times first, but will probably have more success with a size 14 or 16 Hare & Copper weighted nymph. Spin anglers should cast upstream with a small Mepps or Veltic minnow fitted with a single barbless hook.

The immediate area is well stocked with trout and the blind fishing technique should be applied in the absence of obvious fish. The tall trees which shade the river until late afternoon create poor light conditions here.

(7) Ruffe Creek Access: 5.8 km from (6)

This is a spin anglers' venue with a large, deep pool, with restricted back-casting room and a very good head of fish. Park on the other side of the Ruffe Creek bridge, follow one of the steep tracks to the edge of the river and use the heaviest and smallest gold, black or brown minnow available.

Fly anglers should continue driving past the bridge for 200 m, park on the opposite side of the road on a wide gravel verge and walk down the vehicle track leading in the direction of the river. Occasionally this steepish track, which leads to the most delightful picnic and/or overnight site imaginable, is too wet and slippery to use. There is parking room here for two or three vehicles this side of the shallow Shenandoah River ford and more space on the other.

Follow the river to its convergence with the Maruia River, catch the trout at the head of the spin anglers' pool and fish your way upstream with a big fluffy dry fly. There are several channels of broken water descending a steady gradient over stones and rock. It will be necessary to replace the dry fly with a weighted size 10 or 12 Hare & Copper or size 8 Stonefly in the absence of a strike, especially in dull light conditions.

This venue provides days of fishing and it is possible to fish your way up to the gorge, where large browns cruise lazily and feed nonchalantly in the surface film of huge pools but sound at the sight of careless anglers. Skilled fly anglers will enjoy the challenge of the Maruia Gorge; it has few equals on the lowlands and is only surpassed by the fishing in my stamping ground, the wilderness rivers of the South Island's Southern Alps.

This is a strategic camping venue close to prime trout fishing water, but those wishing to remain overnight must contact the property owner for permission. Neil Tyrell, (Ph (03) 523 9303) resides 4.6 km back down the highway (towards Murchison) and welcomes anglers but experiences trouble with deer, pig and goat rustlers and is naturally cautious of strange vehicles. Your personal approach will be appreciated and your request to camp here undoubtedly granted.

Position (4), Maruia River.

(8) Crightons Road Access: 16.9 km from (7)

Request permission to use this road and fishing venue from Dave Sanders in the two-storey house on the hill. Follow this road to the lower river plateau and park by a bridge over the Warwick Stream (this is a sanctuary — no fishing). Follow the stream on foot to the Maruia River.

Good fishing exists here in a river flowing purposefully through successive rapids, pools and glides creating conditions suited to all techniques. It is an excellent venue.

(9) Boundary Road Access: 3.5 km from (8)

Turn right at this signposted junction and continue for 2.1 km to the bridge spanning the Maruia River. Here there is ample parking and easy access to the river. The character of the river here is different from the lower reaches. It now flows over a wide shingle bed instead of stones and rock and the water is even clearer than has been the case so far. The shallow rippling runs, smooth glides and transparent pools will have to be approached with stealth, and the skilful application of the upstream fly fishing technique is crucial.

Fly patterns should be modified to sizes 16/18 Adams, Greenwell's Glory, Dad's Favourite dries and Sawyer's Pheasant Tail, Peacock Herle nymphs. Anything larger will scare the trout seen feeding in the shallows or rising quietly in a gentle turbulence. This location is invariably basked in brilliant sunshine and enjoys hot temperatures so the fish extremely alert.

The most successful method of fishing is to walk slowly upstream and sight the fish before making a presentation, rather than fish blind for any length of time in one position. The searing heat of mid afternoon should be spent resting in the shade. The fish will undoubtably do likewise.

(10) Upper West Bank Bridge: 9 km from (9)

Turn right at the junction leading to the bridge and follow a small gravel drive to the riverbed, where there is ample parking for several vehicles and easy walking access to the water's edge.

The water descends a positive gradient from beneath the bridge and is confined to a deep flow against a stopbank opposite the parking area. It then forms a rapid to bisect the riverbed and parallel the highway embankment. This section of water will provide good fishing and, if possible, the emphasis should be placed on the twilight hours when the fish become more active. Daytime fishing should not be discounted, but it is essential to fish with the stealth similar to that exercised in position (9).

The deeper water calls for long-distance casting and in the absence of a rise it will be necessary to use a weighted nymph, say a size 12 Hare's Ear, Hare & Copper or Pheasant Tail after floating a dry size 10 Humpy down the ripple bisecting the pool and through the broils against the rocks of the stopbank.

Above the bridge the river flows through several braided channels which are pleasurable to walk and search for trout, but the effort will result in poor returns. This questionable fishing only lasts for only a few kilometres upstream until the gravel is replaced by granite stones and silica rock. This ends the fishing on the Maruia River.

13 **Grey River**

The headwaters described in Chapter 14 are separated from this venue by many kilometres of inaccessible mountain country. Whereas the upper section flows through a forest-enclosed gorge of stable rock and huge stones, the section explained here bisects open country in a wide bed of boulders and gravel, typifying a South Island trout fishing river. The main stream and tributaries of this major river system are well stocked with wild brown trout in a pristine environment. Both sides of the river in this location are accessible from roads following its course inland from Highway 6.

Big Grey River: northern side

Drive 1.7 km south of the Ikamatua Settlement and turn left into Golf Road. This rough gravel road is quite negotiable by standard vehicles for 10 km, and provides easy access to several very good fishing venues suited to either spinning or fly fishing methods. The road crosses an elevated plateau for 5.8 km, passes through two gates (leave as found) and then descends to the river flats. The panorama from the brow of the plateau reveals the Grey Valley emerging from distant mountains, and the proximity of the road to the river on the lower level.

Your first fishing access is immediately below this elevated position. Descend the short but very rough slope and park beside a gate near the acute left-hand bend in the road — a distance of only 200 or so metres.

Walk across the paddock and examine the river flowing 4 m below along the base of the bank fringed with thick, prickly scrub and the odd tree or two. The water is very clear and about 1 m deep close to the stone bank extending from a solid rock buttress upstream. Although the rippled surface makes sighting fish difficult, experienced anglers should follow the river upstream and examine the edge of the current at every opening in the vegetation for a distinctive grey shadow holding motionless just below the surface. A heavy weighted nymph (size 8 Stonefly or size 10 Hare & Copper) would be a wise choice of fly unless the fish is breaking the surface, in which case a well-hackled dry (small first then larger if spurned) should be used. In these water conditions, size and buoyant floating action are more important than pattern. I'd use a Grizzly Wulff, Humpy or Palmer-hackled Molefly.

The bank is really too steep to encourage fishing blind with the upstream technique, but do it by all means if you can locate a foothold. Spin anglers should walk upstream to the outcrop of solid rock and spin their way downstream with a slim, deep-running, dark-coloured minnow.

Examine the broils and eddies at the base of the buttress for feeding resident trout before fishing the turbulence at the bottom of the rapid. The water flowing down this incline is generally too deep and swift to be fished with the fly fishing method. However, at times of low water you should examine the shallows while walking upstream — trout frequent these positions and feed on aquatic insects hatching between damp, moss-covered stones during the heat of summer.

The road leaves the river for several hundred metres, but a wide section of old riverbed provides walking access to a selection of shallow rapids, smooth glides and quiet pools. This particular section of riverbed is unstable and subject to occasional realignment during floods, but it does hold a good head of trout — transient though they may be. It is really a fly anglers venue and particular attention should be given to the shallow water between and around protruding stones rather than fishing blind in deeper sections. Do not discount the shallow sections of this river — I am ever amazed by the nonchalant cruising antics of browns on the prowl.

Just 2 km from the first access the road follows the river along the top of a stopbank, where the slabs of hewn rock provide not only a 600-m long, wide, gentle pool but also a perfect fish habitat where anglers may walk (quietly) upstream on a grassy road verge and visually locate their quarry. The clarity of the water and atmosphere, the light colouration of the gravel riverbed and the unruffled surface (except in adverse weather) combine to offer an oustanding fish sighting arena.

Walk slowly, and concentrate on the precincts of the rocky embankment and the sections of water at say an angle of 30 degrees towards the centre of the river. The trout will not be large (0.5-1.5 kg (1-3 lb)), and they are coloured slate grey. Long-distance casting with a small nymph or dry fly will be necessary to tempt the fish midstream. Those holding in feed channels against the embankment demand short, accurate and stealthy casts with small diameter leaders and sizes 16 or 18 lightly dressed nymphs. It is not a spin anglers' venue unless the river is in spate or the wind is breaking the surface film. Such anglers should walk (or drive) upstream, park near the high rock and fish the rough rapid flowing into the head of the pool. This is a well stocked and excellent spin fishing run, as is the small glide and in-flowing current on the opposite side of the river.

En route to the final fishing access, the road is separated from the river by a stand of trees and the gate 900 m beyond the end of the pool may be locked. If so, just climb over and walk the final 400 m to Browns Creek — the cattle yards ahead precede the creek and end the road. (Anglers wishing to reside overnight near the creek/river confluence should contact Ken Ferguson, Waipuna Station, telephone (03) 732 3501 and request permission to do so.) Walk across the paddock toward the trees downstream and note the river rushing swiftly through channels of solid rock on a lower level. This interesting section of river holds resident brown trout that take and fight as violently as the turmoil they live in. Although spin fishing may result in action, a size 8 high-floating, well-hackled dry fly whisked quickly (and adeptly) over the troubled surface will often goad an opportunist fish into a frenzied take. The wonderful red-gold colour of a fit brown trout savaging tumultuous water is worth a broken leader — and lost Grizzly Wulff, Red Humpy or Kakahi Queen dry fly!

Difficult as it may be, clamber down the slippery slope near the upstand of solid rock and fish your way upstream from the river bank through the rapid below. The large pool converging with Browns Creek at the head of the rapid offers good fishing — spinning in the lower section and fly fishing through the shallows in the upper portion. The wide ripple entering this pool upstream provides good fishing, as indeed does all the river from here upstream. Anglers may walk anywhere upstream from their vehicle parked near Browns Creek and encounter good fishing for days on end.

Big Grey River: southern side

This is not just another place to go fishing but rather an opportunity to visit and fish a venue that is more wilderness than most accessible rivers in the South Island. The environs of the valley floor were shattered in the 1800s by pioneers with more brawn than brains, but the surrounding mountains of native forest were more than a match for axe and fire and remain as untouched today as they were before European occupation. The haunting call of the paradise duck heralds the trout season and the roar of the red stag in the autumn banishes the angler from his annual intrusion into this unique corner of the South Island.

Anglers are welcome to fish on this private property and those wishing to reside overnight must extend the courtesy of a verbal request to the owner, Ken Ferguson (phone (03) 732 3501) residing in the first house (right-hand side) just past the Anglers' Access crossroads 8.6 km up the valley from Highway 6.

Highway 6 Bridge Access

Drive south from Ikamatua and stop this side of the bridge crossing the Grey River — a distance of approximately 2 km. The bridge provides a panoramic view of the riverbed in both directions and will probably reveal several slate-grey trout working the current — especially in the right side of the rapid immediately upstream. There is access to the river on the Ikamatua side of the bridge from the small parking area beside the bridge approach. Walk through the gate visible in the paddock and follow the track onto the gravel riverbed where there is unrestricted access to literally miles of fishing water. There is also good vehicle access beneath the willow trees upstream on the opposite side of the river.

Drive over the bridge, turn left and follow the road signposted 'Waipuna Station' for some 500 m. Stop where the road veers right to parallel the trees. There are several vehicle access tracks leading over the stopbank onto the riverbed but do not drive over the stopbank before visual inspection — the tracks are occasionally washed-out and reconstructed or repositioned. The parking provides easy foot access over the wide gravel riverbed to all types of river conditions.

Use a size 8 heavy weighted nymph in the runs where it will be necessary to fish blind and present sizes 12/14 lightly dressed patterns in the shallows where trout will be feeding between round stones and along the very edge of the current. A size 12/14 dry fly, in patterns Molefly, Red Tip Governor or Yellow Humpy (in other words, a solid-bodied fly) would be a wise choice in the ripples.

(1) Waipuna Creek Access: 3.6 km from Highway 6

Continue along Waipuna Road and park near the bridge crossing this black-watered stream. Walk through the gate preceding the bridge and follow the stopbank to the main river. All types of trout fishing water exist here and it is merely a matter of walking to locate conditions suited to your expertise.

Anglers should consider walking the river from the Highway 6 bridge to this access, but if doing so remember to wear protective clothing and apply a sunscreen: the glare and heat of the sun is intense on the gravel riverbed and the warm breeze will certainly burn the unaccustomed.

(2) Anglers' Access Sign: 5 km from (1)

At this crossroad junction, you will see an Anglers' Access sign. Follow the road through three gates to the grassed riverbed and drive upstream towards a stand of shelter trees. This is an outstanding picnic and fishing venue, facing the sun and within a few steps of perfect trout water.

Both spin and fly fishing anglers will be enthused with this location and undoubtedly some will wish to reside overnight and fish the evening rise. They may even care to drift a midnight dry on the pool beside the camper van. In either case, request permission to camp overnight from the property owner Ken Ferguson residing in the next house up the valley from the crossroads — it will be granted willingly.

(3) Old Road (Gate) Access: 8.3 km from (2)

The road crosses paddocks, enters native bush and then skirts land being cleared. This elevated plateau offers vantage positions to visually examine the lower river valley. Stop at an opening in the trees on your left and walk to the cliff edge — the view is quite breathtaking. It is possible to identify the fishing venues I've described on the other side (Golf Road) of the valley — the extent of fishable water available over there is almost unbelievable. The road then descends, crosses a very black stream, and ascends another bush-covered plateau. Attention is necessary to locate this pending access so watch your odometer. At 2.2 km from the black stream bridge the road follows an acute right-hand bend opposite a new fence and gate dividing an old section of gravel road. Stop here, or drive through the gate and park.

Walk down a steep grass track leading onto a large paddock following the river downstream as it disappears from view against the hill in the distance. This is a perfect spin fishing spot, providing a continuous gradient with rippling water flowing against the paddock. Spin anglers would be hard pressed to locate better water anywhere in the South Island. Apply the downstream technique with a 14-gm (½-oz) slim, deep-running, dark-hued minnow, and although a size 8 well-hackled Grizzly Wulff dry would undoubtably lift trout, the geography of the terrain makes its application difficult.

Fly anglers should turn right where the steep track enters the paddock and walk through bush enclosing a narrow horizontal strip of land up to a bluff about 70 metres away. There are several fallen trees to clamber over en route and the river can be seen on the left. The very wide, shallow bar stretching across the river has protruding stones and probably dozens of squawking ducks stealing trout food. This is superb fly fishing water where anglers should ideally cross the river carefully in the knee deep water just below the prow of the ripple and cast upstream to trout visibly feeding or holding station in the shallows. A small, light-bodied Pheasant Tail or Gold-ribbed Hare's Ear nymph or size 16 Adams, Coachman or Twilight Beauty dry fly will do the trick here.

The pool extends for several hundred metres, slowly deepening up to the rock cliff face in view and holds many cruising fish. Stealth, long-distance casting and soft delivery of the fly are essential in the body of the pool. Step carefully off the bank into the river to reach the bar — there's a narrow but deep channel here and one careless step and you'll end up a mile or so downstream. All jokes aside, this is a very good fishing venue whatever technique is practised and will provide many hours of pleasurable pursuit for anglers applying a sensible and thoughtful approach.

(4) Clark Flat Venue: 2 km from (3)

The road climbs to cross undulating grassland with scrub-covered windrows and a backdrop of native forest en route to the convergence of the Clark River. Pass through two gates, the second of which means veering left (do not continue driving straight ahead). The elevated plateau being traversed reveals a panoramic view of an outstanding trout fishing venue. The Grey River emerges from a glassy pool at the base of a bush-sided canyon to flow in an agitated manner down a gentle incline along the base of a hill and then disappear into the native bush to your left. The smaller Clark River emerges from the valley on your right, flows under a bridge in view and follows a similar incline to merge with the Grey to create a large, swirling pool with shallow edges and the most perfect fishing glide imaginable.

Rest awhile and reconnoitre this extensive area properly — then decide on and plan your approach. Immediately before the final descent to the level of the Clark River an obvious vehicle track leads towards the convergence of the rivers. It is negotiable by standard vehicles in dry weather conditions only. There is also a steep gravelled vehicle track leading to the Clark Bridge river-flat a few metres further along the road.

The convergence pool provides good fishing for spinning in deep sections and fly fishing through shallows and among debris floating in swirling currents. The glide and broken water from here all the way down to where the river disappears into native bush offers excellent results to anglers applying any method.

The Clark itself holds larger fish than the Grey and typifies a wilderness river where experienced fly anglers will walk upstream slowly, fish every inch of water blind while

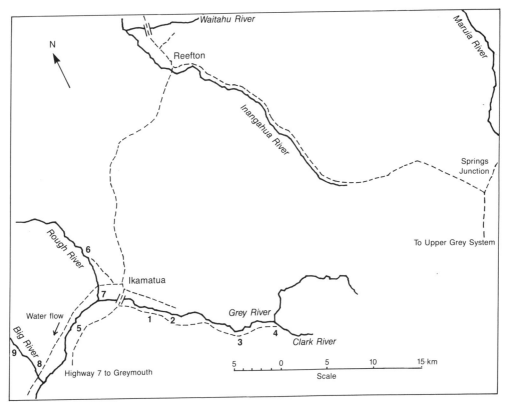

A big brown from the Big Grey River, position (6).

visually searching for a shadow beneath the turbulent surface, and then replace his well-hackled size 8 dry with a size 16 Hare & Copper nymph to catch it.

There is one particularly good fishing venue in the main river downstream from the Highway 6 bridge, as well as two tributaries offering trophy browns. These emerge from the opposite side of the valley and are accessible from a secondary road. Return to the Ikamatua Settlement.

(5) Alcorn Road Access: 9 km from Ikamatua

Drive south from Ikamatua on Highway 6. Alcorn Road is located by a row of trees at right-angles to the highway. The gate must be left as found and provides access to a 500-m long gravel road that terminates just over the stopbank in a fenced enclosure. Park here or drive past the cattle yards and through a gate in the riverside vegetation. Here is a large grassed flat beside the river and a good overnight camping position within a few metres of excellent trout fishing water. This latter position is near a rapid at the lower end of a long, deep, quietly flowing pool providing a good head of smallish (1-kg) brown trout. The steep vegetation-capped gravel bank on this side of the river creates difficult fly casting conditions but it is ideal for spin fishing.

Fly anglers should wade the tail of the pool (carefully, as it is swift) and fish from a long, shallow delta opposite. Any small drab-coloured fly will suffice (use larger sizes during windy conditions) to lift trout during the day and the usual size 12 Twilight Beauty wet is the perfect choice for the evening rise. Any type of spinning hardware seems to fool the silly trout in this location.

The head of the pool and the usually braided in-flowing rapid provides good fishing and is accessible by walking along the top of the stopbank and scrambling through a fence beneath willow trees onto the riverbed. There is unlimited fishing water available on this riverbed and anglers may wander at will for days on end and not cover it all.

(6) Rough River upper section: 5.7 km from Ikamatua

This is a prime brown trout river and acknowledged as such by regular visitors who practise a strict catch and release policy. I implore all anglers to respect and treat it in a similar manner.

Take the road over the railway line signposted 'Blackball', cross the Mawheraiti River bridge, turn right into Mirfins Road and follow it for 4 km to a gate within sight of the sawmill complex. Park on the open grassed paddock, walk along the road and follow a track between trees leading towards the river. The riverbed of stones and coarse gravel is quite open with channels of honey-coloured water flowing exuberantly down a steady incline.

Perfect wilderness fly fishing conditions exist over the whole length of this river from its rain-fed source in the mountains to the convergence with the Grey River. It is possible to follow the river through its tortuous bush valley for days, although two rough gorges do prohibit access to all but keen, physically fit fly anglers with questionable intelligence — it is rough going!

Experienced anglers will walk the river slowly, examining every likely holding position for a faint shadow while casting a size 10 Hare & Copper nymph or Humpy dry fly through agitated runs and onto calm mirrors. This enticement will be replaced with a smaller one when actually casting to a visible trout.

Felt-soled wading boots and neoprene 'hippers' are ideal in this boulder-strewn waterway and, naturally, Polaroid glasses and a brimmed hat are essential — as is sandfly repellent.

(7) Rough Creek lower section: I km (approx.) from Mirfins Rd

Return to the junction of Mirfins and Blackball Roads and follow the latter to the bridge crossing the Rough River, where there is off-road parking. Easy access is afforded on this side to the wide gravel bed strewn with large slabs of hewn rock to arrest erosion immediately downstream of the bridge. This barrier does not inhibit fish movement or fishing and anglers may choose to fish the section downstream to the Grey River confluence or the mid section towards (and perhaps up to) the described sawmill access some 3 km upstream. In either case, anglers are assured of a challenging experience in one of the South Island's prime brown trout rivers.

(8) Slaty Creek: I4 km from Mirfins Road

An interesting and delightful river to fish — a smaller version of the Rough River and holding brown trout of equal calibre. Park the other side of the bridge where there is easy access to the open riverbed and fish in either direction in a manner similar to that applied on the Rough River. The pool immediately upstream should be visually examined from the bridge. It is quite usual to see trout from here.

There is approximately 1.5 km of fishable water between the bridge and the Grey River, and anglers fishing it should walk directly to the confluence and fish their way back to the car.

Another access exists some 5 km upstream and anglers wishing to fish this entire section should allow a full day to traverse the braided riverbed of stones and miscellaneous scrub. It is an interesting and primeval terrain — and the trout are a challenge.

(9) Swingbridge Access: 5.4 km from (8)

Drive over the bridge, turn right into Slaty Creek Road and traverse a farmed valley for 5 km. There is no visible access to the river which is obscured from the road by tall trees and rough scrub. At a gate blocking the road beside an old shed, turn right and follow a vehicle track to a bush clearing a short distance away. An ancient lichen-covered swingbridge leads over a small creek, through an avenue of trees onto the gravel bed of Slaty Creek. There is yet another relic of the past here; a much larger lichen-covered swingbridge with a washed-out approach suspended high above the river.

The river flow has been confined into a single channel for a short section by groynes adjacent to the bridge and it is necessary to walk to either end of the run to reach fishable water. Although there is overnight parking room in the clearing near the smaller swingbridge, the river and terrain are not suitable for evening fishing and it would be advisable to return to the pool above the road bridge 5 km downstream for this purpose.

The largest tributary of the Grey converges with the main river at Stillwater, about 55 km south of Ikamatua along Highway 6. The brooding waters of the Arnold River provide an entirely different fishing episode to those of the Grey. Its source, Lake Brunner, with a crystal-clear tributary, the Crooked River, offers yet another experience.

14 Upper Grey River System

The source of the largest river in Westland, and draining a large catchment area before entering the sea at the port of Greymouth, the Upper Grey River system consists of three tributary streams: the Upper, Brown and Blue Grey Rivers. The first two drain the Pohaturoa State Forest on the western side of the valley, while the last drains Lake Christabel in the east. This lake is 650 m above sea level and actually runs underground for about a kilometre before emerging as the Blue Grey River. The lake does not hold fish.

The Grey and its many tributaries are well stocked with fish and the upper reaches, below the convergence of the three headwater streams, offer excellent fishing using nymph, dry or wet flies. The large valley where these three streams converge has been cleared of bush and is now open grassland providing access to an otherwise inaccessible region of natural beauty. But this remote location does have its disadvantages: fishing in a valley floor some 400 m above sea level makes warm clothing and insect repellent essential. There is a farmhouse in the valley, and common courtesy demands that you request permission to fish the area.

Before they join, two of the streams offer mediocre fishing conditions to a limited stock of brown trout in reasonably slow, rippling water. But the convergence creates a river of an entirely different nature: its swift, broken water is no place for the faint-hearted or infirm angler, and the larger flow is well stocked with active trout that are constantly on the move. For many kilometres after the convergence the river runs through a deep gorge with steep, tree-covered banks. The river is often some distance from the road and generally concealed by thick native forest.

Common sense calls for the use of robust equipment to handle the rough water of this river from its headwaters to the lower reaches on the West Coast, described in Chapter 13. My personal choice is a 9-ft (2.7-m) SAGE 4-piece travel rod, weight 6. This powerfully-shafted unit will stop a threshing trout in its tracks and prevent its frenzied dash through raging rapids and possible rock-inflicted injury. These trout are as strong and dynamic as the environment they inhabit and light rods will not handle trout positively in these circumstances and are cruel on the fish.

Fly patterns in the rough waters of the gorge section are not of paramount importance, but the design, and to a lesser extent the size, is. Full-hackled flies are desirable, and patterns Wulff, Humpy, Blue Dun, Kakahi Queen and Black Gnat are ideal when dressed thoroughly with floatant. As a general rule, the rougher the water the larger the fly, but if a trout is located quietly holding or feeding in a small, calmish backwater it would be wise to change to a much smaller fly for the initial cast(s). The large, full-bodied size 8 used to lift a fish in the turbulence would probably scare such a trout.

The extreme clarity of the water is intensified by the mica-encrusted slabs of rock and deems that a stealthy approach, even walking upstream to gain a casting position, is essential. Long-distance casting is often necessary, especially where there is a section of calm water between the bank and a fast flowing current. Trout will frequently lie directly under the edge of the current just beneath the surface, so you should whisk that dry fly along the converging waters. It is desirable to clamber upstream and locate the trout in calm water before casting, but most of your fishing here will be blind and applied in either the upstream or across and down method.

The ideal approach to fishing this area is to reside overnight at Springs Junction, a mere 15 km away, and spend a whole day on some terrific water. The road, though rough and crossed by several open watercourses, is quite negotiable by standard vehicles and there are ample roadside parking positions for a camper van. There is also a forestry hut available for public use on the open terrain where the road exits from the bush. To gain access to the area, drive from Springs Junction towards Reefton on Highway 7. At exactly 4.3 km from Springs Junction, while ascending the Rahu Saddle, and just preceding an acute right-hand bend, drive into the access signposted 'Palmers Road' directly ahead. Watch carefully for this as it is easy to miss and occasionally one of the local 'lads' will remove the sign after spending a hour or two at the pub. A pleasant drive along a narrow road enclosed by native bush for a further 4.2 km will bring you to the first bridge.

(1) Upper Grey River

This is a mere creek where it is crossed by a culvert while driving beneath the bush enclosure and it is quite unsuitable for fishing.

(2) Brown Grey River Bridge: 4.2 km from Highway 7

Emerging from a bush-lined gully on the right, and converging with the Upper Grey after passing beneath a bridge, it is too small to hold fish. The riverbed is flood-prone and consists of unstable stones and broken rock. It is quite usual, however, to notice a couple of small trout in the shallow pool downstream from the bridge — 'lost souls' no doubt. Less than 2 km down the road, this river again passes under a bridge and by now has become a stable, stream-sized river of brownish-coloured water running over a fine gravel bed between grassy banks. Although there are fish in this region, they are sparse, and the upstream section of the riverbed has limited access and casting room. I would advise driving down the road another 2 km to position (3).

En route to the next position the road traverses a small hill which provides an elevated position from which to reconnoitre both the Brown and Blue Grey rivers flowing to a convergence beside a forest-covered hill. The course of both rivers is discernable and you should plan your approach from here. Park, and walk to the edge of the cliff from the other side of the fence leading off the road.

(3) Blue Grey River

Appearing from the left after an 8-km journey through native bush and grassed river-flats, this stream is larger than the other two and offers excellent fishing to a good stock of trout in boisterous conditions. The water is tinged a grey/blue colour and runs over a gravel bed between grassy banks and occasional rocky outcrops. Before the bridge, the Lake Cristabel

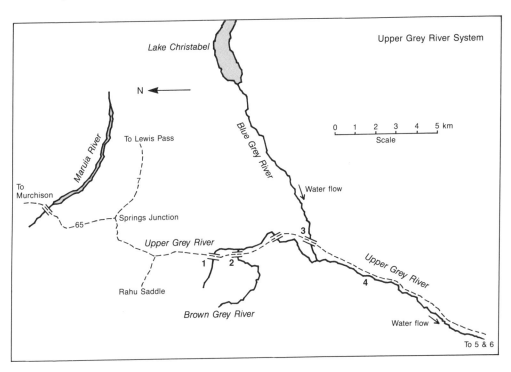

sign indicates the walking track which provides access to about 1.5 km of delightful water flowing through open terrain before it parallels the river upstream through native forest.

Downstream from the bridge, the river traverses open country descending a steady gradient to its convergence with the Brown Grey. This section offers interesting fishing to a good head of trout that may be located visually in the fast current as their colouration is in contrast to their environment, a refreshing change to usual circumstances.

You should seek access permission from the nearby residence before walking downstream through the paddocks to fish this 6 m wide by 1 m deep stream.

(4) Big Grey River: 3.8 km from (3)

This first roadside access is reached after driving across open elevated terrain then through forest on a rough road bisected by several watercourses. It is quite negotiable, but you should drive slowly. The river is well below the level of the road and obscured by thick forest. Park on the wide section of the road as the river appears on the right side. The water is now crystal-clear as it rushes over a gravel bed in which protruding stones and slabs of broken rock create extremely turbulent conditions. The gradient is obvious and consistent, but the riverbed forms a series of long 'steps' where the rapids form fast runs with side eddies and backwaters — perfect fly fishing conditions.

Encroaching forest, a damp atmosphere and dim light merge with the roar of the river to create an amphitheatre of exciting apprehension, and an overwhelming desire to lay a line in this unique corner of the South Island. There is good fly fishing water upstream from here, and it is necessary to clamber through the undergrowth occasionally, wade through cold, waist-deep water in places and strain your eyes to locate a grey smudge — generally holding in calm water against the bank. I suggest that initially you present a size 12 or 14 Twilight Beauty, Grizzly Wulff (or similar darkish-coloured) dry fly, replacing it with a small nymph if spurned a couple of times by a visible trout. You must fish this section of river with a dedicated and thorough approach. It is an excellent venue that will produce results, in the form of violent, fighting trout, equal to the effort put in.

The downstream portion of river crosses rough and more open terrain and calls for a different fishing technique from the one used upstream. Whereas it is possible, and desirable, to walk downstream through the thick undergrowth and fish upstream back to the vehicle it is also possible to fish your way downstream if conditions demand. It will be necessary to stand well back from the water's edge and cast a long line to avoid detection by the fish. Either a dry fly or nymph may be used in this manoeuvre — the former will have to be cast (and dried) frequently and will drift only a short distance each time before sinking. The nymph on the other hand may be left to drift the full length of casting line and retrieved slowly upstream in the manner of a streamer until water disturbance dictates otherwise.

Both approaches have their advantages, and in either case an interesting sojourn awaits fly fishing anglers fortunate enough to visit the location.

(5) Hospital Flat: 3.5 km from (4)

The road to this position passes between avenues of native forest and offers two observation positions (400 m apart) after travelling 1 km. Several large pools in the river are visible from the right shoulder of the road and careful observation will reveal cruising trout despite the distance. The riverbank is steep but quite negotiable by agile anglers who should perhaps allow themselves an hour or two to fish the immediate area properly.

This flat, extending for about 3 km, is cleared forest floor and still rough and swampy in places. Pass through a gate (with a 'No shooting, Private Property' sign), park where possible and walk across to the river that is flowing through a bed of stones between grassed banks and rotting tree trunks. There will be trout holding hard against the bank upstream from your stance and a size 8 or 10 dry fly cast upstream and allowed to drift back along the trailing grass will reveal their presence if you fail to locate them visually.

There are several good sections of rapids, pools and runs throughout this section of river that are well worth the effort to locate.

After traversing about 2 km through the flat, a small creek flows over the road after emerging from an extensive stand of tall dead trees on the left. Park on the other side of the creek and walk to the stand of open bush, slightly downstream, beside the river. Approach the river stealthily through the trees. There are several deep, smooth pools here which will have trout visibly cruising in their depths.

(6) Robinson Hut

Hospital Flat terminates with a gate (leave as found) and the hut is visible on the grassy field to the left. En route to the end of the public road near the implement sheds of a farmhouse it is possible to park, walk 30 m to the right and inspect the river flowing along the base of a cliff 50 m below. Large trout will be visible from here. You must obtain permission from the farmer to pass through the farm gates and follow the road to its end near the convergence of the Robinson and Grey Rivers.

The Grey River from this convergence upstream to Hospital Flat can only be described as superb trout fishing water. It is a large flow, wadeable (just), passes through large pools in a semi-gorge and forms perfect fishing ripples over gravel bars. There are quiet glides in which experienced anglers will be able to detect fish visually.

The river downstream from the convergence becomes a conventional waterway flowing over a gravel/stone riverbed with successive sections of rapids, runs and pools through a valley floor of tussock-covered gravel and stands of forest. My finale to this description of the Upper Grey River system claims that it is an outstanding fishing venue with trout worthy of conservation measures.

A visitor from Montana has a good day on the Upper Grey River.

15 Inangahua River

his major tributary of the Buller River merges with the main stream at Inangahua Junction (Highways 6 and 69), 180 km south of Nelson. It is a large river of honey-coloured water and well stocked with wild brown trout over most of its 80 km course, originating from near Springs Junction (Highways 65 and 7).

Access from adjacent roads is restricted to its open riverbed of gravel and rock by impregnable native forest, scrub and farmland. Once entry is gained, however, anglers have hours of fishing in solitude as the river receives very little fishing pressure.

It fishes well when using either spinning or fly fishing methods, and the trout are less selective about food in this river than most other waterways in the South Island, perhaps endeavouring to compensate for its lack of charismatic appeal.

(1) Junction Access: 1 km south of Inangahua Junction

Strangers intending to fish this position must extend the courtesy of an access request to the property owner Terry Lee, telephone (03) 789 0288, residing in the last house before the sawmill on Highway 69 just south of Inangahua Junction. Drive through the Inangahua settlement where just before the highway junction there is an access gate to a vehicle track crossing a grass paddock and terminating on the riverbed.

Wide expanses of shallow water deepen gradually towards midstream over a gravel bed descending a gentle gradient. This beach extends from the bridge upstream to a high bluff downstream and provides a kilometre or so of easily accessible fishing. This is a venue equally suited to either spinning or fly fishing. Spin fishers should cast a minnow right across the river and cover the whole expanse; the latter may walk upstream and nonchalantly drift a size 10 or 12 dry fly in the ripple while searching for the swirl or shadow of a feeding brown trout.

This ideal position will generally produce an active wet rise at twilight followed by good dry fishing after dark when any pattern size 10/12 dull-coloured, well-hackled fly will coax a take. Try fishing the crack of dawn with a size 12 or 14 Greenwell's Glory wet fly or a 14-g (½-oz) black Tinker/Toby minnow.

(2) Roadside Access: 4 km from (1)

Turn left at the junction and follow Highway 69. The river is occasionally in view en route to the next access, but watch your odometer as this is a difficult position to locate. The highway crosses the railway line, follows the river, then veers left to reveal a long row of tall poplar trees on a strip of land separating the river from the road. Park on the wide gravel verge on the left side before the trees. This is 1.3 km from the railway crossing. The gap in the tall vegetation a few metres ahead locates your fishing access and provides a view of the river flowing against the road embankment after descending a wide shallow bar extending the width of its bed.

Walk past the gap and look carefully in the vegetation for a small creek tumbling from a culvert beneath the highway — only a matter of 70 m from your car. Follow the creek down the bank beneath overhanging trees onto the riverbed. But be careful as these few metres are very slippery.

This is an outstanding fishing venue, where once again both spin and fly anglers may expect good results. The stone beach originates from a high bank about 100 metres upstream of your stance. The wide bar 'feathers out' over a gravel fan with channels which confine the water, deep and fast, towards the high bank below the gap. Spin anglers should cast their minnow across the river above the bar, extending the distance with each throw until the whole expanse of shallow ripples is covered. Retrieve slowly and let the minnow swing with the current into the deeper water downstream. Large trout hold in feed channels deep within the current, while their smaller and more agile counterparts frequent the shallows immediately above the bar itself.

This is also an excellent fly fishing venue, although occasionally the water is too deep to permit its application. The stones are very slippery and the current surprisingly swift and strong. Exercise extreme care when wading over this bar. Use a size 10 or 12 Coch-y-Bondhu, Red-tipped Governor, Humpy or Grizzly Wulff dry fly and cover the water in a similar manner as spinning. Cast slightly upstream and as far as possible into midstream, let the fly drift all the way downstream, and retrieve at the end of travel. Trout in this particular environment will take instinctively — be the fly floating or otherwise.

Fly anglers have an advantage when walking upstream, casting ahead of themselves and letting the fly drift back through the shallows. The dry fly (or small nymph in smooth surface water) will tempt trout sunning themselves as they wait for and feed on hatching nymphs.

This position will provide several hours of fishing for the exponents of either technique, but anglers visiting this particular location should be prepared for a strong environment of big water, rough riverbed stones, prickly vegetation and slippery wading conditions — the sandflies are plentiful and very friendly too. Repellent is essential.

Good fishing is also available upstream, where the river follows the perimeter of a gravel peninsula creating fast rapids, extremely deep pools and smooth glides. It is necessary once again to cross private property and anglers should make a courteous telephone call to Otto Reessink, telephone (03) 789 0233, resident in the house directly across the river and request access permission. It will be granted.

Return to the highway from the 'gap' access, walk ahead for 600 m and pass through the second opening in the electrified boundary fence. A short walk through broom bushes and a scramble beneath poplar trees will give access to the peninsula near the base of a large pool. This wide section of shallow water offers excellent fly fishing. Anglers experienced in stealth, long-distance, accurate casting and delicate presentation of sizes 16/18 nymphs or flies will get results here. Trout are invariably rising in the glide flowing over the bar, as well as in its preceding calm expanse. It is unsuitable for the spin fishing method. Such anglers should walk downstream and en route to the large pool against the cliff fish the rapid by casting into midstream and retrieving their minnow back into the shallows. There are a lot of small fish in this run of water!

Then concentrate on the backwaters and eddies at the head of the pool and fish deep with a heavy minnow. Anglers should expect exceptional results here in the event of slowly rising water resulting from summer rains in the mountains.

(3) Highway Bridge Access: 1.8 km from (2)

Park this side of the bridge and examine the shallows below for feeding trout: they are quite brown and hard to distinguish against the stones. Walk along the base of the bridge approach below the highway to reach this good fishing venue.

Fish the whole of the shallow delta with a high-floating size 12 or 14 lightly dressed (drab-coloured) dry fly — Adams, Twilight Beauty, Greenwell's Glory, or similar-sized Hare & Copper nymph. This whole shallow delta is a particularly good fish holding position and warrants dedicated attention.

The midstream channels always hold feeding fish and provide an excellent spinning venue from the delta. The water is too deep to wade. Very long casts are necessary to reach the fish.

The large, calm expanse of water upstream will probably be broken here and there by an odd rise, but unfortunately it is also too deep to fish with the fly fishing technique.

Although the riverbank on the other side upstream has restricted access it should be walked slowly along the top of the bank and the deep water searched for large trout cruising sedately and feeding on hatching aquatic insects. This venue demands stealth, patience and perfect presentation of sizes 16/18 thin-bodied (Sawyer's) nymphs or dry fly patterns Adams, Pheasant Tail, Twilight Beauty.

Spin anglers may also try their luck here, but will have better results if they walk downstream and fish the exit run from the bridge pool — it is a good position. Of particular interest is the wide gravel beach visible on your right-hand side way downstream. The rapid from the bridge pool extends to here and it is accessible by driving over private property owned by Matt and Jim O'Regan, nearby residents (telephone (02) 896 241 or (02) 896 248).

Continue driving over the bridge, turn left into Browns Creek Road, travel for 700 m to a boundary fence gate on a rise. This gate gives access to a vehicle track descending through paddocks and terminating on the riverbed. It is an idyllic picnicking or overnight venue right beside an unexcelled brown trout fishing water suited to both fly and spin fishing. Anglers wishing to enjoy it will be granted access if they phone Matt or Jim O'Regan (see numbers above) or call at one of the first two houses in the next valley a short distance further along Browns Creek Road. Turn right into this valley road at a junction while descending a slope towards a narrow bridge.

I again stress the importance of requesting access permission from property owners, especially those whom I have mentioned throughout this publication, before transgressing over private land. The sportsmen of New Zealand enjoy a unique privilege — please safeguard it.

(4) Swingbridge Access: 8.4 km from (3)

Return to the highway from Browns Creek road and continue south towards Reefton for 8.4 km. Turn right into a nondescript gravel road opposite an old house on the left side of Highway 69 and follow it to its termination in a scrub enclosure a few hundred metres away. Follow the track to a rickety old swingbridge crossing the Inangahua River — its elevation provides good visual examination of the immediate vicinity. A small creek converges with the river at the base of a rapid upstream offering spin fishing conditions. The shallows on the other side of the stream provide good fly fishing conditions.

Hours of fishing are available in either direction from here: it is an excellent if nondescript venue. And the Stoney Creek, converging with the opposite side of the Inangahua a couple of kilometres upstream, is renowned as a fly fishing venue for large brown trout.

(5) Larry's Creek Tributary: 1.5 km from (4)

Now, this is a beaut river for big fish. Fly anglers must be physically fit and masters of the art to ensure hooking into the largest brown trout of their fishing career. Landing it will be a different matter! First, examine the river from the highway bridge. Note the swift, honey-coloured water, the bed of round boulders, the encroaching gorse and broom downstream and the old road beside the approach on the upstream side of the highway. There is plenty of parking and overnighting room here.

Good fishing prevails in the section from the bridge to the Inangahua, but it is difficult to gain access through the thick scrub to the river's edge. Determined anglers may force their way downstream and fish their way back to the bridge while stumbling and slipping over the steepish bank of boulders. It is worth the effort: the edges of the swift current will have large, golden-hued trout holding or feeding.

Easier access is available upstream. Follow the gravel road over the railway line and park in a clearing near an old steam boiler. It is necessary to cross the river here to be able to fish upstream for many miles.

Despite the excessively large size of the trout, it is necessary to use delicate running gear and terminal tackle. Leaders must be long and have fine diameter tippets. Flies must be small when fishing the shallows and presenting to fish sighted holding or feeding. You should use size 16 or 18 nymph patterns — Sawyer's Pheasant Tail, Peacock Herle or Gray Darter — and dry flies, Adams, Coachman, Partridge/Yellow or Dad's Favourite.

It is essential to use a rod with a tip capable of delivering a minute fly within a couple of centimetres of a fish's nose with the softness of a falling thistledown. Its shaft must have the power to cast a long line, to avoid alerting trout by an unnecessary walking approach, and the strength to control a fish which may weigh over 3 kg (10 lb). Choice of pole is the easiest facet of the operation — SAGE 4-piece travel rod, 9 ft (2.7 m), weight 6.

(6) Waitahu River Tributary: 9.4 km from (5)

Another tributary emerging from the left and passing beneath the road to converge with the Inangahua River within sight of the bridge. You may veer left before the bridge and park on a small grassy terrace within a few steps of a conventional-style gravel riverbed carrying a sedate water flow down a gentle gradient in open country. It has a greater stock of smaller trout in a longer waterway than Larry's Creek, and also offers good fishing in a slightly more open and accessible terrain.

Anglers practising either method may fish their way upstream from the highway, and in fact may fish all the way to the next access (5 kilometres away) and be met by a partner instead of retracing their footsteps.

Flies and tactics similar to those employed in Larry's Creek should be used and spin anglers would be wise to use 7-g Spoons, Tangoes or Veltic (Mepps) minnows in light brown, black or maroon colours — or yellow when willow leaves are falling and floating.

(7) Gannons Road Access: 8.2 km from (6)

Continue along Highway 69 for 3 km, turn left and follow Gannons Road for 5.2 km to its termination near a bridge beside an old coal mine. The character of the river here is quite different to that beside the road. It emits a strange aura in the damp shadow of a coal-seam amphitheatre, where it surges deeply and forcefully through rapids, pools and turbulences beneath cliffs of sandstone and rock. The water near the bridge is difficult to fish and much better conditions prevail a short distance in either direction. Walk through the gate before the bridge, follow the track beneath tall trees through the riverside vegetation and fish the rapids and runs.

A very rough road continues up the valley from the coal mine buildings and follows the river for miles. I would not advise using this road without prior examination, but rather suggest that it be treated as a walking access to reach some excellent brown trout water.

The river is as photogenic as the terrain is forbidding — wide, comparatively shallow ripples descend a gentle gradient between low, grassy banks and stands of native forest. This is a typical South Island West Coast lowland bush river — the fish are but a bonus in such a setting.

The trout respond equally well to a spinning minnow, dry fly or nymph when presented correctly in the appropriate run, and there is more water available here than any angler could ever ask for. This river is indeed a hidden gem, please treat it as such.

(8) Golf Course Access: 1.6 km from Gannons Road

Within sight of Reefton, turn right and follow Andersons Road past the golf course entrance, and park beside the avenue of tall trees. Walk along the grass track through a short section

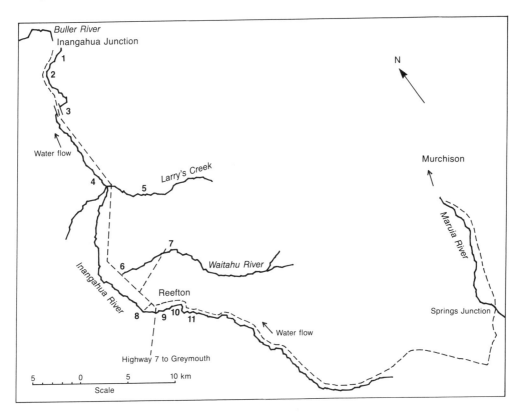

of tall vegetation onto the gravel bed of the Inangahua River. It is now the size of a stream and quite wadeable as it emerges from a curve, flows through a large pool against a cliff, exits down a long rapid and disappears beneath trees downstream. This location is well stocked with small trout and is an interesting venue to fish the evening rise within a few minutes drive from the town centre.

Reefton is a perfect fishing base, well serviced with accommodation, and an excellent motorcamp bounded by the river offers fishing within a few steps of your camper van. A pleasant interlude is available by driving 1.5 km south of the town bridge, turning right at a junction, then right again to follow a short track into a wide gravelled area overlooking the river. This is within sight of the main highway. Only a few steps are necessary to reach the gentle river flowing over a gravel bed which provides easy walking and fishing conditions upstream to the town bridge. This is delightful dry fly water and a pleasure to fish as such during the warmth of an early morning sun or in the soft shadows of twilight.

Highway 7, the main route to Christchurch, now follows the Inangahua River upstream and provides several fishing venues en route to Springs Junction. The initial section offers interesting fishing, but the stock of trout lessens as the river is followed upstream and is not worth bothering with after about 11 km despite several visible runs of appealing water.

(9) Rest Area Access: 3.3 km from the motor camp

En route to this position the river is visible through open bush and its possible to fish nicely rippled water after driving a mere 600 m from Reefton. It is necessary to clamber down a steep embankment from the roadside to reach this excellent dry fly run. Watch carefully for a vehicle access on the right as the highway curves left. It leads back downstream and descends to a small clearing complete with a picnic table and seats. The river flows quite swift and deep against a rock bank here, forms a rapid a short distance downstream, then fans out to ripple invitingly across the whole expanse of gravel bed. This is all good fishing water, generally stocked with small (1-kg) fat, fit and beautifully coloured browns.

Good fishing is available from here up to the base of the Blacks Point pool. The river channels alter occasionally but usually there are two, both of which hold trout especially on the shoulders of and in the tail of rapids. Fish the bar of Blacks Point pool with a size 16 Hare & Copper nymph or size 16 Adams dry fly. A shallow-running minnow might just do the trick here also.

(10) Old Gravel Storage Flat: 2.4 km from (9)

Turn off the road into this large area, now half covered with vegetation, walk to the river and fly fish upstream through shallow ripples which descend a gravel riverbed following a gentle gradient. Full-bodied size 14 or 16 dry flies that bounce the ripples are suitable here, try a Red-tipped Governor, Coch-y-Bondhu, Yellow-bodied Humpy or Grey Irresistible — they'll all move the fish.

This pleasant area extends upstream for over a kilometre and you may step up a low road embankment and follow the highway back to your vehicle.

(11) McConnochie Creek Access: 6.2 km from (10)

Stop beside this small creek which passes beneath the road about 80 m from the river. A swingbridge spanning the river just over a kilometre upstream ends the section of river to be fished from here. Ideally your partner should drive along the highway and wait for you there. (The signposted access road leading to the bridge is 1.2 km further on.)

The river is quite boisterous as it descends a steady gradient over stones and rock rather than gravel. It carries a good head of active brown trout which dart about as though possessed between protruding stones and various current channels. A large dry fly is the answer here. Cast it quickly from place to place until the whole expanse within range has been covered and goad these silly trout into a reflex take.

Should a holding fish be located in the current, replace the large dry fly with a smaller one, say size 16, and change it to a similar sized Hare & Copper or Gold-ribbed Hare's Ear nymph in the absence of a take.

The fast flowing pool beneath the swingbridge will have trout feeding or holding on the bar downstream and in the current against the rock cliff slightly upstream. There's also

Larry's Creek, position (5) on the Inangahua River.

Inangahua River.

a nick in the cliff downstream that often holds a fish — tantalizingly out of reach!

This bridge reserve has a picnic table and barbeque, and is a good position to park overnight (except, perhaps, for the sandflies) and offers non-fishing companions an opportunity to take an interesting bush walk for an hour or two on well-maintained track.

The Branch Creek tributary 50 m upstream terminates the trout fishing on the Inangahua River. I have seldom seen trout in the inviting rapids, ripples and pools upstream from here, but I only frequent this location when hunting and shooting during winter months, so who knows?

16 Lake Brunner Region

Undoubtedly the best-stocked lake for brown trout on the West Coast, Lake Brunner has enticed anglers from all over New Zealand for many years. Having limited road access and surrounds of native bush, scrub and swamps, it is generally fished from a boat. It is a large expanse of water hosting so many big trout that in the quiet of an early morning one can stand on the road and watch them jump clear of the surface from a kilometre away.

Moana is situated on the northern shore of Lake Brunner, adjacent to the main highway from Canterbury to Westport/Nelson via Arthur's Pass, and offers good visitor accommodation at a hotel and motor camp.

Arnold River

This is a large river of brown-coloured water approximately 12 m wide and 2 m deep which drains the lake into the Grey River some 25 km away. It traverses swampy terrain of bush, flax and scrub which restricts foot access from the road that follows its tortuous course. Turn inland off Highway 7 at Stillwater.

(1) Kotuku Bridge: 5 km from Highway 7

Turn left just past the factory and park near the bridge. It would be courteous to request access rights from the land owner in the house on the left side over the bridge before fishing. It is a privilege, not a right, to enter and wander over this property.

The river flows smooth and deep over a weedy bottom between the inaccessible roadside bank and a grassed paddock that provides good walking access to the water's edge. Walk through the gate on the upstream bridge approach to reach this position which is suited to spin fishing for the first 100 m because of restricted casting room. A slim, deep-running minnow of subdued colours will suffice anywhere in this river.

Fly anglers will find good conditions after a short walk up the paddock although they should fish their way upstream if they're able to lay a line from between overhanging willows. A high-floating dry fly will lift trout from the deeper sections where it is necessary to blind fish, try a size 10 or 12 Molefly, Peverill o'Peak, Wulff or Humpy (red). A weighted size 10 rough Hare & Copper nymph hanging from a dropper under one of these dries would be a wise application if you're able to judge the depth of flow. The nymph should just skim the weeds and stones on the river bottom.

Exercise extreme care when wading in this venue, the quiet surface flow belies the river's strength and the colouration of the water disguises the depth and slippery nature of the bed. Wade into the river where conditions allow and cover the entire surface thoroughly with your fly. The geography of the water flow here, and in fact over most of this river, creates unique feeding and holding conditions that entice trout to frequent the whole expanse rather than the recognisable positions so prevalent in the average trout stream.

(2) Power Station Access: 5.4 km from (1)

Turn left off the highway and follow the sign to a carpark beside the power station, where an explanatory plaque details the geography of the area. There is a grassed viaduct spanning the Arnold River adjacent to the carpark from which you will probably see fish cruising and rising in the calm water upstream. A walking track to the dam follows the river upstream and provides many good fishing positions that are generally better suited to fly fishing techniques during mid-summer when the river flow is low. Spin anglers are assured of excellent high-water conditions for the first two and last months of the season, and then again any other time during or after rain.

It is a well-stocked section of river, an interesting and photogenic venue to fish and really the state of the river at any particular time is 'in the lap of the gods' so to speak. Anglers should perhaps examine the water flow from the precincts of the power station whenever passing through as it is not far from the main highway.

(3) Old Oil-drilling Site: 3.7 km from (2)

This access is identified by a white sign on a gate to a railway crossing. Follow the instructions, obtain access permission from the second house visible on the right, then walk along the gravel track to its termination near the trees. The section of water upstream is deep and swift, holding good stocks of trout, but overhanging trees restrict the fishing access to spin anglers only.

An entirely different scene awaits downstream. The water flows over gravel as it follows a long, slow arc, shallow on this side and deep on the other. Guided by a fern-covered clay bank, and dwarfed by a picturesque stand of native trees, this is perfect fly water — and excellent for spinning too.

The contour of the gravel bar makes it possible to walk upstream and sight fish feeding quietly in the shallows. During daylight hours, a size 10 or 12 Hare & Copper, Hare's Ear or Pheasant Tail nymph will take these shallow cruisers, and a size 12 drab-coloured dry will lift the sub-surface feeders along the edge of the current. Examine the surface expanse carefully for rising trout and cast to them initially with a size 14 or 16 Adams, Twilight Beauty or Greenwell's Glory dry fly. If spurned, it should be replaced with a similar sized (Sawyer's) Pheasant Tail or Peacock nymph.

In the event of a 'splashy' rise during the day use a size 14 Greenwell's wet fly and replace it with a Twilight Beauty wet preceding the evening rise at twilight. Occasionally old trees and driftwood become stranded in the river. Pay particular attention to these positions, especially in a water disturbance created by a dragging branch or foliage as there'll be a trout hanging in there waiting for your size 12 dry Wulff, Twilight Beauty or Molefly to drift by.

Insect repellent is essential anywhere on this river as the sandflies are particularly vicious.

(4) Highway Bridge Access: 1.7 km from (3)

Park on the Moana side of the bridge approach from where it is possible to walk down the embankment, step over a low fence, across a small ditch and fish upstream from a grass bank. This is a position ideally suited for spin fishing. Fly anglers should descend the opposite embankment and fish the shallower section of water between the road and railway bridge in view downstream.

After the shallows have been worked over, cast a dry fly right across the river and float it along the grassy bank separating the bridges. Spin anglers may also fish from the upstream side of the bridge, where they can stand on rocks, cast across the current and retrieve their minnow as it traverses an arc then parallels the bank through a deep channel.

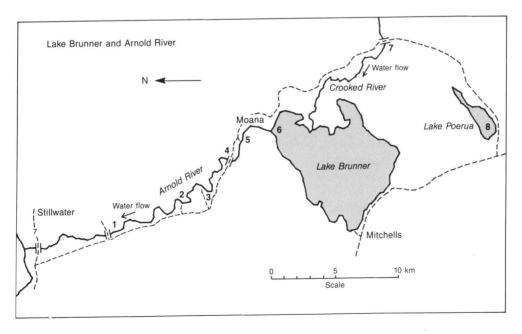

(5) **Railway Siding Access:** 1.4 km from (4)

Watch carefully for a small building near the trees on the right, follow the access road and park near the railway line. Walk along the often swampy track to reach the Arnold River near the emergence of a small creek. This is a small but particularly good area, offering a fast run of water crossing a shallow gravel bed on this side and through a deep run against a cliff face opposite.

The tail of the long pool visible upstream may be fished after crossing the small creek. The rapid, glide and bar should be fished carefully (in that order) with a small dry or nymph while walking upstream slowly. It is a good position for small active trout.

(6) **Moana/Lake Outlet/Arnold River Source:** 3.8 km from (5)

Follow the road through the settlement to a signposted walking track on the right after crossing the railway overhead bridge and before a large carpark on the left side. A well-maintained walking track leads through virgin native forest to a swingbridge spanning the Arnold River at its source. A beautiful and very photogenic setting and a must for anyone visiting Moana — for fishing or otherwise.

Several signposted walking tracks lead from the other side of the bridge, from where it is possible to fish the lake outlet glide and walk the shores indefinately in search of rising or cruising trout.

This venue offers an active evening rise and anglers can expect good results when fishing into the darkness with a size 12 Twilight Beauty wet fly. And it is only a few minutes walk from the motor camp.

The tree-covered Crooked River delta visible from Moana offers good fishing from a boat when trolling, harling or fly-casting to rising trout. Anglers wishing to fish this area should engage one of the commercial boat operators advertised on the community noticeboard opposite the hotel.

(7) Crooked River Bridge Access: 10.6 km from Moana

En route to this position the elevated highway provides a panoramic view of the meandering Crooked River flowing through channels descending a gentle gradient towards its delta in Lake Brunner. This is all good fishing water and within walking distance of the bridge access.

Park on the other side of the bridge where there is easy access to a riverbed which may be walked and fished for miles in either direction. The water is extremely clear as it flows through repetitive rapids, glides and pools and the trout are generally quite visible from a considerable distance away.

It is not as well stocked as the Arnold River, but provides an entirely different environment, calling for a stealthy fish-stalking approach and a high degree of skill in the presentation of size 14 or 16 Adams, Kakahi Queen or Greenwell's Glory dry flies or similar sized/weight nymphs. This is a challenging waterway.

There is another good access to this river some distance upstream. Drive ahead for 2.8 km, turn left at the Rotomoana junction to follow the Ngahere/Nelson Creek Road and you will encounter the upper Crooked River bridge 3 km further on. There are basic rest area facilities at the bridge approach and easy walking access to the river. The clear water here bounces exuberantly over stones between rock pools in a bed descending a steeper gradient than the one encountered at the last access.

(8) Lake Poerua Access: 10 km from the Rotomoana road junction

Return to the junction and follow the Inchbonnie Road for 10 km, cross the railway line, locate and heed the sign 'Legal and physical access to Lake Poerua' to reach the lake shore. There is also another public access a few kilometres further along the Inchbonnie Road. It is identified by a large bulletin board displaying fishing regulations near a shelter-shed inside a fenced enclosure.

Unless you have a dinghy, it is necessary to walk the shores of the lake in either direction and cast to rising and cruising fish or just fish blind if the water is wind-rippled or mirrored by light conditions. The water is shallow enough to permit careful wading (the bottom is quite soft and muddy in places).

The lake is extremely well stocked with brown trout, rainbow trout and a nucleus of sockeye salmon — thanks to the forethought and endeavours of past dedicated and active local acclimatisation society members. Please acknowledge the years of effort spent establishing, retaining and improving the sportfishing in the Lake Brunner region by adopting a 'catch and release' policy when fishing this area. Help ensure the continuity of a diversified sporting fish hatchery.

The Crooked River delta, Lake Brunner, West Coast.

17 Hokitika District

There are two types of water in the rivers of the West Coast. One is brown in colour and froths profusely when agitated by rapids. This holds native eels, whitebait and mountain trout, but seldom imported fish species. The other is clear and may be assumed to have an established stock of either brown or rainbow trout, unless the stones on the riverbeds are heavily impregnated with mica or the water has a milky appearance.

Although the Hokitika district has abundant waterways, in the form of lakes, dams, creeks and rivers, containing brown trout, rainbow trout, salmon, perch and catfish, it cannot be described as a good trout fishing region. The average yearly rainfall is 2775 mm, much of which falls in torrential downpours causing chaos to the waterways, fish and their food sources. Any endeavour to improve trout habitat would be a wasted effort in this climate, so the trout stocks introduced by the pioneers are left more or less to their own resources. There are, however, occasional summers when perfect weather causes trout numbers to increase rapidly, providing good fishing. The fish and game council now allow year-round fishing in most of waterways of the West Coast to make amends for the adverse weather. When planning a specific fishing trip to the region, it would be advisable to contact the Westland Fish and Game Council for current weather and water conditions.

The major river of the district is the Hokitika River. It flows gracefully over a fine gravel and sand bed beguiling the visiting angler with its turquoise water, picturesque stands of willow trees, and backdrop of mountain peaks. However, being large enough to be used as a port for sea-going vessels, it is unsuitable for trout fishing in the lower reaches. Despite this, there are many locations inland which provide good trout fishing with the competent application of the spinning, streamer or fly/nymph fishing methods. Spasmodic salmon fishing results are also enjoyed during that season in the lower reaches as result of the commercial activities which operated in the Kaniere River tributary during the early 1980s. Local anglers are hopeful that a run similar to those established in the South Island's east coast rivers may eventuate.

Arahura River

This clear-watered river descends a constant gradient from the mountains to the sea through an open bed of gravel and stones. It offers many miles of fishing for both rainbow and brown trout. Although once renowned as an outstanding fishery, it may now only be described as average because of fish depletion resulting from major floods and slips in the mountains several years ago. The trout stock is presently holding its own and will undoubtedly increase in numbers when the alluvium from the alpine avalanches ceases to obliterate the food beds.

The lowland section of the river provides good fishing conditions to a reasonable head of trout, but public access to the location is occasionally disputed by local groups. I shall therefore refrain from describing them until such time as an acceptable policy is formulated. Visitors to the region should confine their endeavours to the more productive upper reaches described here.

(I) Milltown Access: 28.3 km from Hokitika

Follow the Lake Kaniere road from Hokitika and turn left at the road junction within sight of the lake. Drive a further 1.3 km through native bush, turn left at the sign 'Milltown' and follow this narrow road carefully for 8 km to the open valley of the Arahura River. This position provides several kilometres of accessible water flowing vigorously over a bed of stones and coarse gravel. There are occasional rocky outcrops and extensive areas of shallows on either side of the main stream where trout may be seen feeding between half-submerged boulders.

The fast runs, smooth glides and sparkling rapids of the central current in this unkempt riverbed of lichen-covered stones, native wildflowers and forest-covered hills will intensify any sportsman's desire to lay a line in the South Island's unique back-country. The location demands solid footwear, as the going is very rough, warm clothing (there is often a wind blowing one way or the other), and solid fishing equipment. The current is surprisingly strong and ideally suited for a 9-ft (2.7-m) SAGE weight 6 graphite rod.

Fly anglers should stalk upstream along the edge of the shallows and search for cruising or feeding trout while blind casting into the main current with a dry fly. The vigorous water conditions call for a well-hackled, high-floating fly such as a size 8 or 10 Blue Dun, Kakahi Queen, Wulff or Humpy. This fly should be replaced with a smaller one (sizes 14/16) when fishing to a trout sighted cruising or feeding in shallow water. A weighted nymph, say size 8 Stonefly, Hare & Copper or rough-textured Pheasant Tail also works well in the depths of this river, but once again it must be replaced with a much smaller one when casting to feeding trout located in shallow water.

Spin anglers may use a slim, single-piece minnow coloured silver, gold or black that will transgress fast, turbulent water without becoming lodged in underwater obstructions. A fast-retrieve spinning reel offers an advantage in these conditions where it is possible, and indeed good policy, to swim the minnow downstream from a pool, over the glide and into the lower rapid. Trout inhabiting this type of environment are alert, active and opportunist feeders and of necessity will snatch at anything which even faintly resembles food, correctly presented or not. But they spook too — one sight of an unwary angler and they're off.

(2) Headwater Bridge: 3 km (approx.) from (1)

You may drive along the road to the bridge and reconnoitre the area before commencing to fish as there are many water variations to choose from. Access is easy, before, after and from either side of the bridge. The stony riverbed is stable and confined by grassy banks. Its crystal-clear water offers a variety of fishing conditions ranging from calm, deep pools to impetuous rapids, all with good stalking and casting positions.

The clarity of the water and open nature of the terrain make the upstream fly fishing technique necessary in the shallow sections of the river. The rougher sections of a rapid or deep runs may be successfully fished with the downstream method.

The terrain offers good overnight parking for a van or tent, and anglers would then have an opportunity to leisurely explore the fishing potential of the area.

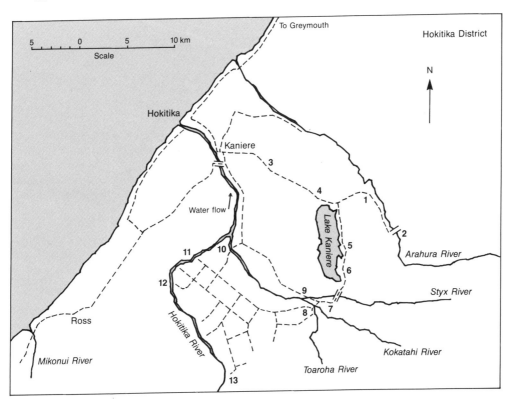

Kaniere River

Lake Kaniere's outlet stream flows through native bush and lowland swamps over most of its 12-km course to converge with the Hokitika River near the township of Kaniere. The waters become coffee-coloured with forest dye as the river descends a steady gradient through a bed of stones to finally flow deep and lethargic in the swamplands preceding the confluence.

Although the lack of visual charisma and restricted access doom this waterway as a trout venue, it contains sections where trout fishing in unusual surroundings offers an interesting interlude for adventurous fly fishing anglers with a little time. The trout are not large, the terrain is covered with gorse and impregnable second growth vegetation and the riverbed of stones and rocks is slippery. But the opportunity to explore a different trout environment has its own peculiar appeal. A size 10/12 yellow-bodied Humpy, Grizzly Wulff, or Kakahi Queen dry fly applied with the upstream technique in knee-deep rapids will often lift the trout, which take and fight with surprising ferocity.

(3) Kaniere River Roadside Access: 9.3 km from Hokitika

Follow the Lake Kaniere road until it veers right to pass over a small bridge and reveal the road signs 'Kaniere Forest' and 'McKays Creek Road.' Just past here there is a steep vehicle track leading from the roadside to the river some 30 m away. Park on the roadside or at the end of the track beside the river if the ground is dry.

This section of knee-deep, turbulent water is difficult to negotiate and should be fished by active anglers wearing felt-soled boots and scratch-resistent clothing as it is necessary to scramble through scrub here and there. An hour or two of pleasurable exploratory fishing is available here.

(4) Kaniere River Top Bridge Access: 2.5 km from (3)

The route to this access passes the Kaniere Power Station which overlooks the river at the head of a long rapid. A small tributary converges with the river here and the immediate area is worthy of inspection and a casual cast or two with a large, well-hackled dry fly. The water is too turbulent to permit visual sighting of trout.

Turn towards the building and use the carpark. This is not a large area, nor is it worthy of a special visit, but rather it provides an excuse for non-fishing members to visit an interesting walking track while anglers test an otherwise neglected venue.

The bridge crosses the river at the lower end of an unkempt scrub-covered flat which provides access to a riverbed of stones. Turbulent water once again presents good fly fishing conditions when using a large, well-hackled, drab-coloured dry of any pattern. I would use a size 10 or 12 Grizzly Wulff or yellow-bodied Humpy. Consider this location an interesting place to fish while passing through rather than a destination in itself.

Lake Kaniere: 18.3 km from Hokitika

Over many years several groups have endeavoured to improve the fishing in this beautiful lake, but, although it now holds a nucleus of quinnat salmon as well as trout, I doubt if present-day anglers have any more success than I did when fishing it as a kid. The lack of sub-surface shelves around the shore restrict spawning and food beds for aquatic insects and smelt. Like the other extremely picturesque West Coast lakes, this lake holds an established but fragile stock of imported fish species.

The eastern side of the lake is followed by a road completely enclosed in native forest which, while offering fleeting glimpses of sparkling water while driving past, provides limited parking or walking access positions. There are, however, two positions offering easy access to venues where shore anglers may expect to locate feeding fish.

(5) Dorothy Falls Access: 9.8 km from the lake outlet

Drive over the bridge and park near a disused vehicle track which follows the course of the creek to the lake. This track emerges into a small bay where a shingle beach conveys the creek water over a shallow delta formed by its own alluvium. Patient inspection may reveal a quiet rise or bow wave of a trout cruising the shallows near the creek convergence or amongst the grasses growing in the water. Such fish should be tempted with a small size 16 Pheasant Tail or Peacock nymph, Greenwell's Glory, Twilight Beauty or Adams dry fly in calm conditions. Increase the size of flies if the water is agitated by wind.

In the absence of trout movement, a size 8 or 10 well-hackled dry fly may be cast, left to drift awhile, and then retrieved very, very slowly. Fishing a fly blind here, or for that matter anywhere around the lake, is a long shot, but concealment, stealth and a little cunning manipulation of a big bushy fly will do the trick if there's a cruiser within eyesight.

(6) Storm Creek Access: 2 km from (5)

Continue along the lake road as it enters open farm land 1.2 km beyond Dorothy Falls and park near the bridge crossing Geologist Creek — a bulldozed gravel channel descending a continuous gradient directly to the head of the lake. Follow this channel on foot to the beach where a large delta extends into the lake and forms extensive shallows. This location probably offers shore anglers the best chance of catching fish in this waterway.

The Styx River

This tributary of the Kokatahi River is a gentle, clear stream flowing through virgin bush country from its source in the Southern Alps to the Lake Kaniere-Kokatahi Road. The upper reaches of some 13 km are more or less followed upstream for miles by a walking track, and the lower section is followed by the road from the bridge for 5 km to its convergence with the Kokatahi River.

The river holds an established but limited stock of both rainbow and brown trout in water of incredible clarity flowing over mica-encrusted boulders offering very challenging fly fishing. It is not a suitable venue for novices, but rather one that will test the skill of the most experienced angler in an environment which appears as pristine as the day of creation.

It is an appealing location in fine sunny weather with sparkling water, glistening riverbed stones and tussock-grassed flats extending from undulating, forest-covered foothills.

Upper Styx Bridge: 12 km from Lake Kaniere outlet via Lakeside Road and 17.6 km from the Kokatahi/Kowhitirangi Junction

Here there is ample parking and easy walking access from the downstream bridge approach, and although anglers may walk at will in either direction, I'd suggest this bridge be used as a base when fishing the upper reaches towards the river's source. The lower section of river is easier fished from the next described access.

Position (2) on the Arahura River, West Coast.

The riverbed is rough, necessitating a slow and careful advance while searching the water for holding or feeding fish. These will be slate-grey, in stark contrast to the golden trout of the Owen River in Nelson or the 'greenbacks' of the Arahura River. May I suggest the use of a size 10 or 12 dry fly in the upstream mode in patterns green- or yellow-bodied Humpy, Grizzly Wulff, Royal Coachman or Kakahi Queen when fishing blind. Use similar patterns in size 16 when fishing to a visible trout and replace it with a size 14 or 16 Hare & Copper, Gold-ribbed Hare's Ear or Speckled nymph if spurned. This fly selection will suffice anywhere in the rough and turbulent waters of the Styx, Kokatahi and Toaroha River systems.

Cover the whole expanse of river with the fly, as there are few holding positions in the accepted sense. Fish which are difficult to detect in the turbulence, clear as the water may be, will be cruising in search of food whenever a hatch occurs.

(7) Dowick's Dilemma Access: 1 km downstream from (6)

Turn right off the road into a vehicle track before the sign indicating the alluvium of this unstable storm creek. A large river terrace provides good parking, excellent wind shelter beneath the trees on the road embankment and easy walking access to the main stream. A short distance downstream the river fans out into braided channels after veering towards and along a sheer rock bank overhung with native bush. The upstream section provides a kilometre of superb fishing water bouncing exuberantly over a wide bed of protruding stones which form a gentle arc originating from another solid rock cliff near the bridge.

The river may be crossed in places and it is possible to walk upstream in knee-deep water while casting a dry fly blind, or walk along a slightly elevated tussock-grassed bank doing likewise and examining the water for trout. This is perfect trout fishing water flowing through appealing terrain. Fish are but a bonus in such a setting.

This location requires several hours to fish thoroughly, and visiting anglers should perhaps contemplate spending at least one full day in the vicinity.

(8) Upper Kokatahi River Bridge: 1.6 km from (7)

The Styx River veers away from the road en route to the next access but it is only necessary to walk across tussock-covered flats to reach its braided channels. There are literally miles of fishing water in this river. Turn left at the junction and you will see the bridge crossing the Kokatahi River 600 m ahead. It offers easy walking access to the stream bed. Park in the grassed flat on this side of the bridge.

The upstream section of river has a fast flow of water confined between stable banks in terrain covered with tussock grass and miscellaneous shrubs extending from the forest-covered hills. The riverbed creates good fish-holding and feeding positions that should be fished blind, initially with a dry fly. Although the water is perfectly clear, the environment makes fish sighting difficult even for the trained eye.

Access and casting conditions are better on the left-hand upstream side of the river and fly anglers should ensure that their fly is well-hackled and dressed to make it float high in the turbulence. It must resurface quickly after being submerged in broken water.

The river from here down to its convergence with the Hokitika, some 14 km away, gradually becomes unstable as the stones give way to a bed of gravel over which the river meanders in braided channels which alter direction with every flood.

Another tributary, the Toaroha, converges with the Kokatahi near the base of the hill visible downstream, and although it is possible to continue along this road over the bridge to gain closer foot access to the riverbed I would advise against doing so. The route traverses the toe of the hill which becomes very wet, muddy and slippery, and it's impossible to drive off the narrow road to turn around.

The Toaroha River which also offers good fishing may be reached by walking across grassed paddocks paralleling the Kokatahi downstream. A long walk certainly, but worth the effort during good, settled weather — this is a delightful stream to fish.

(9) Lower Styx River Bridge: 2 km from Toaroha River road junction

The course of the Styx River is quite discernible en route to the next position and access merely entails a short walk across level terrain to reach its bed. One particular position, while driving downstream, reveals the rippling waters of this river veering away from the road — an appealing and inviting scene on a sunny day. The only parking space near the bridge is on the other side and it is necessary to clamber down steep approaches to reach the water level.

The location offers reasonably good results, especially downstream at the convergence of the two rivers from which either the Kokatahi or Styx may be fished.

(10) Lower Kokatahi Bridge: 1 km from Kokatahi/Kowhitirangi junction, 8.6 km from (9) and 17 km from Hokitika

Follow the Hokitika Gorge road from the Kokatahi/Kowhitirangi junction to the bridge visible ahead. It provides an elevated view of the river in both directions. The section downstream is visibly deeper and more confined than the upper one, where the unstable nature of the gravel bed is quite apparent. The downstream section, from this bridge to the river's convergence with the Hokitika, is ideally suited to the spinning method (or the use of streamer flies and weighted nymphs when employing the fly fishing technique). There is vehicle access to the riverbed upstream of the bridge. From here, many miles of water, with conditions to suit any requirement or technique, can be reached on foot.

It is crucial to use a stealthy upstream approach to any likely fish-holding water in this river to avoid alerting trout cruising or feeding in shallow water. While slowly walking upstream and looking for fish, you may cast ahead, slightly towards midstream with a size 10 or 12 lightly-hackled dry fly similar to a Blue Dun, Molefly, Kakahi Queen pattern. You would be wise to reduce the size of this fly to a 16/18 when fishing to a trout feeding in shallows against the edge of the riverbank and replace it with a small nymph if spurned. It is an easy matter to 'change up' if the fish disregards a small presentation, but the reverse is impossible if it is spooked by a large one.

(11) Hokitika River/Wall Road Access: 9 km from (10)

Continue along Kowhitirangi Road, turn right at the next junction into Cropp Road, then left into Wall Road. The gravel road skirts the toe of the hill and ends in an enlarged space beside a tree shaded stopbank. Do not drive through either of the gates. The track through the one on the right is washed-out, and the left one offers access to a pleasant and sheltered camping position overlooking the river in dry/fine weather conditions only. Walk the 50 m and inspect it before driving in.

The river is deep, wide and flowing quietly against the hill immediately upstream from here. It exits down a long rapid within sight downstream after gliding wide and shallow over a smooth bar. This entire location is a better spinning than fly fishing venue and such anglers should use 14- or 21-g minnows to gain distance and depth of retrieve when fishing over the bar or from the narrow, steep but negotiable base of the hill.

Limited casting distance confines fly anglers to the shallow bar and gravel beaches and they should only walk upstream along the steep bank of the hill in the event of visual fish movement. Trout feed quite voraciously on terrestrial insects against the stones and grasses of the bank and fly anglers may expect results with the presentation of almost any small fly. Take care when walking or fishing along this bank as the stones are a little unstable and the water deep.

(12) Hokitika River Hook Access: approx. 8 km from intersection of Cropp and Kowhitirangi Roads

Return to this intersection, continue straight ahead on Cropp Road, turn right into Nelson Road and follow it to its end on the riverbed. The final few hundred metres pass through farmland, a gate and over the stopbank where there may be wet, muddy and slippery conditions. The vehicle track over the riverbed veers left and passes through stands of gorse and unkempt scrub. It is quite negotiable by vehicles in dry conditions, and terminates at the base of a high stopbank which forms the point of a large curved 'hook'. The river curves through the bottom of the hook, which is being filled in naturally by sand and alluvium, and forms a huge, deep pool at the base of the buttress. This well-stocked water then exits through a rapid towards the opposite side of the riverbed.

This venue provides good spin fishing from a stance at either the base of the stopbank or from the sandy delta directly opposite, as well as along the shallow edges of the entering and exiting rapids. Fly anglers may also apply their technique (using a dry fly) from the two latter positions but will experience 'back cast' problems in the former.

This is a pleasant position to fish the evening rise.

(13) Hokitika River Gorge Access: 3 km from junction of Nelson and Whitcombe Valley Roads

Return to the first junction from the 'Hook Access' and turn right at the sign 'Hokitika Gorge'. This road ends in a carpark enclosed by native forest on the banks of the Hokitika Gorge after travelling 4 km. A swingbridge provides access to the opposite side of the river, but there is no fishing access to the deep, sombre waters of the gorge section — the rising fish are quite safe. The two small creeks which are crossed immediately before the final ascent to this parking area provide a view of the river as it exits from the gorge onto the plains.

I suggest that you inspect both positions (only a few hundred metres apart) for ease of walking access to the main river before deciding which to follow — wash-outs occasionally alter their riverbeds. Generally speaking, the creek nearest Hokitika offers the easiest parking and walking access to the main river, where the water flows from the confines of the gorge through a pool and over a wide bar to exit down a rapid.

This final access described on the Hokitika River provides good fishing for anglers employing either method, although once again fly anglers are limited by the range of their casting ability. The Hokitika River is certainly well stocked with both rainbow and brown trout. It is a large, untamed waterway of major proportions and therefore demands a trout fishing approach far removed to that applied on accepted streams. The trout will frequent the shallows, be they rapids, glides or pools. They will hold and cruise a 'beat' hard against sheer banks beneath overhanging vegetation so concentrate your attention to these positions.

Spring Creeks of the Kokatahi and Kowhitirangi

These inland plains are criss-crossed with spring-fed creeks and drainage canals with perfectly clear water drifting between grassed earth banks and shaded here and there by trees. They represent dry fly utopia, and deserve to be treated as such by angling sportsmen through a strict catch and release approach. I have refrained from describing these valuable streams or revealing their best fishing positions — they are sacred to the fly fishermen of this district whom I'm sure would have no objection to visiting anglers approaching local property owners for permission to fish as long as they release this valuable resource. Please respect and acknowledge the privilege of sharing the trout fishing of this region with the local sportsmen.

Salmon fishing

Recent endeavours have been made to improve the limited salmon fishing in this river by the release of smolt from a commercial salmon farm that was situated on the banks of the Kaniere River tributary. Only time will tell if this has been successful.

18 West Coast

This province of the South Island comprises 200 km of mountains separated from the Tasman Sea by alluvium. A temperate and damp climate, with huge areas of primeval swamps, forests and rivers, have produced an ideal habitat for sandflies, eels and whitebait. Trout have found extreme difficulty in adapting to the local waterways. The horizontal strip of land along the coast averages only 30 km in width and much of it is inaccessible swamp or dense forest. Generally speaking, the rivers either rush violently to the sea over unstable beds of stones and gravel or meander quietly beneath the forest before drifting into placid lakes and lagoons. Neither of these situations is compatible with the trout's spawning or food requirements. With few exceptions, the fast rivers are either snow-fed and tinged blue with glacial dust, or extremely clear-watered storm creeks that rise and fall with the rains. They have beds of unstable rocks and sand that smother spawning grounds and underwater insect life. The slow flowing rivers have water that is usually brown, foul to the taste and obnoxious in odour. Although they present visions of perfect trout streams, with inviting ripples and overhanging foliage, they host only native eels and protected mountain trout. Many of the lagoons into which these rivers flow are open to the sea and do actually possess trout — large ones — but the surrounding terrain is frequently swampy, with large stands of flax, making access impossible, even with a boat.

Therefore, despite the many rivers and lakes visible on a journey through the West Coast, it cannot be described as a good trout fishing region, but rather one in which the uninformed could waste many valuable days on barren sections of water. I shall only describe the trout fishing waterways encountered while travelling in a southerly direction from Hokitika to the Haast River bridge.

The 400 km between Hokitika and Wanaka is remote country that receives excessive rainfall, slips and flooding. Service centres are few and far between and it is advisable to carry waterproof clothing, solid footwear and a basic supply of food and drink in the vehicle.

(1) Mikonui River: 27 km from Hokitika

Pass over the Mikonui highway bridge and turn left into the gravel track which leads to a grassed parking area beneath the bridge approach. This provides easy access to a delightful run of water emerging from the confines of a bush valley. The riverbed is quite negotiable and offers good fishing in conditions ranging from wide, shallow runs and fast, sparkling rapids to deep pools. The pool above the first rapid upstream from the bridge often produces trout and certainly warrants a visit by those with a couple of hours to spare.

The fish are alert in this clear-watered river, necessitating a stealthy approach. Fly anglers are advised to use a floating line with sizes 10/12 weighted Hare & Copper or Pheasant Tail nymphs in fast water, or a similar pattern in sizes 14/16 to fish feeding in shallow or calm water. Use size 12 Black Gnat, Molefly, Humpy or Adams dry flies when trout are rising and feeding on the surface, decreasing this size as the water being fished becomes calmer.

Spin anglers should practise their method in moving water by casting a long line and retrieving deep and slow with a 7-g Tinker/Toby-style minnow coloured black, gold or plain silver with the across and down technique. The bar of glides preceding a rapid, a favourite feeding position for small active trout, may be fished from downstream with a small Mepps or Veltic-type minnow if a fast retrieve spinning reel is employed.

The lower reaches of the river flow into a large lagoon, and the good head of residential sea-run brown trout is dramatically increased during the whitebait season from September to November. The 'river fish' from miles upstream migrate to the brackish tidal region annually and reveal their whereabouts when they chase schools of whitebait which move upstream on each making tide. Spin anglers are able to cover extensive sections of water with their imitation whitebait (Devons/Cobras) minnows which they will retrieve just beneath the surface and parallel to the bank. Fly anglers are advised to fish the rapids just above the tidal flow (keep retreating upstream as the tide makes) with a sink-tip line and streamer fly patterns Jack's Spratt/Grey Ghost (October-December) and Yellow Dorothy/Parson's Glory (December/January). Cast downwards into mid current and retrieve the streamer upstream within a few feet of the bank.

This lagoon may be reached by following the river downstream on a road leaving the main highway 400 m south of the bridge on the seaward side.

(2) Waitaha River: 13.2 km from (1)

This large river emerges from distant hills to flow over a wide, unstable gravel riverbed across an inland valley and beneath the main highway en route to the sea 4 km downstream. The Waitaha is unreliable for fishing in the valley but there is a population of sea-run brown trout in the larger and more stable section of river immediately below the highway bridge near the confluence of the Kakapotahi River.

Access to this venue is from the road signposted 'Kakapotahi' that leads downstream on the northern side of the highway bridge. Follow the road a short distance and turn left into a parking area overlooking the convergence of the rivers, only a short stroll across gravel from the water's edge. The water flow here is large and ideally suited to the spinning technique — use a 14-g deep-running minnow and dredge the depths of the immense pool and the turbulence of the converging streams. It is necessary to walk along the road to spin fish the wide bar and glide preceding the fast rapid visible downstream.

The application of the streamer fly technique, while undoubtedly very effective in this venue, is thwarted by the sheer size of the river, as are all of the other accepted fly fishing techniques. This is not a position I would advise anglers to visit for the sole purpose of fishing. But if time and circumstances allow, it is worth testing this interesting corner of forgotten terrain. And may I suggest a quick stopover at the Pukekura Tavern a short distance down the road for up-to-the-minute fishing information from local anglers.

(3) Lake Ianthe: 7.1 km from (2)

The lake materializes through mists as the highway drifts further into the virgin forest to seek a rest area near sombre waters. There is a short vehicle access from here to a narrow

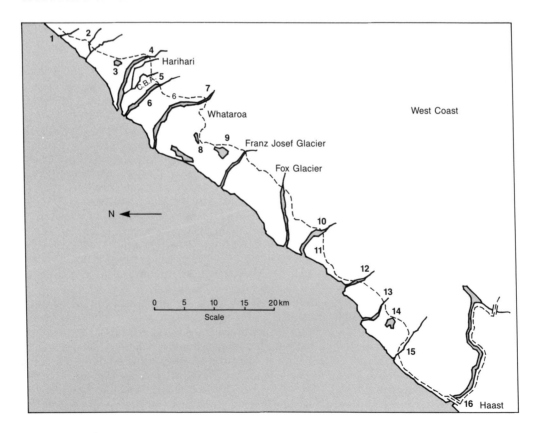

strip of gravel beach leading north. I suggest that after examining the lake from this initial vantage position you drive further along the highway to another rest area with better picnicking facilities beside slightly shallower water.

As with most West Coast lakes, brown trout are established but not plentiful due to the sub-surface terrain, and fishing from the shore is a gamble unless there are obvious signs of feeding. In the absence of visible fish, spin anglers should make long casts into the lake almost parallel to the shore. Let your 14-g black, gold or silver minnow sink slightly, then slowly retrieve it just above the weed. Fly anglers should use a streamer fly to tempt trout moving in an agitated manner near in-flowing creeks, where they will be feeding on smelt or cockabullies (scolpins).

There are usually two periods daily when these lake trout feed sedately on minute dry flies or nymphs. Vigilance is necessary to locate the slight bow wave or rise beneath the shadows of overhanging trees or close to the rushes and flax growing in the water. This feeding pattern is apparent as dawn lifts the mists from the surface of the lake and reveals a jet-black mirror disguising the shoreline with forest reflections. The slightest water disturbance is manifested ten-fold in these circumstances and it is difficult to locate its origin. These cruising fish should be tempted with a size 16/18 Twilight Beauty, Dad's Favourite or Black Spider dry fly, or perhaps a size 18 Peacock Herle or Sawyer's Pheasant Tail nymph. Anything larger will put them to instant flight.

Anglers fortunate enough to experience unique dawn fly fishing on a West Coast forest lake will revel in the silence, then listen apprehensively for the first ringing call of the bellbird that awakens the chorus of the bush. The twilight rise offers a different experience as the breeze stills and the ripples of the lake subside. The trout become active, hard to locate in the agitated water and less alert. Start fishing with size 10/12 dries in the ripple and reduce the size as the water calms. I would not advise anglers to visit this lake only to fish, unless they have a boat (this really offers an interesting variation to fly fishing), but should rather enjoy the surrounds and experience the dawn or twilight fishing as circumstances allow.

(4) Big Wanganui River: 13 km from (3)

The wide, rough and unstable nature of this large river will be seen long before the bridge is crossed to reveal swift water discoloured by glacial dust. It is unsuitable for fishing above its tidal reaches, but these offer excellent spinning and streamer fly brown trout fishing during the whitebait season (October to December) if one is able to locate a fishing stance on the bank. This area is heavily populated with professional whitebaiters during the season and almost every access through the bush is blocked with nets, screens and other paraphernalia peculiar to this fraternity. These fishermen will, however, welcome anyone who will catch the trout which take up feeding position in front of the nets and scatter 'their' schools of whitebait.

Trout anglers so inclined should follow the Wanganui Flat Road from the southern end of Harihari to its termination in a bush-enclosed carpark adjacent to the tidal area and offer their services to a whitebaiting fishermen. You are assured of a welcome, and it will certainly be a different trout fishing experience to anything you've ever tried previously.

(5) La Fontaine Stream, Harihari

This is one of the best fly fishing streams on the West Coast. I fished it as a youth over 40 years ago and the trout population is still excellent. It is the practise of the local kids to catch and take, but visiting anglers, who are privileged to share their domain, should promote conservation with a strict catch and release approach.

The river rises from a swamp 3 km south of the township and passes beneath a small nondescript highway bridge. At this stage, it is little more than a narrow ditch running between flax bushes that almost conceal the flow of water. Over the next 5 km the river flows through farmland, where it has been deepened and widened to serve as a drain. This section provides excellent fishing for competent fly anglers. The water is extremely clear and flows quietly and deeply between 2-m high grassed banks, offering occasional access through cattle furrows onto clumps of solid grass at water level. These fishing stances are quite precarious and must be negotiated carefully or you may have an unscheduled swim through floating water-weed! Separate the grass ahead and inspect the ground below before 'putting your best foot forward'.

As the river enters the lower valley it becomes a gentle stream, alternately flowing over gravel or running swiftly and boisterously between grass banks shaded by the occasional tree. It is possible to cross the river in several positions in this lower section, but you should exercise caution at all times. The clarity of the water belies its depth and strength.

It is necessary to cross private land to gain access to the river and it is essential to obtain permission to do so. If you are in doubt as to your whereabouts, make inquiries at the nearest residence.

(5a) La Fontaine Bridge (return to the Lower Wanganui Flat Road and request permission for access from the residence nearest to the Petersons Road junction)

Turn right off the road and follow the Lower Wanganui Flat Road from the southern end of the township. Turn left at Petersons Road intersection after travelling 1.4 km. Follow this road to the second bridge, a distance of 2.1 km, and park on the other side of the bridge beside a gate — ensure the ground is dry and firm before parking your vehicle here. Walk onto the bridge stealthily and examine the water on either side. There will be a large trout probably sub-surface feeding between clumps of weed about 10 m upstream and an obvious surface swirl or two from others working further upstream. This particular steadfast feeding station will test your expertise of invisible approach and accurate casting.

Step through the fence beneath the willow tree on the opposite side of the river to the parked vehicle, sidle your way down the grassy bank, kneel (to avoid detection) on the lower one and catch that fish with the first cast of a size 18 Pheasant Tail or Peacock Herle nymph — you'll get but one chance at this beauty.

Now, slowly walk upstream along the top of the bank, locate trout that are feeding in the currents between weed-banks and cast to them from the lower bank wherever it's accessible. The stream is extremely well stocked with brown trout. The absence of visible fish indicates that they have been alarmed by your approach or that they're not feeding. Stealth of approach is paramount in this waterway and the accurate casting of small presentations is essential to ensure success.

The downstream view from the bridge often reveals a trout holding hard against the high bank on the left side of the stream. It may be reached from the other side of the river by stepping through the fence or walking back down the road to a gate for access. The straight section of river visible downstream from the bridge converges with a tributary just around the corner and the resulting surge-pool holds a good stock of residential trout. They are, however, difficult to catch owing to the lack of a low or concealed casting stance. Anglers fishing this location should walk well downstream through the open paddocks stocked with cattle and leisurely fish their way back to the bridge. It is an outstanding spring creek worthy of a dedicated and professional approach.

The West Coast waters provide challenging and rewarding fishing.

(5b) La Fontaine Bridge (Bill Levett, phone Harihari 753 3058)

Return to the intersection, continue along the Wanganui Flat Road for approximately 3 km and follow it around an acute left corner into La Fontaine Road. The river now follows the road and presents a view of the perfect dry fly stream before passing beneath the bridge, visible 1.2 km ahead. This 10-m wide flow of honey-coloured water emerges from an enclosure of native scrub. It passes sedately between grassed banks and surges quietly against earth buttresses that guide it towards shelving gravel beaches. The stream disappears behind a small stand of trees, reappears, follows a gentle arc against rocks and passes beneath the road to grace an avenue of willow trees downstream.

Park and walk through the gate on the other side of the bridge (Bill Levett lives in the large house visible on the left side of the road ahead) and fish the river upstream. The conditions here differ from the ones encountered at the previous position as the river now flows over sections of gravel, beneath enclosures of bush and through pools with high, grassed banks. It is advisable to fish the rapids and any likely fish-holding positions blind where the light limits your ability to sight the trout. Use a size 10/12 Hare & Copper/Pheasant Tail nymph or similar sized well-hackled dry fly in this section of river and change to a much smaller size when fishing to a trout seen feeding near the surface.

Impregnable scrub and trees restrict access here and there making it necessary to backtrack and cross the river occasionally and you should keep an eye out for cattle — I have encountered large bulls in this location!

Anglers should ideally plan to spend a whole day fishing this section of river, it's an outstanding venue.

(5c) La Fontaine Bridge Public Access

Continue along La Fontaine Road for 2.4 km and turn right into an open gravelled vehicle track leading towards a bridge. Although this is a public access, you should extend the courteous gesture of approaching the occupants of two houses (one either side of the access track) with a request to wander at large over their property which borders both sides of the river. Drive over the bridge and park on the other side in the grassy space beside a gate (please don't block it). This section of river provides yet another aspect of the fishing available in the 'Spring Creek of the Coast'.

The water is deeper and flows forcefully between banks lined with willow trees. These create a perfect fish habitat but also make it difficult for anglers to place a fly on the nose of a trout feeding on willow grubs falling off a trailing branch. This idyllic location calls for a determined fishing approach where anglers should use a powerful, accurate, positive-actioned SAGE 9-ft (2.7 m) weight 5 rod that will power a fly to a fish feeding within inches of a grass bank — on either side of the 10-12 m wide river. The advantages of such a rod will be obvious when playing trout hooked in this strong water flow: these fish are extremely active, fit and beautifully proportioned specimens.

Anglers may approach the river on either side of the bridge and walk along paddocks while searching for feeding trout (generally beside overhanging vegetation), while casting to every likely position and keeping a taut line to their drifting dry fly. It is an open venue providing good vision to extended runs of water. There are few positions where anglers may stand at the same level as the water and release their catch, but there's nothing wrong with lying on your stomach, reaching down and slipping a barbless hook out of a fish's jawbone.

The three accesses I have described will provide anglers with more fishing than they'll probably have time to spend in the area. I wish you 'tight lines' on this unique waterway — please enjoy, conserve and protect this realm of my youth.

(6) Poerua River: 5 km from (5)

Unstable gravel in the mid reaches of this river creates an unsuitable habitat for trout near the main highway bridge, 4.6 km south of Harihari. The lower section, however, offers pleasant fishing for salmon and sea-run brown trout in open and accessible surrounds. This large, clear-watered mountain stream meanders over a wide gravel bed and presents conditions in stark contrast to the La Fontaine Stream at Harihari, a mere 5 km away. The sunny valley with its stands of native bush will provide an interesting fishing interlude suited to the application of either the spinning or fly fishing method.

Travel 3.4 km south from Harihari, turn right into Oneone Road, follow the sealed road for 2.2 km and turn left at the 'T' junction. Pass through native forest 4 km further on and watch for the first access beside a water tower (painted green) on the left side of the road. Flash floods and the unstable nature of the riverbed make the accurate description of water channels impossible, but generally this position contains a confined flow of deep water ideally suited for spinning with a silver, green or gold coloured 7- to 14-g blade minnow. It will be necessary to park on the road verge and walk through a narrow fringe of trees to reach the river here.

Continue along the road (ignore all side roads leading right) for 500 m to an access onto the riverbed itself. Caution: walk and inspect the gravel of the riverbed as it is occasionally too soft to hold a motor vehicle. This wide riverbed of fine gravel allows easy walking to the water and unencumbered access along its channels when searching for fish.

Anglers using either method should blind fish through the rapids and deep runs in which trout will appear as transparent grey shadows in the clear water flowing over light-coloured stones. Fly anglers are advised to use lightly-hackled dry flies here: Adams, Blue Dun, Greenwell's Glory or Hardy's Favourite in sizes 12/14 would be a good choice when applied in the upstream manner. Don't persevere with this pattern for more than three or four casts if it is ignored by a trout working actively in shallow ripples. Change to a thin-bodied size 16 Pheasant Tail nymph and increase its size if initially spurned.

There is another riverbed access offering similar conditions closer to the tidal reaches 4 km further down the road.

The fishing available in this river does not warrant a special effort to reach but should rather be considered as an interesting diversion while travelling between other destinations.

(7) Waitangitaona River, Whataroa Settlement: 25.6 km from (6)

This river equals the La Fontaine Stream of Harihari with its clear water and established stock of brown trout. It is sourced in the mountains, crossed as an unstable snow-watered river by the main highway 6.4 km south of Whataroa and actually disappears underground near Lake Wahapo to reappear further down the valley as a spring creek. Both waterways share similarities in that they cross alluvium plains formed by the huge turquoise-coloured Big Wanganui and Whataroa Rivers sourced by snow fields and glaciers in the Southern Alps.

They do, however, offer individual and distinctive attributes. Whereas the La Fontaine soothes and caresses the verdant countryside, the Waitangitaona bounces and rushes exuberantly through a gravel bed, crossing open terrain covered with tussock and pasture grasses. Easy access from the valley road will provide anglers with hours of fly fishing where larger dry and nymph patterns to those used on the La Fontaine are necessary in the more boisterous water conditions.

Follow the Whataroa Flat Road from the Highway 6 intersection at the southern end of the township, and drive straight through the Butler and Gunn intersections, past the Whale Road junction on the right and watch for a letter box on the side of the road signposted 'Jetty', a distance of 7 km. Take the next road to the left, stop near the bridge crossing the Waitangitaona and locate a gate access leading to a large parking space on the opposite side of the river.

This position provides a strategic base for long forays to good fishing water in either direction. The lower section meanders over the flats, presenting varied conditions which provide interesting and successful brown trout fishing. There are more good access points to similar water conditions from the road continuing over the bridge and following the river downstream towards the tourism-oriented White Heron Colony Wharf that more or less ends the fishing in this river.

(8) Lake Wahapo: 12.6 km from (7)

The road skirting the shores of Lake Wahapo provides easy access to the rocky shores. The lake is well stocked with brown trout, but a boat is necessary for good fishing. If conditions are perfect, you should spend some time watching the water within casting range of the road, and once fish movement is detected use similar techniques as at Lake Ianthe. The outlet of the lake is at the southern end and a short road leaves the highway to follow the shore to this position. En route there are vehicle accesses to several pleasant picnic areas on the water's edge. The lake narrows considerably towards its outlet, and the vicinity is frequented by cruising fish. These should be tempted with a small dry fly (size 14/16 Twilight Beauty, Adams or Molefly) when surface feeding, or, in the absence of fish movement, a spinning minnow retrieved deep or perhaps a Parson's Glory or Yellow Dorothy streamer fly, which must be used with a sinking or sink-tip line to make it skim over the weedbeds. The waters of this lake always appear dirty, but this does not detract from its visual appeal or affect its stock of trout and salmon.

The Okarito River, which is the outlet of Lake Mapourika, offers very good fly fishing in the short channel from its source 11 km away (9).

The highway more or less follows the river en route to the lake and occasionally reveals its sombre waters flowing smoothly between grassed banks and flax a few metres away.

These unusual fishing venues offer an interesting interlude for exploratory fly anglers with the time and energy to step through a fence, walk a few metres and drift a large, dark-coloured dry fly down the centre of the narrow channel. The trout here appear as a beautiful golden apparition as they nonchalantly lift from the depths to take with incredible softness.

(9) Lake Mapourika: 7 km from (8)

The bridge crossing MacDonalds Creek gives a view of Lake Mapourika — a large waterway which is well stocked with large brown trout and larger salmon. Pass over but do not fish this spawning creek (closed for angling), turn off the highway and park on the large gravelled plateau. There is a particularly pleasant and picturesque picnic area, with basic facilities, just inside the bush enclosing the old road directly ahead.

Follow the river-flat downstream to its convergence with the lake, where the outlet, the Okarito River, is sourced. This position must be approached cautiously during calm conditions, as the fish are extremely alert in the shallow, clear water, especially on the bar over which they are constantly cruising 'on the feed'.

MacDonalds Creek flows into the lake near the source of the Okarito River but shingle frequently displaced by floods alters the actual character of the immediate terrain and makes an accurate permanent description impossible.

You should approach the location with the intention of crossing MacDonalds Creek well before the lake, walking through dense bush to the Okarito River and fishing it upstream towards the lake. The water is swift, clear and deep, and flows between high grassed banks. There are extensive patches of floating weed under which the fish shelter. This outfall should be fished upstream with a small dry or nymph, stripping to keep a taut line to the presentation. Stand well back from the actual bar and fish right across it, using long casts. The water over the bar is generally ruffled by wind during the day and a large, high-floating, well-hackled dry fly should be left to bounce through the ripples and goad any nearby trout into action.

When the bar has been thoroughly fished, walk to the left and around the shores of the lake, fishing blind, while examining the water ahead for cruising or feeding trout. Should the water be ruffled by wind action, and your circumstances allow, you should leave the inshore fishing until evening when twilight stills the waves and lifts the hatch, which will induce trout to cruise and feed.

The size 10 or 12 Humpy, Wulff, Blue Dun and Black Gnat dry flies used during the day in agitated water conditions should be replaced with smaller size 16/18 as the light fades and the ripples abate. Efficient fly patterns for this latter period should include Twilight Beauty, Greenwell's Glory and Dad's Favourite.

The highway follows the eastern side of the lake, providing several obvious walking accesses to fishing positions. There is a jetty and concrete boat-launching ramp in a small bay at the southern end of the lake which is well stocked with fish. However, these trout have been pursued so many times that they are impossible to catch, and rise blatantly just beyond casting range of the jetty.

As is often the case, the most productive fishing water is on the inaccessible side of the lake. A gentle stream drifts through clumps of flax into a small, placid inlet, surrounded by tall native trees. Large trout rise sedately to take insects falling from the branches, offering challenging fishing to the fly angler fortunate enough to have the use of a boat.

The lake is renowned for the quality of its salmon fishing, and visiting anglers should perhaps seek the services of a guide from Franz Josef with a boat if this style of fishing is their thing.

(10) Karangarua River: 64 km from (9)

This is a large, fast river flowing over a wide bed of unstable rock and gravel which alters with every flood. Although it has a stock of trout, it can not be classed as a trout fishing river but rather one which offers an interesting interlude for transit anglers with a little time to spare. The turquoise water flows through successive rapids, glides and pools and presents an appealing scene on a sunlit day. There is safe parking on the verge or through roadside gates on the northern side of the bridge and easy walking over tussock and gravel to the water's edge.

This venue is suited to both spinning with brightly coloured minnows and fly fishing with a large (sizes 8/10) well-hackled dry fly: Humpy, Grizzly Wulff, Molefly or Kakahi Queen in the ripples, shallow rapids and bars of wide glides.

(11) Jacobs River: 12 km from (10)

This wide expanse of water extending the full width of the riverbed between high banks, covered with unkempt vegetation and willows, gives the impression of a canal rather than a river. The fine gravel bed is pale grey and disguises the large trout that will be within visual range of the highway bridge. Unfortunately, this good trout fishing river has restricted public access.

The volume of the flow allows the river to be crossed at the head of rapids but there are extensive sections where the smoothly flowing water is too deep to wade over. Although large expanses of deep water offer better spinning conditions, fly anglers should not be discouraged. There will be large trout holding alongside obstructions in knee-deep water against banks of earth and sand beneath overhanging grasses and shrubs. These trout will be motionless and difficult to see as their colouration matches that of the river-bottom.

Silver, gold or black spinning minnows of the Tinker/Toby, Daffy or slice pattern, in weights to suit the water flow, will suffice in this river. Fly anglers would be wise to try the small, dry patterns Coachman, Adams, Molefly or March Brown when fishing to visible trout and increase the size if the fish ignore the presentation. The same patterns, and size, will also work on the bar of a smooth glide where reflection frequently creates a mirror effect and restricts vision. When fishing blind in the ripples and rapids I suggest that you use a full-hackled fly — Humpy, Grizzly Wulff, Kakahi Queen or Blue Dun, for example.

It is possible to reach, and walk along, the banks just above the water from the bridge approaches. There is a steep track on the downstream side of the bridge providing access to the narrow strip of bank extending in both directions. Vegetation upstream restricts fly casting, and the downstream section, too, is suited only for the spinning method where long casts across the river will swing towards and be retrieved against the current close to the bank.

Acrobatic fly anglers may scramble upstream, cast (using a sideways technique) ahead of themselves and let the fly drift back downstream close to the bank with the current, unless they locate a feeding trout to fish to. This approach may also be applied to the upstream section of river on the opposite bank, where the water is deeper, the bank steeper and the fish more plentiful.

There is a vehicle track providing access to the upstream section of river. It leads from the highway on the southern side of the bridge near an old hut and cattle yards. The road is closed with a padlocked chain and the owner of the property must be contacted personally for permission to enter. Anglers keen to fish this river upstream, where there is excellent water (especially against the stopbanks), should contact Jim Sullivan at Fox Glacier.

(12) Mahitahi River, Bruce Bay: 20 km from (11)

This is a larger river than the Jacobs and well stocked with trout. There is ample access to its riverbed from the southern side of the Bruce Bay Settlement — watch for vehicle tracks leaving the highway through unkempt roadside vegetation, and terminating on the gravel of the riverbed. The bridge will be encountered 3.8 km south of the settlement, and there is easy vehicle access to the riverbed from the highway on the southern side of the bridge.

It is necessary to seek permission from the residents of the house ahead to pass through a closed gate to the downstream section, which offers good parking on a grassed river flat a short stroll from the water. The upstream access is similar, with good parking within a short walking distance of a river stopbank.

There is a good spinning position on the upstream side of the bridge. But step carefully down the embankment to reach your casting stance just above the water. This stopbank may be followed upstream onto the gravel bed of the river. This beautiful clear-watered river will provide hours of pleasant fishing in either direction of the highway bridge. The turbulence below the rock groyne extending the full width of the river below the bridge is an excellent piece of water through which to retrieve a 14-g Black & Gold Tinker minnow.

Going south, the highway follows the course of the river for a kilometre or so and provides a view of several perfect runs of trout fishing water. Access is possible through a lichen-covered wooden gate on the roadside — seek entry permission from the farmhouse on the opposite side of the road.

(13) Paringa River: 15 km from (12)
Another large, clear-watered river, well stocked with brown trout, that materializes from the Southern Alps at the head of the valley. An obvious vehicle track leads from the upstream side of the highway, crosses the old riverbed and offers unlimited parking on the tussock-covered gravel within a short distance of the water. Upstream, the river exits from a rapid to flow deep against a stopbank ending at the highway bridge. It then disappears from sight through graceful arcs alternating from side to side over the valley floor.

Another vehicle access on the downstream side of the bridge passes through a gate and ends on the gravel riverbed which is used as a launching pad for trailer boats. It is also possible to park on the roadside near a monument and walk across the highway to fish from the stopbank described above. Access to good venues is quite easy here.

This large, forceful volume of water offers good spinning everywhere but fly anglers must apply their technique in the shallow edges of pools and rapids which should be fishing blind with a well-hackled size 10 or 12 dry fly while constantly watching ahead for a feeding trout. Shallow ripples and glides may be treated similarly, and the turbulent surface of runs entering pools should be inspected for fish movement or that shadowy shape.

This appealing location offers several days of interesting fishing along a 30-km section of highway and anglers should consider scheduling their itinerary to allow a little extra time to explore this river, and the nearby lakes, Paringa and Moeraki, where there are rental boats, cabins, and caravaning facilities. There is excellent trout fishing to be had in these waterways and their tributaries.

(14) Lake Paringa: 7 km from (13)
There is very restricted access for shore fishing at this end of the lake, which is fished extensively from boats. A drive of a further 1.5 km is necessary to reach a suitable fishing position. Turn off the road into the reserve, which provides an ablution building, a ring-road giving access to several gravelled camper van parking areas between trees, and large areas of sheltered lawn. This facility is built on a small peninsula which offers good shore fishing for trout and salmon, especially at the convergence of the small creek bisecting the reserve. There is extremely good fishing at the convergence of a creek on the opposite side of the lake but a boat is necessary to gain access. This tributary is too small to hold many fish but the semi-enclosed bay it enters is an excellent position for small dry flies cast to rises and spinning.

(15) Lake Moeraki: 17 km from (14)
This is undoubtedly the best stocked lake in South Westland for brown trout, but it has the most vicious sandflies and mosquitoes I have ever experienced! (You must be prepared and have repellent handy.) The elevated highway skirts the western shores of the lake, but provides limited access to the water's edge. However, roadside vegetation is occasionally trimmed and foot tracks created down to the narrow strip of gravel beach, so watch for them while driving past.

The outlet of the lake is situated at its southern end, where it flows under the highway near a motel complex. Salmon are well established in the lake and spawn in its main tributary which is closed to fishing at all times. As the lake comes into view, watch carefully for a gravel road leaving the highway to give access to a boat-launching beach with limited parking space. The Moeraki River enters the lake on the other side of the grassy peninsula, behind the stands of flax on the opposite side of the bay. This river has formed an extensive underwater delta, covered in places with coarse hip-high grass growing in the water. There is a low grass-covered bank beside the fast water flow, and a wide, reasonably shallow bay with unkempt swampy vegetation growing around its perimeter. This is an outstanding trout fishing venue with difficult access through scrub, flax and water. Boats provide easy access to the river's gravel bar near the edge of this position.

Anglers able to reach this venue are assured of excellent sport if they walk slowly and stealthily through knee-deep water with a small dry fly at the ready and cast to trout located visually, or by their water disturbances. The trout are not large at an average 2 kg but they provide an interesting stalk and will take any small, dark-coloured fly delivered in a reasonably competent manner. They are not overly alert or easily spooked here.

The actual shallow gravel bar is cruised constantly by feeding fish which may be taken with a small dry fly placed strategically in the path of their 'beat'. The depths below the alluvium shelf are well stocked and produce good results to the trout spinning fraternity, if such anglers are able to 'beat' their salmon fishing cousins to it.

The bar and river outlet beside the motel offer good fishing but the river too deep to wade and should be fished from a boat. Row into the lake before dawn, and drift downstream over the bar and along the fern-fringed outlet just as the light strengthens enough to silhouette the trees. Use a sink-tip line and a heavily weighted size 8 Pheasant Tail nymph, casting either side of the drifting boat and retrieving slowly so that the presentation skims over the bottom weed. The large fish here hit and play hard, and are impossible to land without the use of a net.

The lake outlet, downstream of the rapid opposite the motor camp, assumes the character of a normal river in the accepted sense, and offers good fishing in a variety of water conditions passing through terrain with restrictive vegetation. Agile and suitably clothed anglers may wish to explore this area if circumstances permit. Access is from a gravelled track leaving the highway on the right side just south of the bridge. You should seek permission from the proprietor of the motel to use this access as it passes through private property.

(16) Haast Bridge: 30 km from (14)

En route to this position the highway crosses the Waita, with its brown water rippling quietly over fine gravel. Although a picturesque setting, there is a limited head of brown trout in this stream, most of which are 'sea-runs' living in the tidal reaches. If circumstances permit, you may follow the access track downstream and apply the streamer fly or spinning techniques. The upstream section of river is shallow, passes through swampland and is of little value as a trout hatchery.

The sheer size of the Haast River renders it unsuitable for trout fishing, though it is undoubtedly well stocked. It drains a huge catchment area and is subject to frequent flooding.

The Haast Hotel is close to the south approach to the Haast Bridge. There are two settlements nearby and a motor camp situated south on the Jackson's Bay highway. I suggest that anglers with time at their disposal should study Chapter 19 Land's End/South Westland. Our direct route now follows the Haast River upstream to leave the West Coast and breach the hinterland of the South Island — Central Otago.

19 Land's End/South Westland

The West Coast Highway continues for another 50-odd kilometres south of the Haast River and ends at Jackson's Bay. It is an interesting drive along the coast, crossing swampland forests and offering an occasional fleeting glimpse into the disappearing pioneering era of South Westland. The plaques are few and simple, yet convey an admirable and moving history. Four of the five rivers crossing the plains are well stocked with large brown trout that provide good fishing close to the road in venues limited by inclement weather and primeval terrain. Two rivers are glacial and two rain-sourced and they leave their mountainous surrounds to flow through swamps and impregnable native forest en route to the sea. Only one is navigable above the lowlands by jet boat; the others surge over or through natural barriers of rock and flood debris and local knowledge is essential to negotiate them on foot or horseback.

The brown trout in the mid and lower reaches of the main streams are nomadic, and an awareness of this predictable pattern will make or break a fishing vacation to this region generally refered to as New Zealand's last frontier. Whitebait, juvenile New Zealand native trout, swarm into the rivers in their thousands from the Tasman Sea to stock the swamps, lakes and streams from August through to late November. This annual event entices the river trout to join their sea-run cousins in the tidal reaches for a gluttonous orgy. The introduced brown trout has adapted well to this yearly spree and they move en masse from many miles up river for this 4-month period. At this time it is possible to walk the river for days above high-water mark and not see a single trout, such is the extent of this pilgrimage.

The trout, cursed by the professional whitebait fishermen, gorge themselves silly on schools of bait, often directly in front of set nets in which they are frequently caught. Trout feeding in this way are an easy target for a deftly manoeuvred Grey Ghost/Jack's Spratt streamer fly or an imitation whitebait spinning minnow. The latter fishing method, while not as effective as the streamer fly technique, has obvious advantages in the large, deep tidal lagoons. Such anglers may stand (and be readily welcomed) on a whitebaiter's platform, or among riverside scrub, and reach a marauding trout made obvious by his feeding antics.

Fly anglers will have difficulty reaching these fish and may do better if they walk the river near the extent of the tidal flow and stalk individual trout that have reached 'the age of discretion' — and are usually very large and rotund. These 'old bulls' may be extremely vigilant for above-surface movement and footsteps but they cannot resist a streamer fly. In fact they are frequently so stupid that I catch them annually with a streamer fly pulled against, with, and even sideways to the current. But, you must approach casting positions with the utmost stealth — one quick movement, one careless footfall on the gravel, and it's all over.

Okuru River: 11.5 km from Haast Junction

A rain-sourced river of clear water crossing the floor of a mountain valley between forest-covered mountains where massive waterfalls cascade over sheer cliffs and plummet through giant trees standing aloof on exposed ridges. The constant clouds of swirling spray which engulf the forests near the falls create an incredibly verdant and photogenic location — complete with a large, powerful, yet gentle, water flow carrying a good head of large brown trout. This is one of my favourite back-country venues that I visit all too infrequently each season. The lower reaches emerge from impregnable forest to bisect open farm land and flow into the sea after being crossed by the Jackson's Bay highway which provides access to several good fishing venues.

The Okuru Road on the seaward side, before the bridge, passes through a small settlement and terminates near a walking track leading to a lagoon. These tidal reaches offer spinning rather than fly fishing conditions. Immediately before the bridge approach a vehicle access leads to a sheltered position which also offers good spin fishing conditions.

The downstream section of river provides an open grassed riverbank with unencumbered walking access to the water's edge. It would be wise to visually inspect the immediate area from the bridge itself before deciding on a particular spot. This location presents an opportunity for fly anglers to ply their technique from open terrain into a wide, smooth flow of water in which unusual surface disturbances indicate the location of feeding trout. Time spent sitting quietly and just looking is well spent in this type of location. Trout have an uncanny knack of suddenly materializing from nowhere, especially as the tide comes in and the large silver-coloured sea-run trout drift nonchalantly with the current just beneath the small pieces of flotsam.

When fishing the tidal section use a Grey Ghost or Jack's Spratt streamer fly from opening day to say mid November, replace it with a Yellow Dorothy or Parson's Glory until the end of March and use a Hamill's Killer, Hope's Silvery or Mrs Simpson during winter — if the trout season remains open for 12 months, as has been the case for the past few years.

Although the tidal reaches may be fished successfully all year for sea-run browns, the migration of river fish back upstream in December drastically reduces the overall population. Gone are the optimistic feeders, the young fish that rush and dash all over the place terrifying more whitebait than they eat. In mid summer and autumn spin anglers may still confidently expect to catch large sea-run trout with their long-distance, deep-water retrieved minnows, but fly anglers should consider moving upstream to fish the following section.

Turn inland and follow the Okuru Valley Road from a junction just south of the bridge. It follows the river for 1.2 km and offers several easy-walking accesses from parking positions amongst the roadside trees. This area is tidal so keep your escape route open. Grassed farmland a few hundred metres along the road also offers walking access over a kilometre or so to the riverbed. Anglers wishing to cross farm land to reach the river from this 'no exit' road should extend the courtesy of an access request to Maurice Nolan (Ph (03) 750 0824), the farmer residing in the first house up the valley. He also operates a commercial jet boat safari business on the waterways of the region and provides otherwise unattainable access to fishing venues on several lakes and rivers as well as the sea coast.

The river flows against the road verge for a short distance 2.8 km up the valley and provides an opportunity to search for trout from an elevated position. Fly anglers active enough to scramble down a 3-m high embankment, cast accurately and present a fly delicately from a difficult stance should expect good sport here. Clear water flows gently through a 20-m wide, 4-m deep channel forming an arc with its apex against the road. The depths are cluttered with driftwood trees and stumps which create a perfect trout habitat. Anglers should study the whole expanse carefully for fish movement.

The trout here are unbelievably large. They drift through the debris slowly and nonchalantly, and it is possible to see their mouths opening to take food such is their size and the clarity of the water. They are, however, extremely alert for untoward movement and you must stay below the horizon while inspecting or approaching their domain.

Once again, use the streamer flies (probably with a sink-tip line to gain depth) until the end of the whitebait season. They should then be replaced with either very small nymphs or dark-coloured dries (sizes 16/18) when casting to trout feeding near the surface, and weighted size 12 or 14 nymphs to in-depth feeders. This venue, as with a similar one on the Turnbull River, must be approached cautiously — the trout deserve it, they're real trophies.

You may drive along the road a further 500 m, step through a fence beside an old hay shed and walk the river along the top of an elevated bank to the next access at the end of the road, a kilometre or so upstream. This final access is an excellent venue with picturesque surrounds and easy access over a riverbed of fine gravel. Clear water, from a pool extending to the extremities of the river, flows into a rapid which confines its flow against the far bank. This run curves gracefully through a wide pool and passes beneath a few willow trees. It then exits down a long rapid, veers left and disappears from sight to create the previously described fishing position.

Ideally, anglers should walk down the paddock and examine the river for trout from the elevated bank as they fish their way back upstream. (If spinning, fish blind.) The glide over the bar of the pool directly ahead is a good holding position and warrants close inspection, but the rapid flowing between the pools either side of your stance is of marginal fishing value. The water flows swiftly over clean, unstable gravel which is dislodged with every flood.

The pool covering the full width of the river upstream is well stocked with trout, but its depth restricts fly fishing to within casting range of the bank. It does the opposite for those using the spinning method. This narrow strip of water offers good fishing to large trout that sedately cruise a 'beat' close to the overhanging bank along which you should walk carefully. Examine this location thoroughly, it is a venue calling for stealth, accurate casting and soft delivery of sizes 16/18 nymphs or dries, unless the river is in spate.

Walk upstream along the grassed bank where the elevation provides good underwater visibility devoid of surface reflection. The head of the pool extends into native forest which eventually restricts further progress and spells the end of lowland fishing on the Okuru River.

Turnbull River: 2 km south of the Okuru River

Another rain-sourced river following the Okuru from the mountains to the sea and offering excellent trout fishing. The upper reaches are barren: the size of a natural waterfall, harnessed to generate electricity, prevents the passage of fish. I have filmed the Turnbull's 'hanging valley' from helicopters and walked its waters to no avail. And yet, I still find it quite inconceivable that a river of such perfect stature, gently descending a long valley between mountains of virgin forest, could be this way.

The lower reaches make amends for nature's oversight by offering big trout in a river that I can only describe as 'the largest spring creek in the South Island'. Its gin-clear water flows over fine, white gravel in a bed undulating its way between grassed farmland paddocks. This river is a must for anglers seeking the 'essence of fly fishing' — solitude, a pristine environment, an intangible silence and a worthy adversary.

The Turnbull river flows into a tidal lagoon shared by the Hapuka River, a true 'swamp creek' sourced by a huge area of impassible flax and ancient alluvium. No brown trout, but the habitat of eels, native trout and birds unique to New Zealand. The section of river between the highway bridge and lagoon may be fished in a similar manner to that of the Okuru, from the bank on the southern side.

Both sides of the river upstream from the bridge are followed by roads offering foot access to good fishing venues. It is necessary to cross private land and anglers should request access

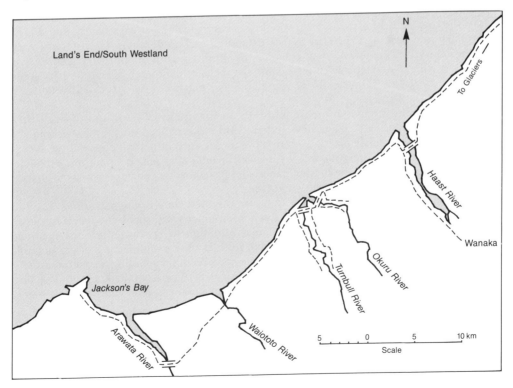

Haast River Valley.

permission from its owner Kerry Eggling, residing in the house directly behind the motor camp situated between the Turnbull and Hapuka River bridges. Bryan Glubb, owner of the motor camp, is a keen angler and an authority on the area and its fishing. Anglers residing in the motor camp should talk to him and ascertain prevailing conditions and fishing venues currently producing good results.

Turn inland at the junction on the south side of the bridge, drive for 900 m, pass through a gate (leave as found) and follow a vehicle track to the gravel riverbed offering better spinning than fly fishing conditions.

Return to the main road and continue inland for a further 500 m. The river flows right against the road embankment and you should park here, walk upstream slowly, and search for cruising and basking fish. This is an outstanding section of water, well stocked with big trout that are extremely alert. It calls for the utmost stealth of approach. The river is about 15 m wide, 5 m deep and flows against the rocks of the road embankment for some 500 m. The clarity of the water is inconceivable and magnifies the large driftwood trees visible below the surface.

Trout hold against, and swim parallel to, the main trunks of trees and through bare branches in search of food. Their slow and graceful movements are extremely difficult to detect in the depths and again I must stress the importance of patient observation. A ten-minute break just sitting and watching is time well spent — it is quite possible, and probable, to notice a 3-5 kg (6½-11 lb) brown trout materialize from nowhere and drift along the gnarled and twisted trunk of a sunken driftwood tree.

Bide your time, and cast with a size 14 or 16 weighted Hare & Copper or size 12 or 14 Pheasant Tail nymph as the trout swims away. Your actions will spook the fish if it is even slightly abreast of your stance. Pay particular attention to the water against the road embankment formed with large slabs of hewn rock, boulders and patches of grass. Large trout drift slowly, with barely a ripple, along the bank feeding on falling terrestrial insects. These fish are easily caught with a deftly placed size 16/18 small-bodied nymph (Peacock) or sparsely hackled dry fly (Adams), but they're spooky and can read your thoughts before you even cast a fly.

During the whitebait season you should use streamer flies, as described under the Okuru River section, in this tidal area.

The upstream piece of road verge is covered with scrub and overlooks a particularly good trout feeding area. This backwater should be examined thoroughly from the top of the bank (it is possible to force a path through the vegetation).

If the cruising trout are unattainable from here, return to the road, walk upstream, step through the fence into the open paddock and scramble down the high bank onto the sandy riverbed and fish from there. The in-flowing rapid offers good fishing and should be walked and fished in the accepted upstream mannner.

Continue driving along the road for a further 1.5 km and park where it veers right, near a distinct roadside recess on the left at the junction of two fences and a wooden gate. This is only a few metres from the riverbed — just out of sight behind and below a few manuka bushes growing on the edge of the paddock. Walk to the edge of the plain and stealthily inspect the river flowing swiftly but smoothly over a grey-coloured gravel bed; it descends a gentle gradient between, and 4 m below, open land.

Ideally you should walk well downstream (or start fishing at the last roadside access) and walk back along the top of the bank while looking for trout. They will be quite visible from up here, and will probably be holding or feeding within or beside the clumps of grass and clay of eroded banks, old forest stumps or piles of driftwood surrounded by water. Stop and inspect these obstructions closely — the only sign of a fish may be its tail and fin moving in the current, or perhaps a darkish hue on the side of a sunken tree trunk. Although it is unlikely to locate a fish in sections devoid of obstructions, you should inspect the whole expanse quickly when walking upstream.

This venue provides hours of fishing, and good results to fly anglers who apply a thorough and dedicated approach. Pay close attention to the grass-covered banks beside deepish water — a square tail twitching in the current beneath the overhang is all you will see of a feeding brown here, and it'll be a big one.

It is possible to walk upstream for several kilometres and enjoy good fishing in wide rapids, runs and occasional deep pools in a bed which has been bulldozed here and there and becomes rougher as the gravel gives way to stones and rock. The lower reaches are too deep to cross but a road on the other bank offers access to venues you may have noticed and desire to fish — return to the main Jackson's Bay highway, turn right towards Haast, cross the bridge and turn inland at the junction.

The first access is revealed as the road veers left to follow the river for a short distance. This position, 700 m from the highway, offers spinning in a deep, fast flow (albeit tidal) from a high stopbank. This side road forms the riverbank 1.9 km inland from the main highway and offers conditions similar to the venue on the opposite side, although this one favours spinning rather than fly fishing, in a deeper, swifter flow of unobstructed water. You may also walk and fish from the road, then scramble through vegetation to reach the shingle bed visible upstream.

There is an excellent fishing and picnic venue 3.7 km from the highway on the top of an old stopbank covered with grass and shaded by trees. Watch for a narrow opening in the roadside vegetation, drive down the slight depression (if wet inspect surface first) and park on the grass. The river runs deep and swift against the bank which has several rock groynes extending into the current — these are natural positions to find trout holding in a vortex and feeding at will in a food channel.

Fly anglers will achieve results consistent with their expertise. Large trout are half-hidden by overhanging slabs of rock and disguised by shadows. Their feeding motion is active and confined to a small area and they must be tempted with a presentation delivered at the feeding depth. Use a weighted Hare & Copper, Gold-ribbed Hare's Ear or Stonefly nymphs unless the trout are rising to the surface at dawn (then use a Greenwell's Glory wet fly) or late twilight (Dad's Favourite or Twilight Beauty dry fly).

You can walk along the top of the stopbank and follow paddocks onto a wide gravel riverbed visible upstream, but the downstream section is very overgrown with impregnable vegetation and is quite unsuitable for fly fishing. It is however an ideal venue for deep-retrieved spinning minnows if such anglers can find their way to a casting position.

The road may be followed a short distance upstream where further access is possible by walking across paddocks. Do not drive into the bush after crossing the next wide clearing — the road is closed by a locked gate and turning is extremely difficult. Anglers intent on fishing the marvellous section of water below the powerhouse outlet should speak to Bryan Glubb back at the motor camp.

I will conclude this description of the Turnbull River with a plea for conservation: This is a unique venue — the trout are confined to the lowlands — subjected to violent floods in a river with very few sanctuaries and only the strongest fish survive. It must be considered an outstanding but fragile fishery. Catch and release these wild brown trout.

The three other rivers on this section of highway all hold fish, but lack of access renders them unsuitable trout fishing venues. The lowlands are covered with impregnable native forest and impassable swamps. Several of their tributaries offer good fishing, but these, too, are inaccessible to those without local knowledge and specialised transport. They remain hidden from all but the fly fishing angler whose questionable intelligence is overidden by an insatiable desire to 'see what's on the other side of the hill'.

The Hapuka River

This river passes beneath the highway 1 km south of the Turnbull River, emerges from swampland as a black-watered, tidal influenced canal and shares the same lagoon before converging with the sea behind the Haast Motor Camp. The lagoon holds a good stock of sea-run brown trout which may be caught from the shore at low water as the tide floods. Scrub along both sides of the river makes shore-line fishing almost impossible, but anglers with a dinghy can expect excellent results either spinning blind or flystreamer fishing to trout feeding on the surface.

The Waiatoto River: 11 km south of the Haast Motor Camp

This river offers good spin and streamer fishing for sea-run brown trout in the estuaries at the correct stage of the tide during any time of the season. Immediately before the bridge there is a vehicle access leading upstream off the highway, through a gate, past a couple of houses, and terminating on an air-strip which parallels the river for quite some distance. It is possible to park on the grass verge overlooking the river and walk along its banks at low tide. The water is glacial and coloured grey/blue which restricts sub-surface visibility.

Blind fishing when using either method must be practised here and, as with other West Coast rivers, there will be lack of standing room come whitebait season from September to November. But if you are prepared to kill trout, the whitebaiting fraternity will willingly share their stands with you during that period.

Further walking accesses, through thick bush, are available from a vehicle track leading downstream on the southern side of the bridge. These lead to banks along deep water, and offer conditions suited to spin fishing only. The road terminates near the beach and offers walking access to a lagoon.

Anglers visiting this river must be prepared to 'roll with the punches' and do a little exploring. The weather, condition of the river and mood of the tide combine with the prevailing state of the terrain to present an unknown factor until the actual time of arrival. Anglers should, however, avail themselves of the opportunity to catch a large sea-run brown trout if circumstances allow when passing through. These trout are really something... and big!

The Arawata River: 10 km from the Waiatoto River

The immensity of this valley is quite startling when viewed from the highway bridge. It materializes as a wraith from a blue haze supporting the distant Southern Alps. The river is large, it's transparent azure-blue colour is accentuated by the white sand/gravel bed, and it is well stocked with brown trout. Unfortunately, it is only the sheer size of the water flow that makes it unsuitable as a trout fishery.

There is a vehicle access to the riverbed leading from the highway on the Haast side of the bridge where spin anglers may ply their technique in a perfect, if large, run of trout fishing water.

The road continues to Jackson's Bay and offers ample walking accesses to the riverbed as it follows the river downstream. Anglers may walk the shallows in the accepted manner along this section, but I consider the odds are with the fish rather than the fisherman here.

Some of the headwater streams of this watershed provide good fishing in crystal-clear water, but they are too far away and inaccessible to the layman.

The author fishing with a dry fly on the West Coast.

20 Makarora River

This northernmost tributary of Lake Wanaka emerges from an immense gorge and flows through an open, tussock-covered valley for some 18 km before entering the lake. The main highway follows the gravel bed of the river and provides ample access to exuberant water hosting good stocks of both rainbow and brown trout.

Three tributaries converge with the river from the western ranges and offer fishing results equal to the main stream. Because it has a large, mountainous catchment, the Makarora is subject to frequent flash floods that alter the channels in gravel sections of the riverbed. At times, these are of such ferocity that the trout themselves are swept back into the sanctuary of the lake. Once the river flow returns to normal, however, they soon restock the river, such are their numbers in the lake.

Although the lake and its immediate surroundings boast an exceptionally dry and stable climate, the upper fishable reaches of the river, only 18 km away, receive regular rainfall, so it is wise to seek information on climatic conditions before making a special fishing trip. Contact the Haast Pass Tourist Centre situated about half way up the Makarora Valley (Phone (03) 443 8372).

The river offers conditions and venues to suit all methods of trout fishing. Most standard flies and minnows work well here, but the ever-changing environmental conditions will dictate the best patterns to use at any particular time. Generally speaking, spin anglers should use Tinkers, Tobies or similar single-blade minnows coloured black, gold, or yellow in the main water flow and small mepps and veltics through the shoulders of shallow glides. I use a 9-ft (2.7-m) SAGE weight 5 rod on this river. It is a no-nonsense power-shafted and resilient-tipped unit, fitted with a weight-forward floating line. Sizes 8-10 dry fly patterns are recommended: Blue Dun, Grouse & Purple, Humpy and Grizzly Wulff in turbulent water conditions and smaller sized similar patterns in the quieter sections of flowing water. The fish sighted in calmish shallows should be tempted initially with size 16 Peacock or Pheasant Tail nymphs or Royal Coachman, Adams and Dad's Favourite dries. In other words, the dominating effervescent conditions of this clear-watered river call for well-hackled, high-floating dry flies.

The water conditions over most of the river are ideal for fishing with a weighted Stonefly, Hare & Copper, or Pheasant Tail nymph, and the use of sink-tip lines is frequently necessary to pull the presentation into the vortex beneath the stream of the main current.

Although it is possible to wade this river in many places, caution is essential. The vibrant rapids, sparkling ripples and gentle glides of water belie the fact that it drains the mountains into the lake and its clarity disguises its depth and strength.

(I) Davis Flat: 66 km from the Haast Hotel

As the road descends to Davis Flat, the Makarora River gorge will be seen on the left-hand side as a gash in the hills. This is the upper extremity of the fishable river. The highway leaves the enclosing forest to follow the perimeter of a small tussock-covered river-flat where there is a rest area and several vehicle accesses to the river.

The flat ends at the highway bridge 1 km downstream and provides good fishing in delightful river conditions where fast runs, shallow ripples and smooth glides are easily accessible over open terrain. The river offers perfect conditions for those adept at walking slowly upstream and sighting their fish before laying a line. You should blind cast slightly ahead and into the vortex beside the midstream current during the stalking manoeuvre to coax holding trout to take. Those feeding in the turbulence itself will reveal their presence by an unusual swirl or flash of colour, but the trout feeding along the edge of the river may be in water barely deep enough to cover their bodies. These fish move sedately so as not to disturb the tranquil water and the insects hatching sub-surface. Extreme vigilance is necessary to locate and catch such trout: they will be slate-gray in colour and will spook easily, even to a minute size 18 Pheasant Tail nymph if presented incorrectly.

The trout are not as prolific in this section of the river as they are lower down the valley, but it is a most delightful venue to introduce visiting anglers to Central Otago.

(2) Kiwi Flat: 1 km from (1)
This flat provides about 2 km of accessible water. It is possible to park on the roadside as you exit the bush and walk a few metres to the edge of a bank overlooking the turbulent water some 6 m below. I suggest, however, that you walk downstream to where the bank descends to the river's level, then walk back upstream and examine the expanse of water carefully for moving trout. The elevation and natural lighting characteristics of this location offer an advantage to the angler rather than the trout (for a change).

Kiwi Flat terminates with a bulldozed gravel storage dump through a gate at the base of a rise on the highway, and offers easy walking access to many hours of fishing water upstream.

(3) Camerons Flat: 2 km from (2)
This is a long tussock flat with a distinct, though gentle, downward slope over which the river flows on the western side, forming pools where it strikes the hills. The river flow is agitated, but less so than previously. The rocky nature of the bed slowly gives way to one of round stones, which, while unstable, do not inhibit the trout or the quality of the fishing to any extent. There is a pleasant rest area on the left side of the road before a creek which crosses the tussock-covered terrace towards the river, now several hundred metres away.

This venue offers 2 km of fishing on a gravel riverbed descending a gentle gradient where successive sections of rapids, runs and glides provide conditions to suit all fishing applications. Ideally, your companion should drive you to the lower end of the flat and allow you to spend a leisurely day quietly fishing upstream through very good trout water, then meet you upstream in the late afternoon. It is then only a short drive downstream to the motel complex of the Haast Pass Tourist Centre, a strategic base from which to fish the Makarora River and head of Lake Wanaka.

(4) Blue River: 1 km from Camerons Flat
Watch carefully for the road sign indicating a foot track through the bush towards the convergence of this small tributary coming from the western side of the valley. It is necessary to wade the Makarora River to fish this bush-shrouded river, an action which should only be undertaken by those reasonably fit.

The Blue River offers good fishing in a true mountain-stream environment. Clear, boisterous water engulfs a bed of rock and stones in bush surrounds and hosts large trout that will test the expertise of the most accomplished fly angler. This river may be considered a sight-fishing venue, in which skilled anglers will scramble upstream slowly and visually examine every inch of water for the grey shadow before actually casting a line.

The feeding actions of fish sighted will determine the correct fly to present. Generally speaking, a trout holding in the shallows on the edge of a pool will take a size 16 or 18 Sawyer's Pheasant Tail or Ostrich Herle-type nymph. The extremely active underwater feeders working a violent turbulence will snatch anything which resembles food; try a size 12 Hare & Copper or sizes 8/10 Green Stonefly nymph. The surface feeders in these tumultuous water conditions present exhilarating visions of colour, especially when they roll over and 'sound' after gulping a size 14 Royal Coachman, Grizzly Wulff or Twilight Beauty dry fly.

This water way and its parallel counterpart, the Young River, 5 km or so further down the valley, offer skilled and opportunist fly fishing anglers a chance to enjoy challenging and enthralling mountain-river fishing seldom accessible from the main roads of the South Island. I wish you well in these two unique catch and release fly fishing venues.

(5) Rainy Flat: 1.5 km from (4)
Conditions here are similar to those at Cameron Flat, but the river runs closer to the road in several places and the flow of water widens and shallows slightly as the contour of the valley flattens towards the head of the lake. Access is similar to the previous positions: it is merely a matter of parking the car and walking across the tussock-covered terrain.

It is necessary to modify the fishing approach in these calmer water conditions and concentrate on the head and tail of the wider and slower runs. The fish will be easier to spot, but likewise they can also see you, and hear your footsteps on the gravel, so stealth of approach becomes important.

Fly patterns will also gradually change with the environment and the heavily hackled and solid-bodied dries so essential in rough, turbulent water conditions should be replaced with sparsely tied varieties such as Adams, Kakahi Queen, Partridge/Yellow and Molefly. Naturally, the calmer and shallower portions of wide flows demand a smaller sized presentation, and the minute size 18 nymphs and long, fine leaders come into their own.

(6) Young River: 2.5 km from (5)

The convergence of this western tributary is indicated by a sign before a roadside fence gate which may be opened to provide walking access over the wide, open, tussock-covered plain to the Makarora River. A long walk and careful river crossing is necessary to reach the Young River, and anglers should ideally allow the best part of a day to explore and fully enjoy the attributes of this lovely waterway.

The Young Valley is of a more open nature than the Blue once the initial stand of bush is negotiated and it offers an enthralling venture to a hidden corner of the Southern Alps.

(7) Information Centre and Motel/Shop Complex: 3.8 km from (6)

Either of these sources will provide information regarding current environmental conditions and the whereabouts of professional air or water transport facilities. The motels offer an excellent operational base for the area. The sign for the Mount Albert Station, on the right-hand side over Whites Creek bridge just south of the shop, indicated access to the Makarora River, where there is literally miles of good fishing water in either direction offering unlimited scope for the application of any trout fishing method.

(8) Wharf Creek Rest Area: 10 km from (7)

The highway follows a gradual descent towards the lake and is separated from the river by a 600-m wide strip of farmland. Two storm creeks, Station and Flaxmill, are crossed en route to the head of the lake and offer walking access to the river on the other side of the

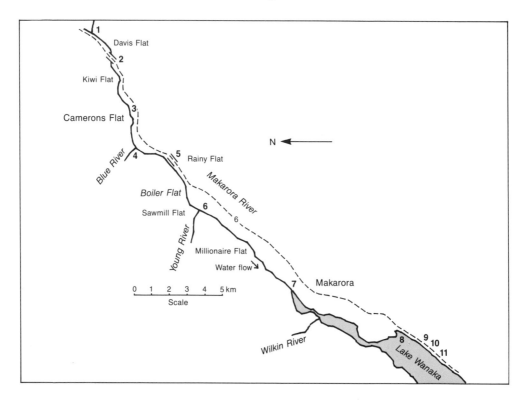

valley. Anglers wishing to fish this region may park their vehicle on the roadside and walk along the bank of one of these creeks to the main riverbed.

A few hundred metres before the rest area, the road passes between a high bluff and thick stand of willow trees. Careful observation will reveal a wide, grassy area large enough to hold several vehicles. On the other side of this parking area there is a narrow section of water. This position offers walking access to the shallows at the head of the lake. It is necessary to walk beneath the willow trees and through long grass above the water to find a position to cross the narrow but deep channel and gain access to the grassy flat. The effort necessary to achieve this crossing will be rewarded with extensive wadeable shallows with patches of rushes and floating weed — an outstanding venue for stalking cruising quinnat salmon, rainbow and brown trout.

These shallow flats, with their many small channels and inlets, extend the full width of the valley floor and terminate against the gravel bed of the in-flowing Makarora River. Not only do the shallows provide almost unlimited fishing, the river itself does likewise and any angler will be hard put to slow down in his rush to see everything. This venue is one of my personal favourites and I endeavour to visit it annually to spend a day or two drifting quietly in a boat through the shallows. It is pleasurable experience catching these large cruisers with an accurately placed dry or streamer fly (determined by the prevailing feeding pattern). The three species of fish frequenting this location, while not large by mountain trout standards, are extremely fit, and once hooked will 'scream the reel' until the backing pulls up tight and fight like the very devil until the very moment of release. Barbless hooks are the answer here as the weight of the fish will keep it imbedded until released.

Turn off the highway at the sign and drive into the first parking area. I suggest that you reconnoitre the area before deciding on your next move. There is a boat launching pad and beautifully sheltered parking area on the lakeshore and this camping area has basic ablution facilities and an honesty box in which to leave your fee (a mere pittance for the use of this real estate).

The lake is deep against the embankment and a channel frequently restricts access to the shallows at the head of the lake. The use of a boat from this position offers unlimited fishing possibilities: trolling along the road embankment, fly fishing through the shallows at the head of the lake and trolling around the deltas of the rivers descending the western ranges opposite.

Makarora River, near position (2).

This rest area is a photogenic introduction to the Southern Lakes District of Central Otago — a vastly different terrain and environment to that experienced on the western side of the South Island from Nelson to the southern descent of the Haast Pass.

(9) Boundary Creek: 4 km from (8)

This position will be seen from the narrow, elevated road skirting the lakeshore. It is a distinct isthmus, with stands of manuka trees on either side of the creek and an old hut. Drive down the steep access road, park near the gate and if the hut is occupied it would be courteous to acknowledge the privilege of unrestricted access to the occupier.

In calm conditions, the northern corner of the bay formed by the isthmus will hold several cruising fish, 'on the feed' but also very much on the alert. This position is well worth close inspection, though it must be approached in a stealthy manner. The mouth of the creek itself, on the other hand, does not require stealth so much as the ability to lay a long line into either side of the current entering the lake. It has always been a good position for the spinning technique and the use of sinking lines and streamer flies. Only the antics and appearance of the fish will determine if it is a rainbow, brown trout or quinnat salmon — the three species live in harmony in this lake.

(10) Sheepskin Creek: 2.1 km from (9)

A large, steep delta guides the rough waters of this small creek into the lake, where the gravel beach is accessible by following a walking track leaving the highway at a wide parking verge on the northern approach to a corner.

This is a good position to fish and, like (9), is suited to both the spinning and streamer fly methods right in the outflow of the creek itself. It will fish well whatever the conditions of the lake (except storm conditions).

(11) Camp Creek: 3.7 km from (10) and 44 km from Wanaka

This creek enters the lake over a small gravel delta, providing consistently good results with both spinning and streamer fly methods. The lake bed is slightly shallower than at positions (9) and (10) and there is a boat launching pad.

Turn inland off the highway on the southern side of the creek and follow the gravelled vehicle track under the bridge onto the large parking space beside the lake. This is a good picnic position, where one may fish the convergence of the stream and lake during the hours of darkness in perfect safety — and with dry feet.

I have found that rainbow trout predominate in this position, and that excellent results may be had when the lake is agitated by wind and the waters are slightly discoloured. In these conditions, small pieces of debris will swirl in the eddies caused by the creek on one side or the other (depending on wind and wave directions), well out but within casting range of the shore. The odd piece of driftwood that will attach itself to your fly or minnow on occasions is a small price to pay for the opportunity to catch one of the fish feeding on and beneath such floating rubbish.

When travelling south from Haast to Wanaka, this is the last accessible position from which to fish the lake. The road subsequently rises to cross a low saddle, revealing the waters of Lake Hawea.

Above: This small tributary of Nelson's Pelorus River typifies the easy access of the district's dry fly trout streams.

Below: Playing an active rainbow trout, taken while blind fishing a shallow ripple with a size 12 Humpy dry fly on the Pelorus River.

Above left: Rugged terrain, excessive rainfall and a primeval environment create a unique brown trout habitat in the Southern Alps.

Above right: The larger, quieter back-country rivers host brown trout that demand extreme stealth.

Below: The author with a brown trout taken on a Hare & Copper nymph on the Makarora River.

Above left: A mountain rainbow taken near Queenstown on a size 16 Royal Coachman dry fly.
Above right: A brown caught on a Stonefly nymph while feeding beside the driftwood in the background.

Above left: One of the Oreti River's small browns.
Above right: This brown from the Inangahua River 'lifted' nicely to John Garnett's English-tied dry fly.
Below left: Another face of the Inangahua River: open terrain and grey-coloured fish.
Below right: The Maruia River produces equally good results for nymph or dry fly fishing.

Above: Lake Clearwater in Central Canterbury is a popular venue, but offers limited opportunities for anglers lacking local knowledge.

Below: The upper reaches of the Ashburton River running 'fresh' following spring rains offer interesting exploratory dry fly fishing.

21 Lake Hawea

Boasting the best climate of all the Southern Lakes, Lake Hawea is well stocked with rainbow trout, brown trout and quinnat salmon. There are times when its whole surface is dimpled with rising fish. Under normal conditions, its waters are surrounded by a small gravel beach extending from the tussock-covered banks. In about 1960, the level of the lake was raised by 20 m and the fish population improved accordingly. Fishing is, however, affected by the fluctuating level of water as it is drawn off for power generation. There have been several occasions during the last 20 years when the lake has been extremely low, causing the fish to change their feeding habits and move into deeper water. The extensive sloping banks, generally covered by water, remain a quagmire for months restricting foot access by anglers, except where the converging creeks and rivers create gravel deltas. The stock of trout is undoubtedly governed by the food available and their numbers diminish during the low water periods that fortunately only occur during the winter months when there is the greatest demand for electricity. It may be assumed that the water level of the lake will rise during the warm spring rains and that trout will follow it to feed on the prolific insects which have infested the parched and cracked lake bed. There is exceptional fishing in these circumstances.

Hawea is not as commercialised as the other Southern Lakes, but is adequately serviced by motels, a motor camp, shops and a hotel at the lower end adjacent to the dam wall. The area has an atmosphere of peace and solitude: it is possible to spend a whole day fishing without sighting another angler.

Although the main highway following the western shore provides many access points, the ones I have described offer the best fishing. Much of the shore is inaccessible and a boat is necessary to reach some very productive and challenging positions. Much of my own angling here is done from a boat, trolling or using it as a floating platform from which to fly fish over the extensive underwater deltas around the perimeter.

(1) Motor Camp: 15 km from Wanaka

The dam wall is on the right-hand side of the road and it carries the road providing access to Hawea settlement. Drive straight ahead on Highway 6 towards Makarora. The boat-launching ramp and the entrance to the motor camp are directly ahead. This is a pleasant overnighting position which provides the usual ablution facilities.

The camp is situated on a small headland that gives easy access to the water's edge. Good fly fishing may be had during twilight hours, using size 16 Black Gnat, Twilight Beauty, or Dad's Favourite dry flies. In the event of a splashy rise, use wet flies of the same patterns in size 12 or 14. The spin angler may expect results at any time with 14-g (½-oz) Tinker or Toby-type minnows in gold or black, though the best spinning minnow in all the Southern Lakes would be the 50-mm (2-in) 'Z' spinner, constructed of copper with a red flash on one side.

The precincts of the camp are fished heavily by holiday-makers during the Christmas period and the catch rate diminishes during the height of summer. During quieter periods, October/December and March/April, however, large fish may be caught in the small bay formed by the road and the large outcrop of rock directly opposite the launching pad.

This is a delightful position, where the skilled fly angler should patiently watch the water's surface in the deepening twilight before casting a size 16 or 18 Twilight Beauty dry fly to the almost indistinguishable disturbance caused by a shrewd old brown savouring an entrée of hatching nymphs.

(2) Craigieburn Creek: 8.5 km from (1)

The road is elevated and separated from the lake en route to this position, where a small isthmus conveys a creek towards a convergence with the lake. There is a large lagoon on the opposite side of the highway.

Good spin fishing is available from the small gravel beach in daylight hours, during which time the lake's waters tend to be disturbed by wave action. In calm conditions during the day, however, and in the still of the twilight, the fly angler should expect to detect cruising fish, by sight or water movement.

Fly fishing results will be inconsistent from the road around the lake between positions (2) and (6). Whereas spin anglers can cover large expanses of water, fly anglers are restricted to the limit of their casting ability.

The fish frequenting the shoreline are cruisers and not domiciled in any one position. But many fly fishing anglers succumb to the challenge of locating and catching these fish, with questionable success.

(3) Section of Old Road: 5 km from (2)
This descends sloping terrain and parallels the shore for a short distance. It offers good spin fishing conditions, up to and including the next small, sheltered bay.

(4) Roadside Access: 5.5 km from (3)
Park either side of the road, from where a 4-m walk provides access to deep water, suited to the spinning technique only.

(5) Access Road: 1.9 km from (4)
This clearly defined vehicle access follows the sloping terrain to the water's edge. The water provides similar conditions to position (4). There is also a similar access road a further 1.2 km along the highway, from where it is possible to launch a small boat.

(6) Hunter Valley Junction: 2 km from (5)
From the Lookout (3.7 km from position (2)) you will notice that the lake is an 'L' shape, with the right arm extending into the mountains and becoming the Hunter River. This road offers access to several good fishing positions en route to the Hunter Valley Station. The inlet directly beneath the road was a separate lake before the level of Hawea was raised by 20 m, and since then it has been an outstanding fish holding area. In the distance, on the left-hand side of the road, there is a small patch of native bush on a cliff. This is where

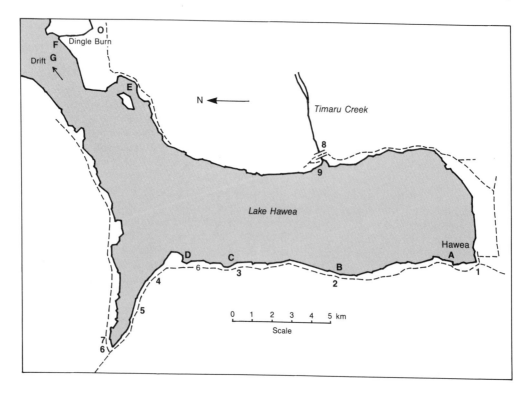

the Neck Creek passes under a bridge before flowing through pasture to enter the lake between the manuka trees in view on the shoreline.

The small inlet below the junction offers good results with the use of either the spinning or fly fishing techniques. Spin anglers would be wise to walk from the inlet towards the body of the lake on the left-hand arm, where it is possible to cast into deep water. Fly anglers should walk on the opposite side, that is, under the main highway, and concentrate on fishing close to the bank and between the clumps of grass.

There is generally a prolific evening rise here, especially as the wind eases. Do not rush frantically into the water the moment the wind stops, but wait until the fish start their noisy, splashy rise. Have your fly rod ready for action with a size 10 or 12 Twilight Beauty wet fly attached to a leader with a stout tippet. The rise will be short-lived, lasting about 30 minutes or so, but very active.

(7) Neck Creek Access: 2 km from (6)
Cross the small bridge, traverse the right-hand bend and drive off the road towards the lake just as the road curves left. Follow the sloping paddock down to the stand of manuka trees near the outlet of the creek. Do not drive to this position if the grass is wet or rain is imminent. The gentle waters of the creek itself, and the shallows of the lake next to it, will provide excellent fishing by either method.

(8) Timaru Creek: 30 Minutes drive from the Hawea Settlement
This delightful stream, renowned for its big fish, is situated on the eastern side of Lake Hawea. Pass though the settlement on the plateau above the lake, follow the road around the shore, and turn left into the signed road at a junction. The road is narrow and necessitates careful driving, especially where it descends a long and steep slope into Timaru Creek valley.

Park on the Hawea side of the bridge and follow the walking track upstream for about 2 km as it passes though gorge-type terrain and enters an open valley. The river from here upstream is perfect for dry fly fishing. Lightly hackled and delicate dry flies of the Molefly, Adams, Greenwell's Glory, Kakahi Queen and Dad's Favourite patterns in sizes 14 and 16 should reap a harvest for the skilled angler.

(9) Timaru Creek Convergence: 400 m from (8)
Pass over the Timaru Creek Bridge and, while climbing the hill, watch carefully for an access road leading to the lake on the left-hand side. This very steep road terminates in a picturesque picnic position beneath deciduous and evergreen trees right on the shore of the lake.

The river is difficult to cast into because of overhanging vegetation, but it offers good fishing for some distance before it enters the lake over a wide shingle fan. The channel through this fan alters occasionally, though it generally runs towards the head of the lake, more or less parallel to the shoreline, and shelves gradually into the depths.

It is possible to walk into the lake and follow the course of this channel. Fish feed voraciously in it: underwater during daylight and on the surface in the twilight. Good fishing may be had during the day when using spinning minnows, as described under position (1), or with the use of medium-density sinking fly lines and streamer flies of a yellow or brown hue. The evening rise should be fished with a floating line and Greenwell's Glory wet fly, in sizes 10/12, while the light is still strong, and a Twilight Beauty of the same size when twilight banishes the silhouette of the mountains.

The Timaru Creek road continues up the lake from the junction to this access. Do not drive along this road, it is private, extremely dangerous, and leads to the Dingle Station. The mouth of the Silver Burn and Dingle Burn are accessible by boat only.

Boat Fishing or Trolling
Lake Hawea offers excellent trolling conditions for rainbow trout, brown trout, and quinnat salmon. The style and patterns of trolling minnows vary among anglers, but I consider the most consistent to be the 50-mm (2-in) 'Z' spinner, constructed of copper, with a flash of red paint on one side. Anglers with harling equipment, as used in the North Island lakes, are assured of success when using a large streamer fly containing predominantly yellow or brown hues.

The following information is general as I am not able to give exact distances for travelling times on water. The correct speed for trolling the 'Z' spinner when using monofilament nylon is about walking pace, and once the minnow has been laid out the boat speed should be altered carefully until it 'works' correctly. This will be felt as a distinct pulse through the tip of the rod. There may be occasions when three separate rods will be employed from the same boat. This should be done by holding the two outside ones at right angles to the hull, and the inside one high and dead astern to avoid tangles.

The following schedule would be a typical day's fishing on this lake, concentrating on the positions shown and travelling at speed between each. The boat would be launched at the main slipway next to the dam wall. Please note that distances are approximate only.

(a) 1 km from the launching ramp

Follow the shoreline on the left to the headland and troll the entire perimeter, a distance of about 1 km.

(b) 6 km from (a)

This area is near the mouth of the Craigieburn Stream. Troll this vicinity close inshore on a course that will permit the bed of the lake to be seen vaguely beneath the surface.

(c) 7 km from (b)

Move on towards the headland on the left-hand side of the lake, where a small sheltered inlet will be seen. Troll close inshore, as at position (b).

(d) 3 km from (c)

This area is opposite position (3) and may be identified from the water by the road ascending a steep slope at right angles to the shoreline. About 10 km of trolling can be had here by following the shoreline into the inlet ahead and doing likewise along the other shore up to Kidds Bush — the only stand of trees on the lakeshore — opposite the starting point. This whole inlet provides good fishing. The lake gets more shallow towards its head, where it crosses the neck of the land that was high and dry before the raising of the lake in 1960, and then deepens as it passes over the previously land-locked lagoon. The bed of the inlet undulates as far as the mouth of Neck Creek, where it assumes a consistent shallow gradient.

When trolling the section between Neck Creek and Kidds Bush it is advisable to exercise care: there may still be one or two tree stumps standing beneath the surface, though all timber was supposed to have been felled and cleared prior to filling the lake.

(e) Silver Island: 9 km from (d)

This position is an island on the opposite side of the lake. Head for the stand of forest on the left-hand side of the barren precipitous cliffs, where it will be seen obscuring the flats over which the Silver Burn flows to enter the lake. Pass around the Hawea township side of the island and continue into the sheltered inlet, which provides very good trolling results.

(f) 5 km from (e)

Follow the right-hand side of the lake towards its head until the Dingle Burn Stream is seen flowing over a delta. Remain well off-shore as you approach and troll this position — the delta is shallow.

This spot produces good results but because of its exposed nature the water becomes very choppy when the wind blows down the lake. If, however, the boat's crew are experienced enough to handle rough, wet conditions, the trolling will be excellent, as the fish feed actively in disturbed bottom debris.

(g) 16 km from (f)

The last 3 or 4 km of the lake is a large, shallow, flat delta — resulting from the flooding of fertile river flats. The Hunter River flows into this, causing further silting during times of flooding. This position should be crossed carefully. There are rows of willow trees completely surrounded by water, and many more stumps rotting beneath the surface. It is possible to drive right into the mouth of the Hunter River and step ashore to fish.

Trolling anglers should practise conservation by fitting their minnows with single hooks and bending the barbs flat with a pair of pliers. This method of making 'barbless' hooks, now standard practice amongst fishermen (sea and freshwater) will hook and land just as many fish, but permits their humane release. Take what you need and return the others unharmed to ensure that the lake remains as productive as it is today.

Boat Access for Fly Fishing

This approach to dry fly fishing is simple. It is merely a matter of driving the boat slowly and quietly into the shallows, where the motor should be stopped and the boat propelled by paddles or oars until a fish is visually located feeding beneath the surface or rising from the depths to take surface-hatching insects. A Hare & Copper nymph (unweighted for surface feeders or weighed for deep feeders) is then cast in the fish's path and twitched as it approaches. Stealth and patience are essential during this operation.

The outstanding places for this type of fishing are in the shallow section of position (d), the grassed and shallow sections of position (e), and the shallows either side of the Hunter River mouth (g), where there are long, small peninsulas covered with tussock extending into the lake parallel to the river's course. The Hunter River itself is one of the prime trout fishing rivers of the South Island.

Neck Creek Access, positions (7) and (8), Lake Hawea.

22 Lake Wanaka and Hawea River

Lakes Wanaka and Hawea are similar in climate and established fish species. Lake Hawea, however, has a greater stock of fish, with easy access from the main highway that skirts its western shoreline. The barren terrain of rocks, snowgrass and tussock provides no relief from the scorching sun or wind and those unaccustomed to a life outdoors will suffer severe burns unless protective measures are taken. Lake Wanaka, on the other hand, is a larger expanse of water and much of its coastline encompasses small bays with occasional stands of deciduous trees that provide welcome shelter from the sun. Much of the shoreline is inaccessible from the roads, so a boat is necessary to reach the best fishing positions.

I would suggest that you focus on the rivers in the immediate vicinity of the two lakes. The geography of the area makes it possible to choose suitable water conditions and locate a position out of the wind, whichever way it is blowing.

(1) Roy's Bay: 3.9 km from Wanaka
Take the road to Glendhu Bay until a signpost marked 'boat ramp' is seen, pointing towards the lake on the right-hand side of the road. A 700-m gravel road leads to the shores of the lake. The clean, unobstructed water and beach make this position more suited to the trolling technique than fly fishing, especially during the bright daylight hours, when the afternoon breeze will invariably cause the lake to become choppy.

The late twilight hours of a warm midsummer's day will provide the patient and proficient fly angler with challenging fishing for brown trout as they cruise inshore to feed on hatching nymphs in the shallows. Stealth of approach and presentation is important. Sawyer's Pheasant Tail nymph, Dad's Favourite or Twilight Beauty dry flies in sizes 16/18 are good patterns to tempt these cruisers to take.

(2) Glendhu Bay Motor Camp: 8.4 km from (1)
This pleasant motor camp is situated right on the shore of the lake and protected from the prevailing winds by a stand of deciduous trees. The waters of the bay are shallow and have a beach of fine gravel, providing easy walking access to any position where a fish may be seen 'on the cruise'. The small rocky headland on the Wanaka side of the camp entrance provides the best fishing. This position may be reached by parking under a stand of trees on the lake side of the road at the base of a small rise exactly 1.4 km from the camp entrance. From here, it is merely a matter of stepping over a low fence and following the shore.

The shallow water should be fished in the same was as in (1).

(3) Glendhu Bluff Inlet: 4.3 km from (2)
Drive 800 m past the camp entrance and turn sharp right at the junction. Look for a sign marked 'Glendhu Bluff', indicating an extremely steep and narrow 2.2-km section of road. This necessitates slow and careful driving. As you follow the road around a left-hand bend on the brow of the bluff, two parking positions will be noticed on the right-hand side. Pull into the second one and examine the surface of the inlet some 30 m below the road. This picturesque bay is very deep, shrouded by trees and holds many fish, some of which will probably be feeding on the surface. There is a steep track to the water's edge, where there are ideal conditions for spinning, and although encroaching foliage makes the fly fishing technique difficult, it is not impossible for the experienced angler.

Spin anglers should use Tinker, Toby or 'Z' spinner minnows coloured gold, black or yellow and retrieve them deep and slowly. Fly anglers should use small, lightly-hackled dry fly patterns Blue Dun, Kakahi Queen or Adams when the trout are feeding quietly from the surface, and replace them with a size 18 sparsely tied nymph if spurned. In the event of a slightly 'splashy' rise, use a size 16 Greenwell's Glory wet fly.

An unusual but effective technique works well in this position. Cast a size 4 Hamill's Killer streamer fly attached to a floating line in the path of a cruising fish and give it a slight jerk as the trout enters visual range. This manoeuvre will often cause a trout to leap forward and take instinctively.

(4) Matukituki River: 6.7 km from (3)

Descend the gradient ahead, turn right at the junction, cross the bridge over the Matukituki River and park in the grassed picnic area near its downstream approach.

The river runs over a wide gravel bed for a considerable distance, providing easy access and unobstructed casting conditions, before converging with the lake. The large flow of swift water is well stocked with trout, especially in the lower reaches where the current loses its strength in merging with the lake.

The best time to fish this area is autumn (March through May), when the fish congregate at the mouth of the river ready for their spawning run up river. This is the period for the streamer fly enthusiast, try a Yellow Dorothy or Parson's Glory for action during the day and a Black Pete, Pukeko or large Twilight Beauty wet fly in the evening.

Fly anglers may also expect good sport with the presentation of a size 8 or 10 Humpy, Mole, Wulff or similar full-hackled dry fly if they cast slightly head of the fish's bow-wave. And, naturally, the spinning anglers will fit a single barbless hook to ease the effort of fish-release from their yellow coloured Dinki-di, Toby or Haulk minnow before 'having a ball' in this position. Conservation, even in lakes of this magnitude, must be foremost to ensure the continuity of our unique freshwater fishery.

(5) Lake Wanaka Outlet, Town Side: 7 km from Wanaka

Drive 600 m from the Wanaka Post Office towards Hawea, turn left into Andersons Road, continue for 1.4 km to a junction, and turn right. This leads to the junction with Lake Outlet Road (1.6 km), which terminates on the bar of the lake opposite position (8). Over the kilometre preceding this position there are several access tracks leading towards the concealed riverbank. Most of them terminate in good, small fishing venues.

The road ends on a sloping gravel beach, from where it is possible to walk well into the river and cover large expanses of calm and moving water with the spinning method.

In the absence of a rise to indicate insect-feeding trout, the fly angler should use a heavy rod, medium-density sinking lines and streamer fly patterns Mrs Simpson, Yellow Dorothy, and Hamill's Killer in size 4.

The evening rise should be fished with a size 8 or 10 Twilight Beauty, Greenwell's Glory, or Peveril o'Peak wet fly until complete darkness, when a size 12 Twilight Beauty dry fly would surpass all patterns as a reliable fish enticement.

(6) Clutha River, Town Side: 6 km from Wanaka

Follow the main highway from Wanaka to Lake Hawea for 5 km, turn left into Kingston Street, pass though the Albert Town settlement, and follow the road to a gate marked 'Fishermen's Access'. Pass through this gate and follow the dirt track to the tall poplar trees beside the riverbank.

Although this position is only 2 km or so from the lake, the outlet stream is now a large and swift river flowing over a deep bed. Conditions are ideally suited to the spinning or streamer fly methods at any time of the day, and although there are occasions when good results may be obtained with accepted fly fishing techniques, the fast current calls for an accomplished degree of skill to ensure its success.

(7) Lake Outlet, Opposite Town: 13 km from Wanaka

Follow the main highway from Wanaka to Lake Hawea, cross over the Albert Town bridge, travel 1.8 km and turn left into the Dublin Bay road. Continue for 2 km, turn left into an unmarked dirt road, and drive for 4.2 km to a manuka tree by the water, opposite position (5).

The water on this side of the outlet is deeper than position (5) and access is more restricted. However, the main volume of water flows towards the high bank just below the bar and presents perfect conditions for the deep-water retrieval of a streamer fly or spinning minnow against the current. This is the natural route for fish to follow when they are moving from the river into the lake.

(8) Luggate Bridge: 10.8 km from Wanaka

Take the main highway from Wanaka to Cromwell. While descending a steep gradient, you will see the Luggate Bridge on the left where it spans the Clutha River gorge. Turn left at the junction at the base of the hill, follow this road for 1.7 km, and turn left at another junction. Travel 400 m and, as you approach the bridge, turn right into a gravel road leading to a large picnic area beside the river.

This is a perfect position for the spin fishing. The water is extremely clear and deep, and the downstream bank is lined with trees. The spin angler should work downstream, cast the minnow across the river and retrieve it slowly against the current, as close to the overhanging bank as possible.

Although the fish rise nicely in this position, it is usually unsuitable for fly fishing, owing to the swiftness of the current, depth of water and inadequate access to the river bed. During low-water conditions however, fly anglers may walk upstream and fish a channel of water separating a small 'island' from the left-hand riverbank. The shallow, shelving riverbed on the midstream side of this 'island' is also worthy of close attention with a fly: the trout hold and feed amongst the tree roots waving in the current. At such times fly fishing anglers may also walk a long distance downstream through the trees and fish their way back to the carpark along the narrow strip of 'beach' and through the shallows at the base of the trees. This is a particularly good fishing venue. Walk slowly, have a small nymph or dry fly ready and cast to the fish you will see holding motionless hard against the bank. Their green backs, not movement, will reveal these feeding trout, unlike those which will be seen cruising slowly between rocks and weed on the shelf slowly descending into the green depths of the river.

(9) Anglers' Access Sign: 1.2 km from (8)

Pass over the bridge at position (8), drive along the straight road for 1.2 km and stop beside a gate on the left-hand side of the road. Walk through the gate to the edge of the terrace, from where there is a panoramic view of the river. It is only a short walk through scattered manuka to reach the stony riverbed, where the water is deep, clear, and boisterous.

This is a good fly fishing position and such anglers should experience success when using large, high-floating dries during the daylight hours and sizes 10/12 wet flies as twilight settles and the trout indulge in their splashy, vociferous feeding antics until complete darkness stills the action.

(10) Anglers' Access Sign (Horseshoe Bend): 800 m from (9)

Continue along the road towards Lake Hawea, ascend the hill, pass through the boundary gate on the left-hand side of the highway and follow the dirt track towards the river. The river at this venue is large, deep, extremely clear, and holds a good stock of quality trout that rise to the dry fly during most of the day under normal atmospheric and water conditions.

The fish are fit because of the environment they inhabit. They have plenty of room to run and will increase the weight on the line with their habit of lying across the current. You should use robust equipment here, the fish must be played hard, with a firm, steady and positive pressure on the rod. Give them an inch and they'll 'throw the hook' or smash the leader. These are tough fish.

The water is too deep for consistent results to be obtained with a nymph and the eddies in the current inhibit the use of a streamer fly. It is a position ideally suited to the dry or wet fly (depending on the rise) and any of the well-hackled standard flies prove to be effective and a size 8 or 10 Blue Dun, Grizzly Wulff, Kakahi Queen, (Palmer-hackled) Molefly or Humpy will often lift a fish even in the absence of a rise.

During a wet rise, I would use a Twilight Beauty, Greenwell's Glory, Dad's Favourite, or Peveril o'Peak, size 12 or 14. In the absence of any visible fish movement during the twilight hour, I would use the same patterns in size 8 with a full sinking line to make them 'swirl' through the underwater eddies and emulate a natural insect caught in the holocaust.

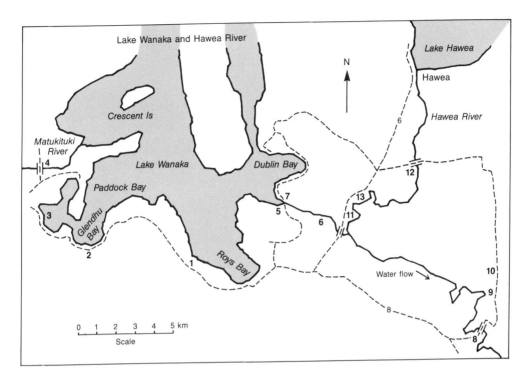

Lake Wanaka and Hawea River

(11) Hawea River: 4.2 km from Wanaka

Drive along the main highway from Wanaka to Lake Hawea, turn hard right after crossing the Albert Town Bridge and follow one of the vehicle tracks to the convergence of the two rivers. Lake Hawea is used as a reservoir for power generation and so it is subject to flow variations during the year. The flow is reasonably constant during the summer months, however, as the gates are generally closed to fill the dam's storage capacity for winter demands.

Over the years, the fish have adapted to a low flow in summer and the opposite in winter, and the river offers some of the most delightful fishing in the Wanaka District. Access to the water's edge is easy from the maze of dirt tracks that criss-cross the rocky ground. The river runs over a gently contoured bed of stones as it follows a curve for about 1 km upstream from this position before it swings sharply to the right and then left to form a huge holding pool. Vehicle access tracks follow the river upstream for approximately 2 km and then double back to the main highway.

The whole area is now a recreational reserve and the right of access is thereby assured for all time — the few restrictions regarding its use are listed on a roadside bulletin board.

(12) Hawea River: 4.3 km from (10)

Continue along the highway towards Lake Hawea and turn right at the intersection into the Hawea Flat Road. Drive a further kilometre and park next to the fence leading to the approach to the Hawea River bridge. The upstream section of this river provides particularly good fishing in broken water conditions suited ideally for the application of large, buoyant dry flies.

Anglers fishing this section must remain on the Queen's Chain access strip on either side of the water flow after gaining access to it from the bridge approach itself. Do not go onto other property without obtaining prior permission.

(13) Horseshoe Bend, Hawea River: between (11) and (12)

This position is approximately halfway between the Albert Town Bridge and the intersection preceding position (12). It is located from the main highway by a signpost overlooking the river flowing through a ravine about 200 m below the highway plateau. Access involves scrambling and sliding down a steep but negotiable bank. The clear water follows a tortuous semi-circle course over rocks and stones creating rapids, pools and surging eddies. These conditions suit the skilled dry fly angler — they are too rough for the spinning method.

There is considerable foliage growing on the banks, and access and casting positions are rough, tough and limited to water that is particularly well stocked with wild fish. This is a venue that will appeal to, challenge and be conquered by only the physically able and adventurous outdoorsman with a high standard of fly fishing expertise.

Other Clutha River Waters

The Clutha River downstream from position (8) at the Luggate Bridge is a waterway of major proportions. It is extremely clear, well stocked with trout and provides good fishing for experienced spin or fly anglers.

North of Wanaka, drive towards Cromwell. Anglers' Access No. 5 (indicated by a square blue panel with the figure of a fish and the numeral 5 on it) is 7.8 km from the intersection. Turn left off the highway and pass over the Luggate Bridge spanning the Clutha at position (8), then turn right and follow the Tarras Road. Drive to the top of the hill, park and examine the river below as it emerges from under the bridge and follows a right-hand arc. Note the gravel road ahead which leads down the slope to end at the water's edge. Access to this road is a few metres ahead on the right beside a gate just where the highway curves to the left.

The river below is unsurpassed throughout the Clutha watershed and is suited to all fishing methods. On the opposite side, the river follows a foliage-covered bank from the trees near the bridge to beyond the bend downstream. Note how clear and shallow the water flow is around the hill. It gets more shallow as it ripples over stones to depths of some 2 m off the bank and is an excellent fish-holding water. Anglers should return to the bridge access described under position (8) Chapter 22 and fish their way downstream. A whole day could be spent fishing this position alone.

Fly anglers should examine the terrain below, follow the steep access road to the river, walk downstream (out of sight of the water) and spend a day fishing back. This venue is for the determined fly angler only, calling for positive identification of holding water. Few fish will be sighted because of the broken flow, and larger dry flies and nymphs than are usually used are necessary to handle the turbulent conditions. Personally, I would use a SAGE 4-piece 9-ft (2.7 m) weight 5 graphite rod, a Cortland weight-forward floating line, 3X leaders and dry-fly patterns Humpy Green, Grizzly Wulff, Royal Coachman or Palmer-hackled Molefly in size 8. Failing a take, I would switch to weighted size 8 Green Stonefly, Pheasant Tail or size 10 Hare & Copper nymphs.

Although fishing upstream is the accepted method of fishing this type of venue, less experienced anglers could expect to catch fish by laying a long line across and down and retrieving in the streamer fly method. The water is agitated enough for feeding fish to take a dragged submerged dry fly.

Return to the Wanaka-Cromwell highway. The following accesses are taken from the Luggate Hotel, a short distance along the road from the intersection. There are six Anglers' Access Signs, Nos. 10 to 15, downstream from the hotel. They are all blue and display a fish alongside the number. (Note that the format of these signs may change with the pending changes to fish management.) All signs are on the left side, on or beside gates, and indicate well-defined tracks leading over the barren plains to the river's ravine some 700-1000 m away. These tracks are rough so drive slowly. Access signs cover a distance of 11 km.

The water flow at all these positions is strong, and fish will frequent the very edges of the current, feeding on both aquatic larvae in the shallows and wind-blown terrestrial insects beside the banks. You should examine the small, swirling surface disturbances in the current for the slightest splash or flash of colour which will indicate a trout sub-surface feeding — such fish are dry fly enthusiasts.

Lake Dunstan: Luggate, through Cromwell to Clyde

At the time of writing, this new lake had just been filled to its capacity but had already proved itself to be a trout fishery of some substance. The lake was stocked with hatchery-bred trout to supplement the wild fish that were well established in the Clutha and Kawarau Rivers and their tributaries. The stocking programme has been an outstanding success and several large fish have been caught to date.

The highway running beside the lake on both sides from Luggate to Cromwell has many accesses to constructed and modified picnic and fishing areas, which have been planted with trees and equipped with basic amenities. The upper reaches of the lake merge through trees and grass on a shallow plateau to providing prime fly fishing venues. However, I feel that the lake requires a year or two to consolidate before it warrants my detailed description of fishing and techniques — 'work' that I anticipate with pleasure. For the moment, I must congratulate the appropriate authorities for their thoughtful endeavours to provide an outstanding fishery and 'playground' for the sportsmen of this country.

The latest South Island trout water, Lake Dunstan in Central Otago.

23 Queenstown/ Lake Wakatipu

The premier tourist resort of the South Island, Queenstown is renowned for spectacular scenery, skiing, water sports, socializing and trekking. Perhaps what is not as well known is the good quality of its trout fishing. Lake Wakatipu, the third largest lake in New Zealand, is well stocked with both species of trout and quinnat salmon. It provides restricted shore fishing venues, however, owing to its barren terrain and lack of shallow inlets containing basic trout habitat. Trolling behind a runabout with spinning equipment is extensively practised on this lake and those with a trailer-boat in tow may approach the area with optimism; there are good camping facilities at Queenstown itself as well as at either extremity, Glenorchy or Kingston. Several bays around the perimeter of the lake also offer pleasant camping positions and good opportunities for fly anglers. In January and February cruising fish rise readily to the dry fly in their quest for the cicadas and beetles that infest the lake at this time of the year.

Of the several other smaller lakes in the district, four are accessible by vehicle (Hayes, Moke, Kirkpatrick and Diamond) and offer good fishing in pleasant surroundings to ample stocks of trout. Of the six major rivers entering the lake, only the Dart and Rees are easily accessible by vehicle and the Greenstone and Von are reached following a tiresome drive over rough gravel roads. The Caples River is a long walk from the road end, and air or water transport is necessary to reach the Lochy. The latter four rivers may be classed as excellent fisheries but the services of a professional guide should be obtained to ensure access to suitable water and thus guarantee success.

The Rees and Dart Rivers are both snow-fed and flow through wide valley floors which offer reasonably easy foot access to water tinged blue with glacial dust. Both rivers are

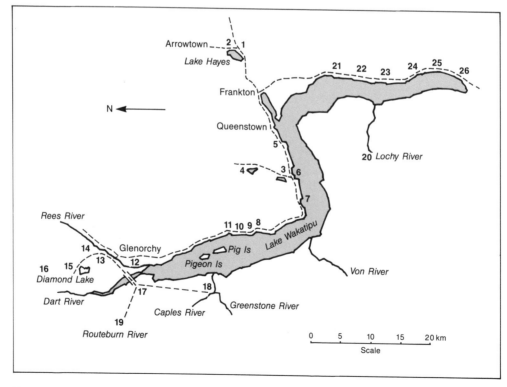

extremely photogenic as they meander over beds of white gravel between tussock-covered banks graced with isolated stands of trees. A backdrop of high mountain peaks completes the scene and it is only the sheer volume of water in these rivers that restricts them to mediocre fisheries.

There are times (too infrequent) when the flow is low enough to cause the waters to almost clear, and reduces their channels to a manageable fishing width. In such instances, it is an absolute pleasure to walk the river during the calm of early morning and visually locate trout — silhouetted by sunlight against the white gravel bed. Catching them is something of an anti-climax: generally, a single cast of a size 16 Hare & Copper nymph or Adams dry fly will do the trick.

Lake Hayes

This lake is approximately 3 km long by 2 km wide, flanked by the main highway at one end and along one side by the access road to Arrowtown, which offers access to the shore. A separate access leaves this road and terminates at the head of the lake, where its waters are shrouded by weeping willow trees. The far side of the lake has no beach, the waters lap the toe of a hill.

This is a unique waterway in that it has always held vast numbers of brown trout. At the turn of the century, these were netted, smoked and sold commercially, and in those days fish in double figure weights were common. Even now, although they are of a more modest weight, the trout must be considered large when compared with the average trout fishery in the South Island.

The trout rise prolifically here and it is quite usual to view the lake from the elevation of the road and notice the whole surface expanse ruffled by rising and jumping fish.

(1) Lake Hayes Picnic Area: 15.7 km from Queenstown

Follow the main highway past the lower end of the lake, take the first turn to the left, marked 'Arrowtown', and turn sharp left 900 m past the junction into an access road leading beneath overhanging trees. The shore of the lake consists of fine gravel and the shallow water is overhung by willows. It is possible to walk stealthily under these to locate feeding or cruising trout within casting range. Although the catch rate will not be large when fishing from the shore, the fishing is challenging and in the most pleasant surroundings imaginable.

It is possible to launch a small boat from this position and use it as a platform from which to reach rising fish or to indulge in the harling technique while the craft is being propelled by oars or paddles. The use of power-driven boats is prohibited at all times, to conserve the waters for swimming, sailing and fishing.

(2) Anglers' Access: 900 m from (1)

Continue along the highway towards Arrowtown and, as you approach the end of the lake, watch carefully for an access road going over the bank on the left-hand side. It is not signposted, but can be located by a wide gravel verge opposite a farm building on the right-hand side. Drive down this steep road (in dry weather only), pass through the gate at the head of the lake, and follow the wheel tracks over the grass to the small stream entering the lake, about 600 m from the highway.

The lake at this position is shallow and overhung with willow trees. A small creek enters it over a small beach that extends into the depths as a shallow delta and provides a walking platform to reach any trout visibly cruising or rising near the convergence of the stream. The full width of the lake here offers excellent fly fishing for anglers wearing chest waders and so are able to reach out with their small dry flies or minute nymphs to a fin or nose rippling the water. Fly patterns are of less importance at this venue than the ability to wade, and make minimal disturbance in the water. These trout aren't silly...

The small bays towards the hill opposite the road also hold cruising fish. They also contain a few stumps and standing trees, which, while restricting casting, provide ideal cover (and dampen your water movement) when stalking fish. There are extensive clumps of flax growing in the water at the base of the hill and the proficient angler may sight his quarry by walking precariously and slowly along the bank above the lake. Although there are several positions in which it is possible to enter the water by walking on a shallow shelf, most of the fishing in this particular section necessitates long-distance casting over the flax and the high bank behind the angler; you will need to apply the 'tower' casting technique. Quite frequently trout can be seen cruising very close to the steep shore.

(3) Lakes Moke and Kirkpatrick turn off: 6.5 km from Queenstown

Follow the road to Glenorchy for 6.5 km, until you reach the Moke Lake signpost. Drive along this steep and tortuous road for 4 km as it bisects a narrow valley in mountainous terrain. Extreme driving care is necessary here. After passing through gates positioned at each end of the lake, park in the paddock on the left, from where it is only a few metres to the water's edge.

En route to Moke is Lake Kirkpatrick. It is a shallow lake about 300 m long by 200 m wide and has a shoreline of grass and rushes, providing unobstructed access and fishing conditions. By walking around the edge, the angler may view the plentiful stock of brown trout cruising and feeding in the depths.

You should endeavour to fish here in the morning before the breeze starts about noon or perhaps in evening as twilight stills the air.

This waterway should be treated as a catch and release venue.

(4) Moke Lake: 3.8 km from (3)

Continue along the same road, passing through a gate marked 'Ben Lomond Station', until you reach the lakeshore. Drive to the far end, where a small outlet stream flows between stunted scrub and rough grass. There are basic picnic facilities here.

This lake is much larger than Kirkpatrick. It is approximately 1.3 km by 1 km, with an undulating shoreline of tussock and a narrow gravel beach in several places. There is walking access around the perimeter, though in some positions the terrain is steep and difficult to negotiate. The lake is very deep and the brown trout are only visible when they cruise or rise to feed.

The lack of shallow beaches restricts fishing, but there are two good positions at the end of each arm of the lake. One of these is visible from the road, where the small outlet stream from Lake Kirkpatrick flows through rushes, while the other is out of sight behind the bisecting peninsular. The use of a small dinghy or inflatable boat would be advantageous in this waterway in which the rings of the rise may be seen over the whole surface during normal atmospheric and water conditions.

Effective dry fly patterns in both of these lakes are sizes 12/14 Greenwell's Glory, Dad's

Moke Lake, position (4),
Queenstown.

Favourite, Humpy and Twilight Beauty. If these patterns are spurned during a quiet dry rise, replace them with a size 18 Sawyer's Pheasant Tail or Peacock Herle nymph. When the waters of Lake Moke are disturbed by wind action, I would recommend the use of the streamer technique using a slow sinking line and a Parson's Glory, Yellow Dorothy, or Mrs Simpson streamer fly.

Lake Dispute: 10 km approx. from Junction at (3)

Return to and follow the Glenorchy Road for about 10 km and watch carefully for a roadsign reading Lake Dispute. This points to a track leading from the road on the right-hand side. A walk of about 20 minutes, steep at the start but gentler as it progresses, leads you along an attractive valley to the lake.

A good head of both rainbow and brown trout are often seen cruising here within casting range, particularly in January and February. These fish, of above average size, dominate the lake. Brook trout of much smaller sizes, released some six years ago, also populate this water. Use the same fishing techniques here as I have suggested for Moke and Kirkpatrick.

Diamond Lake

The 50 km plus drive to this lake crosses undulating country from Queenstown to Glenorchy — the gravel road is extremely rough and dusty. Anglers should consider residing overnight at Glenorchy in the camping ground, or hotel, some 48.9 km from Queenstown to give the waters of this location, including Diamond Lake and its outlet stream, the attention they deserve. En route there are many access positions to Lake Wakatipu, some of which are described below, but fishing any such lake water is a haphazard venture at the best of times and the chances of catching fish are slim.

(5) Sunshine Bay: 3.2 km from Queenstown

This pleasant, sheltered bay may be seen on the left-hand side before you reach the access road. It has picnicking facilities right against the water's edge.

(6) Wilson Bay: 5.7 km from (5)

The road passes through a small valley that conceals the lake from view en route to this position, and the waters of Wilson Bay may be seen as the road descends a long, steep gradient. An access road leads to shaded picnicking facilities next to the beach.

(7) Twelve-mile Creek: 2.1 km from (6)

As the road climbs, this bay becomes visible to the left. Watch carefully for the access track leading from the highway; this leads to a pleasant bay with a creek flowing over a fine shingle fan into the lake at the base of a headland. There is a large rest area next to the water's edge.

(8) Meiklejohns Bay: 16.2 km from (7)

The road descends from its elevated position to follow the shoreline. There are several stands of trees along this section, which give shelter from the sun but do little to enhance the barren coast. A pleasant picnic position may be found 1.7 km further along the road, just before a small creek flowing into a lake.

(9) Geordies Creek: 3.5 km from (8)

Just after crossing the bridge over this small stream, pull into the right-hand side of the road, park and walk left over sloping terrain for about 30 m to its convergence with the lake. Here there is a small gravel beach. This waters of this pleasant position are worthy of inspection for cruising trout when atmospheric conditions are perfect, although the afternoon hours are often spoilt with a strong wind.

(10) Access Road: 1.6 km from (9)

Watch carefully for this small road on the left. It leads to a position where the shoreline assumes the character of several small headlands, approximately 3 m above the level of the lake. These contain small inlets, where the texture of the beach is more of a sandy nature than gravel, unlike the previous positions.

(11) Parking Area: 2.3 km from (10)

The road follows the shore closely for the next few kilometres. Being windswept, the shore is quite unsuitable for fishing, except at times of complete calm, when the convergences of several small streams entering the lake may be inspected for fish enticed close inshore to feed. A further 2.3 km along there is a small bay with a rest area on the left side.

(12) Glenorchy: 48 km from Queenstown

Turn right at the intersection on the other side of this settlement, which has a camping ground, hotel and store.

(13) Rees River: 5.6 km from (12)

Having driven 4.7 km, turn left into the road signposted 'Paradise'. Cross the bridge spanning the Rees River, on the other side of which there is a vehicle access leading to the riverbed. This is a large river of clear water, occasionally tinged blue with glacial dust and flowing over a wide bed of fine gravel which is subject to frequent disruption during floods. There is easy walking access to good water stocked with trout during normal conditions.

There is also good access to the river by turning right at the junction mentioned above and following the Rees Valley Road for approximately 6.5 km. Park beside a gate with a sign restricting further progress to 4-wheel drive vehicles, and even then only when Muddy Creek is negotiable. From this point on, walking access provides anglers with about 10 km of fishing in one of the most beautiful and picturesque valleys in the southern region. Fish, both rainbow and brown, are big (5-10 lb (2.2-4.5 kg)) but they are few and far between, and melting snow from Mt Earnslaw frequently colours the water making sighting the big trout very difficult.

(14) Anglers' Access Sign, Diamond Creek: 1.3 km from (13)

Follow the signs towards 'Paradise' at a junction after driving 300 m from the Rees River bridge, and do the same at the next junction. Seven hundred metres further on the Dart River valley will be quite apparent. An Anglers' Access sign is attached to a boundary fence gate on the left-hand side. Follow the tracks across the grass to the river, which is visible 100 m or so away.

This small stream, from its source at Diamond Lake to its outlet, provides some 5 km of delightful fishing. The water is very clear, flows over fine gravel, and is contained by banks on which tussock grass grows profusely and generally overhangs the edge of the stream. There are good casting conditions and easy access along the banks of this stream that holds a good head of brown trout, some in the 2.7-3.6 kg (6-8 lb) class. Quinnat salmon from Lake Wakatipu spawn in this stream, and to protect them the fishing season closes on 31 March.

Access to the river may also be gained by taking the left-hand turn, signposted 'Kinloch 8 km', at the junction passed en route to position (14). After 800 m, the road passes over a small bridge spanning the stream, from where there is easy access to fish it upstream towards the lake, or for a short distance downstream, where it flows through a stand of flax and then onto the open gravel bed of the main river with which it converges.

(15) Access Road, Diamond Lake: 4.5 km from (14)

Follow the access track on the left after the main road has followed a curve to the right. Be careful — this crosses ground which becomes soft and impassable when wet. The road will take you to the lower section of the lake where there is good fishing in shallow and weedy water conditions.

(16) Rest Area Access: 2.7 km from (15)

Continue along the road and enter a small stand of trees where there is a sign for Mossvale Falls. Opposite this sign, a vehicle track leads to a picnic position with ample parking space. There is easy walking access to the head of the lake, where shallow water with stands of grass and waterweed provide good fly fishing to a good stock of fish. The River Jordan enters the lake some 600 m further upstream, and I would advise fly anglers to make their way past this convergence and continue fishing the shallows of the lake shore.

Above: The author's legacy and heritage — his son fishing a hidden corner of the Southern Alps, where the large brown trout and their surroundings are without parallel in New Zealand.
Below: In a tributary of Southland's Aparima River the aura of anticipation equals the 'thrill of the strike'.

Above left: The Tekapo River is an ideal rainbow and brown trout water, and the quality of the fishing is equal to the picturesque terrain.

Above right: A renowned fishery, the Ahuriri River deserves its reputation, although the terrain and constant wind are better suited to the experienced outdoorsman.

Below: Emerging from virgin forest, the Wangapeka River is an excellent brown trout fishery, and it supplements the Motueka River with quality stock each season.

Above left: Lake McGregor, in the Mackenzie Country, is well stocked with large trout.
Above right: Fly anglers adept at stalking will find enthralling sport at the Mavora Lakes, Southland.
Below left: This small tributary of the Motueka River will astound anglers with the size of its brown trout.
Below right: Few rivers in the South Island exude the same outdoor appeal as the Eglinton.

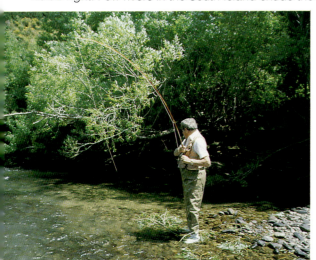

Below: The sheer might and beauty of the Waiau River, Southland.

Above: Central Otago's Hawea River offers good fishing at any of its accessible venues.
Left: Cold, savage and pristine is an apt description of the Routeburn River.
Below: New Zealand's 'last frontier' — the Okuru River — where only the largest and fittest trout survive.

Below: This springtime view of Lake Wakatipu's Dart River will surely entice any trout angler to 'lay a line'.

Calm lake conditions favour the use of small, lightly hackled dry flies such as Adams, Greenwell's Glory or Blue Dun, which will entice quietly cruising trout to take. Agitated conditions call for sizes 10/12 Grizzly Wulff, Humpy or (Palmer-hackled) Moles to bounce buoyantly over the ripples at which stage trout throw caution to the wind and snatch at anything that resembles food — unless the barometer is falling.

This location has a strange aura which defies my description yet coerces me to fish there whenever possible. Yet better results await in the Mataura, Oreti, Aparima Rivers or Lake Hayes, which are also closer and more accessible from Queenstown.

(17) Dart River: 8 km approx. from (14)

Return to the junction preceding (14) and follow the directions to Kinloch. The Dart is a larger river than the Rees, is generally more discoloured (blue/grey) and holds a limited stock of fish. It offers walking access from the bridge approach on one side or the other depending on prevailing water channels.

(18) Greenstone and Caples Rivers

I am unable to provide the exact distance from the Dart Bridge to the carpark offering access to the Greenstone River having only traversed it twice by vehicle; my visits to the Greenstone are generally by helicopter. Nevertheless, it is a long and tortuous drive along the lake shore and anyone visiting the location to fish should contemplate staying nearby. An obvious walking track from the carpark provides access to the convergence of the Greenstone River and Lake Wakatipu, an excellent trout fishing venue. The other signposted track follows the Greenstone River upstream and offers access to the Caples River.

Both rivers carry a large volume of clear water in mountainous-type riverbeds of solid rock beneath bush-enclosed terrain. They are outstanding trout waterways which should be visited and fished by experienced anglers versed in the belief that such trout stock is in fragile balance and only firm conservation measures will ensure their survival.

It is the presence of genuine sportsmen, with years of practical back-country experience, demonstrating and verbally expounding the virtues of this approach to our fishing that will save these high-country trophy fish from depletion. It is gratifying to notice a growing trend throughout the South Island by the Fish and Game Councils to educate the unaware of the importance of this matter through notices at the Greenstone River carpark, the bridge over the Routeburn River, the Fairlight, Makarora, Oreti, Ahuriri and many other waterways of note.

(19) Routeburn River: 8 km from the Dart River junction

The lower section of this river offers interesting and challenging fishing to a small head of large fish from one of the most pleasant camping positions imaginable. The upper reaches are virtually inaccessible, where rough, tough terrain with similar water holds a limited number of huge trout awaiting your presence when accompanied by an experience guide — the only way to reach the location.

Follow the directions to the Routeburn Track on the sign at the junction near the Dart River bridge. As the access road enters bush, turn right onto a rough access road located by a small sign reading 'Lake Sylvan'. This extremely rough vehicle track is 1 km long and terminates in an open stand of bush adjacent to a swing bridge spanning the Routeburn River. There are basic amenities and ample room to camp or park overnight.

The river emerges from a small gorge to pass beneath the bridge and flow out of sight downstream as a wide, smooth, deep pool banked by native bush on one side and lawn-type grassed banks on the other — a pleasant section of river easily fished with a fly.

The upstream section may be walked, and inspected from the high bank covered with standing bush. Sighted trout may be fished to after gaining the riverbed (with a struggle).

The downstream section, on the other hand, bisects vegetation-covered alluvium and represents a typical river flowing through rapids, pools and glides. I suggest that anglers walk downstream to the convergence of the Routeburn and Dart Rivers and spend the day fishing back to the carpark.

Treat the river as you would any other clear-watered stream by blind fishing with a size 10 Humpy, Grizzly, Blue Dun or other well-hackled dry to lift the fish while inspecting the water ahead for visible fish or their movement. The water should be examined thoroughly as the trout will cruise from the shallows a few inches deep to the depths of a pool and up to the surface turbulence of a rapid.

The road ends 6 km further on beside the shelter building at the start of the Routeburn Track where there is another swing bridge spanning a rough section of gorge. There will be several large trout holding in deep water within sight of the bridge.

(20) The Von River and the Lochy River

Both of these rivers flow into the lake on the opposite side to the highway and provide excellent rainbow trout fishing. They are similar in that they rise in hanging valleys and pass through reasonably barren terrain in beds of gravel before entering rocky gorges engulfed in native forest. As they reach the lowlands, they cross river-flats of scrub-covered alluvium which offers good foot access to the water's edge.

Whereas the Von is accessible by road (a long journey from Queenstown, through Five Rivers Junction, Mossburn and then via the Mavora Lakes Valley), the Lochy must be reached by air or boat. I refrain from detailing the accesses and fishing available in these two rivers — they are the domain of professionals who will ensure ease of access and success of fishing for anglers. Most professionals appreciate the fragile nature of the fish stock, and are alert to any misdemeanours committed by opportunist anglers. They guard zealously both the resource and the environment.

Kingston Arm, Lake Wakatipu

This arm of the lake is followed by Highway 6 (the main Queenstown-Invercargill route) and there are several fishing positions worth visiting if time permits while passing through. They offer good spinning conditions during daylight hours when the lake is choppy, as well as good fly fishing in the early morning and twilight when the air is still and the waters calm.

When fishing the calm waters with a fly, I suggest sizes 14/16 Blue Dun, Kakahi Queen, Dad's Favourite and Adams patterns — larger-bodied flies would alert the fish cruising in

such shallow, clear and calm conditions. The wet, splashy rise would naturally call for a size 12 or 14 Greenwell's Glory or Twilight Beauty wet fly.

Spinning anglers may use any pattern to enable long-distance deep-water retrieval, but fish cruising the shallows would probably prefer a small Mepps or Veltic blade-type minnows coloured black or maroon.

(21) Headland Access: 14 km from Frankton Junction

This rocky peninsula is quite obvious from the highway when driving towards Kingston and it is merely a matter of parking on the side of the road and walking 200-300 m down a gently descending grass-covered incline to reach the low bluffs encircling small, sheltered sandy beaches. Observation from the elevated bluffs will locate any fish cruising through the small inlets.

(22) Boat Launching Pad: 7.8 km from (21)

You will have to be attentive when negotiating this gravel track through vegetation. It ends at a launching ramp on the lake shore. There is a large parking area surrounded by scrub about halfway down the incline and I would suggest inspection of the site from the highway before driving down.

(23) Staircase Creek: 6 km from (22)

This small creek flowing over a gravel delta will be seen from the elevated highway as it negotiates the preceding Staircase Bluffs. It is a delightful position with a tree-shaded gravel parking space on the roadside this side of the bridge, and a large open parking area on the other side. It is possible to drive off the highway and park on the gravel beach itself. The inflowing current of the creek is always worthy of inspection, and warrants a few blind casts with a spinning minnow during the day and close attention with a fly in the evening as twilight fades to oblivion. The water around the delta fishes well during agitated water conditions, especially if the creek is running high and dirty following heavy rain.

(24) Rest Area: 4.7 km from (23)

This peninsula, extensively covered with exotic trees fringed with native foliage, offers a strategic and delightful picnicking or camping position. It is a large area with basic amenities offering perfect shelter from wind and sun and a gravel beach which descends gradually to the depths well off-shore. The clarity of the water allows unrestricted vision into the depths for an incredible distance and the light-coloured lake bed silhouettes any cruising trout or salmon.

(25) Rest Area: 1.5 km from (24)

This signposted rest area is a smaller version of the previous one and boasts similar conditions.

(26) Rest Area: 3.1 km from (25)

The final rest area on the Kingston Arm offers an opportunity to view the head of the lake before turning right at the junction 1 km ahead to drive into the Kingston settlement. This position does not provide access to the lake but is rather a chance to reconnoitre the shallow, shelving beaches accessible from the township. You may plan your fishing approach while the other members of the party visit the licensed premises of the Railway Station.

They may even take a ride on the Kingston Flyer and meet you at the Mataura River, 10 km further along the highway.

Staircase Creek, on the Kingston Arm of Lake Wakatipu, Queenstown.

24 Upper Mataura River

T he Mataura River is one of the best brown trout fly fishing rivers in New Zealand. It is more than 90 km long and offers excellent fishing over most of its length; from a small, sparkling stream near Queenstown to a wide, deep major waterway near Wyndham in Southland. Only the upper Mataura is covered here. For the lower reaches see Chapter 32.

(1) Fairlight: 10 km from Kingston Junction
The river is first encountered at a sharp left-hand bend on the main highway. Drive into the rest area which provides good sheltered conditions adjacent to the river.

Flowing from the mountains on the right, the river follows a meandering course edged by willow trees through farmland. Here, and for the next 6 km or so, the river is small, and although it occasionally dries up completely in summer it carries a good head of fish most of the year. These upper reaches are vital spawning grounds and subject to strict conservation measures: they are clearly signposted 'catch and release' from Garston upstream. The river is close to the highway between Fairlight and Garston, a distance of 7 km, and offers three easy accesses (1), (2) and (3).

(2) Angler's Access: 3 km from Fairlight
As the road follows a wide curve to the right a small bridge will be seen in a paddock on the right side. Follow the gravel road over the bridge, drive through a gate (leave as found), on which there is a plaque explaining fishing regulations, and park on the riverbed a short distance ahead. The river is delightfully stream-sized as it flows around the edge of the small flat on which you are parked. It offers idyllic dry fly conditions in both directions, the upstream section is particularly pleasant.

You will pass the convergence of a small creek on the right as you follow the river upstream through a wide pool and then along high, grassed earth banks which confine the water flow to runs and smooth rapids in a bed of fine gravel. The trout will be quite visible to experienced anglers and will rise nicely to a size 14 or 16 Dad's Favourite, Greenwell's Glory or similar winged dry fly. The fish seen cruising through the shallows should be tempted initially with a minute nymph to avoid the possibility of spooking them. The dry may be used if the nymph is spurned.

(3) Angler's Access, Scott Creek: 2.9 km from (2)
Traverse the sharp right-hand curve between overhanging roadside trees slowly, this Angler's Access sign is erected on a gate alongside Scott Creek Bridge and is easy to miss. Parking space is limited and you may have to park a short distance along the road and walk back. A short walk through enveloping vegetation provides access to a delightful run of water which may be fished the few kilometres to the previous access.

(4) Garston Hotel: 1.5 km from (3)
Accommodation at this hotel is limited and it is necessary to make advance reservations if you wish to reside in this strategic base for a day or two.

Ideally, you should use a light, delicate rod that will ensure an accurate delivery of the fly with a short distance cast as willow trees and banks overhung with long grass restrict casting in this river. My 8-ft 9-in (2.6-m), 2-piece, weight 3 SAGE rod is unsurpassed for this type of fishing. It only takes the slightest movement of the wrist to settle the fly on the calmest mirror surface without any disturbance.

Although the river is small, felt-soled footwear is essential for fishing the very productive water beneath overhanging willow trees. It is necessary to walk upstream on extremely slippery stones in knee- or thigh-deep water to reach casting positions in range of rising fish.

Drive or walk towards Queenstown for a short distance from the hotel and follow Hume Road towards a bridge crossing the Mataura River. This appealing and well-fished section of river typifies the dry fly fishing available in Southland. Continue over the bridge, take the first road left and follow the river downstream to where it strikes a bluff and creates a small deep backwater, a total distance of about 100 m. If you are driving, park in the clearing opposite this position.

There will be at least one visible fish in this backwater on the cruise for food. Walk stealthily to the upstream side of the tree growing on the water's edge, look around its trunk in a downstream direction and examine the swirling water flowing hard against the bank. The trout will lift from the depths frequently and be back-on to you approximately 6 m away. You will notice it take food from the surface, turn to the left and 'sound'. Bide your time and cast just at the instant it disappears from sight with a fine-tipped leader and a size 16 dry Red-tipped Governor, Dad's Favourite or Kakahi Queen fly. Fish tend to be alert in such positions and extreme stealth is necessary to gain casting range and coax them into taking a fly.

Continue along the road, which is fenced from the river flowing on the other side of a pasture, and seek permission from the occupier of the house ahead to cross his land to fish. The long, smooth run of water ahead of the gate should be left for nightfall, or fished in the upstream mode if there is a rise during daylight. Walk downstream through the paddock to where the willow trees lining the banks veer right. At this position the river is swift and agitated as it follows a curve and creates a deep run against the opposite bank. Although willow trees overhang the water here, they are high enough to allow unrestricted fly casting as you work upstream and fish through varied water conditions.

I've found that the best fly patterns for this river are, in order, size 16 dry Grizzly Wulff, Red-tipped Governor, Twilight Beauty, Kakahi Queen, Blue Dun or Dad's Favourite. During the wet rise use either a wet Twilight Beauty, Greenwell's Glory or Pomahaka Black in size 12. When the fish are feeding in a very quiet manner during daylight hours and creating the slightest surface disturbance you should use leaders with very fine tippets and a size 16 or 18 Sawyer's pattern Pheasant Tail nymph, and extreme stealth.

Having reconnoitred and perhaps fished the long, smooth section of water during daylight, you should consider returning at twilight and fishing it again during the evening rise with a Twilight Beauty or Molefly dry fly and catching a decent-sized fish.

(5) Side Road Access: 6 km from (4)

Before fishing this position you should seek access permission from the occupant of the roadside house 1.6 km south of the Garston Hotel. The main highway from Garston follows a reasonably straight course for some 5 km before turning sharp left. At this point, continue straight ahead into a rough grassed access track instead of following the bend in the main highway. Drive slowly for a few hundred metres and park on the other side of overhanging willow trees beside a gate. Walk across the paddocks to the riverbank marked by an avenue of willow trees.

This section of water is almost completely enclosed by trees, which restrict casting and access. However, the physical effort necessary to gain access is warranted. The river not only has an extremely slippery bed, but is also extremely well stocked with fish. A full and pleasant day's fishing may be had by following the river all the way back to position (3).

It is possible to leave from here by continuing to drive along the grass track, passing through a gate, turning left and then right onto the highway, about 1 km ahead.

(6) Two Bridges Access: 3.3 km from (5)

Drive over the first bridge, turn right off the highway and park in the gravel area before and below the level of the second one. The river from the bridge upstream is confined between grass-covered banks lined with willow trees and gives the impression of a canal. Actually, this configuration exists from here to Garston, a distance of some 10 km.

From this venue, a small ripple is visible upstream where the river veers left at the end of the 10-m wide canal which is overhung on either side with long grass. There are no gravel beaches: the water is knee-deep at the edges and the trout hold beneath the grass and move into the current to feed as food drifts by. You will spook them as you walk along the riverbank.

Contrary to my usual advice, I advise against holding your presentation until you sight a fish, despite the clear and reasonably smooth nature of the water flow. You should

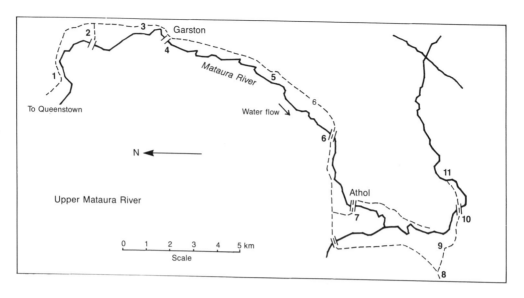

continually cast ahead of your stance and let the fly drift downstream as close to the overhanging grass as possible. The earthen terrain occasionally creates pools with overhanging banks and deep channels of fast water in which the trout are difficult to see. Cast as long a line as can be handled comfortably and strip to keep a taut line to the fly as it floats back to you. The fish will snap at the fly as it is whisked past their feeding station by the current and eject it just as quickly once they feel the hook.

Any of the well-hackled dry flies will generally suffice here where the trout feed as much on terrestrial insects as they normally do on aquatic insects. Incidentally, the river occasionally changes course just above the two bridges, but the dominating canal feature prevails on either side of an occasional gravel bar or corner-beach which may be created temporally. It is therefore possible that my description of any specific position may alter slightly and not apply when you visit, in which case you're on your own.

The river flow below the bridge can only be described as idyllic, as it follows a wide arc to the right where its apex is formed by a 1-m high bank of solid earth above a deep channel which shelves gradually onto a shallow gravel beach opposite — the typical impression we all hold of a perfect stream. Downstream, the water becomes more confined as its course meanders through the precincts of the Athol Settlement.

(7) Athol Settlement: 1 km from (6)

Turn left into Riverview Road just as you approach the township, drive 1 km and turn hard right into the gravel road. The course of the river is ascertainable by the willow trees lining its banks. You may park your car at the end of the road, where there is a walking track straight ahead leading to excellent water.

This section of the road extends only 4.6 km, but the actual river is probably twice as long. It meanders all over the place, offering a multitude of fishing conditions, including sparkling rapids, still pools, and swirling backwaters. The terrain is level, but covered with trees and rough vegetation which restrict access to the riverbed in many places. This is, however, a small sacrifice to endure for an opportunity to fish for such a bountiful stock of brown trout.

(8) Nokomai Valley Junction: 6.1 km from (7)

Slow down as the bridge over the Parawa River comes within view, and turn left at the junction where the main road follows a sharp bend to the right. The turn-off is quite dangerous because of the fast traffic and restricted visibility due to the encroaching trees.

(9) Cyclone Gate: 1.8 km from the Junction

Follow the gravel road to a gate on the left-hand side offering access to the river, which is separated from the road by 30 m of grassed paddock. The river flows reasonably deeply here in a rough bed between high grass-covered banks with occasional willow trees overhanging the water. This well-stocked section of water is difficult to get to for a couple of kilometres, until you pass the first bridge 1.8 km ahead.

(10) Bridge: 1.3 km from (9)

The river comes from the left in a confined course to pass beneath the bridge, on the other side of which there are several fishing cottages. An access track leaves the road near here and offers easy access to the water. The riverbed consists of small stones rather than fine gravel and the water flow is broken and reasonably swift, offering good fishing once a casting position is reached through encroaching vegetation.

(11) Bridge: 900 m from (10)

The river flows from the right after following the headland separating it from the road and assumes a completely different character. The river now descends a gentle gradient through open country where there are stands of stunted scrub on a wide gravel riverbed subjected to channel alteration during floods.

The open aspect of the location provides perfect access and fishing conditions in a gentle flow of water which passes through successive sections of rapids, ripples and shallow pools. It is a venue calling for the presentation of lightly hackled dry flies, Adams, Dad's Favourite, Blue Dun, etc., and small-bodied nymph patterns, Sawyer's Pheasant Tail, Peacock Herle and Twilight Beauty, for example.

The road continues up the valley for many kilometres and there are numerous privately owned fishing huts standing alone or in clusters along the way. Many of the access positions are clearly marked 'Foot access only, no vehicles.'

25 Upper Oreti and Mararoa Rivers

The South Island has an ever-changing environment and the picturesque, tree-shrouded Mataura soon gives way to rivers of a different character. Only 36 km from Athol the whole countryside changes to a wind-blown, sun-scorched plain, relieved only by rows of pine trees. This immense tract is contained by foothills that are dwarfed by the snow-capped Southern Alps.

Upper Oreti River

This clear river changes course frequently over a shingle bed between banks of high grass and clumps of broom. It offers excellent access, perfect stalking and casting conditions, and large brown trout. Although these are not as plentiful as in the Mataura, Aparima or Motueka Rivers, their sheer size makes them reasonably easy to locate visually by the proficient angler. Their slate-grey colour helps in the ripples, where the water is often tinged a faint blue by silica rock-flour. These trout rise nicely to a large, well-hackled dry fly, and they provide an exciting challenge with their cunning nature and vicious fighting antics once hooked.

The river receives heavy fishing pressure during the early part of the season, especially during the Christmas holiday period, with the result that most of the 'easy' fish have been well trained in the art of evasion before the height of the dry-fly fishing months of February and March.

This chapter covers the upper reaches of the river, from the township of Mossburn to the last bridge spanning its course a few kilometres past the Mavora Lakes turnoff — a distance of approximately 50 km. Over this whole section, the river follows a wide, unstable, gravel bed that crosses a valley floor covered with tussock and snow grass. This valley guides a strong prevailing wind down from the Southern Alps to the sea coast. Anglers will suffer a severe burn from wind and sun unless they use sun-block and moisturising cream.

The accesses from (1) to (4) and (16) are on Highway 94 (Lumsden to Te Anau) and the remainder are reached from the Mavora Lakes access road which turns inland from this highway at a junction 13.5 km south of Mossburn. Several of these latter vehicle accesses lead to level ground on the western side of the river, where they join obvious vehicle tracks running parallel to the water. Do not drive along these tracks if the ground is wet or attempt to fish the river immediately after a flood. The unstable loose gravel requires several days to consolidate, allowing the water to clear, before the trout move into the new or disturbed channels.

The best approach to this river is to fish likely holding positions blind while walking slowly upstream and searching for the flash of a fin, tail or perhaps the smudge of a body holding motionless in the current. The water flow is gentle but swift and requires competent line stripping by the fly angler to ensure a tight line to the drifting fly or nymph at all times.

The size and shape of the fly is more important than the pattern when fishing the rapids of this river. It must be well hackled and treated with floatant to ensure that it rises to the surface quickly and floats high after being immersed by wave action or line drag. False casting, which is generally practised to dry the fly, should be avoided as much as possible in this open environment, where there are no solid backdrops to disguise the line flashing through the air. My choice of flies for this river are Wulff, Humpy and Molefly, and Kakahi Queen and Blue Dun in sizes 8-12 when fishing blind through rapids and ripples. Adams, Greenwell's Glory, Dad's Favourite and Twilight Beauty dries in sizes 14-18 supplement the small nymphs in patterns Sawyer's Pheasant Tail, Peacock Herle and Twilight Beauty used when fishing to surface-feeding trout in swirling backwaters, quiet smooth currents or holding between stones along the shallow edges of the stream. The larger nymph patterns Stonefly (brown), Half-back Pheasant Tail and Hare & Copper (rough tie) are without any doubt unsurpassed when fishing blind in a rapid or to a shadowy shape feeding frantically in smooth, deep, fast currents.

(1) Highway 94 Bridge, Mossburn: 19 km from Five Rivers Junction

This position is within sight of the Mossburn township and offers easy access to the river from the approaches on either side of the bridge. There is also ample off-road parking.

The river flows swiftly through several unstable channels above the bridge, which generally confines them into a single channel downstream. You should examine the water flow stealthily (head below skyline) from the bridge. You will probably notice trout moving in the current of the pool immediately upstream of your stance. Intense observation of the downstream rapids may also reveal the flash of a grey shadow indicating a fish feeding sub-surface. The ten minutes or so taken to study the water is time well spent: it is an opportunity to evaluate the conditions that will be encountered upstream for 50 km. It will also suggest the gear you will need: felt-soled wading boots, clothing and headgear to protect from the sun, and a powerful rod which will lay a line into the teeth of the wind, generally, a daily occurrence.

The trout feeding near the bridge are quite catchable if a careful approach is applied. It is warranted as they may weigh as much as 3 kg (6-7 lb). I suggest that you study and memorize their feeding pattern: the two or three fish in the pool will hold, remain in and actively feed within their chosen section of water. You should aim for a particular trout rather than cast willy-nilly through the whole expanse of pool. You may only get one chance to catch one of these beauties.

Approach the position from downstream and present the fly accurately into the fish's feeding area. If the trout is surface feeding, use dry fly patterns Wulff, Humpy, Molefly or Blue Dun, in sizes to suit the water conditions (rougher turbulence calls for a larger, more buoyant presentation). Use the same formula to select sizes of nymph patterns. Stonefly, Hare & Copper or Pheasant Tail all work particularly well in this river.

The river may be fished upstream to access (3), a distance of approximately 3 km, to where your companion has left the vehicle. He may fish a similar length of water and be met at position (4) by yourself with the reclaimed transport.

(2) Mossburn: 2 km from (1)

A small settlement offering basic services; a motor garage, grocery shop, hotel and accommodation.

Upper Oreti River.

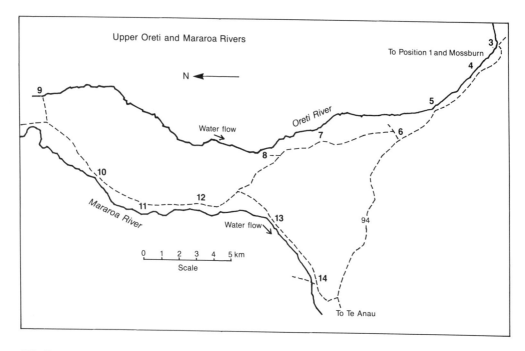

Upper Oreti and Mararoa Rivers

To Position 1 and Mossburn

N

Oreti River

Water flow

Mararoa River

Water flow

0 1 2 3 4 5 km
Scale

To Te Anau

(3) **Roadside Access through Broom:** 1.5 km from Mossburn (2)

As Highway 94 follows an acute left-hand turn watch carefully for an access road leading through the fringe of roadside broom. This road ends in a parking space beside the river which is usually braided with one channel flowing against the road embankment for a few hundred metres. The riverbed is similar to that observed from the highway bridge (1) and will remain so for approximately the next 20 km, when an odd headland of solid rock will be encountered on one side or the other of the valley.

You should walk this riverbed unhurriedly and fish in the manner I have suggested in the introduction to the chapter. The lack of charismatic beauty so characteristic of most South Island trout streams will give the uninitiated angler the impression that the waters are as barren as the landscape. Nothing could be further from the truth — this is an outstanding brown trout fishery that will provide sport for fly fishing anglers who are prepared to stumble over rough stones, get scratched by briars and be blown inside out by a constant and often very cold wind.

(4) **Anglers' Access Sign:** 2.4 km from (3)

Watch for this sign as the road turns left; it is near a corner boundary fence with heavy reinforcing timber. Follow the foot track through encroaching vegetation to the open riverbed and concentrate your efforts on the run of water that looks most established.

(5) **Highway Curve Access:** 4.3 km from (4)

The river is screened from view by acres of broom bushes en route to this position, situated on the apex of a left-hand curve. Pass through the solid wooden gate and follow the vehicle track between thick stands of broom to the open riverbed.

(6) **Mavora Lakes Road Junction:** 4 km from (5)

This insignificant junction is easy to miss. It is marked by a small yellow AA sign fitted to a roadside post opposite a gravel road. Turn right and follow the road signposted 'Centre Hill Station'.

(7) **Anglers' Access Sign:** 6.8 km from (6)

The sign is on a gate where the road veers left and provides vehicle access to a faint track leading over descending grassy terrain towards the river, visible several hundred metres away on the valley floor. The riverbed from here on narrows considerably, and its stones are retained between solid, tussock-covered banks. The confined nature of the river creates rapids, long glides and small, deep pools against solid rock abutments situated every few hundred metres or so.

Anglers may now concentrate their attention on one flow of water rather than in the several braided channels as was necessary in the lower reaches. The trout will be easier to locate, although at times it will be necessary to cross the river to gain better lighting conditions and eliminate the surface 'mirror'. You should examine the whole expanse of water thoroughly, the fish will nonchalantly cruise through the shallows on the edge of the stream in search of food, feed vigorously in the depths of midstream, and splash viciously with a flash of colour as they take dry fly flies in the surface turbulence.

All of the pools will host several residential trout which will hold and feed sedately in the downstream glides during daylight hours, becoming more active in the twilight. You must adopt a gradual and stealthy approach along the glides to avoid alarming these vigilant fish. Generally, such trout will be holding almost motionless just above the bed of the stream and moving only a few inches occasionally to take food. I suggest that you tempt them with a small nymph rather than a dry fly at first. The latter presentation will usually spook such trout unless they are actively feeding from the surface.

(8) 'Centre Hill' Access: 5.8 km from (7)

A no exit sign marks this road, leading straight ahead from the valley highway as is follows a left-hand curve. There is an Anglers' Access sign 400 m past the junction offering similar access and fishing conditions to (7).

This no exit road terminates 4.5 km away on the brow of a hill, where there is a gate which may be passed through to provide a continuation of vehicle access upstream. The road is rough, and initially descends a steep gradient, so drive carefully. You should rest a while on the brow of the hill and reconnoitre the valley floor stretched out invitingly below you. The river disappears behind the plateau on your right, and its course may be traced from the distant mountains as it meanders through open, level, tussock-covered terrain. The gradient is quite gentle and the riverbed of stones is easily negotiable along the sections of successive rapids, glides and pools. Note the first fence crossing the valley floor at right angles in the distance. This is your next vehicle park and walking access to some excellent water, holding large brown trout.

There are literally days of good fishing to be had from this particular venue. It is a position worthy of attention by experienced fly fishing anglers who will undoubtedly catch and release the trophy sized browns that inhabit this unique back-country river.

Before passing through the gate and descending the plateau to this venue, you should request access permission from the occupants of the Centre Hill Station, 2.2 km before the gate. **Courtesy gives pleasure: access is free, and this unique privilege offered the sportsmen of this country is due to those who share their domain so unselfishly.**

(9) Upper Bridge: 25.4 km from (8)

The valley road passes two junctions on the way to this bridge. The first one, following the Mararoa River upstream from Highway 94, is encountered 2 km from the entrance of the no exit road described under (8), and the other, 19 km further on, is the access road to Mavora Lakes. Veer right at this last junction and follow the road leading to the Von River for 3 km and park near the last bridge crossing the Oreti River.

Similar conditions to those prevailing at the previous three access points will be found here, and you should apply the same fishing approach as used in the lower sections of the river. This is the Upper Oreti River — may you enjoy it fully.

The Mararoa River

This river runs for approximately 36 km from the Mavora Lakes before it is crossed by Highway 94, some 24 km north of Te Anau. It then passes through many miles of inaccessible terrain to reappear and pass beneath the Te Anau-Tuatapere Highway and converge with the Waiau River at the Mararoa Dam, 11 km downstream from Lake Manapouri. (This final section of river also offers good trout fishing. See Chapter 29, position (1).)

The Mararoa initially emerges from the lake as a wide, deep, smoothly flowing river passing through virgin native forest. This section is well stocked with large fish but the terrain allows little access to fishing positions between encroaching bush. The sight of huge trout nonchalantly cruising and feeding within range on the other side of standing tree trunks is an exciting but frustrating experience for any angler. It is possible, however, to follow tracks along the riverbanks and endeavour to locate a position from which to cast a line.

The river emerges from its bush enclosure about 8 km down the valley and flows through gorge-type terrain until it nears the Oreti/Mararoa Valley Junction (6) approximately 11 km further downstream. In most instances it is necessary to walk across the grass and tussock-covered plateau to reach the lip of the ravine.

Similar fishing techniques and fly patterns as used on the Oreti River are applicable to this waterway. The fishing accesses are explained in the downstream direction from the Von River/Mavora Lakes Junction 2 km inland from (8).

(10) Anglers' Access Sign: 7 km from (8)
Park on the side of the road and walk towards the hills. The river is out of sight in a small gorge about 20 m below the plain and is accessible by following animal tracks from the

edge of the ravine. The water conditions along this section of river are delightful: a stable bed of rock and stones provides pools, rippling rapids and fast-flowing guts.

Although the portions of open, barren terrain of both the Oreti and Mararoa Rivers suit flies in sizes 8 to 10, the confined and stable nature of the gorge section will produce better results when using sizes 14 and 16. The proximity of bush also effects fly size and the dry patterns Twilight Beauty, Dad's Favourite and Peveril o'Peak now come into their own.

In the event of trout rising very sedately during bright daylight hours in a calm pool, the fly pattern should be changed to a Sawyer's Pheasant Tail nymph in sizes 16/18. If this is spurned, try a wet Greenwell's Glory of the same size as the fish will be feeding on 'emergers'.

(11) Anglers' Access Sign: 3.2 km from (10)

The Anglers' Access signs described under (10), (11) and (12) are small, painted brown and difficult to see at first glance — you should watch for them at the distances shown. This particular one is located beside a stile providing access over a fence to open terrain.

(12) Anglers' Access Sign: 5.7 km from (11)

A dry creek bed precedes this access, which is downstream from an avenue of pine trees. Access to the ravine and river conditions are similar to positions (10) and (11).

(13) Roadside Access: 8 km from (12)

When travelling down the valley, ensure that you follow the right-hand road at the junction 4 km from (12). The river emerges from your right to closely follow the road for about 10 km. You may examine the water flow from the vehicle and fish any section which appeals; it is only a matter of parking on the side of the road, stepping down a low bank and walking a few metres to the river. The terrain is open, tussock-covered and wholly uninteresting. But this sun-scorched, wind-blown section of water will reward the obstinate fly fishing angler with fishing results to equal the anticipation. It is a good venue.

(14) Mararoa Station Road Bridge: 8 km from (13)

After travelling downstream another 7 km, turn right into a no exit road. This leads to a bridge crossing the river 1 km away where the water is generally confined in a single channel of a more stable nature than upstream. There is ample parking on this side of the bridge and easy walking access onto the riverbed. Here the deeper water flow should produce better results when presenting slightly larger flies and nymphs than were used in the confined sections upstream.

Mararoa Station Road Bridge, Mararoa River.

26 Mavora Lakes

The two Mavora Lakes are situated in a mountain valley at an altitude of 610 m. The northern lake, 13 km long, is joined to the southern lake, 3 km long, by the Mararoa River, which flows between tussock banks for 1.5 km. Cold air from the Southern Alps is frequently funnelled through this valley to the plains of Southland, so warm clothing is essential when visiting the region. All the waterways are well stocked with brown trout.

(1) Mavora Lakes Junction: 24 km from Te Anau
Take Highway 94 from Te Anau towards Mossburn and turn left at a junction signposted 'Mavora Lakes'. They are some 33 km inland.

(2) Lake Outlet (Mararoa River): 1.4 km from the second junction
Park on the side of the road; it is only a short walk to the edge of the outlet stream which is flowing wide and deep between earth banks covered by forest. A few metres downstream, the river enters a huge pool where the currents create eddies and backwaters that entice trout to feed in flotsam. Unfortunately, many of the good holding positions are out of casting range for fly anglers, who are already restricted by overhanging trees. Spinning anglers have an advantage here.

The skilled fly angler should be able to catch trout in this position by moving stealthily upstream, locating a cruising fish close to the bank, walking ahead through concealing vegetation, and waiting for it about 7 m ahead. A size 12 or 14 dry fly should be cast with a flick of the rod-tip and left to float naturally in the fish's path. The rod-tip should be held a few centimetres above the surface, at right angles to the bank, and the line kept as taut as possible without disturbing the fly's drift. If this manoeuvre is skilfully executed, the trout will lift and take the fly, and the angler will gauge the correct pause before setting the hook by hardening the line with the free hand. This is an extremely efficient method of catching cruising trout that are feeding close to overhanging vegetation, and only requires stealth, patience and a little practice.

(3) Lake Outlet Bar: 300 m from (2)
There are parking and picnicking facilities a few metres from the swingbridge spanning the outlet stream with easy walking access to small gravel beaches on the lake shore. The open terrain simplifies the casting of a fly or minnow well out into the lake and retrieving it through the current flowing over the bar — a favourite position for feeding fish.

Dry fly patterns Grizzly Wulff, Twilight Beauty, Molefly and Peveril o'Peak, in sizes to suit prevailing conditions, will suffice anywhere in this area and you should change to Twilight Beauty, Dad's Favourite, or Greenwell's Glory wet flies when the rise is splashy and active, especially at twilight.

It is possible, though difficult, to walk downstream in the water close to the bank on this side of the stream, but the opposite side provides better access to several small gravel beaches. Anglers may cross the bridge and walk downstream through the bush to reach the large pool mentioned under position (2), where several positions offer good casting conditions from which to spin or fly fish. The ground is, however, quite soft and swampy underfoot and requires care to negotiate.

(4) Head of the Southern Lake: 3 km from (3)
The road to this position follows the lake for about 2 km, passes through a stand of native forest, and provides a good view of the lake's small shallow inlets. Several of these inlets have stands of rushes growing in the water close to the beach and they provide good feeding areas for trout.

After about 2 km, the road leaves the bush and crosses open tussock land offering an unobstructed view of the head of the lake. The outlet from the northern lake converges with

Lake outlet, position (2), Mavora Lakes.

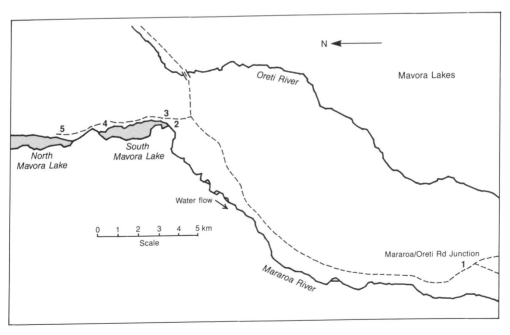

this over a wide, shallow, grass-covered delta where it is possible to walk through the water slowly and locate a fish by sight before presenting a fly. To reach this position you must walk down the tussock slope from the road and across the flat terrain through which the river flows. Although the terrain may look even, the knee-high tussock grass conceals many narrow dried-up river channels, so you should walk cautiously and separate the grass ahead before every step.

Many hours may be spent fishing this end of the lake, which is about 400 m wide. but I would suggest visiting it before the afternoon breeze ruffles the water and makes fishing by sight difficult.

(5) North Mavora Lake: 2.5 km from (4)

The road follows high ground through tussock country to this position, presenting a panoramic view of the river. There are a number of gravel runs and rapids, but the water flow is generally about 10 m wide and 2 m deep, flowing swiftly and smoothly as it descends a gradient of 90 m over 2 km. Several vehicle access tracks lead from the road towards the river's edge. Take these carefully, as in places soft muddy patches are hidden under overhanging tussock.

The swift water flow restricts the visual location of trout, though careful observation will often reveal a rise or swirl of a feeding trout in the current. Ideally a dry fly should be used in the upstream mode, but it is also possible to fish across and down. Many a fish may be taken by this method, though the fly will be half sunken and dragged.

The gravel road ends at (5), next to a shallow beach where there are basic camping and picnicking facilities, a school lodge and several semi-permanent parked caravans. The access track entering the bush ahead leads to the head of the lake but it is negotiable by four-wheel-drive vehicles only. The shore of this lake has a beach of fine gravel and it is possible to walk the shore for many kilometres. The clarity of the water provides good sub-surface visibility and casting is unrestricted to trout that may be seen cruising or feeding within range.

The outlet of the lake, 800 m downstream, also offers good fishing where the tussock bank gives way to a small beach of fine gravel. Unrestricted casting conditions allow the application of conventional fishing practices, by either technique, in the shallows before the water accelerates over the bar.

Although the whole location is a particularly good fishery, I would suggest that you concentrate your efforts on positions (2) and (4), with the emphasis on (4). These are excellent venues.

Improved vehicle access now allows large numbers of anglers, equipped with power boats and treble-hooked trolling minnows, to visit this lake. This action has drastically reduced the population of large brown trout for which these lakes were renowned only a few years ago. All trout anglers must practise sensible husbandry to conserve those large fish that are left.

27 Eglinton River, Te Anau

T e Anau is a good base from which to fish the Waiau and Eglinton Rivers. The town is on the shore of Lake Te Anau, where air and water transport is available for anglers wishing to troll the shoreline or fish the remote rivers entering the lake. There are also three delightful fly fishing streams within easy reach of Te Anau, the Upukerora, Whitestone and Mararoa Rivers. Although they receive considerable fishing pressure from visiting anglers, they are constantly replenished by fish from the lake. The occasional disruption to habitat, and consequently the resident trout stock, caused by weather is a phenomenon anglers have learnt to live with.

The Waiau is the largest river in Southland and gains its source within 4 km of the town, as explained in the chapter on the Waiau. The Eglinton, described here, is accessible from Highway 94 leading from Te Anau to Milford Sound. The Eglinton follows a long valley and offers fairytale conditions, with crystal-clear water flowing through successive rapids, pools and glides in a bed of gravel interspersed with abutments and shelves of solid rock. The terrain, covered with tussock and stands of native forest, provides easy walking access to some of the most pleasant fishing venues available in the South Island. It is prone to flash floods but fortunately has a natural restocking reservoir of rainbow trout with Lake Te Anau.

En route to the first access 37 km from the Te Anau, there are several good fishing positions on the lake within easy reach of the road, which follows it closely for a considerable distance. The highway parallels the lee shore of the lake which, through exposure to wind and waves, has small shallow beaches of gravel or sand. These provide reasonably easy access. The terrain next to the water's edge is generally tussock, bracken and manuka scrub, in contrast to the native forest on the other side of the lake. A heavy concentration of underwater weed near the shoreline provides both protection and food for trout. It also ensures that a permanent trout population is retained within casting range of the beach.

The fly angler should visit these lakeside positions during the morning, while the water is calm. When fishing to trout located visually or by water movement I would recommend a size 14 or 16 Dad's Favourite, Blue Dun, Twilight Beauty or Adams dry fly. If this fails, try a size 16 Sawyer's Pheasant Tail or Peacock Herle unweighted nymph.

When the water becomes agitated by the wind you should use a medium-density sinking line, with streamer fly patterns Yellow Dorothy, Hamill's Killer, Parson's Glory or Mrs

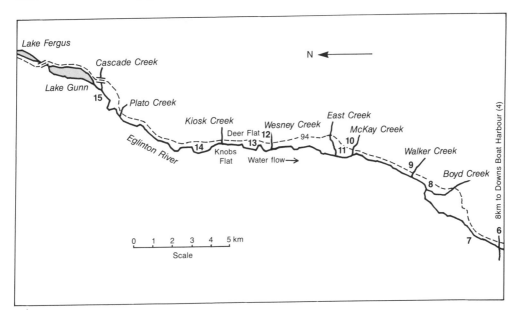

Simpson. Twilight Beauty, Dad's Favourite and Greenwell's Glory wet flies are a natural choice when fishing the wet rise as twilight fades into darkness.

(1) Lake Te Anau Access: 8.7 km from Te Anau

There is a rest area on the left-hand side of the road, providing easy access to the water's edge.

(2) Vehicle Access: 5.1 km from (1)

Watch carefully for this small gravel vehicle access leaving the left side of the highway. It passes through thick manuka scrub and terminates on a small gravel beach beside the lake.

(3) Camping/Picnic Area: 10.4 km from (2)

This is a picturesque area surrounded by bush in a sheltered bay aptly named Pleasant Bay. There is good access to a long beach, and the water is protected from the prevailing wind by a small peninsula. Several vehicle access tracks lead from the highway through the manuka to the water's edge.

(4) Downs Boat Harbour: 4.6 km from (3)

This large enclosed inlet is used as an anchorage and has launching facilities for pleasure boats. It also has a hotel, motel complex and picnicking facilities.

Eglinton River

The fishing in this river is subject to strict conservation measures which are altered from time to time, and it is necessary to refer to the regulations shown on your locally issued

Eglinton River.

license. You should seek this information from the Te Anau sports shop if your license was purchased elsewhere in New Zealand.

(5) Eglinton River Mouth: 4 km from (4)
A few metres past the entrance to the boat harbour there is a nondescript gravel road leading off the highway to the left. This terminates near the Eglinton River, which flows wide and clear over a large shingle delta extending into the lake. The shape of the delta and its numerous water channels changes with every flood, and the odd driftwood tree and miscellaneous rubbish are deposited on the shingle. It is quite firm underfoot, and negotiable with the use of hip boots, though light-weight chest waders would be advantageous when crossing deeper channels.

This is an area for the adventurous fly angler who is experienced in reading the water, willing to walk long distances and criss-cross channels of flowing and calm water in search of fish. The calm backwaters created by the channels and lake water waves hold cruising trout with eyes like hawks and ears to match. You will sight these fish from quite a long distance away as they cruise over light-coloured gravel in shallow water or rise on the quiet surface of a smooth glide. You must approach casting range with the utmost stealth — one noisy footstep, or your shadow within the fish's vision, and it's all over.

The end of the shingle fan slopes steeply into the depths of the lake, and is frequented by cruising and feeding fish — which are harassed and terrorized by the powerboat trolling fraternity. Particular attention should be paid to the rocky shoreline downstream from the shingle fan, where there is a deepish channel running parallel to shore. This usually holds a few trout sheltering from passing boats.

The trout feeding in the waters of the delta are easy to catch with almost any small dry fly or nymph. An undetected approach and delivery of the presentation is of far greater importance than a mere fly pattern here.

(6) Dunton Creek: 8.1 km from (4)
The highway leaves the undulating scrub country before this position and crosses a small, fertile valley carrying a gentle spawning stream. Stop by the bridge and follow this creek to its convergence with the Eglinton River, which flows over an unstable gravel bed. There is easy access, unrestricted casting and good dry fly fishing water in this location during settled atmospheric conditions.

(7) Access Gate: 1.4 km from (6)
This gate is on the left-hand side of an elevated section of the highway which gives a panoramic view of the river. A 'firm' stream of water passes over gravel after emerging from the confines of a wide gorge, accelerates down a slight incline, and creates a large, quietly flowing pool against a small cliff. Pass through the gate and drive 50 m to the parking area above the river.

Before walking upstream, try a few casts in the debris-littered backwater swirling against the cliff on the other side of the main stream. It is generally possible to wade the river above the fall and fish a considerable distance into the gorge. The water here flows over gravel rather than through the rock pools and thundering torrents usually associated with gorge-type terrain. This is a good position for trout fishing in a reasonably stable environment.

(8) Boyd Creek: 5.2 km from (7)
Park near the culvert and follow the creek for 1 km to its convergence with the Eglinton River, which now flows over a stable bed after passing through several kilometres of insecure gravel. Good fishing is available anywhere along this section.

(9) Walker Creek: 3.9 km from (8)
The highway forms the riverbank while passing through a stand of bush on the way to this position and it offers excellent access to a section of rippling water — perfect size 10 dry-fly territory (Grizzly Wulff, Blue Dun or Humpy). It then passes through open tussock flats, providing a view of the river's course and further accesses. Walker Creek itself is unsuitable for fishing.

(10) MacKay Creek: 4.7 km from (9)

The road to this position provides similar conditions to those on the way to position (9). There are several walking access points to the river from the road as it passes through a fringe of bush and crosses the tussock flats. The river is close to the road and generally flows over an unstable gravel bed. About 6 km upstream from Mackay Creek it emerges from native forest and the water is confined to a course of solid rock rather than gravel. These stable positions provide sanctuary for trout when the gravel beds are threatened and dislodged by floods.

(11) East Branch Eglinton River: 2 km from (10)

This river is unsuitable for fishing. The convergence near the forest offers good fishing in water flowing over a reasonably stable bed and is well worth a visit by anglers with time at their disposal. It receives limited fishing pressure because of the long walk necessary to reach the river. This highway bridge is separated from the river by 2 km of tussock-covered terrain.

(12) Wesney Creek: 5 km from (11)

This creek is unsuitable for fishing. Continue to the Eglinton River, about 800 m away through the bush, to where it flows through a rocky riverbed with rapids, pools and generally rough water conditions. Exhilarating sport awaits the fly angler here. Conditions are confined, however, and the rocks of the riverbed are slippery and jumbled.

(13) Deer Flat Access: 1 km from (12)

This access to the riverbed can be seen as the road turns left to pass over a small creek, and it leads to many kilometres of dry-fly fishing water. It is undoubtedly one of the outstanding positions on the Eglinton River. It is about 72 km from Te Anau.

(14) Smithy Creek: 5.2 km from (13)

The road to this position passes through standing forest before crossing a tussock-covered plateau. There is easy walking access to the river over several visible tracks. Smithy Creek does hold trout where it crosses the tussock plain, but the water flow is small and has the appearance of a channel rather than a natural stream. The lower reaches, just above the creek's confluence with the Eglinton River some 600 m away, offer good access and fishing.

(15) Cascade Creek: 10.8 km from (14)

Although the Eglinton River is often out of sight when following the highway through native forest, access may be gained by walking though the trees to the left. There is a particularly good position exactly 2.4 km from Cascade Creek, where a small gravel road leads from the left side of the highway to the riverbed. Conditions here are perfectly suited to the rainbow trout that inhabit the waters. The rock formation creates turbulent water through rapids, pools and runs providing superb conditions for the application of the dry-fly technique. The full-hackled patterns Humpy, Grizzly Wulff, Blue Dun and Irresistible (well dressed with floatant) are ideal in this environment.

There is a camping ground at Cascade Creek, about 1 km from the Eglinton River, and several walking tracks lead from the camp to the river and its source at Lake Gunn. The forest grows to the water's edge at this section of the lake and restricts access and casting to an otherwise good, well-stocked fishing spot.

Mararoa, Whitestone and Upukerora Rivers

These three streams, within half-an-hour's drive of Te Anau, offer delightful fly fishing conditions. They are small enough to cross almost at will and the accepted approach of upstream fishing with dry flies during the day, nymphs under dull conditions and winged wet flies in the twilight will result in success.

The Upukerora is only 2 km from the town centre and ideal for that pre-breakfast or twilight session. Leave Te Anau on Highway 94 in the direction of Milford. The first bridge encountered crosses the Upukerora. Before and within view of the bridge, turn left and follow the gravel road to its end near the convergence of the river with the lake, a distance of about 2 km. The fishing from here back to the bridge can only be described as delightful.

The Whitestone is renowned as a dry fly fishery and is about 8 km from Te Anau on Highway 94 heading towards Mossburn and Queenstown. The stream runs close to the road for a kilometre or so offering ample and easy walking access. There are also a couple of positions where one may remain overnight in the camper van — a gravel storage area on the left where the river is first encountered and in a rest area, complete with facilities, beside the Highway 94 bridge.

The river descends a gentle gradient over a braided gravel bed free of casting obstructions and anglers must fish the region with the stealth and expertise it deserves — upstream with small dry fly patterns (Adams, Kakahi Queen, Red-tipped Governor and Dad's Favourite). This river may also be fished some 13 km inland from Highway 94, where it meanders for miles over the floor of a gentle valley. Turn left up Kakapo Road, 4.3 km from Te Anau on Highway 94, and turn right into Dale Road (no exit) which leads to a bridge spanning the river. It is possible to turn off Dale Road to the right and park on the riverbed immediately before the bridge, from where you can walk in either direction and enjoy good fishing for days.

The Mararoa River, already described in chapters 25, 26 and 29, is certainly worthy of more exploration. It is a delightful river, larger than the other two, and necessitates a bolder and more active approach. The Highway 94 bridge crosses this river 24 km on the Mossburn side of Te Anau. There is ample parking on either side of the bridge, from where it is possible to walk in either direction. Two anglers using the one vehicle should perhaps consider fishing upstream from this bridge for about 4 km to the bridge mentioned under position (14) in Chapter 25, using the 'leap frog' approach. The first angler will fish from the first to the second bridge and collect the vehicle his partner has left parked before fishing upstream towards a position where the Mararoa River and Mavora Lakes Road are only a few metres apart.

Lake Te Anau represents an enormous volume of water and is very well stocked with fish. This sustains the population of resident trout in the tributaries described. The fishery, however, is under heavy angling pressure and an awareness of conservation must be foremost in the thoughts of all genuine sportsmen — be they Kiwis or visitors.

28 Waiau River

This is the largest river in Southland, draining Lake Te Anau into Lake Manapouri through a deep and tortuous gorge which is approximately 20 km in length, with limited access and fishing positions. The water is extremely clear, very deep and flows comparatively slowly through the base of the gorge, where the ground is covered with fern, bush and scrub; it is well stocked with both rainbow and brown trout. The flow fluctuates as a result of hydroelectricity generation, but the level is relatively low and stable during the midsummer months, when the control gates at the outlet of Lake Te Anau are closed to build up storage for peak electricity demand in winter.

Although the river is generally fished with the streamer fly technique, good results may also be obtained with spinning or fly fishing.

There are many more accesses to good water conditions than the four I describe: the plateau above the gorge is covered with scrubby manuka trees through which dozens of tracks, both vehicle and foot, criss-cross the dry terrain and descend the steep banks of the gorge to the river. It would be impossible to list them all and I'm sure that fit, active and inquisitive anglers could spend days exploring and fishing in this region.

(1) Control Gates: 4 km from Te Anau

Turn right into the Lake Manapouri road at the intersection at the southern end of Te Anau and, after travelling 1.6 km, turn right at the junction into the road signposted 'Golf Course'. Continue for 2.3 km to another junction and follow the road to the Kepler Track. About 500 m on, there is a carpark within view of the control gates. A walking track leads from here to the gently inclined bank which offers easy access to the riverbed, which shelves steeply into the dark and often cloudy water. This position is perfect for the anglers practising the streamer fly technique. The fly angler is also assured of a morning and evening rise

Waiau River, en route to position (2).

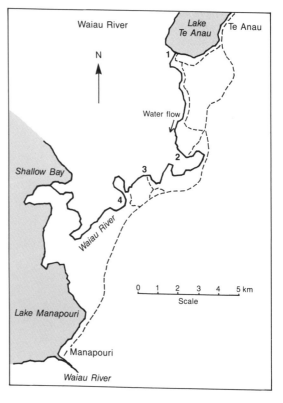

and, though the river is very wide, trout will feed over its entire surface, providing ample opportunities for casting to fish within range of the shore.

The dawn rise is a delight to fish. The angler may stand in the dim light on the very edge of deep water and watch large trout rise from the murky depths, take a minute insect from the surface and disappear. It is seldom that they will take a dry fly during this rise because they are feeding on small nymphs rising to the surface to hatch. I would suggest using a size 16 or 18 thin-bodied Pheasant Tail nymph or size 18 Greenwell's Glory wet fly, as well as long leaders with a .007 inch diameter tippet. The fish are plentiful but alert for the slightest sign of movement, so anglers must cast carefully while remaining concealed. The same stealth is not necessary in the evening, when the trout generally rise wet, active and boisterous, just as the light fades, and cease when it is completely dark. During this rise, the fly pattern is unimportant, and the commonly used patterns of Twilight Beauty, Dad's Favourite or Greenwell's Glory, in size 12, will suffice.

Enthusiastic fly anglers should visit this position about an hour after dark with a rod fitted with a floating line, a 3-m (9-ft) leader, and a size 10 or 12 Twilight Beauty, Molefly or Wulff dry fly. Cast as far as possible towards midstream and strip to keep the line taut as it drifts downstream. The resulting take will be almost indistinguishable and will feel like line drag in the current. Harden the line with your free hand as soon as you feel this drag — the ensuing action will be unmistakeable; it will be violent.

Spin anglers may also expect spasmodic results at any time of the day in this area. They should cast towards midstream, in a slightly downstream direction, with a 14-g single-blade minnow which should be given time to sink into the depths. Retrieve it slowly to allow it to travel just above the weeds growing on the riverbed. Better spin fishing may be had further down the river, however, where fast-flowing water enters pools, creating concentrated sources of food and holding positions for trout.

(2) Queen's Reach: 6 km from (1)

Return to the intersection on the river side of the golf course and turn right. This road more or less follows the lip of the gorge and offers several positions with steep access to the water over a distance of 3 km, before veering away from the river. After travelling a further 1 km, turn right at an intersection into the road signposted 'Queen's Reach', which descends a steep slope and terminates at a picnic area 1.5 km away.

This is a pleasant position, offering shelter from the sun and wind, a boat ramp and reasonably good access to the water's edge from a low bank. There is also, depending on the water level, a gravel shelf extending well into the river, which provides a good stand for casting into moving currents or reaching the backwater, where food is concentrated in the small eddies.

(3) Rainbow Reach: 5 km from (2)

Return to the plateau above the river, turn right at the junction, drive for 200 m and turn right at the intersection. Follow this road for 4.6 km as it skirts the edge of the river gorge, and turn right at a signpost marked 'Rainbow Reach'. Drive along this rough road for 400 m, and pull into a parking area just past a foot track leading to the right. You can follow this steep track down to the river, where a gravel beach provides several hundred metres of fishing into moving water from reasonably good access venues. Conditions here are better suited to the spinning rather than the fly fishing technique owing to the forceful flow of the river.

The road continues from the carpark for about 1 km to a picnic area next to the river; from here a walking track leads to the Kepler Track swingbridge. The river at this position is contained between banks that restrict fly casting, but it is ideal for spinning. The water flows over a rocky bottom and it is possible for the spin angler to clamber down the low bank and stand on the stones at the edge of the water. You should cast well out into the river and retrieve the minnow slowly upstream to allow it to pass over any trout feeding along the edge of the current.

The view downstream from the bridge approach reveals a section of gravel beach some 40 m away through the trees. It is necessary to walk through the bush to reach this position, which offers good access and conditions for both spinning and fly fishing.

(4) Balloon Loop: 4 km from (3)

Return to the road, turn right, and turn right again 1.2 km from the junction into the Balloon Loop road. Follow this road for 1.4 km to a good camping area next to the river. This is a pleasant position, where you may spend the day fishing from a gravel beach 400 m long with easy access and good conditions for both fishing techniques.

Balloon Loop offers the best fishing in this upper section of the Waiau River. The wide curve of the river's course has created extensive deltas of sand and gravel which form feeding beds during the summer months when they are exposed to sunlight and shallow water with the closure of the dam. Anglers can walk all over these deltas and spot trout from a considerable distance because they are silhouetted against the white sand. These fish follow a definite feeding 'beat' and stealth in both approach and fishing is essential. You must bide your time, memorise the trout's beat, and cast a size 14 or 16 Hare & Copper nymph into the fish's path once it has passed beyond your stance. Twitch the line and make the nymph jump as the fish returns — it will certainly inspect the movement and generally take the bait. As the trout lifts away with the nymph in its mouth, set the hook by tightening the line slowly but firmly with your free hand before lifting the rod.

If spinning or fishing a streamer fly, concentrate on the shallow ripples and swirling backwaters. Reconnoitre this location from the road before descending onto the riverbed.

The return to Te Anau may be shortened by travelling straight ahead at the intersection mentioned under position (3).

Balloon Loop, position (4), Waiau River.

29 Monowai River

This river is an excellent trout habitat. The water level is controlled at its source from Lake Monowai and flows through an artificial channel for some 2 km of its 9-km course to a power-generating plant on the banks of the Waiau River. The scrub-covered wasteland crossed by the river provides a permanent source of food and shelter for trout, which reside in a constant flow of cold, clear water approximately 2 m deep. The riverbed of rock is covered with masses of weed, which undulate in the current. Without any doubt, this waterway carries one of the best stocks of large brown trout in the South Island.

The Monowai River converges with the Waiau about halfway between the Mararoa Dam and Tuatapere, some 90 km north-west of Invercargill. I shall describe it in conjunction with the other tributaries and the main stream of the Waiau River from Lake Manapouri to Tuatapere. The Waiau River is 185 km long, drains a huge catchment area of undeveloped mountainous country, but has limited access to its predominantly gorge-like course. Its water is well stocked with both rainbow and brown trout, with an average weight of only 1.3 kg (3 lb). Although it contains larger trout, the 'small fry' are easier to catch, and thus determine the low average weight result. The fish are, however, easy to catch compared to those in many South Island rivers.

(1) Mararoa River: 11 km from Manapouri

The elevated highway provides a panorama of the Waiau's Mararoa Dam situated at the confluence of that river. Stop and park on the other side of the highway bridge spanning the Mararoa, and reconnoitre the location. Before the bridge there are vehicle tracks leading from both sides of the road to parking areas. The downstream area has picnic tables (and is an ideal venue for overnight camping), and the upstream one provides shelter amongst stands of broom from where there is easy foot access to delightful fly fishing water.

A well-hackled and dressed size 8 or 10 Humpy, Grizzly Wulff or Blue Dun dry fly should be applied in the upstream manner through the boisterous water towards and through the miniature gorge as far as access will allow. This is good trout water, broken by large stones and protruding rock into holding eddies extending the full width of the stream. Sighting the trout is difficult, (except from the bridge — there'll be a couple holding against the shoreline downstream) and the dry fly should be cast and drifted to cover the whole expanse of water.

Competent casting or line control is of little consequence here; the violence of the water flow will disguise any discrepancies and goad the fish into snatching anything that resembles food.

The course of the river descends steadily across a sloping valley floor to converge with the dam water. The access road to this position is clearly identifiable as it follows the edge of the plateau on the opposite side of the river and ends with an easy foot approach to the dam. The river flow is swift and disturbed as it bounces over a bed of stones and rock, offering perfect conditions for physically fit fly fishing anglers. Anglers intending to fish the shallows of the dam are advised to examine the water as they walk along but well back from the shore and sight their fish before casting a presentation. They can be located by water disturbance as well as by sight. Use a size 16 or 18 Pheasant Tail nymph if the fish are cruising in water a few centimetres deep and replace it with a size 10 or 12 Hare & Copper nymph when they are hugging the bottom in the depths.

In the event of wind-ruffled water conditions, fly anglers should blind fish the shallows with a 10 or 12 dry fly of the Kakahi Queen, Humpy or Wulff pattern — full-hackled, high-floating varieties.

(2) Monowai/Waiau Bridge: 26.6 km from (1)

On the way to here the highway passes through undulating country and crosses several small streams that are unsuitable for fishing. Turn right into the road signposted 'Lake Monowai' (about 23 km from (1)), and follow it to the bridge spanning the Waiau River, 3.8 km further on. Park this side of the bridge and follow a track leading upstream through the bush to a rocky outcrop at the head of the pool extending from beneath the bridge.

The terrain restricts casting for fly fishing anglers but offers perfect spinning positions. Fly anglers may, however, test the waters: try a size 16 or 18 Sawyer's Pheasant Tail nymph if the rise is barely discernible; sizes 14/16 Adams or Dad's Favourite dry fly if the rise is 'firm', that is creating distinct surface rings; or a size 12 or 14 Twilight Beauty or Greenwell's Glory wet fly if the rise is active and splashy.

Playing and landing brown trout hooked in this position can be tricky. They tend to dive into the deep, powerful current against the cliff face on the other side of the river and lay athwart in the accelerating water until the leader breaks under the pressure. Rainbow trout, on the other hand, will leap out of the water as though stung in the tail and skitter over the entire surface of the pool, before heading downstream at high speed in an endeavour to gain the sanctuary of the rapid.

(3) Monowai Village: 3 km from (2)

Turn right at the junction on the other side of the bridge. Follow the Lake Monowai Road for 2 km and turn right into the Monowai Village road. Follow this through the quiet village to a picnic area on the banks of the Waiau River, just upstream from the powerhouse. This is a particularly pleasant area in which to park and fish. The large pool on the edge of the domain is well stocked with both species of trout in a water flow agitated by the spillway from the powerhouse. The fish are generally out of fly-casting range, but easily reached with spinning minnows.

A gravel bank extends some distance into the river upstream from the pool providing fishing access to an inflowing current. A foot track leads downstream from the powerhouse to the lower reaches, which lend themselves to fly fishing in water that gets shallower towards the bar.

(4) Monowai River Bridge: 1.5 km from (3)

Return to the junction, turn right towards the lake, park and examine the river beneath the bridge. This canal follows a straight course from a low dam upstream to pass under the bridge on its way to the powerhouse. The clear water flows 2 m deep over a heavy concentration of bottom weed between stopbanks overhung with grass, scrub and flax. Occasionally this channel is cleared of its foliage and although this improves the performance of the power station it disrupts the trout's habitat temporarily and spoils the fishing.

In all probability there will be several fish visible on either side of the bridge. Those downstream will slip away quietly as soon as they see you, while the ones upstream will remain on station and tantalise the most composed of anglers. These slate-grey brown trout are unbelievably large and remain stationary in the current, only occasionally moving quietly to one side or the other to take food before returning to their original position.

Fly anglers adept at casting accurately under extremely difficult conditions may step over the fence on the village side of the bridge, walk along the top of the stopbank and fish in an upstream manner towards and past the small lagoon ahead. If they are left-handed, they should walk along the top of the opposite stopbank and fish their way to the next access position some 500 m upstream.

Most patterns of small dry flies will suffice in this river, which flows through terrain with the perfect habitat for myriads of savage and annoying flies and bugs. Personally, I would use a small Twilight Beauty or Pamahaka Black unless the rough turbulence called for the more buoyant Grizzly Wulff or Palmer-hackled Molefly.

(5) Water Level Control Dam: 2 km from (4)

Drive 400 m, turn left and follow a dirt track to a parking area offering access to a small concrete dam controlling the water flow to the old powerhouse 2 km downstream. The overflow channel is unsuitable for fishing, but the pool has good access around its perimeter and provides excellent fishing with sizes 14/16 wet or dry flies, depending on the type of rise. You should use a size 16 Greenwell's Glory wet fly if rising trout spurn dries or nymphs — they will be taking emergers.

The river enters the dam near the stand of small trees opposite the concrete wall. From here upstream, it flows through its natural bed and provides very good results in rough and confined conditions.

(6) Water Tower: 4 km from (5)

The road to this position crosses flat, scrub-covered wasteland, providing a view of the small cliff on the left against which the river flows. Do not attempt to walk across to the river unless you are experienced with swampland — it can be treacherous. Drive down the grass track to the water tower on the left. The riverbank has stands of flax growing in the water, and the only access is just behind the tower where there is a small creek.

The river flows swiftly and smoothly over stones and water weed. It is very clear, about 1.2 m deep and 12 m wide. The water becomes shallow as it runs over a shingle bar downstream, whereas upstream there is a flowing pool. There are excellent stocks of trout here where the terrain calls for chest waders, felt-soled boots and physical fitness. Impregnable riverside vegetation makes it necessary to wade upstream to fish with a size 14 dry fly or lightly weighted Hare & Copper nymph. Cast as close as possible to the overhanging vegetation and let the fly drift in the current while you examine the water ahead for grey shadows. The willow tree with branches trailing in the water on the opposite bank slightly upstream is a particularly good holding position for trout; they tend to be stationary just under the turbulence created by the trailing leaves.

The shallow bar may be fished in the downstream mode by laying a long line to the right side of the flow and letting a nymph or wet Greenwell's Glory fly swing to the left bank, from where it should be retrieved slowly in the manner of a streamer fly. Do not attempt to fish this venue alone unless you are experienced in rivercraft. The conditions are quite treacherous and, come nightfall, the large eels are hungry!

(7) Lake Monowai: 900 m from (6)

The road ends at a carpark next to a concrete spillway and the walking track follows the banks of a small inlet containing extensive areas of fish weed and good stocks of trout. Unfortunately, the water is too deep to wade, though an occasional trout will stray within casting range and may be tempted with a small dry fly.

The whole lake offers good fishing around its forest-fringed perimeter, but a boat is necessary. The outlet flows onto a bed of large stones, creating turbulent, tumbling water conditions that are too rough for fishing. There is, however, a small accessible position on the left bank, just below the dam wall, where it is possible to stand and cast into the eddies below the stones. Trout caught in this position are strong and difficult to land.

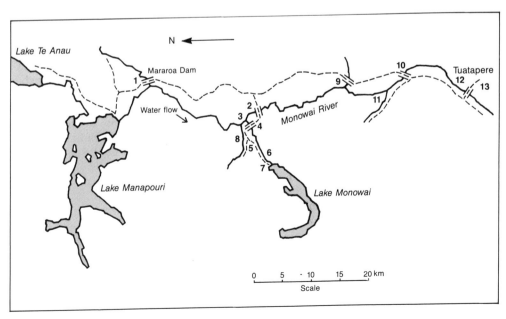

As the river flows downstream, its banks become cluttered with willow trees, stunted native scrub and grass, restricting access to all but the most determined of anglers. This section of water provides challenging fishing with a well-hackled size 10 dry fly of any pattern or size 8 weighted nymph of the large-bodied Pheasant Tail or Hare & Copper pattern. Of necessity, these have to be presented downstream using the wet fly technique.

(8) Borland Burn: 8 km from (7)

Return down the valley, after 6 km veer right at the intersection near position (5) and continue for another 500 m. Watch carefully for an obscure vehicle access leading between the manuka flanking the left-hand side of the road. Drive down this rough dirt road and park near a derelict house some 700 m away. Do not attempt to follow the road further without prior examination as the steeply descending track is generally too rough for a standard car and the muddy patch at the bottom is often too soft to cross. The river will be seen from the elevated plateau as it flows through reasonably open country for a short distance, after emerging from its forest-enclosed course. It is only a short walk down the slope and across the flat to reach the rocky bed of the river.

The river is a delight to fish with its entire course surrounded by native bush and a water flow small enough to allow foot crossings at will. It is well stocked with both rainbow and brown trout, providing exhilarating fishing for anglers experienced in casting within confined conditions. The water ripples and tumbles exuberantly from pool to pool and extreme accuracy is necessary in placing a size 14 or 16 Twilight Beauty, Dad's Favourite or Wulff dry fly in the smallest of eddies and backwaters under a canopy of forest.

(9) Wairaki River: 27.8 km from (8) and 26 km from Tuatapere

Return to the highway, turn right, drive for 27.8 km and stop on the other side of the Wairaki River Bridge. The gentle stream here, flowing over a wide bed of gravel and stones, offers good fly fishing to anglers adept at fishing upstream with light tackle. The fish are difficult to sight in the rippling water of the river and the technique of fishing blind should be applied. Size 10 Adams or Kakahi Queen dry flies are ideal during the bright periods of the day. The dull morning hours should be fished with a floating line and sizes 10/12 unweighted Hare & Copper or size 8 weighted green stonefly nymphs, while the wet rise at twilight may be fished with the old standbys, Twilight Beauty, Dad's Favourite or Peveril o'Peak wet flies in sizes 8, 10 or 12.

Access to the water is good, either by walking through the gate signposted 'Fishermen's Access' and following the river downstream to its convergence with the Waiau or from the highway bridge upstream. This latter venue is particularly good during March and April. Park your vehicle on the roadside as the gate offering access to a large gravel storage area near the upstream bridge approach is now locked.

The Waiau River has now entered flat, open country through which it flows for the remainder of its journey to the sea and it offers wide expanses of slow-moving pools and shallow ripples. The gently contoured shingle riverbed provides easy walking access to the water, which is well stocked with trout. Although they are clearly apparent during rises, long walks are frequently necessary if you wish to visually locate and cast to individual fish.

The river from here downstream offers very good spin fishing, and such anglers may cover huge expanses of water with each cast and retrieve. Fly anglers should use small fly and nymph presentations when fishing to visible trout and revert to the well-hackled more buoyant patterns in the many sections of shallow ripples and runs to be encountered from here on.

(10) Clifden Bridge: 12 km from (9)

Travel for 11 km, turn right, follow Highway 96 at the intersection and after a further 1 km park on the other side of the Clifden Bridge. Access to the gravel riverbed on the seaward side is possible by clambering through long grass on the bridge approach embankments. The river here is wide and slow flowing as it emerges from beneath the old swingbridge upstream (11) and follows a curve to the right downstream of the highway bridge.

Good fishing is available by following the riverbank downstream to the shallows created by the river's change of direction — particularly for the fly fishing fraternity. Spinning anglers

Lake Monowai, position (7), Monowai River.

are assured of results if they cast their minnow right across the river into the deep run against the far bank either up or downstream from the corner gravel bar.

(11) Old Clifden Bridge Historic Reserve: 14 km from Tuatapere

There are signs to this location on the junctions either side of the main highway bridge. This is one of the most pleasant fishing venues on the Waiau River. Before this position, the river flows gently over a wide braided gravel bed and then makes a left-hand turn to run between rock buttresses on both banks. The river is deep and gently flowing beneath the bridge, then it fans out over a shallow gravel bar just downstream of the highway bridge visible some 400 m away. There are also picnic facilities on either side of the historic bridge. The one on the inland side is particularly pleasant. It is a small grass reserve beneath the shoulder of the old road, sheltered from the wind by a stand of trees, and boasts basic amenities including fresh tap water.

It is an ideal camping position, from which there is a gravel path to rock ledges just above and running along the river's surface. The rock formation on either side of the river provides perfect spin fishing conditions and such anglers should cast their presentation well into midstream, let it sink, then retrieve it slowly to allow the minnow to swim close to the rocks and crevices downstream.

Of particular note is the section of river upstream from the southern rock buttress. The river flows from the plains, makes a right-angle turn towards the bridges and has over the years created bars, backwaters and small peninsulas with gravel and sand deposits. This ideal fish habitat is accessible from the road leading to a gravel pit from the old highway on the Monowai side of the historic bridge. Follow the signposted 'underwater stream' track from the reserve to the river. Approach the deep, swirling hole furtively, cast a size 16 or 18 Twilight Beauty dry fly on the nose of that cruising trout barely discernible amongst floating debris, and see what happens...

(12) Lilburn Stream: 6.3 km from (10)

After travelling 1 km from position (10), turn right at the junction into a road signposted 'Lake Hauroko 32 km'. This follows the banks of the Waiau River for 2 km and offers limited access to its waters. A road junction is encountered 5.2 km from the main highway and the road to the right leads to a bridge over the Lilburn Stream, 500 m away.

There is easy access from here to rather poor localised fishing conditions, where the water flows quietly between high banks covered with long grass and overhanging trees. It would be better to continue straight ahead at the junction and stop beside an angling hut on the side of the road after travelling 1.4 km. The river is small and meanders through flat pasture land, providing easy access. A few trees grow along the bank, but they do not hinder progress in any way. There are 5 or 6 km of these idyllic conditions close to the road. Anglers wishing to fish them should pay a courtesy call to either of the two houses in the vicinity. The river should be approached in a leisurely but stealthy manner to avoid alerting the trout and then fished in the technique applicable in such waterways: have a small fly at the ready and examine the water thoroughly for holding or feeding trout before casting the presentation. Sizes 16/18 Adams, Blue Dun, Dad's Favourite and Greenwell's Glory will do the trick here.

(13) Tuatapere: 14.1 km from (11)

Return to Highway 96, turn right and continue to the bridge over the Waiau River, 300 m before the town. There is road access on the near side of the bridge leading to a large parking area beside the wide, slow-flowing river. Under good atmospheric and water conditions this position will provide a prolific evening rise, offering fly anglers challenging dry fly fishing until about 20 minutes before complete darkness, when they should change their pattern to a size 10 or 12 Twilight Beauty, Dad's Favourite or Greenwell's Glory wet fly.

The riverbed consists of gravel and small stones, sloping gradually towards the depths against the far bank. This provides an easy upstream approach to fish feeding in the shallows. Long-distance casting is neither desirable nor necessary: the competent angler will walk slowly upstream in gently flowing knee-deep water and lay a line to the half-seen rise in the twilight, keeping a tight line to the presentation, before hardening with his free hand at the moment of strike.

The river from here to its outlet into the sea is a major flow. Although it undoubtedly carries good stocks of fish, it presents difficult fly fishing conditions because of its size. The spin angler, however, may cover extensive sections of water and expect spasmodic results. There are many other fishing positions on the waterway between Manapouri and Tuatapere, but those I have described will provide any angler with enough choice to enjoy good fishing on most occasions.

30 Aparima River

The Aparima is an excellent trout fishing river, perfectly suited to both spinning and fly fishing methods. It has abundant stocks of brown trout, averaging 1 kg (2.2 lb), in clear water flowing gently over a bed of fine gravel, with occasional stands of willow trees providing shade and shelter for anglers and fish alike. The inclement weather of Southland is its only disadvantage. This chapter describes some 70 km of the river from the sea coast inland to its head-waters near Mossburn, where it is bridged immediately before the highway leading to the Oreti River at Dipton. The route described in this and the following chapter will enable an angler to use Invercargill or Mossburn as a base from which to fish the Aparima and Oreti Rivers — both of which are brown trout fisheries of renown.

(1) Gummies Bush: 3.1 km from Highway 96

On the northern side and within sight of Riverton, turn inland into the Otautau Road and follow this to the bridge, where there is good access to the riverbank on the downstream side. The water is deep and slow, with banks of long grass and occasional willow trees. Although this is a favourite position for local anglers to fish with a worm, it also produces good results when applying the spinning and fly fishing methods.

Fly anglers should stand on the edge of the earth bank and back cast over the water, unless they are accomplished 'tower' casters and can avoid the high vegetation. It is difficult to visually locate cruising fish here and in the absence of a rise you should blind fish with a size 14 or 16 Dad's Favourite, Greenwell's Glory, Twilight Beauty or Adams dry fly. If fish ignore the dry fly, when all indications point to a dry rise, use either a size 16 Greenwell's Glory wet fly or a size 16 Pheasant Tail nymph. The evening wet rise should be fished with the standard patterns: sizes 12/14 Twilight Beauty, Greenwell's Glory or Dad's Favourite wet flies.

(2) Fairfax Bridge: 13 km from (1)

Pass through the small settlement and turn into the next road on the right which leads to a bridge. Turn left before the bridge and follow a vehicle access track that ends in a parking area on the riverbed. The fishing conditions here are excellent; clear, rippling water flows quietly through a shallow run and into a deep pool on the opposite bank with a gravel beach sloping gradually into the depths.

During normal atmospheric conditions the trout are quite visible as they cruise or remain on station, feeding quietly. These fish must be approached with stealth and cast to in a similar manner, preferably from behind. I would recommend a size 16 or 18 Greenwell's Glory wet fly in the dawn light, a size 12 or 14 Pheasant Tail nymph from an hour after sunrise until mid-morning, and sizes 14/16 Dad's Favourite, Adams or Greenwell's Glory dry flies until mid-afternoon, when the fish will stop surface-feeding during the heat of the day. A size 10 or 12 Hare & Copper nymph will suffice during the late afternoon period until the trout rise and feed dry again as the sun loses intensity.

During the wet rise, about 40 minutes before dark, try a wet size 14 or 16 Twilight Beauty, Dad's Favourite or Greenwell's Glory wet fly until the rise stops at nightfall. Anglers wishing to fish after dark and catch a large brown should use a dry Twilight Beauty fly, sizes 12/14.

Return to the main highway and turn right.

(3) Otautau Bridge: 11.6 km from (2)

The river, railway line and highway follow each other on the way to this position and access to fishing positions is limited. Pass through the town and turn right at an intersection to follow the road to Winton. The bridge over the Aparima River can be seen 700 m ahead. There are vehicle accesses on both sides of the bridge, leading to gravel beaches extending into rapids or small pools dependent on prevailing riverbed channels, which alter occasionally during flood conditions.

The immediate location has a delightful run of water, well stocked with trout, and can provide anglers with good fishing. Unfortunately, there are times when earth-moving equipment extracts gravel from the riverbed, rendering it unsuitable for fishing. If this is the case, drive to the following access points, as the 14 or so kilometres between positions (4) and (7) may be described as a fly anglers' utopia. The numerous ripples, runs and pools, in a clear river flowing down a shallow gradient through a course lined with grass and overhanging willow trees creates a perfectly balanced habitat for brown trout.

(4) Anglers' Access Sign: 1.6 km from (3)
Do not return to the main road, but continue past the bridge and turn left at the junction into a road signposted 'Wrey's Bush 19 km'. An Anglers' Access sign on the left-hand side indicates a gravel road that leads to the riverbed. Positions (4) to (7) are accessible from this side of the river.

(5) Anglers' Access Sign: 4.8 km from (4)
This sign is at an intersection and marks a gravel road leading to the left. The road is 1 km long, passes through a gate (leave as found) and terminates on the riverbed. **It would be impossible to find a more perfect section of dry fly fishing water in New Zealand. Fly fishing conditions are unexcelled here.** Clear water flows over a fine gravel bed with a gentle gradient from the beach to the depths against the high bank overhung with willow trees and flowering broom which deflects the prevailing wind.

The water downstream drifts quietly over a wide glide to flow swiftly and smoothly between earth banks covered with long grass and occasional willow trees. Upstream, on the other hand, the river flows over open gravel beds between stands of willow trees and offers shallow ripples and small pools with perfect lighting conditions for stalking, sight fishing and applying the upstream fly fishing technique. The fly selection described under (2) may be used with confidence at this venue.

(6) Gravel Road Access: 4.8 km from (5)
The sign 'Anglers' Access' locates this road leading to a venue with a river offering similar conditions to (5).

(7) Nightcaps Highway 96 Bridge: 5.1 km from (6)
Turn left at the intersection before but within view of this bridge and park on this side of the bridge to enable a reconnaissance of the location. The upstream section emerges from a wide gravel bed descending a slight gradient between stands of willow trees — a view possibly spoilt only by the sight of a mechanical digger removing gravel a short distance upstream (more acts of vandalism). The groyne of hewn rock forming the upstream bridge approach will have trout feeding sub-surface in the turbulence. These are accessible by walking under the bridge (from downstream), standing on a slab of concrete and casting ahead of your stance.

The downstream section flows quite wide and extends from a grass-edged gravel beach on your left to willow-shrouded depths opposite. The long pool exits through a rapid which confines the waters to narrow channels beneath the shade of overhanging trees. This pool is well stocked with small trout — try a few casts with a small dry fly through the turbulence created by driftwood caught in what appears to be old bridge piles midstream.

A rough access road leaves the highway beside your parked vehicle and follows the riverbed for some distance downstream offering numerous access positions to excellent runs of productive water. The whole location warrants time to explore and fish thoroughly.

Pass over the bridge, turn right and follow the route signposted 'Wrey's Bush'. The river will now remain on your right-hand side as far as position (13).

(8) Anglers' Access Sign: 2.7 km from (7)
This position is within sight of the Wrey's Bush settlement, where there is a hotel offering accommodation. It is necessary to park on the road and walk along a gravel track between vegetation for a short distance to reach the riverbed. From here upstream it becomes rougher as the gravel is replaced with stones. The gradient steepens slightly and confines the water

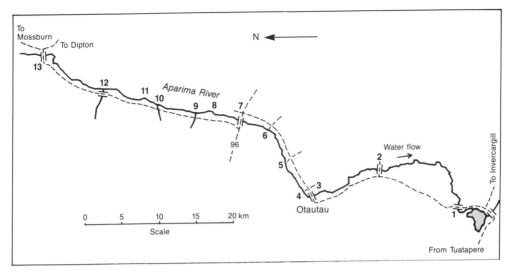

Nightcaps Bridge, Aparima River.

flow into discernible and relatively stable channels. The fly patterns will also change, becoming larger and more buoyant — Grizzly Wulff, Yellow Humpy, Blue Dun and Kakahi Queen in sizes 10/12 for use in rapids and Hare & Copper, Pleasant Tail (weighted) nymphs for similar conditions and in deep pools.

(9) Anglers' Access Sign: 4.1 km from (8)
On the way to this access point there is a sign advising against trespassing. Do not attempt to gain access to the river along this section of highway, despite its appealing appearance. The Anglers' Access sign is on the roadside near a low stopbank which obscures the river. There is easy access here to conditions similar to those at (8).

(10) Anglers' Access Sign: 3 km from (9)
The river is very close to the highway at this sign and access is easy to good water conditions.

(11) Anglers' Access Sign: 4.5 km from (10)
This sign marks a rough vehicle track leading through high vegetation towards the river and is within view of an AA sign on the opposite side of the road reading 'Gowan Hills Station'. The access track is very rough and it would be wise to walk it before driving down to determine if it is roadworthy.

(12) Anglers' Access Sign: 5.2 km from (11)

Pass over the Etal Stream bridge and watch carefully for this sign, which is beside an old wooden gate before some tall willow trees flanking the road as it veers sharp left. Access to the river's edge entails a short scramble through thick scrub, but the effort is warranted; the water conditions and resident stock of fish in the confined and boisterous water are nothing short of excellent.

The perfection of this section of river may be viewed by driving ahead a further kilometre, to where the river is separated from the highway by only 20 m of paddock. The river approaches from your right side as it descends a distinct gradient in a stable channel and brushes a stand of flax and trees growing on the upper extremity of the paddock. These superb fishing conditions extend downstream from the next and final access in a course which meanders from one side of the riverbed to the other.

(13) Highway Bridge Access: 8.8 km from (12)

A rest area beside this bridge provides easy vehicle parking and walking access to a wide riverbed of stones, covered liberally with stands of gorse and broom which, with other vegetation, provide a constant supply of terrestrial insects to the fish whenever the wind blows, as it does with annoying regularity in this region. The 8-km section of water from here downstream to (12) is particularly well stocked with trout. It is necessary to blind fish most of the time as the water is too boisterous to permit visual sighting except along the very edges of the current.

An active and positive approach is necessary in these upper reaches if the sport available is to be enjoyed. The terrain is comparatively open but demanding underfoot and the constant down-draught from the mountains not only causes severe burns but calls for the use of a powerful rod to deliver a fly accurately into the teeth of the wind. A SAGE 9 ft (2.7 m), weight 6, and Cortland does this with ease, and likewise will handle the 2-kg (4-lb) brown trout that fight like demons possessed in this outstanding trout river.

This is one of my favourite South Island lowland rivers and I visit it all too infrequently each season. My personal preference for flies for the 20-odd kilometres of the river from positions (9) to (13) are sizes 8/10 Grizzly Wulff, Yellow-bodied Humpy or Kakahi Queen dry flies and similar sized nymph patterns, Brown Stonefly, Hare & Copper or Smith's Pheasant Tail (weighted). May you also enjoy this marvellous waterway, and mark your appreciation with a catch and release approach.

Aparima River.

31 Oreti River

The Oreti and Aparima rivers run parallel to each other, some 20 km apart, and have abundant stocks of brown trout. In some respects, however, they are different. The Aparima gains its source from small springs and lowland streams to flow gently over a gravel bed lined with trees along its entirety, whereas the Oreti River system presents two contrasting characteristics: the mid reaches, described here, echo those of the Aparima but on a much larger scale, whereas the upper reaches traverse many miles of wind-parched high country tussock valleys and provide outstanding fly fishing to brown trout which must be deemed **trophies** by any standards. (The upper section of the Oreti, from Mossburn to the Mavora Lakes, is described separately under Chapter 25.)

The Oreti is a long river gaining its source from the Southern Alps, which tend to discolour the water with melting snow in the early and late periods of the fishing season. During the peak fly fishing months, January to March, the flow is generally clear and stable. Although the riverbed is too wide for the willow trees to provide shade, it is excellent for fishing, and the streamer fly, spinning and dry or wet techniques may be successfully practised.

The mid reaches of the Oreti River, from Dipton to Winton, are dealt with here, where it flows beside Highway 6. I have described access to fishing positions in a downstream direction.

(I) Dipton Bridge: 26 km via Castle Downs Swamp Road from Aparima River Bridge near Mossburn

Preceding the southern side of this bridge the road runs alongside the river, providing an opportunity to reconnoitre the terrain and water flow. Watch carefully for a gravel vehicle track on the left leading to the riverbed, from where there is easy foot access to the water's edge.

The river flows down gentle gradient as it passes under the bridge. It is deep and fast against the right-hand bank for a short distance and then spreads out into shallows. (It should be noted that the course changes frequently as a result of flash floods.) The water flow near the bridge is reasonably small, permitting foot crossing in many places and enabling anglers to fish the whole expanse of the river.

Although the water is clear during the height of the season, its flow is generally too strong and agitated to spot fish in, and fly anglers are obliged to fish blind most of the time. I would suggest the use of full-hackled dry fly patterns Kakahi Queen, Molefly, Humpy and Grizzly Wulff in agitated water conditions and the lightly hackled Dad's Favourite, Twilight Beauty, Adams and Greenwell's Glory in shallow runs and backwaters where trout may be seen cruising on the feed or rising quietly.

Should dry flies fail to lift a fish in rough water try a size 10 or 12 weighted Hare & Copper, Hare's Ear or Pheasant Tail nymph. These nymphs, especially the Hare & Copper, are very effective when used as wet flies; that is, across and down with a slow retrieval. Quietly feeding trout that are hesitant to take a small dry fly should be tempted with a size 16/18 Greenwell's Glory wet fly, Sawyer's Pattern Pheasant Tail or Peacock Herle nymph — deployed in the same manner.

Spin anglers may use Tinkers, Tobies, Tango, Daffy or any other single-blade minnow in predominantly black or gold colours in fast water and revert to Mepps or Veltic (spinning blade) patterns when fishing shallow, slow-flowing and calm water.

These fly and minnow patterns will suffice anywhere in the river system described here, but naturally individual locations will determine the size and pattern which will be most effective.

(2) Dipton Bridge Access

Pass over the Dipton Bridge and follow a gravelled access road leading through trees on the upstream side. This ends on the wide riverbed adjacent to a concentrated flow of water preceding the bridge, and offers easy fishing access and conditions. Actually, there are several vehicle accesses leading off the highway on either side of the bridge and anyone of these will provide access. You should consider checking the location quickly before making a decision on which one to use. Shade from the sun and shelter from the inevitable afternoon wind will influence your choice.

(3) Rest Area: 1 km from (2)

Turn right at the intersection and follow Highway 6, signposted 'Winton'. This highway provides the accesses to the river downstream to Invercargill. The rest area is on the right shoulder of the road, below which large rocks have been placed to alleviate scouring by the river. The water is fast and disturbed, providing better conditions for spinning than fly fishing. There is also foot access to the actual riverbed from where it is possible to fish both confined and wide sections of water.

(4) Benmore Bridge Access: 7.4 km from (3)

Drive 6 km from (3), turn right at the intersection and continue for 1.4 km to the bridge, from where there is easy access to the riverbed. The water is confined between stopbanks and willow trees and the channels provide good conditions for both the spinning and fly fishing techniques. The environment and terrain here typify the mid sections of this river — open, sunlit and pleasant, be you fishing or otherwise.

(5) Centre Bush Bridge Access: 12 km from (4)

Return to Highway 6 and turn right towards the coast. There is no access to the river for the next 12 km, though its course may be identified from the road. After travelling 11 km from (4) turn right at an intersection towards the bridge 1.3 km ahead. As you approach the bridge watch for vehicle accesses leading from either side of the road towards the riverbed. I suggest that you park before the bridge and make use of its elevation to study the lay of the land. Then make your choice as to which access track to follow.

Although the river is confined during its passage under the bridge, the water follows various braided channels both upstream and downstream. Identify and fish the channel that looks most established — the stones and rocks sub-surface will be stained and tarnished, holding an established nucleus of insect larvae.

(6) Tuatapere Road Bridge Access: 10.1 km from (5)

Return to the highway from (5), turn right and continue for 9 km before turning right into Highway 96, signposted 'Tuatapere'. The bridge is 1.7 km further on. Both bridge approaches provide vehicle access to the riverbed, over which they meander for long distances. There are ample parking and fishing positions to water which is generally flowing more quietly here than upstream.

At this position, the river is large enough to offer spin anglers unlimited scope to apply their talents, but fly anglers must exercise patience, observation and a little contemplation. It is of little use to thrash every inch of water in the river, despite the sizeable population of resident trout, as there are large barren spaces.

The ideal times to visit this section of river are in the morning, before the breeze ripples the surface at noon, and in the evening, when the heat of the sun subsides with the wind. The fly angler should walk slowly upstream along the bank and locate a trout visually or by their movements, ascertain its direction of travel and then gain casting range before presenting a fly from a stance obscured from the fish. It should be noted, however, that the fish in the bodies of such large shallow expanses tend to cruise in all directions and not always upstream. Should the pool have a distinct and concentrated movement of water in a fixed position, then generally a single trout will follow a regular 'beat' which is quite discernible to an experienced fly fishing angler.

The circumstances here call for small fly patterns, the style being determined by the rise form. Sizes 14/16 Dad's Favourite, Twilight Beauty, Kakahi Queen and Adams will suffice in the dry patterns. Sizes 14/16 Hare & Copper, Pheasant Tail, and Hare's Ear are effective nymph patterns, and sizes 14/16 Greenwell's Glory wets should be used at dawn, or any time during bright daylight hours if there is even the slightest splash with the rise. The

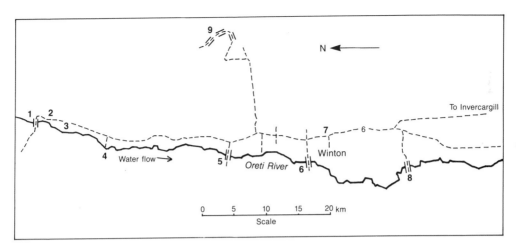

evening rise, if disturbed and splashy, should be fished with sizes 12/14 Twilight Beauty, Dad's Favourite or Greenwell's Glory, though almost any winged variety is effective.

(7) Winton Post Office: 2.2 km from (6)

(8) Lochiel Bridge Access: 14.2 km from (7)

Pass though Winton, follow Highway 6 towards Invercargill for 6.4 km and veer right at an intersection near Lochiel Garage into the road signposted 'Riverton 37 km'. There is another intersection 800 m further on where you turn right into Lochiel Bridge Road, signposted 'Riverton', and after a further 2 km turn left into the Waianiwa road. Travel 250 m, turn right at the junction, and drive 800 m to the bridge.

The river here is large and moving slowly between banks of earth and mud rather than clean gravel. Good results may be obtained with the spinning method. Although the fish rise well for fly fishing, they have a habit of doing so just out of casting range. Walking access to the riverbed is reasonably good from the bridge approaches.

(9) Otapiri Stream: 23 km from (7)

This is a prime dry fly fishing stream: you should appreciate its worth and apply stringent conservation measures. It is one of several streams and drainage canals that form the Makarewa River, which flows into the Oreti some 25 km on the seaward side of Winton. The whole Makarewa River system flows through farmland and the water flows are reasonably slow, descending long, shallow gradients through courses with earth banks overhung with grass, scrub and the odd tree. The environment and terrain create a natural habitat for brown trout, whose survival is ensured by an adverse climate and long inaccessible sections of riverbank.

The average size of the fish caught will be 1 kg (2.2 lb) because the small fish 'dash in' and snatch the fly before the large ones get moving. The flies I have listed under (6) are ideal in these small streams. They must be presented skilfully and accurately to avoid alerting the trout, which will probably be on edge after hearing your clumsy footsteps along the top of the bank. Stealth of approach in such confined areas is as important as concealment.

Leave the Winton Post Office, follow Highway 6 in the direction of Lumsden for 7 km, and turn right at the road junction into the road signposted 'Browns via East Limehills'. Continue past a railway line, ignore four junctions and one intersection, and having travelled 7 km turn sharp left into Hendersons Road. After 2 km, turn right into the road signposted 'Otapiri Gorge 5 km', follow this for 3 km, and turn left into the road signposted 'Otapiri Gorge 2 km'. Follow this for 1.5 km, ignoring one junction, pass over a small bridge, and park on the grass verge next to a gate on the right-hand side. Pass through the gate onto a grass paddock, around the perimeter of which the stream flows in a semicircular course.

I would suggest that you walk to the right and fish the stream in an upstream manner and direction, using a 5X leader and a small dry fly of the Dad's Favourite, Twilight Beauty, or Kakahi Queen patterns. These should be changed to a size 14 or 16 Pheasant Tail nymph if they do not entice a feeding fish.

Although the flow of the water is small, the course provides rapids, backwaters and pools, between grass banks and beaches of fine gravel. Small stands of trees create casting difficulties. The water is well stocked with small brown trout, but a high degree of expertise is necessary to coax them into taking a presentation.

Once this position has been thoroughly fished, you should return to the car and follow the road through the gorge for approximately 5 km. There are many positions over this distance from which there is access to the riverbank.

32 Lower Mataura River

T he Mataura is one of the best stocked brown trout rivers in the South Island. It flows through low foothills and plains for approximately 160 km from its source at Moonlight near Lake Wakatipu, Queenstown, to the sea at Fortrose, near Invercargill. With the exception of a 20-km gorge, the entire river offers reasonable access to water conditions ranging from a small, sparkling stream to a major flow. The river is gentle during good weather, providing good fishing for the novice and expert alike. It must be stated, however, that Southland is renowned for bad weather and subject to frequent flooding; anglers should therefore make inquiries about conditions before embarking on a fishing excursion to the area.

The upper reaches of the river comprise a small, clear, shallow stream flowing gently through farmland, but the section covered here is wide and generally too deep for crossing on foot.

(1) Anglers' Access: 27 km from Invercargill

Drive through Invercargill in the direction of Bluff and turn into Highway 92, signposted 'Fortrose', on the outskirts of the city. Follow this route for 25 km, turn right at a road junction, and pass through the small settlement of Gorge Road. After travelling 1.3 km, turn left into a no exit road at a junction which indicates Fortrose and Waikawa to the right. Follow this road for 800 m and turn right into a gravel vehicle track descending a long incline towards the river, 1 km away. This track, marked 'Anglers' Access, fasten gates', passes through a gate, crosses a small bridge and ascends a short but steep stopbank with parking on a paddock a few metres from the river.

The river is wide and deep at this position. It flows smoothly between grass-covered banks, offering conditions better suited to spinning than fly fishing when there is no obvious fish activity on the surface. There is a high bridge in the centre of the river; but is it unattainable as both approaches have been washed away.

Wyndham Bridge Access, position (4), Lower Mataura River.

It is possible to walk long distances in either direction from here and fish from venues which suit prevailing water conditions. The effort of walking, locating and reaching such locations is certainly warranted — this particular section of water is very well stocked with resident trout.

Spin anglers are advised to use 14-g (½-oz) minnows of the Tinker, Toby, Dinky-di or Slice pattern in gold, black or brown when fishing deep water. Shallow ripples and backwaters littered with debris will produce better results with yellow-coloured 7-g spoons, tangoes or red/black Mepps/Veltic lures.

The type of rise will determine the style of fly to be used by fly anglers. Dry rises, quite normal during the day in smooth water, should be fished with Dad's Favourite, Greenwell's Glory, Twilight Beauty and Adams, that is, lightly dressed, fine-bodied patterns in small sizes 14/16. These sizes may be increased if the fish ignore the initial presentations. The fast flows, or rippled water, may be fished with flies of a more buoyant pattern, Humpy, Wulffs, Black Gnat or Kakahi Queen for example, which should also be of a small size when initially presented.

Fish that are rising sedately, and barely breaking the surface, would undoubtedly prefer a size 16/18 Peacock Herle, or Sawyer's Pheasant Tail nymph moistened (including the leader) with saliva to make it sink in the surface film. These stealthy feeders are generally the big trout.

Lack of visible fish movement does not indicate lack of trout, but reveals their feeding pattern. At such times, fly anglers should use a weighted nymph of say the Hare & Copper, Stonefly or half-back Pheasant Tail patterns. These fly and minnow patterns should also be the basis of the Anglers' selection when fishing the other sections on the lower Mataura.

(2) Anglers' Access: 8 km from the Gorge Road Settlement

Return to the road junction at Gorge Road and veer right into Seaward Downs Road. Look for an 'Anglers' Access' sign near a vehicle access track leading right and descending a long gradient. This sign is situated where the road turns left. (Care is necessary when following this route from Gorge Road. Several road junctions (and their signs) cause confusion and you should consciously bear right to follow the river, which flows a considerable distance away through a valley floor.) This vehicle access terminates about 30 m from the river, which is wide, deep and flowing forcefully between grassy banks. It is a position that suits spinning perfectly and fly fishing anglers must, in the absence of a rise, be prepared to make long casts and similar drifts with a dry fly to lift fish feeding sub-surface.

(3) Mataura Island Bridge: 6 km (approx.) from (2)

Return to Seaward Downs Road and continue upstream for about 3 km. Veer right into McCall Road (signposted 'Mataura Island 6 km') and follow it to the bridge. En route there is another Anglers' Access sign — No. 4 — indicating a vehicle access leading towards the river. From here to a couple of kilometres past the side road leading to the Mataura Island Bridge, the river runs close to the road. It is separated by a fringe of willow trees and a narrow strip of paddock. The water is quite visible at times and beckons anglers to fish in the ripples and smooth glides leading from pool to pool. This is good water: a solid flow calling for a determined and positive fishing approach with spinning equipment or powerful fly rod (a SAGE 9-ft (2.7-m) RPL, weight 5 model would be ideal here). There are several houses along this section of road and anglers must approach the occupants for permission to 'jump the fence'.

Turn right at the intersection within sight of the bridge (on the right). The signs reveal that this is only 37 km from Invercargill via Edendale (a direct route anglers may use to reach this bridge instead of following the described 'dog-leg' via Gorge Road). The bridge offers an elevated panorama of perfect water, picnicking and fishing conditions. The river emerges from a long sweeping arc, along the peak of which there is good walking access on a sand/grass terrace which slopes gradually into the depths. This gentle riverbank extends for some several hundred metres down to the bridge itself, and provides fly anglers with an excellent platform to walk along slowly and examine the shallows for feeding fish. Such anglers will no doubt fish ahead of themselves with a size 16 Gold-ribbed Hare's Ear or Peacock Herle nymph while they are 'working' upstream.

The river continues downstream from the bridge in a wide, positive, smooth flow which is slightly broken by small turbulences as it passes between a grassy bank on one side and restrictive willows on the other. All in all, this is an excellent fishing venue, whatever technique you prefer, and access is easy. Drive off the road onto the river plateau from the other side of the bridge and follow the track over paddocks to reach the beach. Many hours of fishing are available in this venue.

Return to the intersection described above, turn right and follow the road as it parallels the river for about two of the 11 km to Wyndham.

(4) Wyndham Bridge: 9.5 km from (3)

After 7 km, watch for an Anglers' Access sign indicating a long vehicle access track leading right. This leads to a very good venue with similar fishing water. This bridge offers similar conditions to Mataura Island, and it is possible to drive off the road and follow the river upstream along a paddock which descends gradually into the water. This provides an extensive section of superb fishing water emerging from an arc to flow quite shallowly over a bar of fine gravel extending from the inside of the arc.

The river exits below the bridge, still paralleled by the grassy bank, and veers left over a wide, shallow bar extending the full width of the stream. The upstream side of the river is unfishable — it is covered with impregnable willow trees — but the downstream portion offers an elevated bank ideally suited for spin fishing. This location provides unsurpassed brown trout river fishing conditions.

(5) Mimihau Bridge: 1 km from Wyndham

The Mimihau Stream follows a meandering course through farmland in its lower reaches before converging with the Mataura River approximately 1 km upstream from Wyndham. It has a gentle water flow contained between grass banks, with pools, runs and rapids. Before fishing this stream, you must call into the house next to the bridge, on the Wyndham side, and request permission to cross private land.

The water is well stocked with small brown trout, which offer challenging sport to fly anglers. A delicate and accurate touch, a stealthy upstream approach, and the use of size 16 flies and nymphs is necessary to entice these fish to take. The size and shape of the fly rather than the actual pattern is most important. I would suggest Dad's Favourite, Twilight Beauty or Adams — that is, small-bodied, lightly hackled wing varieties — which should be replaced with a small-bodied nymph if rising fish disregard the dry fly. If these patterns fail to attract rising fish, use a size 16 or 18 Greenwell's Glory wet fly. This is an excellent standby and will often produce results.

Trout feeding quietly on the bottom should be tempted with an unweighted size 14 Hare & Copper nymph. Cast slightly ahead and to one side of the fish, enabling the nymph to sink slowly towards the feeding station. The boisterous wet rise should be fished with a size 14 or 16 Twilight Beauty or similar-shaped wet fly.

Fish the 1.3 km of river preceding the confluence by walking downstream and fishing your way back to the bridge. The section of water upstream from the bridge provides pleasant fishing for approximately 900 m, where it is crossed by a second bridge which may be reached by turning right at a junction 700 m along the road from the first bridge. Another particularly good section is upstream from the second bridge. Pass over it, park and fish your way upstream through encroaching vegetation. The results will make the effort worthwhile.

Return to the main road and turn right.

(6) Road Access: 9 km from (5)

The 14-km section of river followed by this road has only one identifiable public access. The Anglers' Access signs, so prevalent in the past, have been removed and there are now several 'private property' signs erected on boundary fences. Do not cross fenced property without prior permission from property owners.

This vehicle access is quite identifiable and leads from the road as it veers right. It terminates on the rough riverbed itself. The access is open to the road, but fenced on both sides and quite steep. The water is confined to a definite channel here, flowing over a stone beach this side and against a high rocky bank on the other. The flow is reasonably swift as it approaches your stance and forms a short rapid downstream where it surges past a small rock abutment. This is a good fishing position for both methods and fly anglers should use large, full-bodied and well-hackled flies of the Humpy, Grizzly Wulff, (palmer-hackled) Molefly and Kakahi Queen patterns in this forceful current. Sizes 8/10 heavily weighted Hare & Copper or Stonefly nymphs, fished blind, are also a good choice here.

An hour or two of good fishing is available from the grass bank on this side of the river.

(7) Mataura Bridge: 5.6 km from (6)

Pass over this bridge only if you wish to gain access to the town. The fishing route below continues up the right-hand side of the river. The next 13 km from here to Gore provides what is probably the most pleasant fly fishing available on the lower Mataura River. The river is quite wide, reasonably shallow and flows over fissures of gravel and rock, creating sections of turbulent rapids, runs, ripples and swirling backwaters. There are occasional long, wide, smooth-surfaced pools drifting quietly with one shoulder sheltered from the elements by tall, overhanging willow trees. It is perfectly suited for fly fishing — the rise form will dictate the style: dry, wet or nymph.

The accesses are quite obvious; generally walking tracks leading through the roadside grass and passing beneath a solid fringe of willow trees. Use the sections where there is no roadside boundary fence. If you wish to pass through one of the several gates or the short sections of fence along this route you should seek access permission from the nearest residence. It will be necessary to park on the roadside and, in most instances, the river is only a few metres away.

This is the final description of the Lower Mataura River. At Gore further inquiries regarding the trout fishing available in the district should be directed to specialist trout fishing establishments.

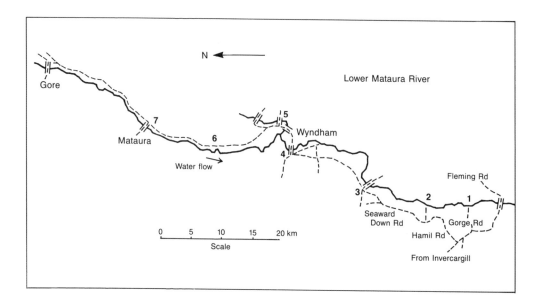

33 Pomahaka River

This tributary of the Clutha River is one of the South Island's brown trout greats. It flows through undulating hills and farmland for well over 80 km and is very well stocked with brown trout. Its meandering course between miles of willow trees creates a natural hatchery, but restricts fishing access. The small section of river I have described here follows Highway 90, the direct route from Gore in Southland to Alexandra in Central Otago via Raes Junction and Highway 8. It will provide transit anglers with an opportunity to test its waters in passing. A full day's good fly or spin fishing is available within a very short distance of the highway.

Leave Gore on Highway 1 heading towards Dunedin, turn left at McNab after 4.6 km and follow Highway 90 inland. After travelling 26 km from the road junction at McNab, you will reach a bridge crossing the Pomahaka. The road is wide enough to park on the other side of the bridge, where it is possible to walk down the approaches to fish in either direction. The downstream section flows for some 400 m between high, grassed earth banks from which it is possible to step down to a stance just above the water. The width of the river and the high bank make this venue difficult for fly fishing. The water is about 3 m deep, dark-coloured, covered with a thick layer of weed and full of brown trout.

Fish your way downstream using a yellow 7-g (¼-oz) Spoon or Tango minnow. It must be retrieved very slowly just above the weed. The river upstream, while also a good spin fishing venue, should be fished with a size 14 or 16 fly (wet or dry depending on the hatch). This is a delightful position with grassed sandy banks along which anglers may fish upstream as the river slowly curves to the right. Before fishing this position, request access permission from the residents of the house on the Gore side of the bridge.

Continue through the intersection ahead and follow Duncan Road for 1.2 km. Turn left at a junction and follow the road signposted 'Waikaka 24 km'. A short drive of just over a kilometre reveals a bridge spanning the Pomahaka River. Pass over the bridge, turn right and park in the large area below the road. This is excellent trout fishing water and spin anglers may work their way downstream on the Waikaka side of the river. Use minnows as described above and expect to catch any number of fish — this is trout water equal to the best in the South Island.

Fly anglers are advised to reconnoitre the upstream section from the bridge and then fish from the riverbank (difficult, but possible) through the section of water broken by layers of visible rock. This whole section of river is well stocked with brown trout which rise nicely to a correctly presented small dry fly.

Return along Duncan Road, turn left at a junction 1.7 km away then left again to follow Highway 1 after travelling 4.1 km. After driving 1.3 km, turn left into the road signposted 'Heriot', which, after passing over a small rise, follows the willow-fringed course of the Pomahaka River through the deserted settlement of Kelso. Veer left at the junction here and follow the road to a bridge crossing the river a short distance ahead.

It is necessary to park on the roadside near the bridge and walk down its approaches to fish the river in either direction. This venue offers superb dry fly fishing in a gentle flow of water passing over a bed of fine gravel between avenues of willow trees growing on grassed earth banks.

Pomahaka River, Rankleburn Access: 19 km from Tapanui

This is a venue suited to anglers with camper van transport and desirous of fishing an outstanding section of brown trout water within a short walk of their overnight camp.

Leave the southern end of Tapanui township on a subsidiary road signposted 'Rankleburn', which traverses undulating country along the base of foothills for 17 km before descending a long, steep incline towards the Pomahaka River valley. While descending this very dusty gravel road you will notice the Rankleburn Reserve, a forestry hut and a small stream on a lower level. There is a junction where the road reaches the level of the river. Turn left here and the entrance to the Rankleburn Reserve is visible and signposted 'Blue Mountains Recreational Hunting Area', or something similar. This is a good overnighting venue on a large grassed area, sheltered by trees and serviced by a small creek. The hut offers basic shelter and similar ablutions only.

The road follows a small terrace between the hills and the Pomahaka River which is partly obscured by a fringe of trees and long grass. Glimpses of the river, permitted by the encroaching scrub, reveal a delightful run of broken water descending exuberantly over long shelves of solid rock and pools interspersed with huge stones and slabs of broken rock. There are also isolated heaps of flood debris, caught up here and there, which adds to the desolate and neglected appearance of the 2-km section of river followed by the road before it leaves the river to climb into the hill country.

It is necessary to walk, or drive, along this road and find walking accesses through the scrub to the river — a hassle indeed, but one which adds to the satisfaction of earning that big brown trout domiciled in this rough portion of an otherwise sedate river. The riverbed is extremely rough, with slippery rock, deep guts of water, rushing torrents and sombre glides brooding beneath overhanging gorse and vegetation. This is an arena for physically fit anglers wearing non-slip footwear, preferably aluminium cleats rather than felts. A strong rod is essential here to power a large dry fly or heavy nymph over impassable water to cover the rises which will be quite apparent but just out of reach for those conventional 'poles'.

The configuration of the riverbed provides a couple of days fishing in this 2-km section where every nook and cranny may hold one or several fish, unlike a normal waterway, where clean, unobstructed rapids and pools allow you to see every fish — or allows every fish to see you! — on the first pass.

This 'gorge' section extends in either direction from the portion described. You may walk upstream along a private road, but the downstream section necessitates walking along the edges of a ravine.

There is a particularly good spot for overnighting beside the river 1.9 km downstream from the Rankleburn Reserve. Turn off the road and follow a vehicle track over long grass behind the roadside trees and stop beside an dilapidated concrete picnic table — a relic from a bygone era. It is possible to continue along this road and eventually cross the Clutha River at Clydevale to rejoin the main highway. It is 'just' a matter of following your nose and choking on clouds of dust from the gravelled roads for about 20 km.

34 **Alexandra Reservoirs**

Alexandra is the largest town in Central Otago, a district which experiences the hottest — and coldest — temperatures in New Zealand. It has the most barren terrain in the country, is renowned for the quality of its fruit and is crossed by the longest river in the South Island. The Clutha is the outlet of Lake Dunstan, a recently constructed hydro-electric storage lake commissioned in 1993. I would not advise anglers to make a special visit, but rather to enjoy the area while on the way to more 'special' waters. The legacy of reservoirs constructed last century by our gold-seeking pioneers, along with old water races and derelict mud huts, offers a trout fishing interlude in stark contrast to anything else available in the South Island yet entails a deviation of less than 60 km. Of the six reservoirs described, I consider Butcher's Dam to be the most interesting and pleasant to fish. Although the trout are not large, they are plentiful. The dam is situated alongside Highway 8, within 6 km of Alexandra, and provides a fishing experience in an accessible and pleasant environment.

(I) **Butcher's Dam:** 5 km from Alexandra

Drive along Highway 8 in the direction of Roxburgh for 5 km. As you descend a long, straight incline towards the dam, stop for a few minutes in the elevated position and study its environs. The left shore of the main arm extending away from you is covered with trees while the other is open and rocky, covered with tussock and briar near the main highway as it curves left. The water is very deep at this end of the dam and gets shallower at the head 1 km away, where there is a small converging tributary. Vehicle access to the shore is over open terrain and also at the head of the dam.

Follow the highway around a left curve, ignore the side road on the right, and follow a small dirt access road on the left. This leads to the water's edge. Several small inlets on this side of the dam provide easy access to the water, with adequate room for casting. The water, however, is deep and quite unsuitable for fly fishing during daylight hours, unless

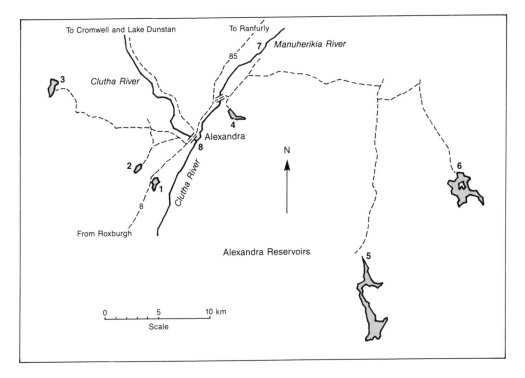

To Cromwell and Lake Dunstan

To Ranfurly

7 Manuherikia River

85

3 Clutha River

4

Alexandra

8

N

2

6

1

8

Clutha River

From Roxburgh

Alexandra Reservoirs

5

0   5   10 km

Scale

there is an obvious rise. It may be successfully fished with either the spinning or streamer fly techniques at any time of the day or evening. A 7-g (¼-oz) Tango or Spoon minnow, in yellow or green, would be a wise choice for the spin angler. The streamer angler should use a medium-density sinking line and size 4 Hamill's Killer (yellow), Parson's Glory or Yellow Dorothy lure pattern. Anglers employing either of these methods should make long casts at an angle permitting the presentation to be retrieved very slowly, deeply and as parallel as possible to the shoreline.

When the fish are rising dry, use sizes 14/16 Peveril o'Peak, Grouse and Purple, Twilight Beauty or Blue Dun dry patterns. The normal procedure of replacing these presentations if spurned with a size 16 or 18 Sawyer's pattern Pheasant Tail nymph should be followed. The wet rise during the twilight hours should be fished with either a Dad's Favourite or Twilight Beauty size 16 wet fly.

Although the terrain on this side of the dam is rough, and there are numerous clumps of briar, it offers good access to the water's edge in many places. To gain access to the top of the dam, return to the main highway, travel towards Roxburgh, and turn left into a gravel road as you start to ascend a hill. This access road gives an elevated view of the shallow bays and I suggest that you stop in strategic positions and look for fish movement. This style of approach during calm conditions can be very rewarding in locating feeding fish, which, once sighted, must be stalked and fished to in a stealthy manner.

The road leads to the upper reach of the dam, where the tributary stream enters its waters — a position that entices fish to feed. The dam is well stocked with small brown trout, with an average weight of 1 kg (2.2 lb), but anglers adept at fishing after dark with a dry fly (size 14 Twilight Beauty) may expect to catch considerably larger fish.

(2) Conroy's Dam: 6 km from Alexandra

Leave Alexandra in the direction of Roxburgh, turn right into Earnscleugh Road, having crossed the bridge spanning the Clutha River, and turn left into Chapman Road after travelling 1.4 km. Drive the entire length of Chapman Road (3.3 km), veer left at the intersection and follow Conroy's Road towards the dam. Pass though the gate at the junction 1 km further on: this road provides access to the dam.

The dam is less than 1 km long and is surrounded by tussock-covered terrain. It should be fished with similar flies and minnows to Butcher's Dam. There is a good supply of brown trout, averaging 600 g (1.3 lb) in this waterway.

(3) Fraser's Dam: 16 km approx. from Alexandra

Drive towards Roxburgh from Alexandra, turn right into Earnscleugh Road just after crossing the bridge, and follow it for 5 km to the junction with Conroy's Road. Veer to the right, drive for 300 m, turn left into Blackman Road, continue for 2.5 km, and immediately after following a sharp curve to the right, turn left into an unmetalled track. Follow this rough vehicle access for 9 km to the dam. It is necessary to pass through gates on the way, please leave them as found.

The dam is about the same size as Butcher's Dam, and its altitude of 647 m suggests that warm clothing may be required as the sun loses intensity. The terrain, while steep, offers reasonable access to the water's edge, especially if you cross the stream and fish from the other side. The same fly and minnow patterns as described for Butcher's Dam should be used. The water is well stocked with 600 g (1.3 lb) brown trout.

(4) Lower Manorburn Dam: 5 km approx. from Alexandra

Leave the centre of Alexandra on Highway 85 heading towards Omakau and turn right at a junction to follow the road signposted 'Little Valley'. Follow this road over a bridge spanning the Manuherikia River, turn left at the junction, and continue for 4 km to the edge of the dam.

This dam is well stocked with small brown trout and perch and while it produces good results to the spinning method, it is of doubtful value as a fly fishing venue.

(5) Upper Manorburn Dam: 40 km approx. from Alexandra

This is a large dam by Central Otago standards, consisting of two very deep reservoirs connected by a gorge to produce a waterway of some 9 km in length. Unfortunately, there

Butcher's Dam, position (1), Alexandra Reservoirs.

is no road access to the banks, except at one end, and the surrounding steep, rocky terrain restricts foot access from elsewhere.

The water is at an altitude of 740 m. It is well stocked with rainbow trout averaging 1.3 kg (3 lb) and good fishing may be had with either the spinning or fly fishing techniques. However, the sheer depth of the water and the steepness of the surrounding banks create conditions more suited to the former than the latter.

Leave Alexandra on Highway 85 in the direction of Omakau and, after travelling 3.5 km, veer right at a junction as the highway veers sharp left. Follow this road over the bridge, around a right then left turn towards Galloway, and take the second turn to the right into Crawford Hill Road. Follow this road for approximately 15 km, until it ends at a junction. Turn right here and follow this very rough road for about 17 km to the fishermen's huts next to the dam. Do not attempt to drive along any of the many tracks leaving this road, as they are suitable for four-wheel drive vehicles only.

The fly fishing technique may be used when there is fish activity in the small bays, and the spin and streamer methods may be practised anywhere. Fly anglers should use similar patterns to those suggested for Butcher's Dam, and spin anglers may consider enlarging their selection of minnows with 14-g (½-oz) Tinkers, Tobies and Spoons, to gain extra casting range and depth of retrieve. Brighter-coloured minnows may be used to attract the rainbow trout.

(6) **Poolburn Dam:** approx. 50 km from Alexandra

Drive towards Omakau on Highway 85 and turn right at a junction signposted 'Ida Valley', opposite the golf course before the township. Follow this road over the Manuherikia River bridge, turn right into Ida Valley Road, and turn right again into Moa Creek Road — a total distance of approximately 9 km from Highway 85.

Follow the Moa Creek Road for 8 km (ignoring the seven junctions), turn left into Webster Lane, continue for 3.2 km, and turn right at a junction to pass the Moa Creek Hotel. This road leads to the Poolburn Dam, some 11 km further on. The last 9 km are unmetalled and should not be attempted during or immediately following heavy rain.

Both sides of the dam provide good fishing conditions. On the right-hand side you should fish between the huts in view, and on the left-hand side follow the road until you encounter the first hut, situated in a sheltered bay. This left branch may be followed all the way to the dam wall, where good fishing is to be had with the spinning or feather lure methods. The same fly and minnow patterns as described in the Upper Manorburn section should be used here. There are shallow beaches to fish from in many places.

(7) **Manuherikia River**

This small stream flows though the plains for over 50 km, followed by Highway 85, the route from Alexandra to Ranfurly. There are many access positions to the riverbed from the highway and its arterial roads.

The clear water flows over a gently contoured riverbed of gravel between open banks of tussock and avenues of willow trees. Although it typifies the perfect brown trout stream it provides mediocre fishing over most of its length due to the lack of aquatic insects. The intense heat of mid summer, the searing brilliance of the sun and lack of rainfall are not conducive to the formation or retention of trout habitat.

Reasonable fishing is to be had by the competent dry-fly angler, however, in the lower reaches, where access is possible from the bridges mentioned under positions (4) and (6).

(8) **Clutha River**

Alexandra is positioned on the banks of this river which, despite being well stocked with both rainbow and brown trout, is unsuitable for fishing because of its huge volume and lack of access. Spin anglers may fish from the beaches beneath the bridge within the precincts of the town and try their luck with any pattern 14-g (½-oz) minnow. There is always a chance of catching a trout in this position.

Fishing from the shoreline of Lake Dunstan, a few kilometres upstream is already producing encouraging results less than a year since the dam was filled. It will undoubtedly become a fishery of substance once the hatchery-bred trout which were released into the dam at its inception become acclimatized and spawn.

Waitaki River Valley overlooking position (1).

35 Upper Waitaki River Valley

The Waitaki River gains its source from the Ahuriri River, passes through three hydro-electric storage dams and is followed for over 100 km by Highway 83 from Omarama and Oamaru. It is crossed at each extremity by Highways 8 and 1, linking Christchurch with Wanaka and Dunedin respectively. The lower 61 km is renowned for salmon rather than trout fishing and it carries a large volume of water through frequently changing courses in an unstable gravel bed.

The river flow fluctuates depending upon power generation demands and this disrupts the trout habitat and necessitates vigilance on the part of anglers, who must always watch for a sudden rise in water level. They must ensure that their retreat cannot be blocked by sudden flooding.

The upper section, on the other hand, offers controlled and stable water conditions where most of the available fishing is in dams, offering excellent results due to the abundant stock of trout residing in a favourable habitat. Of the three dams, Lake Aviemore provides the most consistent fishing. There is easy access to positions and picnicking facilities constructed and maintained by local authorities. Bountiful stocks of fish mean that this region is a good prospect in dry and stable weather conditions.

Because of the length of the river, the unstable nature of its lower section, and the proximity of the dam region to the fishing route, only the upper reaches of some 46 km are described here.

Lake Aviemore, Otematata: 93 km inland from Oamaru

This is the central lake in a series of three linked together by water discharged through canals from power stations. It is 16 km long and 4.5 km wide, well stocked with both rainbow and brown trout and, being completely encircled by a road providing adequate access, requires only a general description.

All methods of fishing are practised successfully here. Although most of the shoreline is better suited to the spinning and streamer fly methods because of their long distance casting capabilities, there are several outstanding positions to suit fly fishing.

(1) Convergence of Otematata River and Lake Aviemore: 800 m from hotel

Drive or walk from the hotel in a downstream direction along Highway 83, turn left, and follow an access road leading towards the lake on the hotel side of the bridge. This road runs alongside the river, leads past a boat harbour on its left side and ends in a large grassed parking area adjacent to the convergence. This is only a short walk from the river, which flows through shallows over an extensive shingle delta extending well into the lake.

There are several small inlets around the perimeter of the delta interspersed with willow trees growing in both the water and shingle banks. These trees provide welcome shade and shelter from the elements and it is usual to notice trout cruising the precincts of the inlets in the early morning and twilight periods.

A good method of fishing this location is to walk as far as possible into the lake along the delta, parallel to, but out of sight of the river, in which there will trout feeding in the ripples. Fly anglers should fish the disturbed flow of water entering the lake by applying the wet fly technique (across, down and slow retrieve) with a size 10 or 12 Greenwell's Glory, Twilight Beauty or any similar winged wet fly. In the absence of a strike, you should try a few casts with a size 8 or 10 Pheasant Tail, Hare & Copper or similar heavy nymph.

In the event of a rise during the day, you should use dry fly patterns Kakahi Queen, Blue Dun, Grizzly Wulff or Molefly in sizes to suit the conditions: small if the lake water is calm, but large and well dressed when the water is choppy. The boisterous wet rise in the twilight should be fished with a size 12 wet Twilight Beauty or Dad's Favourite fly.

Once the ripple entering the water of the lake has been thoroughly fished over, anglers may consider working upstream with a small dry fly or Pheasant Tail nymph. The river, while normally small, is well stocked with trout which take and play with enthusiasm. Do not take this gentle stream lightly, despite its shallow runs, small eddies and pools that give

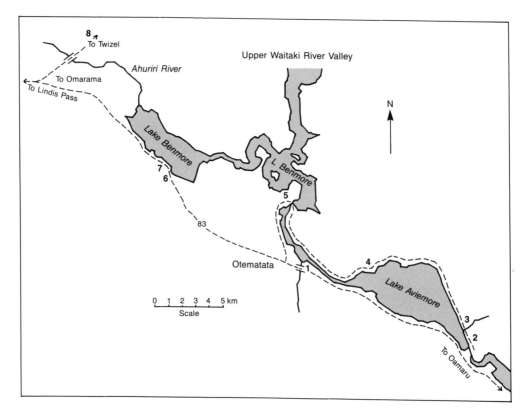

the impression of being too shallow to hold trout — they will be there. It is possible to fish right back to the bridge, though the vegetation will frequently restrict casting.

The patient angler, competent at sighting fish, moving cautiously, and adept at laying an accurate line, should concentrate on the shallows adjacent to and under the willows downstream from the convergence. The precincts of the boat harbour should be fished in a similar way as there is often a fish or two on the cruise here. I would suggest that the best presentation to entice fish in this position would be a size 16 Sawyer's pattern Pheasant Tail nymph which, if disregarded by the fish, should be replaced with the same pattern one size larger. Of course, should the fish be obviously rising dry, the natural choice would be a size 16 Twilight Beauty, Dad's Favourite or Greenwell's Glory dry fly.

Although it is not extensive, this position will provide interesting and relaxing fishing in the calm morning or evening of a summer day. It is not suited to the spin or streamer fly method, with the exception of the deep water at the end of the delta. Spin anglers fishing this location would be advised to use a 14-g (1/2-oz) minnow of almost any pattern, while the streamer fly angler should use a medium density sinking line with a size 2 or 4 Parson's Glory, Hamill's Killer red, or Dorothy red lure. These should be cast as far as possible into the lake and retrieved across and along the edge of the flow entering it. The speed of each retrieval should be varied to allow the lure to cover the various levels of the lake. Once the convergence has been thoroughly fished, concentrate on retrieving the streamer fly or minnow at varying depths parallel to the edge of the delta.

(2) Lake Overflow: 15.5 km from Otematata

Drive along Highway 83 in the direction of Oamaru, turn left at the junction after travelling 14.5 km, follow the road as it traverses the dam wall and turn right into an access road that leads to a parking area next to the outflow. Highway 83 follows the lake shore, offering many places from where it is possible to stop the car and walk a few metres to fish from the shore into deep water.

These positions are unsuitable for the dry fly technique in the absence of a rise, but may be fished successfully with either the spinning or streamer fly methods. The outfall from the dam provides concentrated, fast and disturbed water which offers good conditions for spinning or streamer fly fishing throughout the entire day. It may be fished with the dry fly technique during the morning and evening hours when the fish are rising.

(3) Deep Creek: 1 km from (2)

Return to the road crossing the dam and turn right, that is, follow the lake upstream on the opposite side to Highway 83. The road is in an elevated position and does not give access to the water. After travelling 1 km, the road traverses a culvert, on the right side of which there is a small dam backed against a high cliff. The dry fly angler should study the surface of this water quietly for a short period and if fish movement is detected use a size 16 Sawyer's pattern Pheasant Tail nymph to fish the rise. The area is small and offers limited access but it does provide good-sized trout that may be caught by the expert dry fly angler.

(4) Picnicking and Camping Areas: 7 km from (3)

The road follows the steep lake bank in an elevated position offering no access to the water's edge for 7 km. It then descends to cross gently sloping terrain for the next 4.5 km. This section of the lake shore has been developed to provide several camping and picnic areas next to the water, where there are small inlets, gravel beaches and extensive stands of trees.

The lake bed adjacent to the shore is generally shallow, with a gradual gradient into the depths providing perfect conditions for the sighting and stalking of fish during calm conditions. Several small creeks and streams flow into the lake and form natural feeding positions for trout, which will frequently be seen on the cruise.

(5) Benmore Dam: 10 km from (4)

The road to this position is also too elevated to allow access to the lake. Cross the dam wall, drive to the observation position and reconnoitre the outfall of Lake Benmore. This large flow of water is channelled into a course that runs parallel to the road returning to Otematata, which provides easy access to its banks. Just below the dam outfall, the water flows around the perimeter of a small peninsula to which there is road access. This provides fishing positions into deep, fast-flowing water — ideal for the spinning or streamer fly methods.

In all there is about 2 km of accessible fishing water within walking distance of the road downstream from the peninsula, providing good stocks of trout with fishing more suited to the spinning or streamer fly methods than fly fishing.

The dry fly angler experienced in fishing heavy, fast water, such as the Buller River of Nelson, the upper Clutha River of Wanaka or the Waiau of Te Anau, would be quite at home in this section of river. It demands considerable physical effort, quick reflexes and the ability to strip line competently. When fishing this type of water, my choice of dry flies are sizes 8/10 Grizzly Wulff, Palmer-hackled Molefly, Blue Dun and Kakahi Queen.

The route to Otematata is quite straightforward and less than 5 km from the observation position at Lake Benmore.

Lake Benmore

This is the original and largest of the recent dams on the Waitaki River. At an altitude of 361 m, it is 93 m higher than Lake Aviemore. Despite its size, however, there is very little access to the shoreline. It is fished extensively by the trolling method. The lake is more or less a 'U' shape, with the western arm being fed by Lakes Ohau, Tekapo and Pukaki, and the eastern arm by the Ahuriri River. This river gains its source in the vicinity of the Lindis Pass, the main route (Highway 8) from Tekapo to Wanaka. The left arm of the lake is parallel to and accessible in places from Highway 83 (Oamaru to Otematata/Omarama) and provides excellent fly fishing. The positions described below are approached from Otematata.

(6) Lake Benmore Boat Harbour: 10.8 km from Otematata

Drive towards Omarama along Highway 83, which crosses the Ahuriri Pass at 500 m and offers an elevated view of the lake's left arm. After travelling 10.8 km, turn right into the vehicle access leading to the boat harbour, which is situated on a small peninsula offering delightful picnic facilities among the trees.

The boat harbour is positioned at the convergence of a small stream, providing a natural feeding ground for fish. The area is not large but is suited to all techniques of fishing. The spinning and streamer fly methods may be applied during bright daylight hours. The fly angler, however, should visit the area in the morning — before the wind ruffles the water surface, creating difficulty in sighting the fish or their feeding pattern — and again in the still air of twilight.

The water shelves steeply at this position and the spin angler should use 14-g (1/2-oz) weighted minnows of the tinker, toby, dinki-di, spoon or 'Z' patterns in predominantly bright colours. The streamer fly fisherman should use medium density sinking lines and size 4 lure patterns — Hope's Silvery, Scotch Poacher or Parson's Glory (red).

The fly angler must use small, lightly hackled dry flies of the Dad's Favourite, Twilight Beauty, Greenwell's Glory and Adams pattern in sizes 14/16 or sizes 16/18 Sawyer's pattern Pheasant Tail nymphs, when the fish are rising dry. The standard wet patterns, Twilight Beauty, Greenwell's Glory and Peveril o'Peak, will suffice during the wet rise at twilight.

(7) Ahuriri/Benmore Convergence: 12 km (approx.) from (6)

The convergence of the Ahuriri River with the head of Lake Benmore is an excellent position for trout. It is worthy of several days exploratory fishing by anglers using either technique. I suggest that the Glenburn Camper van Park be considered as a strategic base from which to fish the region. This lakeside accommodation is situated on Highway 83, opposite the head of the lake 7 km downstream from Omarama, and the staff will suggest the best walking accesses to the location.

The river converges with the lake over an extensive gravel delta which offers easy-walking terrain to the excellent fishing available in and near the inflowing current. It should be taken cautiously, however, because the sand is very soft in places, especially on the edge of the water.

The spin and streamer fly angler would be advised to concentrate on the actual flow of the river while working downstream well into the lake along the delta. The fly angler, on the other hand, may also fish the same river flow but should also concentrate on the shallows extending to his right from the convergence. This location provides shallow water in which there are stands of grass through which trout cruise in search of food. You should walk parallel to the water's edge (but out of sight to the fish) and watch the shallows closely for fish movement, especially during calm conditions. The fish will cruise among and along the edge of the grass growing in the water, revealing the presence by small bow waves or distinct water disturbance when they take food. It is essential to use stealth and a rear approach to such fish. Should they be obviously feeding on the surface, use a floating line, 3-m leader with a fine tippet and a size 16 or 18 Sawyer's Pheasant Tail nymph, Coch-y-Bondhu, Red-tipped Governor or Humpy dry fly. If these patterns are disregarded, or the fish appear to be feeding on sub-surface food, use the same line, leader and a Hamill's Killer streamer fly, which should be cast about 60 cm to one side of its head or in its path. Once the fly has settled underwater, it should be given an occasional twitch to attract the fish.

The area for this type of fishing is extensive and is better fished in the calm morning hours before the inevitable wind starts blowing about noon. The windy afternoons may be spent casting a streamer through the current of water entering the lake, or walking upstream and fishing the main river with the conventional fly fishing technique. The fishing here is also extensive.

Ahuriri River, Omarama

This is an excellent trout fishing river, from its headwaters inland from the Lindis Pass to its convergence with Lake Benmore. It is a vigorous flow of clear water, often tinged blue by melting snow, descending a gradual and constant incline over a bed of unstable stones, gravel and sand. Open tussock-covered terrain, liberally interspersed with native briar and matagouri scrub offers easy access to the riverbed where occasional willow trees create the only stable pools in the waterway.

At first sight the appeal of the turquoise water, flowering lupins and emerald willows overshadow that of trout fishing, which in fact could be overlooked by the average angler. Fast water rushing madly over jumbled stones beneath a blazing sun and scorching hot wind is a far cry from the accepted vision of perfect dry fly water — indeed, the grassy banks of a quietly flowing stream shaded by overhanging trees and cooled by a zephyr would be a godsend in this hot, windswept environment. It is imperative to take protective measures here, as the wind, let alone the sun, will cause severe burns within a few hours.

The composition of this fishery makes it necessary to walk upstream continuously and visually search for trout while blind fishing all likely looking water with emphasis in the rapids. The trout, predominantly rainbows, are coloured a slate-grey and are difficult to see against the stones unless they are actively moving — there are very few sections of calm water in this river system.

Ahuriri Highway 8 Bridge: 2.2 km from Omarama

Follow Highway 8 towards Twizel and reconnoitre the location from the bridge itself. The water approaches the bridge through an undulating course in a gravel bed covered with flowering lupins and low vegetation. It is lined with avenues of trees and the right bank is quite open, covered with tussock and crossed by a road offering good shaded picnicking positions. This vehicle access track runs parallel to the highway, which can be seen climbing a steep hill as it veers left towards the mountains. This is a good base from which to fish the river upstream. It is generally well stocked with fish despite its proximity to the road.

It is possible to park in a gravel storage area on the downstream side of the bridge and walk downstream through reasonably open terrain and fish the river back towards your parked vehicle.

Excellent access and fishing conditions are available by driving over the bridge and turning right off the highway to follow a gravel road signposted 'Ben Oma Station'. This road follows the river and passes through another gate (leave as found) which displays a meaningful invitation to fish — 'Access is a privilege, not a right'. Please adhere to this message. Follow the road a short distance, and turn towards the trees lining the course of the river as you pass the Rodeo Stockyards visible on the right after emerging from behind a small hill. Park near the trees and walk through the 2-m high vegetation to the river, which is flowing through pools, boils and rapids formed by the roots and trunks of willow trees. This small area of disrupted water is well stocked with trout that are difficult to sight, catch or land in this 'unkempt' environment — but have a go anyway.

Hours of fishing is available in either direction from this position. Personally, I prefer the upper one, where it is possible to wade the river in places and visually locate trout as they hold sub-surface in rapids. Pay particular attention to small backwaters remaining in old channels and the swirling boils between clusters of tree roots or driftwood.

The fish in this river generally lift to sizes 10/16 (dependent on water flow) Wulff, Humpy, Kakahi Queen or Molefly dry fly, but don't persevere with it if its spurned in the first two passes. Change to sizes 10/14 Gold-ribbed Hare's Ear, Hare & Copper or Smith's Pheasant Tail nymph and you'll be assured of a strike.

The angle of the sun in this location creates perfect lighting conditions for sighting fish, but the wind does the opposite. However, it is an outstanding venue nevertheless, as is the whole river.

Ahuriri River: Omarama to Lindis Pass

Highway 8 from Omarama to Wanaka runs alongside the Ahuriri River for some 17 km, offering several accesses through a strip of encroaching briar and matagouri to an open riverbed. The river flows through braided and transit channels which alter character with every other flood, making an accurate description impossible. Even the established willow trees which provide a little stability to the riverbed are currently threatened with extinction.

The riverbed must be walked and the entire expanse of water searched — and fished blind — if the trout are to be caught with regularity. There are no holding pools in this river downstream of a few kilometres above the Lindis Pass Junction. The terrain offers ample opportunity to walk from the road to the river and there are also three gates offering passage through the roadside boundary fence, positioned at 10.4, 15.1 and 16 km respectively from Omarama.

Ahuriri River/Lindis Pass Junction: 17.4 km from Omarama

The access road following the Ahuriri River upstream is signposted 'Ben Avon' and 'Birchwood Station' at the junction and 'Access is a privilege, not a right' a little further up the valley. The river gradually alters character and flows through gorge-type terrain where there are stable channels, permanent rapids and resident trout. Anglers may explore this domain, and enjoy good fishing, for days on end — the river extends for miles.

36 MacKenzie Country Lakes

The high country lakes Ohau, Pukaki and Tekapo form the source of the Waitaki River and are situated in a region that enjoys stable, fine summer weather. Their waters are used for power generation. While the levels of Pukaki and Tekapo fluctuate with demand, those of Ohau remain constant apart from a natural variation, and its height is controlled by a weir across the river outlet. Although both Lakes Pukaki and Tekapo are picturesquely coloured deep turquoise with glacial dust, they both hold fish. The fishing in Pukaki must be described as mediocre but that of Tekapo is good and improving slowly year by year. The waters in front of the motor camp near the Tekapo township will verify this. The trout rise prolifically (but often just out of fly casting range) in the still hour before darkness. This area also offers some of the most impressive and breathtaking mountain scenery in New Zealand. The region is strategically positioned on Highway 8, the main route from Christchurch to the Southern Lakes via the Lindis Pass.

The 80-90 km length of highway between Lake Tekapo and Omarama embraces some of the most pleasant trout fishing in the South Island. In making this observation I have considered the three MacKenzie lakes, their outlet canals, rivers and dams, Lake Benmore and Aviemore, as a singular identity.

Lake Ohau: 30 km (approx.) from Omarama

Travel north towards Tekapo from Omarama on Highway 8 for 15.7 km, turn left at the Lake Ohau Lodge sign and follow the road for approximately 15 km to the lake shore. The lake is only 5 km wide and its shores are generally solid rock with occasional narrow beaches of broken rock and small stones. The terrain at the head of the lake is grass-covered alluvium which extends into the water.

(1) Lake Shore: 15 km (approx.) from Highway 8

This position offers unreliable fishing results from a rough, rocky beach.

(2) Creek Mouth: 5 km from (1)

Lake Middleton, 700 m in length, will be noticed on the left on the way to this position. It is used for recreational purposes and although it holds a small stock of trout it is not worth the effort of fishing.

Position (2) offers good access over a rough gravel beach to the convergence of a small creek with the lake. Like any lake with steep beds, these small tributaries attract fish to feed in the current as it enters the calm lake water. In the absence of an obvious rise or visible fish movement close to the surface, the angler should use either the spinning or streamer fly method. Spin anglers should use 14-g (½-oz) minnows in spoon, slice, tinker or toby design, determining their colour by the rule of thumb method 'the brighter the day, the brighter the minnow'. Start fishing with a gold Tinker/Toby minnow as this is always a good choice to start with.

Streamer fly anglers should use a medium density sinking line, with size 4 lures in brown, yellow or black, such as Mrs Simpson, Parson's Glory, or Craig's Night-time pattern. The rabbit patterns in these colours would be a good choice for this lake.

Should there be cruising fish visible just beneath the surface, fly anglers should use a floating line with a size 8 wet Twilight Beauty fly or size 6 (streamer) Hamill's Killer. Cast as far as possible into the current entering the lake and retrieve it with short strokes and frequent twitches to attract the fish which will frequently streak and take instinctively.

The manner in which surface-feeding fish behave will determine the fly pattern. If the fish are 'humping' or 'porpoising' with only their backs breaking the surface, use a size

10 or 12 unweighted Hare's Ear, Hare & Copper or Pheasant Tail nymph. When they are feeding off the surface with very little water disturbance, use a size 14 Greenwell's Glory wet fly, size 16 Sawyer's pattern Pheasant Tail nymph or small dry fly patterns — Adams, Dad's Favourite, Black Spider, etc. A positive surface-feeding pattern should be fished with a small, full-bodied fly similar to Red-tipped Governor, Coch-y-Bondhu, Humpy, etc. The active, splashy wet rise should be fished with the old standby, a wet size 12 Twilight Beauty.

(3) Creek Mouth: I km from (2)

This position offers similar conditions and fishing to those described under (2).

(4) Lake Ohau Lodge: 2.1 km from (3)

The Lodge is reached by turning to the left and climbing a gravel access road. Opposite this position there is a wide, flat gravel beach, providing easy walking access to the water. I suggest that you park your vehicle, walk 600 m back down the lake and fish the convergence of a small stream in the manner described under position (2).

The beach gives way to shallow water over a rock bed a few metres above this position. Here there is also another creek entering the lake.

(5) Boat Launching Ramp: 2.8 km from (4)

The road to this position is narrow and skirts the edge of the lake but offers no walking access to the water's edge. Turn right at a junction and follow the access road to the Round Bush peninsula where there are numerous trees to provide shelter from the wind and sun.

The surrounding water is deep, and only suitable for the spinning or streamer fly methods unless there are obvious signs of fish activity on the surface or if they are visibly on the cruise.

(6) Road Access: 3.4 km from (5)

Follow this side road to its end in a rest area next to the lake, which offers fishing conditions similar to those at (5).

(7) Head of the Lake: I.8 km from (6)

Veer right at a junction after travelling 1.1 km and follow the road, from which there is walking access to the shore. This section of the lake provides excellent conditions to suit the fly angler. Although the spin fisherman may also expect results, the water is really too shallow and calm to suit this method.

There are approximately 3 km of fishing from the shore, which may be followed to where the Dobson River enters the lake. The shore and bed of the lake are sand and mud, with a shallow gradient covered with grasses and large patches of floating fish weed. Exercise extreme care when walking in or adjacent to the water as there are sections of very soft silt; these may appear solid, but will engulf the unwary angler to his knees and perhaps even his waist. I advise you to walk slowly along the water's edge and search the water for fish movement, in barren stretches and especially near stands of grass and fish weed. Fish located there will be alert for unusual movement within their cone of vision and easily disturbed by anglers wading through the water. The angler must approach these feeding fish cautiously and, when within casting range, lay the presentation so that the line does not pass through the fish's vision.

Do not consider the time spent searching the water surface or stalking a rise as wasted — it will pay dividends in catch rate. There is little point in frightening fish into flight, when patience and stealth will ensure that half their number are caught.

The rise pattern, not the flying insects, determines the fly pattern to use. During calm conditions, my choice of artificials would be, in order of preference, a size 16 Sawyer's pattern Pheasant Tail nymph, size 14 Greenwell's Glory wet fly or size 16 Red-tipped Governor dry fly. Should a trout actively cruising sub-surface ignore these presentations, I would use a floating line, 3-m leader and size 4 Hamill's Killer (red) streamer fly. This would be cast ahead of the fish, to be given a twitch off the bottom when within its range of vision. When the water is slightly agitated by wind action, the natural fly to use would be a size 10 or 12 well-hackled dry of the Twilight Beauty, March Brown, Grizzly Wulff, Humpy or Molefly pattern. In this situation, the angler is obliged to fish by instinct into any likely feeding station.

If time permits, the angler may work his way right across the shallows extending across the head of the lake and fish the Dobson River in an upstream direction from the convergence. This position presents good conditions for the spinning and streamer fly methods. The flat terrain en route to the river has many small inlets, back-waters and side streams, all of which should be inspected for feeding trout.

(8) Maitland Stream: 1.5 km from (7)

Continue up the valley from the junction and park either side of the bridge spanning the Maitland Stream. This flows over rough alluvium from the bridge to the river-flat below the road, after which it passes quietly though a course of gravel and earth to its convergence with the Dobson River. The banks of the river are covered with scrub, which restricts access and casting.

The river provides good dry fly fishing for the experienced angler adept at stripping to keep a tight line in fast water. In these conditions, fish will impulsively take as the fly flashes past their feeding station, but will eject it just as quickly when they feel the hook. The fly pattern is immaterial and good flotation is the prime factor. A size 8 or 10 Palmer-hackled Molefly or Grizzy Wulff would be adequate.

I would suggest that you fish the vicinity of the bridge for a short period and, rather than walk down the incline to the river-flat to fish calmer water, drive a further 1.5 km up the valley and turn right to pass through a gate. This gives access to a rough vehicle track leading towards willow trees growing on the banks of the river. The terrain is quite flat and the river meanders through small runs and deep pools where stands of trees unfortunately restrict casting. These do, however, provide perfect cover and feeding positions for trout.

While the section of river near the bridge may be fished vigorously, this lower section calls for expertise in sighting fish movement, a cautious approach and skill in laying a line softly and accurately. Surface-feeding fish should be tempted with small presentations similar to those used at the head of the lake, but the deep pools (in the absence of a rise) should be fished with a sinking-tip line and weighted sizes 8/10 Pheasant Tail or Hare & Copper nymphs, which must be retrieved extremely slowly. While the streamer fly would undoubtedly be effective in this vicinity the pools are generally too short to permit efficient casting.

(9) Temple Stream: 3.5 km from (8)

The road follows the river for approximately 1.5 km before this position, providing easy access to the water a few metres away. This section of the river flows over unstable alluvium, which causes the channel to alter with every flood. It should therefore be fished only after a prolonged period of settled weather. Stable riverbed and terrain may be found immediately below and upstream from the bridge, where there is ample parking room and reasonably good access to the banks on either side of the road.

The section of river upstream from the bridge provides particularly good conditions in its pools and runs. These may be seen from the road up to where it emerges from the confines of a small gorge. During normal conditions, the water is just over knee-deep in the runs, permitting the fly angler to work upstream, with a small dry fly or nymph, and cover all of the pools from the tail to the head, while remaining concealed from the fish.

The physically fit angler may work his way right though this 1.2 km gorge to an open valley floor adjacent to a picnic ground a few metres below the convergence of the two branches of the Temple Stream. The gorge section is suitable for experienced anglers only, because of the restricted casting and wading and the wary nature of the trout in the deep, clear pools.

(10) Temple Forest Picnic Ground: 1.5 km from (9)

Pass over the bridge at (9) and, after travelling a few metres, turn left into the side road. The road ascends a hill offering a panorama of gorge and valley. Stop for a few minutes in one or two strategic places and reconnoitre the best sections of water with the easiest access.

The valley provides good shelter from wind and easy access to perfect river conditions. These would suit a size 10 well-hackled dry fly of the Molefly, Kakahi Queen, Twilight Beauty or Grizzly Wulff patterns in the ripples, or a size 16 Red-tipped Governor dry, Greenwell's Glory wet, or Sawyer's pattern Pheasant Tail nymph in the calm pools.

(11) Access Gate: 2 km (approx.) from (10)

Continue up the valley from the junction at (10) and a few metres after passing the Huxley Station sign pass through a gate on the right and follow the rough vehicle track to the banks of a small stream.

This waterway gains its source from a swamp a few kilometres up the valley. It is the only sockeye salmon stream in the region and has a very restricted fishing season — November to January only. As a small, clear stream meandering through river flats covered with tussock and grasses, it provides miscellaneous pools, runs and backwaters which demand accurate presentation of flies to ensure successful fishing.

(12) Hopkins River: 2 km (approx.) from (11)

Drive up the valley, stop and walk to the main stream of this river from the most advantageous position. Fish it with the streamer fly or spinning method. This is a large river flowing swiftly over a wide, unstable bed of gravel and rocks. While it carries a good head of fish, they must be deemed 'cruisers' rather than 'residents'. Since the river course alters direction with every flood, the best time to visit is after a prolonged period of settled dry weather. This permits the insects and their larvae to become established, halting the nomadic habits of trout.

Lake Tekapo: 60 km (approx.) from Lake Ohau

Lake Tekapo is a tourist and recreational centre promoting all water sports. It provides good trout fishing in rivers, canals and two small lakes a short distance from the town centre. Lake Alexandrina is 7 km long by 1.4 km wide and lies parallel to Lake Tekapo, which is approximately 1.8 km away over high ground. The water level is maintained by springs and one small tributary, while its small outlet passes through another lake en route to a convergence with Lake Tekapo.

Lake Alexandrina is so renowned for its large brown and rainbow trout that there is a

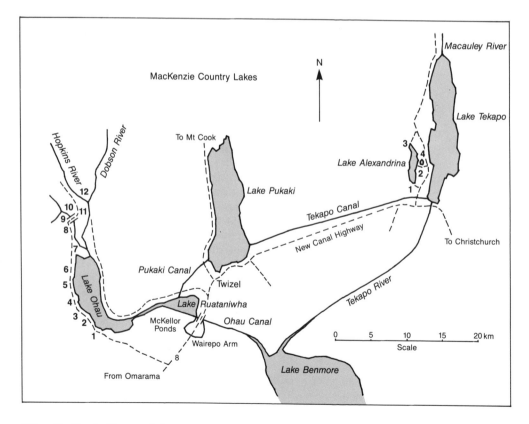

sizeable village of holiday homes overlooking its waters. The Fish and Game Council protects this resource by prohibiting powerboats on the lake, and any angler fishing from a boat within 100 m of the shore must have it securely anchored.

The lake does not have true beaches but steep, open terrain from which the anglers must fish. The steep terrain and lack of shelving underwater deltas around the perimeter of the lake restricts insect life, and the trout are deep underwater feeders. This makes the streamer fly method essential here and about the only time that conventional flies are used to any extent is during the manuka beetle hatch in mid summer.

Lake McGregor is formed by the outlet of Lake Alexandrina and is 1 km long by 600 m wide. It is quite deep but has shallows on its southern and western sides adjacent to and accessible from the access road to Lake Alexandrina. Although this lake is also fished extensively by the streamer fly method, it offers good fly fishing, especially near the outlet that passes under the Godley Peaks Road skirting the shores of Lake Tekapo.

(I) Lake Alexandrina, South End: 6 km (approx.) from Highway 8

Leave Tekapo on Highway 8 in the direction of Ohau, ascend the hill and turn right at the junction marked 'Lake Alexandrina' after travelling 1.8 km. Follow this route through undulating tussock country for 4 km and watch carefully for a nondescript sign depicting 'Alexandrina' erected on a single post inside the fenceline on the left side. Pass through the gate and follow the rough vehicle track as it climbs to the level of the lake, where it ends after following the shore for 800 m.

Stands of bulrushes and occasional trees on or near the banks make it necessary to locate suitable casting positions to fish into deep water. The streamer fly method should be used in preference to other fly fishing techniques — unless there are trout rising within casting range.

(2) Lake Alexandrina, outlet, mid section: 10.8 km from Highway 8

The signed access leads from the road at a junction 8.8 km from Highway 8 and within sight of Lake MacGregor. It runs along the shore of Lake McGregor before ascending the ridge separating it from Lake Alexandrina and ending near the shores of that lake. There are sections of narrow gravel beaches at various positions along Lake MacGregor that permit reasonable casting into deep water. Please note that the outlet stream is closed to fishing at all times.

(3) Lake Alexandrina, north end: 7 km (approx.) from Lake MacGregor

Continue inland for approximately 5 km, turn left at the first junction and then left again at the next junction. Follow this road to where it ends next to some holiday homes within sight of the lake. This end of the lake is very deep. It provides good fishing with the streamer fly method, unless there is an obvious rise, in which instance small dry flies or a size 16 Sawyer's pattern Pheasant Tail nymph may be used with confidence.

(4) Lake MacGregor: 9.6 km from Highway 8

Before fishing this lake, turn left into the Lake Alexandrina access road, park and walk up the hill to spend a few minutes reconnoitring. The outlet from Lake Alexandrina will be seen flowing into this lake between stands of willow trees on your left. The shore directly in front of you forms several small bays with shallow water shelving into the depths. The shores on the other side of the lake are steep, but provide walking access around the perimeter of the entire lake.

This lake offers good streamer fly fishing on the far side, where the water is very deep. Similar results may be obtained from the shallows using conventional fly fishing methods. Particular attention should be given to both the area where the tributary enters from Lake Alexandrina and the outlet channel leading to Lake Tekapo.

Although casting positions are limited, the fishing is excellent. Of these two lakes, I prefer Lake McGregor, where I am able to use the dry fly technique near the tributary in the early morning. Because the rising sun shines from behind, I cannot be seen by rising fish. The outlet channel may be fished similarly in the evening, when the light from the opposite direction repeats the conditions of the morning.

Tekapo River and Hydro Canals

Lakes Tekapo, Pukaki and Ohau are joined by massive canals which now provide excellent fishing resulting from a fish-stocking programme in the 1970s. Leave Tekapo, drive towards Pukaki and turn left into an obscure road on top of the hill 1.5 km away. The sign reads 'NZED Power Station, Private Road, Tourist Recreational Traffic Only'. Descend the slope, cross the bridge, turn left and fish anywhere in the canal leading to the control gates in view upstream. This is the start of the canals, which may be followed downstream after this initial fishing session.

My suggestions regarding fishing techniques here may be applied throughout the entire length of the canals. In the absence of a rise mid-morning or late afternoon, fly anglers should fish the water very close to the bank with a size 14 or 16 Hare & Copper nymph or plumpbodied dry fly — Coch-y-Bondhu, Red-tipped Governor, Humpy, etc. The trout feed on terrestrials blown into the water, and, at times, gorge themselves on freshwater whitebait. This latter food source ensures success for anglers using streamer flies (try a Jack's Spratt or Parson's Glory), and spinners should cast a white Devon, Cobra, or similar minnow.

There are occasions when the fish rise like crazy over the entire surface of these wide canals and the fly pattern is of less importance than the ability to get it down onto the water — personally I'd use a size 12 Grizzly Wulff in such circumstances.

The highway embankment forms many miles of the canal as it more or less follows it all the way to Lake Ohau (via Lake Pukaki), approximately 50 km away and crosses Highway 8 a few times. The canals are very well stocked and it is quite feasible for anglers so inclined to stop on the verge of the sealed road and cast a line anywhere as the whim takes them.

The dams (Patterson Lakes) alongside the canals are artificial and have small trout populations remaining from the original stocking programs. They offer easy walking access and idyllic fishing conditions. The access road leading to these dams is easily identifiable as it descends the high embankment towards the lower plateau.

The Tekapo River, often dry at its source from the Tekapo Dam wall, provides excellent fishing in its lower reaches. There are two main accesses to this location. Follow Haldon Road, signposted 'Lake Benmore, North Branch', from a junction on Highway 8, approximately 12 km north of Tekapo; this is a long drive over a rough gravel road and gives access to the river of clear water flowing over a bed of gravel, lined with willow trees. The terrain is quite open, though interspersed with patches of briar and scrub. This road also provides access to Lake Benmore. The other access is described in the Twizel paragraph below.

Twizel: 57 km from Tekapo, 30 km from Omarama, 63 km from Mount Cook

A good strategic base for the whole MacKenzie Basin, complete with an excellent motor inn, camping ground and shopping centre. The Twizel River bisects Highway 8 just 1 km north of the town. Here there is a large, tree-shaded rest area beside the bridge. This is a small stream offering delightful fly fishing in a flow of clear water passing over a gentle bed of gravel lined with willow trees and lupins.

Anglers may walk in either direction from the rest area, and ideally sight their fish before presenting a small dry fly or nymph. This environment calls for an LL-8-ft 9-in (2.6 m) SAGE 2-piece weight 3 rod, sizes 14/16 Adams, Dad's Favourite, Greenwell's Glory dry flies and sizes 16/18 Peacock Herle or Sawyer's Pheasant Tail nymphs.

Anglers should endeavour to fish the morning and evening hours only — the mid afternoon temperatures, wind and sun are extreme here during midsummer.

Lower Ohau River, Twizel

The lower reaches of this river provide excellent fishing and are within a short drive of Twizel. It is necessary to follow Highway 8 towards Omarama for 2 km and turn left to follow the Ohau Canal downstream at the junction on the Twizel side of the canal. The sealed road follows the final section of the canal described in the Tekapo chapter to its end at a power station ahead.

Before descending to the lower plateau, you should stop and reconnoitre the terrain surrounding the power station discharge channel, the bed of the Lower Ohau River and, in the distance, the placid waters of Lake Benmore. The trees ahead offer good parking, sheltered from the wind and sun and with good walking access to the shallows of the lake.

The Tekapo River enters the lake to the left of the trees and to get there means quite a long walk over rough terrain. It will be necessary to walk across the old bed of the Lower Ohau River to fish the small stream of water it still retains, but moves are afoot to modify and increase the existing flow. Only time will tell what effect this action will have on this particular fishery.

The Tekapo River flows shallow over a gravel bed which creates ripples, runs and an occasional deep but flowing pool. This is an excellent rainbow trout fly fishing venue — one of my favourites. The fish rise nicely to a dry fly — or nymph when conditions dictate — and anglers will surely use barbless hooks and release the bountiful rewards which await the proficient sportsman. Fly fishing anglers wishing to really enjoy the best of the Tekapo River rainbow trout fishing should contact a professional guide as there are several outstanding venues on this river that can only be reached by those with local knowledge and 4-wheel drive transport.

Wairepo Arm and McKellor Ponds, Twizel

These waterways provide a fishing experience unique in the South Island. These two small lakes, extensions of the Ohau Channel, have azure water shimmering between low tussock-covered banks offering easy walking access around their perimeters: they provide perfect conditions for dry fly fishing — calm water, ease of access, unrestricted vision and casting space — a few steps from the vehicle and an excessive head of sizeable trout.

The larger expanse of water, Wairepo, extends from the main canal for 1 km into shallow inlets amongst evergreen trees. These not only provide shelter for people and sustenance for fish but present the most picturesque fishing scene imaginable. The smaller canal, separated by the highway, offers an interesting and pleasant fishing interlude where anglers may walk quietly through level tussock terrain and cast their dry fly at visible fish, or their rises, along the undulating edges of small inlets. This relaxing and absorbing technique should be undertaken during the calm, cool hours of morning and twilight — the mid afternoon sun, heat and wind are unbearable. These two waterways are only 5 km towards Omarama along Highway 8 from Twizel.

Lake Ruataniwha, Twizel

This large lake, formed by the hydro scheme, is used extensively for boating activities and other aquatic sports in conjunction with fishing. There is a large motor camp situated on its shores and the fishing approach is quite straightforward. It is a matter of driving, or walking, around the perimeter of the lake and fishing where you will. Personally, I am not attracted by the fishing in this particular waterway and would rather drive the 25 km towards Omarama along Highway 8 and fish a real river — the Ahuriri — as described in Chapter 35.

Lake Alexandrina,
MacKenzie Country.

37 **Ashburton Lakes**

The Ashburton district of Canterbury extends from the coast to the Southern Alps, a distance of approximately 110 km. It is bounded on either side by two major salmon fishing rivers, the Rakaia and Rangitata, whose parallel courses are some 60 km apart. Two small trout fishing streams cross the plains over beds of gravel and stones. They offer good fishing conditions in clear water, generally overarched with willow trees, with easy access. The larger of the two, the Ashburton River, has its source next to a series of lakes situated in the low foothills, while the Hinds is formed by several tributaries originating in the alluvium of the plains. Several large irrigation canals convey water to farms throughout the region. These are used as trout hatcheries when restocking is necessary.

Most of the waterways in the district hold brown trout, which tend to be smaller than elsewhere in the South Island. They, and their environment, are better suited to fly fishing than spinning and are subject to stringent regulations.

Mount Somers is more or less in the centre of the district and I shall use it as a base from which to describe the distance to fishing venues on the rivers and lakes. It is 137 km north of Tekapo. Follow Highway 8 to Fairlie, turn left into Highway 79, continue to Geraldine, and turn left into Highway 72, which leads to Mount Somers.

There are two systems of lakes inland from here, which are reached by turning either left or right at Hakatere Junction, approximately 25 km inland. Because of the distances involved, several days are necessary to fish them efficiently.

(1) **Ashburton River:** 15.5 km from Mt. Somers

Turn left at the northern side of Mount Somers and follow the Ashburton Gorge Road, which is signposted 'Lake Heron' or 'Lake Clearwater'. Drive for 15 km and stop this side of the bridge spanning the Stour River — a tributary of the Ashburton River. This stream, although small, offers reasonably good fishing when it is carrying a full volume of water.

It is necessary to clamber down the bridge approach and follow its open bed of stones, grass and low gorse to the convergence with the Ashburton River. The immediate location, embracing both waterways, provides delightful dry fly conditions, especially during the early and mid-morning, before the heat of the sun instigates the afternoon breeze. Light rods, similar to my SAGE 8 ft 9 in (2.65 m) weight 3 are ideal for this venue. Walk upstream from the Ashburton River and fish the ripples on the far side of the Stour, beneath the overhanging trees extending up to the highway bridge.

The broken water upstream from the bridge also offers interesting fishing through miles of open tussock country with the presentation of sizes 14/16 Adams, Greenwell's Glory or Kakahi style dry flies.

The Ashburton River also allows easy access to a bed of gravel overarched with willows carrying a stream-sized flow of rippling water, which forms feeding pockets in small pools and backwaters between occasional stones.

Fly anglers should use floating lines, 5X leaders of 3-m length and lightly hackled dry flies such as a size 16 Dad's Favourite, Twilight Beauty or Greenwell's Glory. If visible fish ignore these dry fly patterns and are undisturbed by their presentation, I suggest you use a size 16 Greenwell's Glory wet fly or Sawyer's pattern Pheasant Tail nymph. Should they also ignore these, increase the size and try again. Stealth of approach is essential when fishing the clear water of these rivers.

(2) **Ashburton River-Bridge Access:** 2.5 km from (1)

Continue along the Ashburton Gorge Road for 2 km, turn left into a side road and park adjacent to a large mail box marked 'Mt Possession'. Walk the few metres to a bridge from which the boisterous river may be fished in either direction. It is ideally suited to a well-hackled, high-floating dry fly of size 12 or 14. The angler should wade slowly against the current, use short casts and strip (or use the rod tip) to ensure a tight line at all times. Fish

Position (7), Ashburton Lakes.

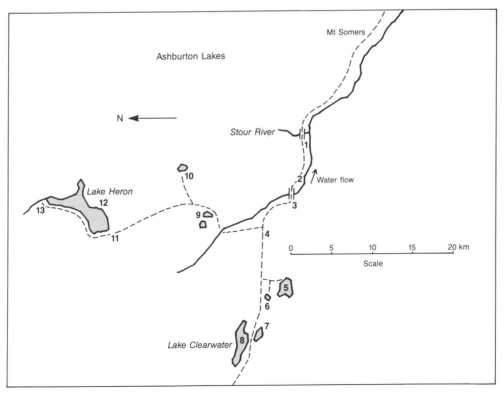

feeding in this type of water take as instinctively and vigorously as they do when feeding wet during twilight periods. It is not necessary to pause before striking in these circumstances.

The riverbed consists of stones with small clumps of broom and grass lining the 12-m wide flow of water and is backed with shoulder-high broom and stunted willow trees. Access is difficult and the unstable stones are awkward to negotiate in the channel-type configuration of the river either side of the bridge. Despite the access, anglers should endeavour to fish this venue, as it is particularly well stocked with trout feeding in the ripples.

(3) Ashburton River-Blowing Point Bridge: 4.3 km from (2)
This bridge is positioned at the base of a bluff signposted 'Blowing Point' (at times, an apt description). The river here flows over a wide bed of unstable stones and gravel between banks covered with broom and rough scrub. The braided channels offer easy access and casting — and good fishing once the beds consolidate and insect larvae becomes established after occasional floods. It is an interesting location to fish during these conditions, and there are several sheltered parking and overnighting positions offering easy walking access. Before the bridge, an access road leads left through the thick broom and the opposite side of the bridge allows vehicle access from both approaches onto the riverbed.

(4) Hakatere Junction: 4.2 km from (3)
On the way to this position, the road follows the course of the Ashburton River which is adjacent to, but initially concealed by, thick avenues of roadside willow trees. The road then climbs to offer a panoramic view of the river descending a very wide valley floor between tussock-covered foothills with a backdrop of mountains. The water flows through braided channels and offers easy foot access and conditions to suit the upstream fly fishing technique. This is a good venue within a few minutes walk of the highway and anglers may chose their own access approach here.

The junction is well signposted and indicates Lake Heron/Maori Lakes to the right and Lakes Clearwater/Camp directly ahead.

(5) Lake Emma: 4.5 km from (4)
Follow the Clearwater Road for 4.5 km across undulating tussock country and watch carefully for the sign 'Lake Roundabout', indicating a dirt vehicle track passing through a gate on the left side of the road. This provides access to Lake Emma, 1.4 km away. (The small lake on the right is Lake Roundabout, described below.) Lake Emma is approximately 1.8 km long by 1.5 km wide, with a horseshoe shape, and is situated in a small valley next to a stand of fir trees. If the weather is calm and the ground dry, you should drive past these trees and follow the road to a small tributary that crosses it. (Four-wheel drive vehicles may negotiate this ford.) Follow the track as it bears slightly to the left while rising slightly, turn right after travelling 300 m and continue for a further 1.8 km to the small cottage next to the lake.

Good fishing may be had where the tributary enters the lake, especially with the spinning or streamer fly methods. The most effective patterns are predominantly yellow in colour. You should concentrate on the side of the lake opposite the tributary, where there are stands of bulrushes growing in the water.

Fly anglers should walk towards the hut on the left where, after passing high ground, they will locate shallows with sub-surface patches of waterweed within casting range of the shore. Trout inhabit this weed and will rise to a correctly presented fly which, during normal conditions, should be cast well into the lake and left to drift naturally and slowly with the wind generally experienced in the region. I would recommend a small but well-hackled dry fly, such as a size 14 or 16 plump-bodied Red-tipped Governor, Coch-y-Bondhu, Humpy or Irresistible. It is important to keep the line taut but without dragging the fly in an unnatural manner.

There is also good fishing close to the stands of bulrushes, where the angler should walk along the banks and cast into the lake through any openings encountered. This naturally requires a high degree of casting ability.

When the water is disturbed by strong winds, it is best to fish on the lee shore — into the teeth of the wind and waves. Use a floating line and streamer fly of the Hamill's Killer,

Yellow Dorothy or Parson's Glory pattern. The waves disturb insect larvae from the weed, frequently goading trout into a feeding frenzy.

Late February to March is a good time to fish this lake, when the weather is settled and warm and the trout are in their best condition, physically and temperamentally. Fishing regulations covering these inland lakes are many, varied and frequently altered from season to season. It is important for visiting anglers to obtain copies of these instructions from license sellers or sports shops.

(6) Lake Roundabout

Return towards the Clearwater road, drive through a signposted gate on the boundary fence and follow a very rough vehicle track for approximately 700 m. This 500 m by 400 m lake has good foot access on the near side, but is inclined to be swampy on the far one. Occasional trees growing on the shore do not hinder casting to any extent. The lake hosts both brown trout and perch and its fishing season is similar to that of Lake Emma. It is reserved for fly fishing only and boats are prohibited from its waters.

(7) Lake Camp: 3.5 km from (6)

While driving towards this position you will notice a stream, shaded by willow trees, in a small valley on the right — I will explain this area later. Lake Camp will be seen on the left after passing over an elevated cattle stop. Lake Clearwater is still obscured from sight by high ground on the right side. A few minutes' observation of the terrain is warranted before descending the road leading to the stand of shelter trees at the end of the lake (an ideal position to spend the night in a camper van). The entire shoreline can be seen from here, as are the easy walking and fishing accesses. You may wish to take advantage of the wind-shelter structures clearly visible here and there, as the valley is frequently blasted by a prevailing wind from the mountains.

It is possible to walk right around the perimeter of this 1.4 km by 600 m lake. It holds good stocks of rainbow trout only and may be fished by the fly or spinning methods. Fishing from a boat is prohibited, though this is the only lake in the region on which powerboats are permitted. Stringent regulations are clearly explained on a bulletin board at the head of the lake.

Good catches of rainbow trout may be obtained with brightly coloured streamers, spinning minnows and conventional dry/wet flies and nymphs as used when fishing for brown trout. Use sizes 14/16 Greenwell's Glory wet flies until 2 hours after dawn, sizes 12/14 small-bodied Pheasant Tail or Hare & Copper nymphs until mid-morning, then sizes 12/14 Dad's Favourite, Kakahi Queen or Molefly dry flies until the heat of early afternoon. The mid afternoon period should be spent using the spinning or streamer fly methods (or sleeping) until the air cools, when the same dry flies should be employed again until the splashy wet rise erupts half-an-hour before dark. This rise should be fished with either a Twilight Beauty or Dad's Favourite size 12 wet fly.

The lake produces good results when dry fly fishing at night but, at this altitude, it is very cold and warm clothing is essential.

The northern end of the lake is accessible from the road leading to Lake Clearwater.

(8) Lake Clearwater: opposite Lake Camp

This lake, on the opposite side of the road to Lake Camp, is 3.8 km long by 1.3 km wide and is stocked with brown trout. Its fishing season is generally from the first Saturday in November to 30 April, when only the fly fishing technique may be used and anglers' boats must be moored at least 70 m from the shore. Please study the regulations before fishing here.

The water is surrounded by tussock-covered terrain, which, although steep in places, generally gives walking access to the shore. Both ends of the lake may be reached following a short walk. Access to the eastern end involves turning right near the cattle stop before Lake Camp and following a rough track through the tussock as it descends to the level of the water. This track is approximately 900 m long and terminates against the small outlet stream from the lake. It should not be negotiated by car in wet conditions.

The lake is better suited to the streamer fly method than fly fishing, though the latter may be practised in the hours following dawn or during the twilight period. Anglers visiting the outlet end of the lake should fish the immediate location thoroughly and then walk up the lake on the right-hand side towards the trees in the distance.

The western end of the lake is reached by driving a further 1.5 km along from the cattle stop and turning right to pass through a group of fishing cabins. It is necessary to walk to the head of the lake, where the ground is soft and swampy in places. The tributary is crossed by a footbridge, enabling anglers to work their way across the flat terrain towards the high ground on the other side of the inlet.

This area provides good results for anglers who can lay a long line to trout visibly feeding on terrestrial insects blown off shore.

(9) Maori Lakes: 6 km from Hakatere Junction

When returning to Hakatere the outlet stream from Lake Clearwater follows a valley parallel to the road. It flows through a series of small pools and swamps liberally interspersed with willow trees. This is a good venue for trout, but the ground is very swampy and soft, creating hazardous walking conditions. Extreme care must be taken when fishing this location, accessible by a short walk down a tussock-covered incline from the road. The road leading to Lake Heron is clearly signposted at the Hakatere Junction.

A bridge over the Hinds River is crossed 4.5 km from Hakatere Junction and while the downstream section of the river appears to be prone to flooding, the upstream one has a stable bed of stones with low tussock banks and, on a small scale, emulates the upper Oreti River of Southland. This is a reasonably good fishery in which anglers should walk upstream and fish the water ahead with a small dry fly. If you have time on your hands, I suggest that you park next to the bridge and work upstream on the side of the river that suits you best and apply the upstream technique with a size 12 or 14 Red-tipped Governor, Coch-y-bondu or Humpy dry fly.

The Maori Lakes are actually a shallow, swampy depression approximately 1 km square, covered with bulrushes, flax and small pools of open water. Although it is undoubtedly well stocked with trout, it is difficult to fish and the only readily accessible position is alongside the road, where there is a parking area. Unfortunately, large numbers of Canada geese and ducks have polluted the shore, making walking conditions unpleasant. Anglers willing to endure the dirty grass banks are, however, assured of good fishing, especially if they are able to cast an accurate line and deliver the fly gently against the vegetation in or overhanging the water.

This small, open section of the lake is only about 500 m long by 200 m wide and is sheltered from all but the strongest winds. Red-tipped Governor, Coch-y-Bondhu or Black Gnat dry fly patterns (that is, plump-bodied varieties) in sizes 14/16 are effective in this position. They should be cast to a predetermined position and left to drift naturally in the slight current or retrieved extremely slowly. Refrain from false casting over the water to be fished, but do so over the land until the desired length of line is under control in the air and then lay the presentation.

When employing the streamer fly method, you should use slow-sinking or sinking-tip lines, with size 4 Mrs Simpson yellow or Hamill's Killer yellow lures.

The Maori Lakes have the same fishing season as the others in the district. Fly fishing only is permitted and a boat may be used if it is anchored.

(10) Lake Emily: Access 2.8 km from (9)

This is one of the few waterways in the South Island to hold American brook trout. The lake is more or less circular in shape, with a diameter of only 500 m. One bank is steep tussock terrain, while the other is flat and swampy in places. The spinning method and the use of boats is prohibited.

There is no road access to the lake and anglers must walk about 3 km to reach its shores. Drive up the valley from the Maori Lakes and after travelling 2.8 km continue straight ahead through the junction as the road follows a sharp turn to the left to cross a stream. Park by the gate and walk along the old track ahead, ignoring the private road climbing a steep hill on the right-hand side. It takes approximately one hour to reach the lake. The walk to this lake should only be undertaken by the reasonably fit angler; although the distance is not excessive the gradient is physically demanding.

(11) Lake Heron: 7.5 km from (10)

With a length of 5 km and a maximum width of 3 km this is the largest of the Ashburton lakes. Lake Heron is T-shaped, with the main section running more or less north-south, and is situated on the brow of a pass at an altitude of 694 m. Despite the lake's size there is limited access to the shore. All legal methods of trout fishing are permitted, as is fishing from a boat, provided that it is anchored. Brown trout, quinnat salmon and rainbow trout may be caught during the season which generally extends from 1 November to the 30 April for trout and the last day of February for salmon. Current regulations pertaining to this lake will be explained on your local license.

Follow the road from the Maori Lakes over an open plateau from which Lake Heron is visible on the right, bear left and descend to the level of the lake where there is a motor camp near a small tributary. I suggest that you stop on the roadside during the descent and study the terrain. The head of the lake is a deep U-shaped inlet surrounded by willow trees, the sides of which are quite steep, with little or no walking access to the water. The gravel peninsula on the left, however, offers easy access and good casting conditions. The right-hand side of the peninsula is covered with overhanging trees, which create perfect fish habitat but restrict casting. It is possible to fish into this section of water from several positions between the trees. Endeavour to place your presentation between the willow trees growing in the water — a position frequented by cruising trout. Although conditions are better suited for spinning, the experienced fly angler will locate a position to suit his technique. Return to the plateau, from where a walking track descends the bank. It is possible to fish all the way into the inlet formed by this peninsula.

(12) Lake Heron Shoreline: 3.4 km from (11)

Before proceeding into this position, you must obtain permission to cross the private land from the occupant of the house just past the motor camp mentioned under (11). Return to the brow of the plateau and follow the road back towards the Maori Lakes for a short distance to where there is a boundary fence gate on the left. This provides access to a vehicle track leading towards the lake, which terminates next to the Swin River tributary, from where it is a short walk to a shallow shingle delta. Conditions at this position are suitable for all fishing techniques.

(13) Lake Stream: 8 km from the head of Lake Heron

The road follows the shore of the lake for approximately 2 km on the way to this position, providing ample walking access to the shore. The deep waters are better suited to the spinning method rather than fly fishing — unless there is obvious fish movement within casting range.

After some 2 km the road leaves the side of the lake to cross an old shingle fan created by the Cameron River. This comes from the mountains on the left to converge with Lake Stream and flow into the Rakaia River, about 15 km away from the outlet of Lake Heron. The last kilometre or so of this road crosses low-lying swampy ground so the drive should not be undertaken if the lake is flooded from recent rains. Under normal circumstances, however, the road is rough but quite negotiable.

Lake Stream is not large, averaging about 6 m in width. It has clear water, about 2 m deep, flowing swiftly over a bed covered with long trailing strands of green weed. Further upstream there is swampy ground covered with grass and occasional trees, creating hazardous walking conditions. The water, however, is very productive and should be fished with size 16 flies or size 14 Hare & Copper nymphs.

The downstream section follows a course lined with trees growing on the lee side of the stopbank, making casting extremely difficult in most instances. This is a perfect environment for fish, but it is surrounded by inhospitable terrain. Do not attempt to walk on the low ground away from the stopbank, as it is very swampy and hazardous.

38 **Hinds and Ashburton Rivers**

The Hinds and Ashburton Rivers follow a parallel course some 15 km apart across the Canterbury Plains. The terrain is open pasture or farmland with a base of alluvium providing a bed of gravel and small stones for the gentle water flow of both rivers. The banks are lined with dry grass, brambles and stands of willow trees, making a good habitat for the insects on which the fish feed. The Ashburton River has two main branches which converge about 3 km inland from Highway 1 at Ashburton. The southern branch (coming from Mt Somers) is normally well stocked with brown trout, but the northern branch is barren.

My choice of equipment for this region is the SAGE 2-piece, 8 ft 9 in (2.65 m) weight-3 rod, a Cortland weight-forward floating line and 9-ft (2.7-m) leaders with a .005 inch tippet. The fly pattern is less crucial than its size. I suggest that you use a size 16 or 18 Sawyer's Pheasant Tail or Gray Darter nymph when fishing to trout feeding just beneath the surface film. A size 14 or 16 Hare & Copper or Gold-ribbed Hare's Ear nymph will suffice for those which are bottom feeding in shallow water.

Fish rising quietly in calm water should be tempted with a very small Adams, Partridge & Yellow or Dad's Favourite dry fly, and a size 14 or 16 Red-tipped Governor or Coch-y-Bondhu dry fly would be effective when fished blind through the ripples. A Greenwell's Glory or Twilight Beauty wet fly of the same size would suffice in the half-light of dawn or when the fish are rising in a boisterous manner.

The single most important factor when fishing these small clear-watered streams of the South Island is the ability to place, or rather settle, a minute presentation bang on the nose of an alert trout. Your rod is the key part of your equipment in these conditions. The patterns described above may be increased to sizes 12/14 when fishing the Ashburton River downstream from the convergence of the branches.

The Hinds and Ashburton Rivers are bisected by Highway 1 near Ashburton and I describe the upper sections clockwise using Mount Somers as a base. I shall use Ashburton as a base from which to describe the lower sections of both rivers from Highway 1 to the sea.

(I) **Ashburton River Bridge:** 10 km from Mount Somers

Drive towards Ashburton along Tramway Road; this follows a slight curve to the right 300 m before a junction, where a left-hand turn is made to cross a bridge spanning Bowyers Stream, a tributary of the Ashburton River. A picnic area on the other side of the bridge offers foot access to the river which provides good fishing in water rippling beneath overhanging willows.

A short period only should be spent fishing this stream, before walking downstream to its convergence with the Ashburton River, which may be fished for several kilometres in either direction.

(2) **Olivers Road Access:** 16.5 km from (I)

Drive along Tramway Road for 3 km, and turn right into Ashburton-Staveley Road and follow this road for 12.3 km. Then turn right into River Road and when within sight of the Greenstreet public hall continue for 1.2 km until you reach the river.

There is easy access from the parking area to the wide gravel riverbed. This carries a good head of water, providing conditions ranging from exposed ripples to quiet pools partly concealed beneath overhanging vegetation. Ideally, the fly angler should walk upstream, fish the ripples blind using the upstream method, examine the tails of the pools carefully, locate feeding trout and fish to them from behind to avoid alerting them. Alternatively, the fly angler may fish with the downstream method in wide, deep or fast-flowing ripples if he is not able to keep a taut line by stripping. In this situation, a long line should be cast and the dry fly or nymph used in the manner of wet fly fishing, but without the slow retrieval; the line should be retrieved only to provide a suitable length for casting.

(3) Blacks Road Access: 6.6 km from (2)
Return to Ashburton-Staveley Road by going down Olivers Road after leaving (2), turn right at the intersection, travel for 3.3 km, turn right at the junction into Blacks Road and follow this road for 1.9 km until you reach the riverbed. Conditions here are similar to those at (2).

(4) Hills Road Access: 5.5 km from (3)
Return to the Ashburton-Staveley Road and turn right at the junction. Travel straight ahead for 2 km, turn right into Hills Road, and follow for 1.6 km to the river. Conditions here are similar to those at (2) and (3).

(5) Hinds River/Winslow Bridge: 19.6 km from the intersection of Highways 77 and 1
Pass through Ashburton and, after travelling 11.3 km from the intersection of Highways 77 and 1, veer slightly right into Winslow Road. (Do not turn hard right at the intersection.) Follow Winslow Road for 8.3 km, until it reaches a bridge spanning the Hinds River. From here, there is easy access to the gravel riverbed, which carries a small but well-stocked flow of water. The Hinds River is much smaller than the Ashburton and provides ideal conditions for the dry fly angler experienced in the use of light tackle.

(6) Dicksons Road Access: 3.1 km from (5)
Drive towards Ashburton on Winslow Road and turn left into Swamp Road at an intersection 800 m from the bridge. Follow Swamp Road for 1.6 km, turn left at the junction and continue along Dicksons Road to the riverbed, some 700 m away.

The position provides easy access to a particularly pleasant section of river, which may be fished in either direction.

(7) Cracroft Bridge: 5.6 km from (6)
Return along Swamp Road, turn left and proceed to Maronan Road, 4.1 km away. Turn left and drive 800 m to the gravel riverbed carrying a gentle flow of water.

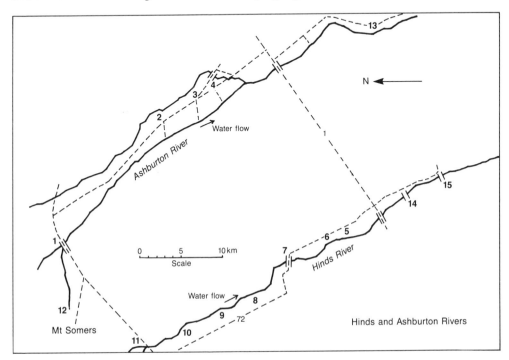

(8) Lismore School Road: 6.1 km from (7)

Drive over the bridge at (7), follow Maronan Road for 2.9 km, and turn right into Carters Road at the first intersection. Follow this road for 2.4 km and turn right into Lismore Road at the intersection just past the school. This road ends at the river after 800 m.

The river at this position is small and may dry up completely after a long period of drought, but during normal conditions it offers pleasant fishing with a good stock of small trout.

(9) Hackthorne Bridge: 7.2 km from (8)

Return to the intersection near Lismore School, turn right, follow the Lismore-Mayfield Road for 4.8 km, turn right at an intersection, and follow Hackthorne Road to the bridge over the Hinds River 1.6 km further on.

Although the river is small at this position, it generally carries a larger head of water than that at (8). Anglers should study the prevailing conditions before deciding which direction to take.

(10) Oakleys Road: 6.2 km from (9)

Return to the intersection of Hackthorne Road and Lismore-Mayfield Road, turn right, drive 3.4 km and turn right into Oakleys Road at a junction. Follow this road for 1.2 km to where it crosses the river over a ford. This position offers similar fishing conditions to (9).

(11) Highway 72 Bridge: 4.4 km from (10)

Return to the Lismore-Mayfield Road, turn right, drive for 1.9 km, turn right into Highway 72 and proceed to the bridge spanning the Hinds River, some 1.3 km further on. Similar fishing conditions to those at (9) and (10) will be found here.

(12) Mount Somers: 14 km from (11)

Follow Highway 72 to Mount Somers, after making a left-hand turn at the intersection 1 km inland from the bridge at (11). The northern branch of the Hinds River follows Highway 72 for approximately 7 km, but is too small for fishing. The southern branch of the Ashburton River is crossed 1.2 km before Mount Somers. It provides good fishing in a reasonably fast flow of water and is accessible from vehicle tracks leading upstream from either side of the bridge.

(13) Wakanui School Road Access, Lower Ashburton River: 11.3 km from Ashburton

At the southern extremity of Ashburton (600 m north of the bridge) turn downstream at the junction into Beach Road. Follow this road for 6 km, veer slightly right at a junction into the River Road, continue for 4.6 km, and turn right at an intersection into Wakanui School Road. Follow this road for 700 m to the riverbed. Here, there is good access to a large, agitated flow of water.

The gentle nature of the upper section of the river is replaced by one where foot crossing is difficult or impossible, with a current in which the angler is obliged to fish blind rather than try to sight his fish before casting. Even the accomplished fly angler may experience difficulty in sighting a rise in these circumstances and the best approach is to use a well-hackled size 10 or 12 dry fly of the Molefly, Kakahi Queen, Blue Dun or Twilight Beauty pattern. The angler should walk slowly upstream in the shallows, fish the water directly ahead and progressively cover the whole width of the river with the fly. Should this technique fail to lift a fish, repeat the manoeuvre with a size 12 nymph of the Hare & Copper, Green Stonefly or Pheasant Tail patterns. When the fish are actively feeding in a boisterous and splashy manner, the pattern should be changed to a size 10 or 12 wet Dad's Favourite, Molefly or Twilight Beauty.

This section of the Ashburton River lends itself to the use of the spinning technique, where 7-g (¼-oz) minnows of the Spoon, Slice, Tango, Tinker or Toby patterns with subdued colours should be employed.

Good salmon fishing is also available during the season (February to April). The angler equipped with the necessary equipment should follow River Road to its termination at Hakatere, some 8 km downstream from (12). There is easy access from the carpark to either the edge of the river, where it flows through a channel into the sea, or to the beach itself. Good results may be obtained by fishing into the surf of the South Pacific Ocean. The ideal salmon fishing combination for the river is a light, hollow fibreglass rod 2.7 m (9 ft) long, a medium-size, open-faced spinning reel fitted with 200 m (650 ft) of 6-kg (13-lb) monofilament nylon line and 21-g (¾-oz) silver slices or spoons. The salmon angler fishing in the surf should use a 4-m hollow rod, a large, open-faced spinning reel fitted with 200 m (650 ft) of 6-kg (13-lb) monofilament nylon, and 28-g (1-oz) silver slices or spoons.

(14) Boundary Road Bridge Access, Lower Hinds River: 5 km from Hinds

At the northern end of Hinds, turn downstream at the intersection into Isleworth Road, continue for 2.9 km to an intersection, turn left into Boundary Road and drive 2.1 km to a bridge spanning the river. There is good access from the bridge to the gravel bed of the river, which carries a flow of water providing ideal fly fishing conditions.

(15) Surveyors Road Bridge Access: 7.6 km from (14)

Return to the Boundary Road/Isleworth Road intersection, turn left, follow Isleworth Road downstream for 3.3 km, turn left at an intersection into Surveyors Road and continue for 2.2 km to the bridge.

   Although the channel is narrower than further upstream, and the vegetation creates casting difficulties, the quantity of fish in this position makes up for these disadvantages.

Author fishing a typical spot on the Big Grey River.

39 The Golden Bay Fishery

Although Golden Bay of the Nelson province is renowned, and certainly patronised, as a holiday destination where an unsurpassed variety of ocean, shell and fin fish attract anglers annually, it also offers some unheralded trout fishing in the rivers and streams.

Golden Bay is a unique destination for both local and international anglers wanting to share an adventurous vacation with their families. There is a multitude of activities here to satisfy everyone's interests and desires. The 'others' can do their own thing, from beach-combing, art 'n' crafting to caving, while you indulge in your chosen sport of trout fishing in idyllic conditions.

The Takaka River

The Takaka River is Golden Bay's longest stream, flowing parallel to but much smaller than the Aorere River. Its source is a mountain lake in a tussock-grassed valley and it initially bisects bush country. Its lower gorge section passes through open, dry land. It has a gentle nature and offers easy access to prime fishing conditions. The hydroelectric dam in its upper reaches provides good fishing for predominately small rainbow trout in contrast to the river itself, which is stocked throughout with brown trout complemented with a run of salmon in the lower reaches. The river has three different environmental characteristics and I will describe the fishing accesses likewise in three sections, using Takaka town as a base.

Takaka River Lower Section

This section of the river is adjacent to Takaka and passes through the precincts of the town itself (quite literally during times of flooding).

(1) Waitapu Bridge Access: 2.3 km from Takaka

Drive through the town and follow Highway 60 towards Collingwood. Turn left off the highway into an obvious large open gravel park on a lower level than the highway as you sight the Waitapu Bridge. This area extends beneath the bridge supports and terminates at the water's edge and offers ample parking and camping positions on either gravel or grassed areas. (It is a tidal region, so be careful when parking your car.)

The river follows a downstream right-hand curve through an immense pool, which deepens from the gravel 'beach' to a stop-bank of hewn rock opposite. The Waikoropupu (or Pupu) River converges with this large pool beneath tall overhanging willow trees on the opposite bank, upstream from the beginning of the stop-bank. Despite easy walking access along the gravel bed sloping into the water, this venue could not be described as a good fly fishing one simply due to the size of the pool. However, the opposite is the case for spinning enthusiasts, who will appreciate the lack of casting and minnow retrieval obstructions. The deep water calls for heavy 14-g blade minnows to facilitate long-distance casting and deep water retrieval, while the location calls for the use of subdued colours, copper, red or black, unless the salmon are running (annually), in which case brighter colours are in order. Fly anglers, however, should not despair. The pool becomes shallower just below the bridge, where there will be a few driftwood logs obstructing the smooth flow over the 'glide' — good positions for 'holding' trout.

In the absence of a 'rise' it would be wise to apply the streamer fishing technique and use a large-sized fly (Grey Ghost or Jacks Sprat in the whitebait season (October to December) and Yellow Dorothy, Parson's Glory, Hamill's Killer (green or red) and Pukeko at other times). A large weighted Pheasant Tail/Hare's Ear/Stonefly nymph on a dropper beneath a floater (use a large dry fly) during similar no visible action periods could be a good move. When there are surface signs of feeding fish by all means use a dark-coloured medium-sized dry fly, such as Dad's Favourite/Twilight Beauty/Pomahaka, black in size 12 in the evening, and a same-sized fly, Greenwell's Glory/Blue Dun or Coachman pattern at dawn/in the daylight. But when the fish are splashing boisterously just on dark you should use a wet fly — just about any pattern will suffice here. My choice would be a Twilight Beauty, Love's Lure, Peveril O' Peak or Black Gnat.

There is excellent fly fishing water just around the left-hand curve of the river upstream, where the horizontal gravel bank is replaced by a raised one (originally an earthen stop-bank) covered with grass and scrub. Anglers may fish upstream to the next access position (2) behind the town through water flowing more or less quietly over a gravel bed. There is easy walking access either along the top of the stop-bank or wading along its base on the horizontal gravel/stone (though deep in places) riverbed. This venue presents perfect conditions for the accepted fly fishing technique of casting upstream to rising or visible fish in a very pleasant section of a typical South Island trout fishing stream. The spinning method is also very effective in this portion of river, but the weight of the blade minnows should be kept lighter than 7 g to avoid catching underwater obstructions. Your companion has probably driven your vehicle from the Waitapu Bridge to this access (2) position (or vice-versa in the case of spinning anglers who will probably prefer to walk and fish downstream).

Back at the pool the hewn-rock stop-bank beneath the bridge on the deep side offers a good elevated stance from which to visually search the river carefully for trout cruising and rising close by. It is possible, if perhaps a little precarious, to scramble down onto one of the stop-bank rock slabs. Undercast to that (probably) large fish rising to gulp 'things' out of the flotsam line in the current with a size 14/16 small-bodied nymph (which doesn't splash when it lands on the water near the fish's head). Try a size 16 Adams, Pheasant Tail or Kakahi Queen dry fly if the nymph does not work, but keep the enticement small and scarcely hackled in such calm water conditions, where the (generally) large old shrewd browns have eyes bigger than their bellies.

Just downstream of the bridge you will notice that the current is deflected from the bank and creates a large swirling backwater. Careful visual inspection between the pieces of flotsam foam will probably reveal a shadowy shape cruising a regular 'beat' as it rises to sip something out of the surface film. Cast that tiny nymph or small scarcely tied dry fly onto the projected 'beat-line' and be ready for action. Spinning anglers should also fish this backwater with initially a light (Veltic/Mepps) spinner and increase its weight to 'dredge' deeper if nothing happens. There will be trout or salmon in this position and there is another good spinning position upstream.

Walk (or drive) back to the 'Pupu springs' road and turn upstream. Drive to the start of the first right-hand turn that disappears around the road embankment, turn hard left and park in a gravel and grassed clearing, large enough to hold half a dozen vehicles. The white wooden deflecting barrier on the roadside ahead conceals a walking access (through tall scrub) leading down to the water's edge, where there is a large (one person) standing rock immediately downstream of the converging Pupu River. The convergence creates a swirling flotsam-covered vortex within casting range of either a spinner or competent 'tower casting' fly fishing angler, and what a marvellous feeding position for trout it is too! All in all, this style of spot/stalking fishing in such a venue is a very efficient way to catch a 'lunker', if one has the expertise to do it. Patience and stealth pay dividends here!

(2) Takaka Town Access

Drive northwards (towards Collingwood) through Takaka and turn left into Reilly Street (near the centre of town). Continue past (right side of) the Citizen's Band blue-coloured shed and through the wire gate (please leave open/shut as found). Follow the gravel track onto the raised section of the riverbed, which provides ample parking in open conditions, or turn right into either of two grassed spaces enclosed between tall poplar trees. This elevated position reveals a delightful section of water with a gravel bed sloping gradually from this side to a visible rock stop-bank on the other against which the river flows as it passes through a large flowing pool. The physical character of this venue may be altered occasionally as a result of gravel extraction and this will effect the trout and their habitat temporarily, but no more so than do the frequent floods.

Visit this venue with an open mind and 'go with the flow' to locate a piece of water that has an established appearance (stained stones or tufts of grass and weed growing on the edges of the bank). This is a prototype venue where a fly angler will just sit and watch for a rise before walking quietly to within casting range with a size 16 Hare & Copper or Gold-ribbed

Hare's Ear nymph during daylight hours. As the shadows herald twilight, turn to a similar or smaller-sized Molefly, Kakahi Queen or Partridge Yellow dry fly. When it is too dark to retie the leader knot and the fish are splashing like mad making those fumbling fingers even worse, move to a common old size 14 Twilight Beauty wet fly. The trout will rise during the evening in that small vortex carrying flotsam in the current about 1.5-2m out from and paralleling the rocky stop-bank and will cruise the shallows, sipping off the surface of the calm pools during the hot morning/early afternoon hours. The Anatoki River (see access 13) converges with the Takaka at the lower (other side) end of this pool and the wide extensive area of water created offers excellent fishing by either method. This access (2) is a most pleasant and relaxing fly fishing venue.

(3) Riverside Access: 2 km from (2)

Leave Takaka and drive towards Nelson on Highway 60. Turn right at the sign marked Kotinga (1 km) and pass over the bridge spanning the Takaka River. (There is lovely fishing water here, but access is restricted. You must clamber down under the bridge approach.) Continue across the bridge and turn hard right as you drive off to follow a narrow gravel road between rough roadside vegetation. This track continues for 500 m and terminates on an elevated horizontal section of riverbed, providing easy (though a little rough underfoot) access to the (stones rather than gravel) riverbed that slopes from this side into the other deeper bank, before forming a huge, wide, shallow, smooth-flowing pool, visible downstream.

This is a position better suited for blind fishing a nymph or spinning minnow, rather than sight fishing, although careful inspection will reveal a stealthy rise or two as the nymphs hatch in the mid-morning heat. And again in the evening as the flies return to deposit eggs after mating during the afternoon, and shortly afterwards to fall dead on the water, thus creating the small nymph, dry fly and splashy wet rise respectively.

It is possible, though physically trying, to walk all the way upstream from the town access (2) through the water and fish to this position. It is also possible to go upstream from here by crossing the river to reach the bridge mentioned in the second sentence of this section. The parking area itself is quite extensive, has ample vehicle manoeuvring room and a few trees — a very pleasant position for both angler and family. Now, ideally an energetic angler suitably dressed should make the effort and fish upstream from here to the Payne's Ford access (4), where a member of the party will be waiting in the car.

This section of the Takaka River will provide an experienced angler with several hours of enthralling upstream nymph/dry fly fishing from 9 am through to mid-afternoon, in a venue which can only be described as idyllic. Shallow rapids (knee-deep) with underwater rocks create perfect trout lairs, locatable by the 'whitecaps' in the currents extending from 'glides' flowing from wide calm pools visible upstream.

As you walk upstream through the water along the edge of the rapid, watch carefully for trout 'holding' in the shallows (10-35 cm deep) ahead and pay special attention when inspecting the smooth 'hump' of a glide immediately above the first ripple of the rapid. If you cannot see any fish in the hump then you should cast a small (size 16) Greenwell's Glory, Dad's Favourite or Wulff dry fly well upstream and watch for fish movement as it passes over this position. (Or line-spook. Careful now!)

As you approach the visible Payne's Ford highway bridge you will encounter the convergence of the Waingaro River flowing in from your right. Now this is a real fly fishing river.

Takaka River Mid Section

The river from Payne's Ford, access (4), to the Blue Hole, access (8), on the upper Takaka to Cobb Dam road, may be considered as the mid section. It passes through valley plains and represents the envisaged average South Island trout stream of clear water flowing smoothly and sedately through pools, ripples and glides in a physically easy environment with similar accesses.

(4) Payne's Ford Access: 4 km from (3)

Drive from Takaka towards Nelson along Highway 60 until you sight the reserve while traversing a right-hand curve. Pull over to the left and drive into the (signed) grassed reserve,

The Takaka River is a superb trout fishing environment. Postion 3, shown here, can be accessed from the bridge approach or at the end of the track (see p. 234).

which is complete with picnic tables and toilets. There is easy access from here into the river itself and there is also a walking track leading upstream for a kilometre or so from the far end of the reserve, which provides easy walking back to the car after fishing the river upstream for a couple of hours. Water conditions in this whole location may be described as perfect.

(5) Waingaro River

Access to this wonderful trout stream is possible from Payne's Ford reserve by walking downstream in/along the Takaka River to the convergence with the Waingaro on the left, a few hundred metres below the highway bridge. With water clearer than that of the Takaka, this river has also bisected the plains after descending from one of those misty valleys in the distance. The rugged riverbed terrain and incredible water clarity make the trout easier to see, but it is also easier for them to see you — making it harder to catch them.

Extreme skill in stalking and presentation is necessary here to ensure results in what I would describe as an 'experienced anglers only venue'. The river offers several hours of intensive, concentrated dry-fly fishing through the plains before it reaches steeply up through a rugged gorge to a source in the mountain peaks far beyond the reach of average anglers. Strangers to the region should not attempt to fish this gorge on their own. It is rough 'n' tough with deep unwadable pools in sheer rock-walled canyons, offering no access around the edges and separated by fast deep rapids.

(6) Lyndsay's Bridge Access: 15 km from (5)

The course of the river is identifiable by the trees overhanging its banks away to the left. Unfortunately there is no public access to the river from the highway or the East Takaka road running parallel on the other side of the river. The highway follows a left curve (while still travelling from Takaka towards Nelson) to reveal Lyndsay's Bridge adjacent to a large grassed clearing surrounded by tall trees on your left. It offers an idyllic overnight camping position beneath a couple of huge trees on the verge of a timbered reserve complete with toilet amenities, and within a 'stone's throw' of really good trout fishing water by either method.

The river downstream from the bridge is broken into two or three separate channels, while that upstream from the bridge consists of a single channel flowing deep against a stop-bank on the other (Takaka) side.

Cast blind and float either a size 10 dark-coloured well-hackled dry fly or size 8 weighted Stonefly/ Hare & Copper/ Pheasant Tail nymph though the turbulent water flow, while waiting for the rise to start in the tail section of the wide shallow pool, visible to your left upstream. I would advise fly anglers to work their way through some excellent water upstream from the bridge during the day — there is a faint track in the scrub on the left bank — and spin anglers to do likewise in the opposite direction. The 'run' coming from the shallow pool passes beneath the bridge, providing a good evening rise. Try a size 10 Peveril O' Peak, Black Gnat or Twilight Beauty wet fly, before warming yourself in front of the campfire and savouring a 'nightcap'.

Takaka River Upper Section

This section of river, from the plains to the hydroelectric powerhouse, is a typical mountain stream passing through an undeveloped valley of native forest (open dry scrub here rather than rain forest) providing interesting exploratory fishing in fast rapids, deep pools, calm glides and gentle ripples. In short, it offers adventurous fishing within a few paces of the comfort of your vehicle parked on a sealed road. The ease of access, however, is counteracted by the physical effort required to wade and cross the often turbulent stream.

Warning! The levels of this river fluctuate with power generation activities. Be careful and ensure your escape route at all times! The road up the valley is narrow but sealed and in good order. Take your time, enjoy the scenery and then the challenge of fishing in this unique unspoiled venue.

(7) Upper Takaka Intersection Access: 105 km from Nelson, 64 km from Takaka

Turn off Highway 60 at this signed junction towards the Cobb Powerhouse.

(8) Blue Hole Reserve Access: 5.5 km from (7)

Watch carefully for this sign, it is low down on the right side, almost hidden in roadside vegetation. Follow the gravel track into the grassed reserve where there is a toilet block and picnic tables set up beneath native manuka trees and within walking distance of a large gravel-banked pool. A prettier or better camping venue would be impossible to find. But watch out for the sandflies! Keep your insect repellent at the ready. The backcountry anglers maxim applies here: 'The more sandflies, the more trout'.

The pool is easily fished from the gravel bank below your campfire, if you want to spook the trout, which are frequently scared out of their wits by kids swimming, dogs and spinning 'hardware'. Alternatively walk about 20 m downstream and follow the track leading to the rapid below the pool. Cast your small (size 16-18) Twilight Beauty, Black Gnat quill, Dad's Favourite or Adams dry fly, or size 18 Peacock Herle/Pheasant Tail nymph at the barely discernible rise in the line of turbulence carrying flotsam flowing near and parallel to the high rocky bank on your right. Don't waste your time with large fly presentations or any of that spinning paraphernalia. The fish in the pool have been tormented regularly by other optimists.

There is good fishing (and much better chances of results) in the fast turbulent rapid either end of the pool where, in the absence of sighted trout, you may use a large well-hackled size 8/10 March Brown, Molefly, Blue Dun or similar high-floating dry fly with every confidence. Dress it well for these turbulent conditions. It is necessary to 'work your way' downstream through some rough going. Fishing your way down is ok, even if it is not strictly 'correct' in some fly fishing circles. The water is rough enough to disguise both you and your floating line.

The section of rapids upstream from the pool is easier to approach by just walking along the bank and following the foot tracks through the manuka trees. Strangers, watch out! Don't touch those thin vines with small oval green leaves that drape over the manuka bushes in places. It is 'bush lawyer', a clinging, very prickly briar that is impossible to remove from exposed skin without lacerating it and drawing blood.

Step to the edge of the river occasionally — it is undercut, so be careful — and carefully search the water either side of those stones, until you locate a telltale grey smudge or pink-edged tail fin. You should initially cast a small size 14/16 Twilight Beauty, Greenwell's Glory or other winged variety dry fly into the feed-line. In the absence of action I suggest you try a small (weighted perhaps) nymph and increase its size until something happens. This is a good fish holding section that continues up around the left corner, through a pool (a goodun!), then further on veering right to lead up to and under the elevated road bridge in view ahead where your partner is waiting in the car.

(9) Roadbridge Access: 1.5 km from (8)

Continue up the valley on the road, which veers left to provide a quick view of the river below, then sharp right to reveal the bridge upstream and a stand of desolate/dead tree trunks (look hard right) on the edge of the river beside a small seepage stream convergence. I suggest that you start fishing at this dead tree access and work your way up through some very good (turbulent) fish holding water to the bridge. It is easy enough to clamber in and out of the river along this section, although the roadside vegetation is a little rough in places. There is a nice run of water visible extending upstream from this bridge and you might sight trout in the smooth flow leading downstream from the bridge.

(10) Sam's Creek Convergence Access: 66 km from (8)

This creek emerges from a small gulch and is bridged where the road follows a sharp left turn visible up ahead. The road is wide enough to park near the corner where there is also a rough (four-wheel drive) track leading onto the riverbed itself. The river up to and beyond this position is quite visible from the road while driving and the good sections of fishing water can be easily identified and reached, if you can locate one of the few wide parking spaces en route between the accesses. Of particular note is one such good section visible just after leaving Sam's Creek, transcending a small bluff as the road follows a slight right curve and passes a huge tree fern growing on the left side, with its palms extending over the road surface. A nice smooth golden gravel river bottom between protruding rock here creates perfect fish habitat. Look for a grey shadow 'holding' in front of those large submerged stones and use a size 14 weighted Hare & Copper nymph if you sight one.

(11) Appletree Flat Access: 13 km from (10)

You will pass some more very good sections of fishing water en route to this flat, which is clearly visible long before you reach it. Pull in beside the large sign erected above the river. It is an easy walk down the bank to the edge of a large pool, which continues around the perimeter of the grassed reserve behind the small stand of native trees. There is a fireplace constructed from slabs of river slate rock. This is a very good overnight camping venue beside a good swimming hole for the kids. Look upstream while standing beside the sign. See that shallower fishing pool above the fast run? Stealthily approach it upstream, with a size 16 Molefly or Pheasant Tail dry fly at the ready.

(12) Drummond's Flat Access: 15 km from (11)

The elevated road en route to this last camping position provides panoramic views of the river, which offers good fishing in turbulent water conditions in a bed slightly steeper and rougher than experienced so far. Scrambling access is still possible from the roadside, although parking spaces are limited. Drummond's Flat offers several excellent picnicking/camping positions in a grassy reserve, with trees providing shade and shelter. The flat is in two sections. The first space is only large enough to hold a couple of vehicles, is nicely sheltered on both sides with trees and has a rough table and an open fireplace neatly constructed of slate rock set into a raised bank. There is an easy, gravelled walking track which leads to the large pool that the space overlooks. It is an idyllic camping position. The other area is considerably larger, with more open space and is completely surrounded by trees. The river passes through two pools offering quieter fishing — fly to fish rising in the flotsam line — than has been the case so far. There is also good fishing where a wide 'staircase' rapid enters the top of the upper pool. (The river follows the perimeter of the reserve.) Now watch out for the sandflies. If anything, they are more aggressive than downstream.

This is the end of the fishing in the Takaka River. The Cobb Powerhouse is just around the corner to the right and the road to the left leads up and over the ridge and terminates at the Cobb Dam. It is an extremely rough and steep gravel road, more suited to four-wheel drive vehicles than cars or campervans.

In conclusion, I would suggest that, if circumstances allow, you should drive the length of river described in this upper section before starting to fish, in order to locate the fishing water best suited to your expertise with the closest parking/camping position. It would be time well spent and it is certainly a scenic drive!

Anatoki River

The Anatoki is another Golden Bay 'hidden' dry-fly stream of clear water descending a gentle gradient through farmed land to converge with the Takaka. But unfortunately, it has limited public access. The environmental aura of this small stream deems it suitable for experienced fly anglers only using the smallest of presentations. The trout are reasonably easy to see and easier to 'spook' with a careless footfall, line shadow or human silhouette.

(13) Anatoki Bridge Access: 4 km from Takaka Information Centre

Leave Takaka on the main Highway 60 in the direction of Nelson and travel for 1 km. Turn right at the junction signed Kotinga, continue over and past the bridge, turn right and follow 'one spec road' until you encounter the (only) bridge spanning the Anatoki River. Park on the road verge this side of the bridge and scramble down its approach onto the wide and open gravel riverbed. The river channels swiftly under the bridge from that very wide shallow pool visible a hundred yards upstream. These idyllic conditions typify the river for several kilometres, offering an enthusiastic dry-fly angler many hours of intensive, concentrated action.

(14) Anatoki Riverside Access: 4.5 km from Takaka Information Centre

Here is a really nice fishing venue beside an equally pleasant parking area. Continue over the bridge described under access (4) and turn sharp left to follow a very rough gravel track running parallel to the river upstream. Pull left into a large grassed open space after travelling 300 m from the bridge. The river is visible from here, but do not drive down the gravelled track towards it, even if you are in a four-wheel drive vehicle! There is plenty of parking offered here and it is only a few steps to reach the riverbed level.

Now, as one experienced dry-fly angler to another, tell me that I do not have to elaborate further on this little piece of heaven! Use a size 16-18 Peacock Harle, Gold-ribbed Hare's Ear nymph, or similar size Adams, Partridge Yellow or Blue Dun fly with a Sage 'Spring Creek' graphite rod here.

(15) Sawmill Access: 6 km approx. from Takaka Information Centre

Drive over the Kotinga (Takaka River) bridge as described under access (13), but continue straight ahead to follow the 'long plain road' (and the signs 'tame eels'), which will lead you to the right turn into McCallum's Road. Follow this road past the game farm/restaurant complex to an obvious sawmill building on the right side of the road. Park unobtrusively on the road verge here. Perhaps nose into that unused loading dock recess on your right. Walk past the mill into the river that follows the arc-shaped perimeter of the sawmill paddock. The river flows (more purposefully here than you will have encountered downstream) through a bed of numerous rocky stones providing unexcelled fish spotting conditions. Eagle eyesight, pinpoint casting accuracy and feather-light delivery of size 16/18 nymphs or dry flies are the only requisites to ensure success in this marvellous fly fishing venue! Do not drive further along this very rough and narrow road. I have no idea where it leads to and it is almost impossible to locate a wide enough space in which to turn a motor vehicle around.

This last access more or less sums up the fishing available in the Takaka River and its tributaries. It is a most pleasant watershed, reasonably well stocked with fish. Please enjoy this river and refrain from decimating the existing trout (take the salmon instead). These browns deserve admiration and respect for their fighting skill, not death. I enlist your support in practising and endorsing conservation.

The Aorere River

The Aorere River is the major waterway that drains the northern most ranges of the Kahurangi National Park into the sea at the commercial fishing port of Collingwood. Its source is found many miles inland at two tributaries; the Burgoo and the Spey — born of a slender waterfall cascading from the rim of Lake Aorere, a high-country mountain snow-water tarn. This river plunges, perfectly clear, through many miles of tortuous ravines and open riverbeds and rages through an immense valley, which receives rainfall of incredible intensity.

The entire length of riverbed, from its source to the tidal reaches, consists of round abrasive granite stones and huge outcrops of solid rock. It does not have beaches or underwater beds of sand and gravel, as do average rivers, and consequently the going is extremely rough, tough, dangerous and physically demanding, especially when wading over round stones which are unstable and roll when stepped upon. This is a dangerous region when compared to the average New Zealand backcountry river. The trout of this river reflect their environment. They are of magnificent stature, extremely fit and antagonistic, with a cunning nature to match that of the most experienced angler. Such brown trout of the South Island's Southern Alps will 'throw the gauntlet' at the most proficient fly fisherman by 'holding on station' and treating a perfectly delivered fly with scornful disdain. Anglers must tread this river carefully, for both their own safety and the success of fishing endeavours. It represents one of the South Island's wildest (in all senses of the word) brown trout fisheries.

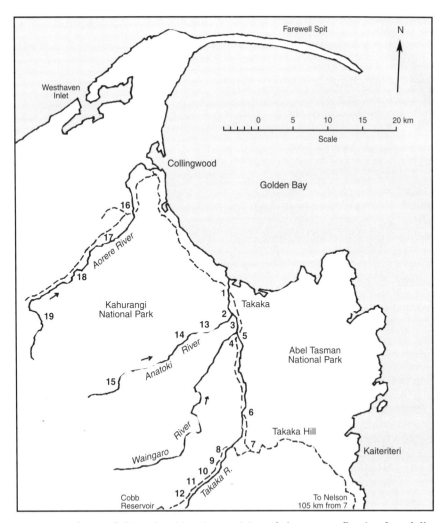

The description 'a good trout fishing river' inspires a vision of clear water flowing forcefully through a negotiable bed of smooth water-polished stones and rock buttresses where gently inclined beaches of gravel and sand provide safe and easy walking. The Aorere River does not match this description, but well stocked with large brown trout it certainly is, and can be fished with every confidence by experienced 'back country' outdoorsmen.

Aorere River Accesses
Rough terrain and lack of roads in this isolated region restricts the number of easy public fishing accesses to four only.

(16) Rockville Bridge Access: 7.8 km from Collingwood Intersection
Turn left (inland) at the intersection immediately preceding Collingwood and follow the signs to Rockville. Park on the road verge on the other side of the bridge and survey the river surroundings from this elevated position. High rock banks confine the river to a very deep course well below the level of the bridge, from where there is an indistinct access leading from the downstream northern approach to a rock shelf just above water level. This stance has restricted space and is better suited for the spinning method than the fly technique.

The water is very deep as it flows over huge slabs of solid horizontal rock over which large trout will be quite visible from the elevation of the bridge, moving in feeding 'beats'. An experienced spin angler will have no difficulty in casting (initially) a small Veltic or Mepps minnow into the path of such trout, to then increase the presentation size in the absence of a 'strike'. Trout in such positions are, by virtue of the surroundings, extremely alert to any unnatural sight or movement, and stealth on the part of anglers (including onlookers' silhouettes up there on the bridge) is essential to success. The steep nature of the riverbanks here makes walking access along the river impossible in either direction. The raised riverbed of dry stones visible upstream from the bridge is reached from access (17).

(17) Gillies Road Access: 2.1 km from (15)

Drive straight ahead after passing over the Rockville Bridge, turn left into Mckay Pass Road at the junction just past the Rockville Hall and then drive for a further 300 m before turning left into Gillies Road. Follow Gillies Road past the farmhouse on your right side. (Please be courteous and request permission to pass over the farmer's land.) Follow the road as it veers right to run parallel to the scrub lining the riverbank.

Your fishing rendezvous is that small wooden gate on the left, set in the wire boundary fence. There is plenty of parking room on the grass paddock this side of the pipe/wire gate up ahead that signals the end of the public road. The track that passes through the wooden gate offers easy walking access onto the extensive 'beach' of large round (difficult to walk over) stones that extend into the water. Now, although this is not a particularly picturesque venue because of the lack of the usual sandy/gravel horizontal type beach and sandy bottomed pools, it nevertheless provides good fishing for accomplished fly anglers, and to a lesser degree spin anglers, who will walk quietly upstream near the water's edge and scan the shallows for a grey shadow stealthily cruising among half submerged stones. Such trout are foraging for hatching nymphs and should be tempted with a very small Hare & Copper or Peacock Hurl nymph, or similar minute presentation if they are indeed foraging below the surface. But should they be surface feeding then you should use a very small Adams, Partridge Yellow or Pheasant Tail dry fly.

In no circumstances should a large fly be presented to a trout feeding like this, otherwise it will take off like a rocket, scared out of its wits. But yes, float that large high floating fly (size 8-10 Blue Dun, palmer-hackled Molefly, March Brown or similar) along the edge of the current in front of you, after you have ensured that there are not any fish cruising the shallows. A blade spinner (black, gold or yellow) cast well into the current and retrieved along its edge may also be very rewarding. Once again patience and stealthy observation will pay dividends.

(18) James Bridge Access: 5 km approx. from Rockville Hall

Return to Mckays Pass Road, turn left (inland) and continue upstream. Turn left and follow James Road as it initially bisects open farmed land to veer left and pass through a grove of native trees running parallel to the river to the suspension bridge spanning the river upstream. The bridge is supported on sheer rock banks offering no access to fish the very deep flow of water beneath, but it is possible to walk through the open trees on the corner just where the road veered left behind you. This offers a rough but negotiable access onto the usual (for this river) bed of stones, which may be fished as described under access (16).

Spinning with a heavy blade dark-coloured minnow is effective here. Those large trout visible from the bridge may be hungry! There is also an access leading downstream through thick scrub on the other side of the bridge. Walk through the old gate visible on the roadside. The track leads to the small stone beach you can see downstream on the right from the bridge. Yes, it is a rough scratchy walk and the venue is suited only for the spinning fraternity — deep water with big cruising brown trout. It is possible to park up in the shelter of the trees on either side of the bridge. The space on the other side is complete with a picnic table but is also very wet underfoot. Vehicle manoeuvring room is quite adequate in both venues.

(19) Fifteen Mile Creek Access: 14.4 km from Rockville Hall

This signed bridge is encountered while passing through a stand of native bush and it is merely a matter of parking in the widened space on the other (right hand, inland) side of the bridge, walking along the road (uphill) 30 m and following a very visible foot track down to the usual riverbed of round stones.

The river flows deeper here than in the two previous positions and is suited only for the spin fishing method. This venue terminates my description of the Aorere River. The gravel road from here to the start of the walking track is very rough and passes through three fords which, in the event of (very regular) rain, can rise quickly and trap you miles from anywhere.

I reiterate my opening comments about this river; it is a huge, dangerous waterflow in an inhospitable region. Be careful!

40 Trans-Alpine Trout

The mountain plateau of the Southern Alps contains myriad spring-fed streams, tarns and small lakes in terrain yet to be weathered by time. This exposed environment, reminiscent of the ice age, softened by acres of golden tussock, wild mountain flowers, and stands of mountain beech, depicts the youth of the New Zealand landscape. It offers a contrasting fishing experience to the exhilarating physical challenge necessary to conquer the large western rivers or the languid meandering required to enjoy the eastern lowland's small and delightful dry-fly streams. Here is a unique environment, within the tranquillity of high altitude mountain silence, which may be enjoyed by travellers exploring the South Island. This isolated region is serviced by several excellent accommodation establishments from which short daily fishing ventures may be made. I will locate and describe them 'in passing'.

Follow Highway 73 (the main route) from Christchurch, through Sheffield and Springfield to Greymouth on the West Coast. This highway provides access to four lakes and several streams, which I shall describe. There are also several other similar waterways throughout the region that are accessible only by four-wheel drive vehicles and will be the subject of a subsequent publication.

(1) Springfield: 67 km from Christchurch
Via the old West Coast Highway 73.

(2) Lake Lyndon Access: 21 km from (1)
Highway 73 gradually ascends the foothills, and passes several (well signed) rest areas, suitable for overnight campervan stopovers, preceding Porter's Pass, at the base of which (on the other side) the small picturesque Lake Lyndon is located. The lake becomes visible on your left when you traverse a right-hand curve and it is merely a matter of turning left off the highway into the second stand of trees. Here there are basic amenities — a roofed, concrete open shelter and a separate toilet block. The stand of trees on the Christchurch side of this gravelled parking space provides shelter from the wind in a grassed reserve, complete with a large picnic table overlooking the lake. If staying overnight is contemplated, it would be advisable to survey the immediate vicinity on foot and determine the position offering the most protection from the prevailing wind (down the lake, from the West Coast towards Christchurch). This feature is the only hitch in this lovely venue, which is large enough to accommodate several vehicles and tents. There is also a small hill covered with trees on the left side offering a safe place for the kids to 'let off steam' after being confined in the car for several hours. It is possible to walk along the shoreline in either direction from here.

Spinning anglers should fish blind with 5-g (or lighter) minnows (blade or Veltic/Mepps style, coloured copper, black or yellow) to trout which will be cruising and feeding in the shallows. Watch for those telltale water surface disturbances. Fly fishing anglers may also fish blind in the absence of fish movement with a brown-coloured high-floating dry fly, such as a patterned Mole, Humpy or Wulff in size 10/12. Also, where the water is deep enough (this is quite common practice with many fishermen), tie a weighted Hare & Copper nymph to a dropper while still using the same dry fly as an indicator. Whichever technique is applied, anglers should ensure that the shallows right up to the semi-submerged shore grasses are fully covered with the presentation. The silly little rainbow trout in this lake frequent its whole expanse.

The elevated road skirting the northern (Springfield) shoreline provides access to the other end of the lake, which offers very good fishing en route to Lake Coleridge. This rough gravel road offers an excellent vantage point from which to visibly locate trout cruising or feeding close to the shoreline. Once located, they are easily approached to within casting range by walking down the open grass-covered gravel bank. Fly anglers: I would suggest using a size 16 (or even 18) Twilight Beauty, Red-tipped Governor or Cochy Bondhu dry fly for trout visibly located surface feeding. Alternatively, use a similar sized (weighted, if available) Hare's Ear,

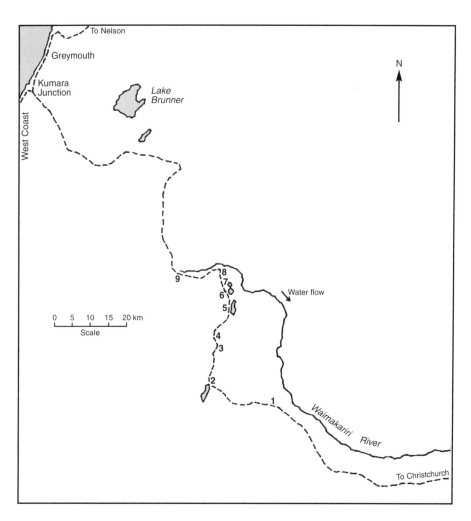

Hare & Copper, or Pheasant Tail nymph when they are obviously bottom feeding — watch for that tail disturbing the surface film. The secret in these tarns and lakes is to 'fish small' during calm conditions and increase the size of the fly when the water is ruffled by wind action.

There are several parking areas on the same level as the road, situated along its 2 km length. In addition there are several obvious vehicular tracks leading onto small gravel peninsulas extending into the lake itself (ideal access for disabled anglers) and one undeveloped gravelled boat-launching ramp on the opposite side of the road to a corrugated iron building. The lake is in the shape of a dumbbell, both ends of which are considerably wider and shallower than the mid-section. Both ends of the lake are too shallow to permit the application of the streamer fly (Yellow Dorothy, Parson's Glory and Hamill's Killer) technique which may be satisfactorily used in the narrow, deeper mid-section. This fishing method is actually very effective in this and other captive waters of the region. However, should the shallow water be agitated and dirty from wave action, anglers would be advised to try the streamer technique and use a slow sinking or sink-tip fly line, which will assist in preventing the streamer fly running too deep and snagging in the weed and stones of the lake bed.

The lower end of the lake is very shallow and inclines very gradually towards the depths. Anglers must walk/wade extremely carefully and quietly over this area, which is quite solid and safe underfoot, to avoid alarming cruising fish. A very careful approach in this expanse is essential to avoid alerting trout cruising the area in search of food, such as nymphs rising from the mud to hatch into flies on the surface. Now, don't take it for granted that the fish are feeding 'dry'. They will be doing so only if the surface disturbance is in the form of an even unbroken 'wave.' It will be more likely the trout will be 'humping' — feeding on nymphs as they float to the surface — and you will see their back and fin break the surface film quietly. In such instances I would suggest the use of an unweighted size 14/16 nymph Hare & Copper,

Gold-ribbed Hare's Ear or similar. Size more than pattern is the answer in these circumstances. Spin anglers, I would suggest the use of a very small Mepps or Veltic spinner rather than a blade or spoon in this shallow venue.

As you drive (or walk) to this lower end of the lake you will notice a band of floating weed just out from and running parallel to the shoreline. It is a good place for trout to feed on the things that inhabit such rubbish. A large dry fly floated blind over the surface above this weed will surely 'lift' a curious rainbow, so be ready to keep the pressure on the line when it takes. It will take ever so softly. Try a size 8/10 Coachman, Blue Dun, Kakahi Queen or Molefly. Now while you are sitting around the campfire near the van during the hours of darkness you will hear a few splashes and out of the corner of your eye you will notice that the surface of the lake is rippled by something more than the breeze. Tie on a size 10/12 (unless the fish are really splashing, then use wet) Twilight Beauty/Dad's Favourite/Peveril O' Peak dry fly on to the leader extending from your dry line and go catch a fish.

(3) Broken River Access

The highway follows an undulating course through open tussock-covered rocky terrain to this venue, which is immediately preceded by the 'Broken River' bridge at the bottom of a small ravine. Do not stop here (yet) to fish this river but continue on to the summit of the rise ahead and turn right into the Cave Creek lookout parking reserve at the end of which you will find a sign showing a map of the two rivers' courses and convergence. It is only a few steps from here to the edge of the bluff overlooking the river from where you can plan your approach to fish your way back to the bridge mentioned and your waiting vehicle.

Although Broken River is very small, and certainly does not warrant a special journey to visit, it provides an interesting interlude for anglers in transit. It flows through barren rocky terrain at the base of mountain peaks. It is an interesting and intriguing venue to say the least, where a fly fishing angler will use (ideally) a weight 3 or 4 rod, floating line and dry fly patterns, size 12/14, such as Cochy Bondhu, Molefly or Wulff. Revert to size 10/12 nymph patterns if the sighted trout is foraging in the shingle bed or 'gulping' caddis husks off the side of the solid rock. Generally these trout will 'rise' to a small dry floated down a ripple and will provide an invigorating fight.

(4) Flockhill Resort: 9.3 km from (3)

This is a unique and excellent establishment on a high country station offering parking facilities for recreational vehicles, adjacent to a top class restaurant complete with a friendly country bar. In addition, there are the backpacker, country cottage and 'luxury motel' accommodation facilities of the complex. This is your ideal strategic base from which to fish the venues described in this chapter.

In addition to providing free and easy access to Lake Pearson, this spot also allows access to several very good trout streams on private property sites that are generally inaccessible. Professional guide services are available to convey you to these sites or you may be given directions and permission to drive your own vehicle through the property upon the payment of a nominal charge. This contributes to the cost of maintenance of the private road system — a generous, friendly and commendable gesture to the exploring angler fraternity.

I would personally recommend this facility and the use of its services to international visitors wanting to enjoy what the New Zealand high country has to offer; be it fishing, sightseeing, tramping or whatever. Opportunity missed is experience lost! The entrance to the resort is clearly signposted on the highway.

(5) Lake Pearson Access: 2 km from (4)

As you follow Highway 73 the lake is visible on the other side of a large grassed paddock (Flockhill Resort property) leading to and creating the (Christchurch end) lower shoreline. It is possible to park on the grassed road verge opposite this end of the lake, step through a wire fence, clamber through a bit of rough vegetation and walk along the grass paddock to reach the shores. Fish from here in the accepted manner of just casting blind into the water with either a minnow or fly in the absence of fish movement. Personally I would still prefer to continue to walk slowly (and probably pass up a few fish) until I detected a fish by sight or movement before 'laying a line'. But there again on a warm sunny calm day you could be forgiven if you choose to sit on the grass and watch a size 8/10 large, well-hackled dry Molefly, Kakahi Queen or Blue Dun drift over the surface, while idly viewing nature's sculptures on the surrounding mountain peaks and looking for that damned kea which is constantly haunting the silence with its plaintive call. Until ... splash! Fisho! Is it a rainbow, brown or macinaw (American lake) trout?

From this end of the lake the elevated highway runs parallel to the shoreline for some 5 km or so, providing dozens of visible vehicle access tracks through the scrub to the water's edge, where there are many grassed camping positions. The lake is quite narrow and deep along this shoreline and offers better spinning than fly fishing. This section is recognised as the best location on the lake for the residential macinaw trout, owing to restrictive vegetation and deep water. It is also an ideal venue for the use of an inflatable dinghy or float-tube. The easy vehicle access to the lake's edge through stands of low vegetation continues until the top of the lake comes into view against a hill on the right, on the other side of all those willow trees growing in the water along the shoreline.

Road access to this position is gained through a gate situated on the top of the rise ahead. As the highway follows an upward left-hand curve, watch carefully for an iron boundary-fence gate from where several obvious vehicle tracks pass over the brown grassed terrain towards the lake. They are quite distinct with short green grass worn flat by vehicles. Once inside the paddock (after shutting the gate), it is simply a matter of following one of the two main tracks, heading in the direction of your choice. The track on your right, which heads back in the direction from which you have come, leads past that small stand of conifer trees surrounding a hut to terminate beneath one of the willow trees growing in the water at the edge of the bank. Now, a more delightful position would be impossible to imagine. Step out of your vehicle onto a level grassed paddock that leads beneath the overhanging willow tree into the very water itself. What a fantastic spot to pitch the tent or park the van. But first please extend the courtesy of a 'request for permission' to the folks at the Flockhill Resort at the lower end of the lake. You will be able to light your campfire in one of those 'rings of stones' already erected on the grass for that very purpose.

As the shadows lengthen, the prevailing wind will drop to an acceptable off-shore draught to aid your casting the size 12/14 Twilight Beauty, Dad's Favourite, Peveril O' Peak or Greenwell's Glory dry fly into the projected path of that fish that has been 'on a beat' and rising quietly to the surface to feed. Your main difficulty now is to decide which one of those several rising fish to go for. Now, don't be greedy and spook them all in your mad rush to cast at the largest rise. Just 'take' the nearest one, the others will rise all night anyway, unless disturbed. You will have to change that fly from a dry to a wet one ten minutes before nightfall and revert back to the dry when the splashy rise finishes half an hour later. The whole width of the lake here is very shallow and has quite a solid bed of alluvium. It is best suited to experienced fly anglers adept at laying a long cast and landing the fly (and line) as softy as thistledown in precisely the correct position to coax a cruising trout to 'err' slightly from its path to 'take'. This is one of those idyllic positions that we long-toothed anglers have passed up for many years in a hurry to get somewhere we should not have bothered with. May you enjoy it to the full!

The other grassed track leading straight ahead from the boundary fence gate leads to the tributary entering the top of the lake. It is necessary to pass through another gate on the way to the lake's edge. The inlet stream keeps the water slightly deeper here, especially where it flows around a couple of stands of mid-stream raupo 'islands'. This is a particularly good position for anglers competent at accurate delivery to fish with either fly or minnow. Tender the fly or minnow as close to the base of the raupo as possible to 'draw' the trout from its lair among the stalks. The terrain just here is quite open and slightly swampy and is not really suitable for camping, unlike the tree-sheltered position described above. However, if anything, the fishing is better.

(6) Lake Grassmere Access: 3.3 km from (5)

Watch carefully for this lake on the right side of (and well off) the highway at the base of a hill with a visible stand of bush fringing the shoreline. A small but well-defined stand of tall poplar trees becomes visible at this (Christchurch) end of the lake. This will be your fishing rendezvous. At the mileage shown above the highway descends a well-defined depression at

This is the top end of Lake Pearson. Access can be gained through the iron boundary-fence gate as described on page 244.

the bottom of which is a metal gate with a sign depicting Lake Grassmere and giving a summary of regulations. Pass through the gate (that hole of muddy water has a solid gravel base) and follow either one of the two vehicle tracks through the grass towards the stand of poplar trees. There is ample parking on a slight rise overlooking the water. This perfect overnight venue has a delightful setting, a high country lake with swampy grass banks on the left (highway) side, sheltered by a stand of native kanuka trees at the base of a hill on the right, with a backdrop of snow-capped mountains silhouetted against an azure sky.

The rarefied atmosphere and eerie silence of high altitude is quite intense in this unique venue, where fly anglers will have a ball catching brown and rainbow trout with small dry flies, such as a size 14/16 Molefly, Kakahi Queen, Blue Dun, Adams, Wulff, or for that matter any pattern that takes the angler's fancy. The small trout here will take anything resembling an insect.

Although the whole shoreline provides good fishing, I would suggest concentrating on your left side along the swampy shores. Here the fish cruise in and out of the little muddy inlets — the inlet nearest to the lower grassed track is a good one — feeding on dry flies and nymphs on the lake bed or attached to grass stems. (The use of waders is essential here.) Should the trout be bottom feeding, then replace the dry fly with a very small nymph that may be left on the mud and twitched. Alternatively, cast near to and to one side of the fish's head from behind! Insect repellent is also essential when fishing along this swampy shore, although there are times when I think that the stuff attracts rather than repels the hundreds of annoying sandflies.

Spin anglers may also expect good results here if they are able to retrieve their 7-oz blade minnow or Veltic/Mepps spinner above the bottom weed, but I would suggest that they walk around the lake and fish the deep water from between the kanuka trees on the opposite shore.

However, this endeavour will be quite frustrating, as forcing one's way through thick and scratchy undergrowth is necessary in order to reach an almost identical and impossible casting stance.

Warning! If the lake is high you must be extremely careful of a barbed-wire fence that will be just beneath the surface running parallel to the bank at the lower end of the lake near your tent/van site. Low water conditions are no trouble, as you will see it before you catch it, or it you.

(7) Lake Sarah Access: 10.2 km from (6)

Now here is a delightful little mountain tarn! Continue along the highway from Lake Grassmere, turn right at the junction signed Craigieburn and follow this rough gravel road over the elevated railway track embankment. Cross the line carefully — the Trans-Alpine Scenic Express passes through here twice daily! Park on the other side of the line to visually reconnoitre this small lake positioned in a slight depression. Access to this end of the lake, which is quite swampy with a raupo-covered shoreline, is through the iron gate in view ahead. However, I would suggest that you drive another 2.4 km and park on the side of the road from where you can examine the whole area from an elevated stance. This provides a better panorama of the lake and its environs.

Those visible stands of raupo create difficulty in gaining foot access to the water's edge and it is advisable to cross to the sections of open dry grass-covered banks and cast from there into the open expanses of water. Endeavour to place the size 16/18 dry fly Cochy Bondhu, Molefly, Grizzly Wulff or Humpy with any coloured body close to the semi-submerged stems of raupo. Twilight Beauty, Pomahaka Black or Love's Lure in similar sizes would be the best enticement during twilight hours. In short, I would recommend a nondescript light-brown coloured fly during the bright periods and a dark one in poor light, if the fish are 'sipping' off the surface in a quiet manner. Should the feeding pattern be boisterous, yet not splashy, you should use a size 14/16 unweighted Hare's Ear or Pheasant Tail nymph on a dry floating line. In the event of a splashy rise, I would consider presenting a size 12/14 Twilight Beauty or Dad's Favourite wet fly to the small rainbow and brown trout inhabitants of this mountain tarn.

(8) Waimakariri River Access: 7.1 km from (6)

Now back to the accepted method of trout fishing, western mountain style — known to be psychologically absorbing, physically demanding and soul invigorating, if running upstream over rough stones and slipping headfirst into cold rushing water in order to keep tags on a 2 kg jumping trout could be considered as such.

The highway gradually descends to run parallel to the wide shingle bed of Canterbury's major river. The massive floods encountered in this mountain region frequently alter the location of water channels and anglers are forced to 'go with the flow' on every other visit to locate a channel with an established appearance (stained stones). As you approach the railway bridge spanning the river on your right, look out for two vehicular entrances (note the upstream one) on the right that provide access to a rough gravel track, which runs parallel to the highway for a short distance on the other side of the fence (between the highway and railway embankment). This is your vehicle access to some great fishing. But don't stop yet! Continue along the highway to the top of the bluff ahead where you should park and reconnoitre the whole area. The wide riverbed with its many braided channels and a panorama of the Southern Alps is indeed an awe-inspiring sight.

After examining the scene return to the railway bridge and park in the wide gravelled space on the upstream side — there is plenty of room for overnight camping here. Walk from here, cross over the grassed stop-bank and make your way by the easiest track onto the gravel riverbed itself. Be careful crossing the stream of water nearest the stop-bank as it is deceptively swift and deep. This is the domain of experienced and skilled fly anglers, who will walk slowly upstream and scan the water for a 'telltale shadow' holding in the current (often within 10 cm of the bank) or on the edge of a current flowing into the head of a pool, or, without any doubt, in the sub-surface vortex near the head of a shallow (knee-deep) rapid extending across the width of the channel. Many years of experience is required to master the skills necessary to locate and 'take' fish regularly in these unique venues, so here is an opportunity to improve your technique.

These wide, comparatively shallow rapids in such unstable riverbeds are particularly good 'holding' stations for feeding trout. But you must walk across the rapid slowly and quietly well downstream from the presumed 'lay' of the fish, because, despite the roar of the rapid, they will still be vigilant. Once the trout is sighted beneath the turbulent surface, cast to it with a size 8/10 high-floating Blue Dun, Kakahi Queen or Grizzly Wulff dry fly. Do not persist with the dry fly if the fish fails to rise, but quickly change to a nymph, a Stonefly or Hare & Copper (size 8/10 weighted in this powerful waterflow) and cast in the same manner as with the dry presentation.

Walk upstream along the shingle as quietly as possible and pay particular attention to the very edge of the water. These trout will 'nose' almost right into the dry stones in search of nymphs and they will remain here as still and quiet as a ghost unless disturbed by a bird's shadow or your presence. Use a size 14/16 Hare & Copper, Gold-ribbed Hare's Ear, or whatever, but you must use a small-sized one. In the absence of sighted trout the blind fishing technique may be applied, especially at the edge of a current flowing against calm water or that which is moving at a slower pace. Such situations require competent 'line mending' to avoid 'drag'. The extent of fishing offered by this venue is limited only by the angler's personal physical fitness and determination.

> **Note:** The small clear-watered streams on this flat have become major salmon spawning beds and the location has now been closed to all types of fishing by the Fish and Game Council. You may record this scene photographically from the roadside, but do not pass through the boundary fence.

(9) Bealey Hotel: 6 km approx. from the railway bridge at (8)

The highway runs parallel to, but is a distance from, the Waimakariri River between positions (8) and (9) and does not offer anglers any access to the river. The hotel is strategically positioned on a peninsula leading from the highway and provides a well elevated panoramic view, especially from the bar, of the downstream section of the river with its bed of many braided channels. The hotel offers a base for people with self-contained campervans from which to make day trips to fish the venues described in this chapter (as well as the Lake Brunner region described on pages 112-115). The 'in-house' and motel accommodation is ideally suited for the requirements of transit anglers and their families.

The historic Arthur's Pass town and government conservation department and information centre is only a short distance further along Highway 73 and offers several excellent overnight camping positions for self-contained travellers and a couple of roofed 'open shelters' for those who are not. You should perhaps tarry a little along this route and enjoy the backcountry environment and dwell in the pioneering history that shaped New Zealand's mainland such a short time ago.

Geographical Index